Inner Development Goals

# Inner Development Goals

—

Stories of Collective Leadership in Action,
Volume 1: From "I" to "We"

Edited by
Mauricio Campos Suarez and Eleftheria Egel

**DE GRUYTER**

ISBN 978-3-11-133706-7
e-ISBN (PDF) 978-3-11-133791-3
e-ISBN (EPUB) 978-3-11-133811-8

**Library of Congress Control Number: 2025931337**

**Bibliographic information published by the Deutsche Nationalbibliothek**
The Deutsche Nationalbibliothek lists this publication in the Deutsche Nationalbibliografie;
detailed bibliographic data are available on the internet at http://dnb.dnb.de.

www.degruyter.com
Questions about General Product Safety Regulation:
productsafety@degruyterbrill.com

Ruth D. Moore

The piece for the book cover is entitled

WA

和

Wa (和) is a Japanese cultural concept usually translated into English as "harmony". It implies a peaceful unity and conformity within a social group in which members prefer the continuation of a harmonious community over their personal interests.

45.5 cm x 30.5 cm

Acrylics, pencil and mixed papers on 300 gm cotton paper.

The work draws inspiration from rock sculptures and ancient cairns, structures nestled within the landscape. Built to endure eternity or collapse in a strong breeze, they ask: Will we work on ourselves to thrive in the world that sustains us, or will we succumb to the next strong storm?

**The artist**: Ruth D Moore is a British-Trinidadian artist and systemic coach living in Switzerland, who started painting seven years ago after over 15 years as a body therapist and Shiatsu practitioner.

# Foreword

Welcome to *Inner Development Goals: Stories of Collective Leadership in Action*. As we navigate this first of two volumes in the collection and its accompanying digital workbook, we embark on a reflective journey from personal transformation to global action, aiming to inspire and mobilize our extensive community towards sustainable change.

My personal engagement with inner development began during my tenure as chair of a small banking group in Scandinavia in the 1990s. Originally introduced to me as leadership development, it quickly became apparent that it encompassed so much more. This formative experience opened my eyes to the broader implications of inner growth and development – not just for individuals or organizations but also for society at large. Just as inner development today is a prerequisite for organizations to stay competitive and survive, so it is a foundation for the functioning of democracies in an increasingly complex world.

This realization came against the backdrop of multiple global crises – a sustainability crisis, widespread psychological ill health, and a collective leadership crisis. These are not isolated challenges but interdependent issues that create complex adaptive problems for individuals, families, organizations, societies, and the planet. Our collective incapacity to address the dynamics and complexity of our world spurred me to found or co-found initiatives like the Ekskäret Foundation, Perspectiva, and Emerge. The Inner Development Goals (IDGs) initiative came to grow out of this small ecosystem of initiatives. The IDGs aim to build awareness of the importance of the inner dimension and the need to cultivate the individual and collective capacities necessary for navigating and leading in our complex, interconnected social environment. The focus is more on organizational and societal cultural shifts rather than focusing solely on individual change. Our challenges are systemic and need to be addressed systemically. "Inner" does not equal "individual".

When the idea for this book and collection of stories was first conceived, I envisioned it as a crucial platform for disseminating the diverse and innovative ways the IDG framework has been applied globally. My hope was that it would not only serve as a repository of knowledge but also as a source of inspiration for continuous growth and transformation.

This book focuses intently on the IDG framework, providing a foundational understanding through various dimensions and the skills they encompass. It gathers an array of diverse tools and methods, all co-created by our intentional and purposeful global community. The contributions span a broad spectrum of genres and styles – research essays, case studies, storytelling, practical guides, visual art, and poetry – each adding depth and breadth to our understanding of inner development.

Of all the aspects of this collection, what resonates with me the most is the palpable sense of collective wisdom that permeates these pages. The contributions not only enhance our understanding but also demonstrate the practical applications of the IDG

https://doi.org/10.1515/9783111337913-202

framework across different cultural and professional contexts, reflecting the transformative power of collective leadership.

Looking ahead, the IDG movement will continue to grow as an open-source initiative, thriving on the continuous contributions and co-creations of its expansive community, which now spans over 35,000 individual members and 600-plus hubs and networks across more than 80 countries. Our vision for the future is one of sustained transformation, where continuous learning and adaptation are at the core of our approach to complex global challenges.

This collection plays a pivotal role in advancing the IDG movement's objectives. By documenting and sharing the myriad ways in which our framework can be applied, it not only broadens the dialogue among our members but also empowers new audiences to engage with and contribute to our collective efforts. It is a testament to the power of collective action and leadership, and a tool for fostering the skills necessary for both individual and collective freedom.

As you explore these contributions, I invite you to reflect on how the insights gathered here might influence your own journey and that of your organization, not only to become better at navigating the present world with its social system, but also to become able to see, realize, and exercise the collective freedom we have to change the system we all now feel a bit trapped within.

Thank you for joining us in this critical endeavor to not only understand and navigate but also actively shape the world we create.

Tomas Björkman
Chair of IDG Foundation
Founder of Ekskäret Foundation

# Acknowledgments

The creation of this book has been a collaborative journey, enriched by the support, encouragement and contributions of many individuals and organizations.

First and foremost, we extend our deepest gratitude to all the *authors* for their willingness and openness to co-create this work with us. Your insights, dedication, and shared vision brought this project to life.

We are profoundly thankful to our *families* for their understanding and patience as we devoted countless hours—on weekends and evenings—over many months to this endeavor. Your encouragement has been our bedrock through every step of the journey.

We wish to acknowledge *Impact Hub Basel*, whose vibrant community and innovative space provided the home where the idea for this project first took shape. Your commitment to empowering changemakers has been a constant source of inspiration and motivation.

We would also like to recognise the incredible support from our *Basel IDG community*. Your inspiration, shared commitment to fostering positive change, and support of this initiative from its inception has been invaluable. A special note of appreciation goes to our Basel IDG community member *Hape Muelle*r for your pivotal role in supporting our communication efforts and website.

We deeply appreciate being part of the vibrant IDG Movement & Community, which has been instrumental in bringing this project to life. Special thanks go to Tomas Björkman for your unwavering presence and inspiration, and to Fredrik Lindencrona with the IDG Researchers Circle for your support from the beginning.

We extend our sincere thanks to Judi Neal, CEO of Edgewalkers International, for your invaluable advice in helping us identify the perfect publisher. Your guidance has been critical to our success.

Lastly, we are deeply grateful to De Gruyter Brill for your openness and partnership in making this publication a reality and for embracing this non-conventional book project. Your collaboration has allowed us to reach a broader audience and share this work in its fullest expression.

To everyone who has been part of this journey, we offer our heartfelt thanks. Your belief in our vision, your generosity, and your unwavering support have made this book possible.

— The Editors

https://doi.org/10.1515/9783111337913-203

# Contents

## Section 1: **Being nature**

## Section 3: **Interbeing**

# Editor biographies

**Mauricio Campos-Suarez**

Mauricio's journey as a transformative leader spans over 20 years, encompassing healthcare, technology, leadership development, and innovation in more than 40 countries. With a background as an engineer, MBA, and certified Integral™ (ICF PCC) and Systemic Senior Team Coach, he integrates inner development with business strategy through cultural transformation. After holding pivotal roles in large global corporations, he now collaborates with organizations and supports leaders as an independent coach and transformation catalyst. His dedication to organizational and leadership transformation fuels his drive to elevate awareness and create a better world. Deeply committed to fostering the sustainability shift needed to address humanity's most pressing challenges, he supports companies globally from his base in Switzerland, helping them expand their purpose and build their legacy. As a father of two and a long-time yoga and mindfulness practitioner, Mauricio's mission is to help organizations embrace change, enhance well-being, and drive personal and systemic transformation in a rapidly evolving world.

**Dr Eleftheria Egel**

Eleftheria is a scholar, board member, business mentor for female entrepreneurs and the co-founder of EOS Academy, an Edtech social startup. The focus of her work is on social sustainability. Her research and publications are in the fields of spiritual, female and sustainability leadership. She has published in academic journals and book collections and presented her work at international conferences worldwide. Eleftheria currently serves on the Executive Board of One Planet Education Networks and is a member of the Advisory Board at Ethics International Press. Previously, she was Board Member of the "Management, Spirituality & Religion" Division of the Academy of Management. Her vision is to drive positive change by challenging conventional thinking, fostering compassion and pushing the boundaries of what is possible in individual and socio-organisational contexts. A fervent community supporter, Eleftheria co-founded #SheHustlesAfrica in Nigeria together with the indigenous NGO AKAWI. Together, they empower local women entrepreneurs to tackle business challenges and grow. Close to her heart lies girls' education in developing countries. Her guiding motto is "*The phoenix cannot rise out of the ashes until the past has been laid to rest*".

https://doi.org/10.1515/9783111337913-205

Mauricio Campos Suarez

# Introduction to Volume I

When I first encountered the Inner Development Goals (IDGs) framework in 2021, it felt like a homecoming. Here was a convergence of transformative ideas, scholars, and communities dedicated to embedding the profound importance of inner work into our global efforts to address today's most urgent challenges. What inspired me most was how the IDGs don't just focus on personal transformation – they recognize that the path to a sustainable future is rooted in cultivating the inner capacities that enable empathy, collaboration, and systemic thinking across diverse cultures, sectors, and worldviews.

At the time, I was working in a large corporation, grappling with the constant pressure of delivering profit and navigating complex business strategies. Yet, I began to feel a deeper, more urgent calling. My experiences outside the boardroom – immersed in practices that nurtured my own inner development – stirred something inside me. The stable job, paycheck, and title alone no longer felt enough. I realized that leadership must evolve – bridging corporate realities with the urgent need for sustainability and well-being. This realization led me to engage more deeply with the IDGs and to bring empathy, purpose, and connection into organizational life.

Looking back, I realize this calling wasn't new. Like all of us, I was born with a deep sense of care, connection, and awareness. Yet, for many, life brings challenges we struggle to digest. In response, we often shut down, disconnect from ourselves and others, and push harder in pursuit of what we've been taught to value most: a successful career, making more money, and staying busy to avoid deeper reflection.

# The systemic challenges we face: A world at a crossroads

Today, despite living in the most comfortable and affluent era of human history, we find ourselves facing an unprecedented array of crises. Archbishop Desmond Tutu once observed that we are the most medicated, obese, addicted, and lonely generation in human history (Tutu, 1999). We stand at a critical juncture where a profound shift in our global narrative is not only desirable but imperative. The factors that once enabled humanity to thrive – leading to a global population of over eight billion – are no longer sustainable as we approach ten billion by 2050.

The prevailing paradigm of infinite growth within a world of finite resources is fundamentally flawed (Jackson, 2017). Societies around the world are grappling with increasing inequality, political polarization, ecosystem collapse, and climate change. These are not isolated issues; they are symptoms of an outdated worldview that no

https://doi.org/10.1515/9783111337913-001

longer serves our collective well-being. Instead, this worldview threatens the future of humanity itself (Rockström et al., 2009).

# The power of inner development: From personal to organizational transformation

In my work with for-profit organizations across different sectors, I've noticed a common trend: concerns for people and the planet are often addressed only after profit-driven strategies – focused on short-term gains – are already in place. A mindset rooted in competition, where one party's success comes at another's expense, continues to dominate decision making. This narrow focus overlooks the deeper, systemic impacts that organizational decisions have on the world around them. The result is a finite game where we deplete our limited resources and squander opportunities for long-term, sustainable growth.

The transformation we need requires a new paradigm. This shift must be rooted in individual perspectives, systemic understanding, empathy, and collaboration. We need to move beyond linear, competitive thinking and act from the emerging future in service of our highest purpose (Scharmer & Kaufer, 2013). By doing so, we won't only become more sustainable – we'll rethink how we approach strategy itself. This shift will allow organizations to move beyond the "profit-first" mentality, integrating the triple bottom line – people, planet, and profit – into the heart of strategic decision making. This creates a new dimension that goes beyond well-being, toward a deeper, holistic alignment.

When we integrate inner development into the core of organizational processes, we invite a mindset shift – from "ego" to "eco" (Scharmer, 2009). This shift enables leaders to access a deeper level of wisdom, where immediate outcomes for shareholders remain important, but the broader, long-term impacts on future generations, ecosystems, and communities are non-negotiable. By approaching strategy with this integrated perspective, organizations unlock new dimensions of sustainability, impact, and benefit.

Rather than viewing investments in well-being programs or environmental initiatives as additional costs, organizations can build their strategies on these core pillars. This holistic approach ensures that profitability and competitive advantage arise not from exploitation or short-term wins, but from a sustainable, long-term vision grounded in care for people and the planet.

# References

Tutu, D. (1999). *No future without forgiveness*. Doubleday.
Jackson, T. (2017). *Prosperity without growth: Foundations for the economy of tomorrow* (2nd ed.). Routledge.

Rockström, J., Steffen, W., Noone, K., Persson, A., Chapin, F. S., 3rd, Lambin, E. F., Lenton, T. M., Scheffer, M., Folke, C., Schellnhuber, H. J., Nykvist, B., de Wit, C. A., Hughes, T., van der Leeuw, S., Rodhe, H., Sörlin, S., Snyder, P. K., Costanza, R., Svedin, U., Falkenmark, M., . . . Foley, J. A. (2009). A safe operating space for humanity. *Nature*, *461*(7263), 472–475. https://doi.org/10.1038/461472a.

Scharmer, O. (2009). *Theory U: Leading from the future as it emerges*. Berrett-Koehler Publishers.

Scharmer, O., & Kaufer, K. (2013). *Leading from the emerging future: From ego-system to eco-system economies*. Berrett-Koehler Publishers.

# This book story and structure

This transformation starts with each one of us – each leader shifting from a mindset of separation to one of interconnection. This essence of leadership is at the core of this first volume in our collection and the heart of the global IDG community.

In April 2022, we launched the Swiss IDG Hub, embodying the spirit of co-creation and purpose. It was during one of these gatherings that Dr Eleftheria Egel and I began envisioning this book. We recognized the vast wisdom within our global IDG network and saw the need to create a cohesive body of knowledge that connected its diverse insights.

When we put out a call for submissions, we were overwhelmed by the response. Nearly 100 papers flowed in, transforming our initial vision into two volumes. We dedicated countless nights and weekends to reviewing contributions and collaboratively shaping each article. This book is not just a collection of ideas; it is a living testament to the collective wisdom and experiences of individuals from across the globe.

This work embodies a commitment to holistic growth, integrating the intellectual, emotional, and spiritual dimensions of our lives. As we navigate the complexities of our time, the insights within this book are intended to nourish the mind, feed the soul, and heal the heart. They are not simply theoretical concepts but serve as enablers of practical, meaningful action.

We aspire for this book to become a dynamic body of knowledge, a living space where emerging ideas and concepts connect, showcasing collective efforts to shift our global narrative. It is a space for dialogue, understanding, and connection – a catalyst for new ecosystems of collaboration.

This book is supported by three key pillars:

1. The first theme is *inner development*, which brings together insights from various schools of thought to create a diverse representation of ways to foster transformation and drive meaningful change. Inner development extends beyond personal growth; it encompasses how individuals, communities, and organizations relate, collaborate, and act to contribute to a fairer and more sustainable future.

2. The second theme emphasizes the power of *collective leadership*. Facing the fact that the "heroic" leadership model won't solve the world's challenges, we need to rethink our approaches and systems to better work together. Collective leader-

    ship is essential for creating real impact, leveraging diverse perspectives and experiences to address the complexities of today's world.

3.   Finally, the meaningful *action*: inner development and collective leadership form the foundation of impactful action. This section explores how we can translate these principles into tangible steps toward a more sustainable, equitable future.

The structure of this work reflects the journey of inner and collective development, transitioning from "I" to "We".

    We begin with the section **Being Nature** that explores how deeply intertwined we are with the natural world, even though we often speak of nature as something separate from ourselves. Many of us feel disconnected from nature, forgetting that we are not just in nature, we are part of it. This section invites us to cultivate a deeper state of being, where we recognize that our true nature is one with the whole. As we embrace this connection, our sense of self expands, guiding us toward greater harmony with the planet, others, and ourselves.

    The next section, **Interbeing**, is rooted in the idea that "I am because you are" (Tutu, 1999). This concept reflects the interconnectedness of all life and the understanding that our existence is inherently tied to others – humans, animals, plants, and Earth itself. This section explores how relationships shape us and how collective wisdom and shared experiences are crucial for our development.

    The final section, **Ancient Wisdom**, looks beyond modern science-based knowledge and acknowledges the vast reservoirs of wisdom passed down from ancient civilizations and indigenous cultures. While science offers valuable insights, it is not the sole source of understanding. This section explores timeless wisdom that our ancestors – across cultures and continents – have nurtured for centuries.

    As you hold this book, I invite you to see it as a catalyst for new ecosystems – networks that unite individuals, sectors, countries, and organizations across the globe. These ecosystems foster dialogue, sharing insights, and inspiring one another.

    Imagine yourself sitting in front of a grand bonfire in a pristine forest, surrounded by diverse people sharing stories and insights. This book is about diversity – not only of voices but of perspectives and experiences. The stories within come from all continents, spanning art, academic research, and business applications. We hope it will inspire you and nurture meaningful action.

    This book is not a static collection of stories and ideas; it's a living space, an ongoing conversation. As a reader, you become an integral part of this ecosystem, joining a movement that transcends race, beliefs, and personal orientations. Together, we can create a more tolerant, sustainable, and peaceful future while balancing the present needs of all beings on this planet.

    The time for action is now, and the journey begins with each of us. The connections we forge, the inner work we undertake, and the collective leadership we embrace are all crucial steps toward the sustainable, equitable future we must create – together.

As editors, we are grateful for the collaboration and insights shared by each contributor, whose expertise and perspective makes this work a rich resource for readers.

We invite you, the reader, to engage deeply with the ideas presented, to reflect on their implications, and to consider how they may inform your own work and thinking. It is our hope that this book not only provides knowledge but also sparks dialogue and inspires action.

Thank you for joining us on this journey, and we look forward to the conversations and transformations this work may inspire.

## The Inner Development Goals (IDGs)

In 2015, the United Nations introduced the Sustainable Development Goals (SDGs), a comprehensive blueprint with the noble intention of achieving a sustainable world by 2030. Yet, almost a decade on, progress has been alarmingly slow, and it seems increasingly unlikely that these goals will be met on time. One critical reason for this shortfall is the lack of a fundamental inner dimension in our policy approaches, education, societal structures, economic models, and production systems. To confront and effectively address the complex challenges we face today, we must urgently enhance our collective abilities. This is where the IDGs become essential.

The IDG framework, developed with the insights and collaboration of over 4,000 scientists, experts, and practitioners, outlines the inner capabilities, qualities, and skills necessary to accelerate progress toward the SDGs. Comprising 23 specific attributes grouped into five dimensions, the framework offers a structured approach to cultivating the essential capacities of the human mind and heart – those inner qualities and abilities critical for addressing the multifaceted challenges of our time.

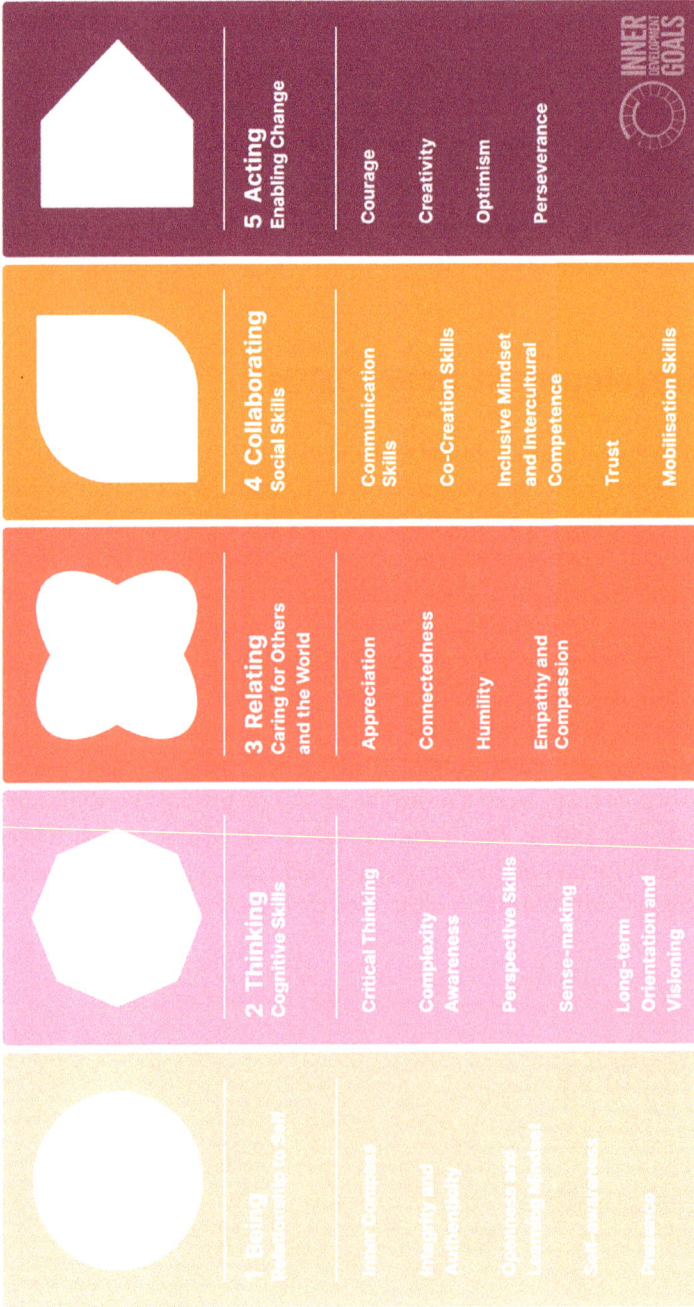

**Figure 1:** The Inner Development Goals framework.
Note: This framework outlines the 23 attributes, grouped into five dimensions, that are essential for developing the inner capacities necessary to achieve sustainable development.
Source: Inner Development Goals https://innerdevelopmentgoals.org/

Section 1: **Being nature**

Ana Gabriela Mata Carrera, Paul Jeffcutt, Mauricio Campos Suarez

# Chapter 1
# Prelude

We are nature, yet we often struggle to perceive our intrinsic connection to it. The *being* dimension of the IDG framework is defined as the relationship to self. In this section, we delve into this relationship through two distinct lenses. The first three chapters explore the *human-centered* experience, while the remaining chapters shift to an *eco-centered* perspective on our being development.

As you journey through this section, you will start by exploring being as the "core" of Inner Development Goals. You will delve into the stillness of your own presence to find a reservoir of intuition and insight, a guiding light on the path towards authenticity and accountability.

The next chapter will explore being from the artistry of a bread-baking perspective. In the gentle kneading of dough and the patient rise of the loaf, you will find a refuge from the chaos of the modern world, a reminder to cherish the moments of quietude and simplicity that nourish the soul.

Connecting with your soul, you will step into the embrace of nature, where the earth becomes your teacher and the sky your witness. Through the dance of outdoor eco-embodiment, you will explore how to cultivate a better connection with yourself and other beings, with, and even as, nature through sensory awareness.

With outdoor eco-embodiment, you will be able to open your heart to the rhythm of life, where every breath is a prayer and every step a dance of interconnectedness. Embrace the shift from seeing yourself as separate from nature to recognizing your place within the tapestry of existence, where every action ripples through the web of life, shaping the world around you.

As you experience your interconnectedness with nature, you will complete this section by exploring sustainability through an artistic lens and the state of flow. Here, the canvas becomes a collaborative medium to reflect on our individual and collective patterns and behaviors while we fully immerse in the experience.

May these chapters inspire you to embrace the fullness of your relationship with yourself and the nature within you, guiding you to navigate by the compass of your inner wisdom.

https://doi.org/10.1515/9783111337913-002

**Figure 1.1:** *Life flows through us* (2010).
Photograph by A. G. Mata Carrera, Istanbul, Turkey
*"The figure in the picture embodies the concept of presence, as the movement of water mirrors the rhythmic dance of thoughts against the backdrop of our past experiences and the potential of our future."*

*Watershed*[1]
*Gushing between glaciers*
*and the ocean bed,*
*a vast, unremitting tide*
*sculpts the reluctant land*
*as the moment needs,*
*sweeping particles for sediment*
*or in raging spate, whole trees.*

*Tugged from the awkward bank,*
*undertows twist and swirl us*
*beyond the shallows.*
*You roar onwards*
*in sleek rolling waves,*
*plunging deep and dangerous*
*into the cascade.*

**Paul Jeffcutt (2024)**

Author's note. Inspired by the fundamental power of nature and the challenge of climate change.

---

1 The poem appears in Paul's new collection *True*, published by Eyewear Publishing (2024).

*Identity*
*The "Being" is round*
*The Self is whole.*

*We are circling*
*around our identities,*
*lights and shadows,*
*tears and laughter.*

*We are one,*
*and we are many*
*curious explorers*
*around the fire,*
*with an open heart and open mind.*
*Coming together*
*with courage and humility,*
*caring for each other*
*and caring for the whole.*

*Asking the question:*
*"What does life want from me?"*
*Keeping the flame alive,*
*Holding the space,*
*Deep listening.*

**M. Campos Suarez (2014)**

Author's note. This poem reflects on the power of connection found in circles. We explore our identities, both shared and unique, within this supportive space. Since becoming a coach, I've been captivated by the power of team circles. Witnessing teams and individuals connecting deeply, shedding layers, and discovering themselves at so many levels. It felt like serving life's core need for connection and growth.

Lukas Til Vogel

# Chapter 2
# "Being" as the core IDG methodology: Why being holds successful IDGs together

**Abstract:** This chapter explores the depth of *being* and its scope within the Inner Development Goals (IDGs) narrative. The central assumption is that deepening rootedness in being serves as a prerequisite and goal for authentic inner development, leading to the cultivation of wisdom. The author argues that wisdom, not intelligence, is the catalyst for the successful implementation of both IDGs and the Sustainable Development Goals (SDGs). For a comprehensive understanding of being, a synthesis of viewpoints from different traditions is provided, highlighting related practices for its cultivation. It further contextualizes the findings within the IDG framework, while elaborating on related risks and requirements.

**Keywords:** systems theory, ecology of mind, holism, wisdom cultivation, social change

## Introduction

### "Being" in the IDGs

The IDG movement has emerged in response to the pressing need for change. It proposes catalyzing transformation from within. Central to this endeavor is the fundamental question: Who must we become in order to create a sustainable future for both humanity and the planet?

The first dimension of the IDG framework is that of *being*. Often overlooked in the clamor for action and achievement, being holds the essence of authentic presence, mindful awareness, and interconnectedness. Defined as "cultivating our inner life and deepening our relationship with our thoughts, feelings and body", being serves as the foundation for holistic action (Inner Development Goals, n.d.). As a state of being present, intentional, and nonreactive in the face of complexity, being represents a radical departure from the dominant culture's notions of development, which tend to prioritize external achievement over internal growth. Within the IDGs, being is further elucidated through the sub-dimensions of "inner compass", "integrity and authenticity", "openness and learning mindset", and "self-awareness and presence". However, while being is a fundamental aspect of the IDGs, its interpretation and implementation remains subject to debate and scrutiny.

https://doi.org/10.1515/9783111337913-003

## Caveats of interpretation

In reflecting on the representation of being within the IDG framework, it is important to acknowledge both its strengths and its limitations. On the one hand, the introduction of being into mainstream discourse represents a significant milestone, offering an opportunity to expand its meaning and application. By integrating being as a fundamental dimension of inner development, the IDGs underscore the importance of a being. While the integration of being into mainstream discourse represents progress, there is a risk of oversimplification. As the mind tends to fixate on singular concepts, there is a danger of overlooking their deeper manifestations.

Furthermore, within the IDG framework, being is often perceived as a discrete step in a sequence of actions or as a separate component, distinct from dimensions 2–5 (Inner Development Goals, n.d.). This compartmentalization of being limits its integration into holistic approaches to inner development and reinforces a dualistic mindset that separates being from other IDG dimensions like *thinking* or *acting*. However, drawing on insights from wisdom traditions, being is understood as inseparable from all dimensions of life and a driver for intrinsic motivation. Rather than a set of values or virtues, being involves a profound recognition of the interconnectedness of all phenomena that transcends egoic boundaries. The IDG framework runs the risk of reducing being to a superficial conditioning, devoid of deeper insight into the interconnectedness of things. This approach can lead to the loss of the beginner's mind, stifling curiosity and openness to the deeper dimensions of being.

Critics of the IDGs argue that this reductionist approach fosters conflict and confusion, as it fails to provide a comprehensive understanding of the multidimensional nature of being. By presenting being as a set of prescribed values, the IDGs risk perpetuating ideological conflicts and undermining their transformative potential. Furthermore, without a nuanced understanding of interconnectedness, actions seemingly arising from being may remain rooted in egocentric perceptions of self, limiting their capacity for genuine transformation. In this vein, what is needed is an understanding of well-being that integrates inner and outer dimensions of change. The tendency to isolate complex concepts can thus lead to a superficial understanding that fails to capture its depth and nuance. Thus, treating being as a discrete component within a larger framework risks overlooking its intrinsic interconnectedness with other dimensions of human experience.

## Hypothesis

Rather than viewing being as a linear process within a predefined framework, it is proposed that insight into being reveals the interconnectivity of all consciousness, which in turn cultivates wisdom. This wisdom, which transcends simple description, serves as a foundational basis and essence for holistic change, as it makes one drop the notion of self to gradual extents. This hypothesis challenges the dualistic notion that *inner* development – often framed as *self*-development – is secondary to outer achievement. It underscores the integral value of cultivating wisdom, which is the source of many other qualities, including intrinsic motivation and compassion. As all problems are a set of system dynamics, efforts to implement the IDGs or SDGs without some understanding of and connection to being may lack depth. As suggested in Figure 2.1, the cultivation of a sense of interconnectedness, presence, and alignment is a condition for individuals to engage in collective leadership in action, which represents the ultimate objective of the IDGs.

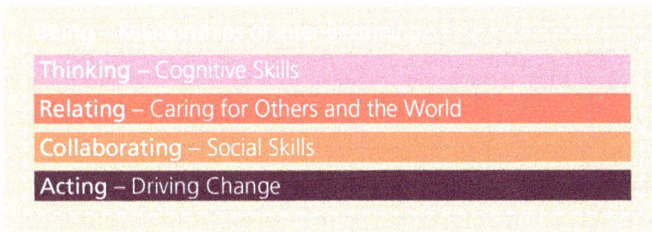

Being – Foundations of Inter-becoming

Thinking – Cognitive Skills

Relating – Caring for Others and the World

Collaborating – Social Skills

Acting – Driving Change

**Figure 2.1:** The omnipresence of being in the IDG framework. Own work.

# Descriptions of being

The emergence of the IDG movement and its fragmentary treatment of being reflects broader cultural trends and historical developments. Primarily aimed at a Western audience, the origins and intentions behind the development of the IDG framework emphasize the individual, thereby risking contributing to a reductionist portrayal of being. In contemporary Western culture, the concept of being is increasingly marginalized and overshadowed by growth incentives that emphasize productivity, efficiency, and measurable results. The prevalence of management practices derived from military models further reinforces a utilitarian approach to human development, prioritizing external goals over internal states of being.

In addition, the process of secularization has severed the traditional links between wisdom and knowledge, relegating spiritual insights to the periphery of public discourse (Wilber, 2000). As language shapes our understanding of reality, the term "being" itself has become commodified and diluted, stripped of its deeper philosophical implications. Historically, the concept of being can be traced back to the Greek word *ousia* (οὐσία), which influenced the Latin term *essentia*, both conveying notions of essence or existence. In the Arabic philosophical tradition, the concept is represented by the term *wujūd* (وجود), which similarly means existence or being. Today, being is often reduced to a superficial state or condition, divorced from its ontological meaning.

Furthermore, the dominance of left-brain thinking in modern society has contributed to a pervasive sense of fragmentation and alienation that has brought humanity to the brink of ecological and existential crisis (Bateson, 1987). The linear, reductionist worldview propagated by discursive, rational thought processes has fueled a race to the bottom characterized by competition, exploitation, and ecological degradation. In contrast, practices such as meditation and mindfulness offer pathways to accessing right-brain modes of consciousness, fostering a deeper connection with being and promoting holistic forms of cognition (Davidson et al., 2003).

## Wisdom traditions

The concept of being is expressed in a variety of cultural and spiritual traditions, each offering unique insights into the nature of human consciousness and inner awareness. As mentioned, being is often referenced as the source of wisdom as opposed to knowledge. To gain a deeper understanding of being, we can draw on insights from both Eastern and Western traditions. Eastern traditions, rooted in contemplative practices, offer very systematic insights into the nature of being and consciousness. In contrast, Western traditions, influenced by Western thought and religious frameworks, offer complementary perspectives that are often culturally easier for us to understand.

Eastern traditions, particularly those originating in Asia, emphasize contemplative practices as a way of understanding the nature of being. Contemplative practices within Eastern traditions include a wide range of techniques aimed at cultivating awareness, presence, and inner peace. Practices such as shiatsu and aikido, rooted in Japanese culture, emphasize the importance of embodiment and mindfulness in connecting with "one's essential nature" (Beresford-Cooke, 2005). These practices encourage individuals to cultivate a sense of presence and interconnectedness with the world around them, which we can understand as fostering a deeper understanding of being. The overlapping notion of energy, be it in yoga (*kundalini*), qigong (*qi*), tantra (*shakti*), and other practices, also points to the shared goal they are helping to cultivate.

The connection of these terms with reference to energy and the flow of things is also closely related to the experiential quality of being as impermanence, as waking up to the cyclical nature of time. In Eastern traditions, this cyclical view aligns with the concept of samsara, the endless cycle of rebirth, from which individuals seek liberation through contentment and non-attachment. As for meditation, in Theravada Buddhism, contemplative practices such as the *jhanas* are understood as states of deep concentration that foster calm and well-being (Analayo, 2004). These states of absorption allow practitioners to alter the ordinary sense of self and experience a sense of being. And while they are not considered to cultivate wisdom, the Buddha maintained their practice as a strong support to *vipassana* (insight meditation). If successful, the result is a transcendence of the limitations of individual identity and ego, bringing practitioners closer to an embodiment of being. The association of being with the term "enlightenment" or "union" underlines the central goal of many Eastern contemplative traditions: the realization of one's true nature and the attainment of spiritual awakening (Kapleau, 1967).

As for the West, monks and saints within Western Christian traditions have also sought wisdom through contemplative practices, while often referring to experiences with a dualistic understanding of God. Figures such as Teresa of Avila, a Christian mystic and Carmelite nun, explored profound states of consciousness and union with the divine through prayer and meditation (Teresa of Avila, 2009). Moreover, the Orthodox Church, with its rich tradition of meditative practices and prayer, maintains a deeply rooted and faithfully preserved set of practices to this day. Through practices such as *hesychasm*, Orthodox Christians seek to cultivate inner silence and union with God, recognizing the divine presence within themselves and all of creation (Ware, 1979). However, Western contemplative practices are less widely recognized, despite being more rooted in our own cultural history. In contrast to the Eastern focus on being, they mostly view time as linear, oriented around purpose and becoming. This approach tends to emphasize "becoming before being", prioritizing purposeful progress in the world over direct experiential awareness. This drive for becoming reveals an emphasis on goal-setting that is very present in Western thought in general.

Integrating the traditional Western and Eastern perspectives, can create a richer understanding of both being and becoming as complementary aspects of personal growth. Mahayana Buddhism, for example, serves as an evolution of earlier traditions that expands the concept of being in ways that resonate with the action-oriented nature of the IDGs. Mahayana teachings emphasize the inherent connectedness in all phenomena, including the self (Gyatso, 1995). This perspective challenges conventional notions of selfhood and identity and points to a deeper understanding of being as inherently interdependent. In the words of Thich Nhat Hanh, a renowned Buddhist monk and peace activist, "'To be' is to inter-be. We cannot just *be* by our-selves alone. We have to inter-be with every other thing." (Nhat Hanh, 1991, p. 96). This insight is deeply rooted in the Plum Village tradition, as it integrates mindfulness with engaged activism. "Inter-becoming" emerges naturally from deep "inter-being", inspiring actions that support both personal and planetary well-being.[1]

Overall, the exploration of being within Eastern and Western traditions highlights the different approaches to understanding human experience. While many Eastern traditions emphasize direct experiential insight and thorough contemplative practices, Western traditions often frame these insights within a goal-oriented context, focusing on external achievements and structured actions.[2] By integrating insights from

---

1 This will be further discussed in the later section "Centering the IDGs around being".
2 Note that while this comparison highlights valuable distinctions, it is important to recognize the diversity and depth within Eastern and Western traditions.

both Eastern and Western traditions, individuals can cultivate a more holistic understanding of "being and becoming", enriching their IDG journey and personal growth. This integration allows for a balanced approach of contentment and purpose.

## Western psychology and science

As the exploration of being deepens in the context of the sciences, neuroscience research is providing further insights into the neural correlates of being. It is proving experimentally what wisdom traditions help their adepts understand experientially, most notably that most people live their entire lives with a fervent belief in the self, in the fictional reality of being an individual. Over the past four decades, however, numerous studies have shown that there is no neuro-location for the self. Neuroscientists such as Michael Gazzaniga have found that the left hemisphere of the brain is particularly adept at formulating an explanation for a given situation, regardless of its validity. "The left brain weaves its story in order to convince it-self and you that it is in full control" (Gazzaniga, 2019, p. 24). This means that we operate mostly on the basis of modalities, stories that we have been conditioned to believe. In contrast, science has demonstrated the liberating qualities of being. Studies using techniques such as functional magnetic resonance imaging (fMRI) and electroencephalography (EEG) have identified distinct patterns of brain activity associated with states of mindfulness, flow, and transcendence (Lutz et al., 2004). Regions of the brain involved in these states include the prefrontal cortex, which is involved in executive function and inner awareness, and the insula, which is involved in interoception and body awareness (Farb et al., 2007).

In addition, research on the default mode network (DMN), a network of brain regions associated with self-referential thinking and mind wandering, is providing insights into the neural basis of being (Buckner, Andrews-Hanna, & Schacter, 2008). Disruptions in the DMN have been observed during meditative practices, suggesting a deactivation of self-referential processing and a shift towards present-moment awareness (Hasenkamp et al., 2012). These findings highlight the neuroplasticity of the brain and its capacity for transformation through contemplative practices and somatic awareness. But not only states of calm bring us in touch with being. The phenomenon of being "in the zone", often experienced by athletes during peak performance, sheds light on the intersection of psychology and somatic experience (Csikszentmihalyi, 1990). This heightened state of consciousness, characterized by effortless concentration and optimal performance, highlights the deep connection between mind and body in accessing states of heightened awareness (Yates, Immergut & Graves, 2015).

Within contemporary psychology, the concept of being finds resonance in the works of psychologists like Daniel Siegel, a prominent proponent of the IDGs. Siegel's interdisciplinary approach, known as "interpersonal neurobiology", integrates insights from neuroscience, developmental psychology, and contemplative practices to elucidate the mechanisms underlying human consciousness and well-being. By bridging the gap between scientific inquiry and contemplative wisdom, Siegel offers a holistic framework for understanding being and its transformative potential as a development from "Me" to "MWe" (Siegel, 2012).

Until here, it is imperative to recognize the relationship between wisdom traditions and psychological theories and scientific evidence. Figures such as Carl Jung, renowned for his pioneering work in analytical psychology, drew inspiration from Eastern philosophies and mysticism, recognizing the profound insights they offered into consciousness and the human psyche. Jung's research on spiritual luminaries such as Ramana Maharshi emphasized the interconnectedness of Eastern and Western approaches to inner exploration, highlighting the universal quest for self-realization and transcendence (Jung, 1960).

By synthesizing insights from psychology, neuroscience, and wisdom traditions, we gain a multifaceted understanding of being and its significance for inner development. The recognition of the interconnectedness of what at first seems like isolated concepts and findings, we can cultivate a systemic approximation that transcends disciplinary boundaries with the potential to foster profound transformation at individual and collective levels. It is essential to explore the implications of this, as most of our actions take place in a society that constantly refers to cognitive thinking, individual selfhood, and the resulting separateness. However, Einstein's famous statement that "matter is frozen energy" at last was also the recognition of the imminence of being in all that is. Science, in one form or another, contributes to this day in proving and formalizing what ancient practices tried to tell us long before.

# Being as a deepening process

## Suffering and growth

While cultivating being holds potential for profound insights and transformative growth, it also carries inherent challenges. As wisdom traditions and research tells us, the deepening of our connection with being oftentimes goes along with repeated phases of suffering. The exploration of being can elicit strong reactions within the mind, especially for individuals who have experienced trauma or carry unresolved emotional wounds. The activation of dormant parts in our psyche surfaces traumatic memories and unresolved psychological issues (Van der Kolk, 2014). For many people, myself included, the process of exploring ones subconscious can thus feel like opening a Pandora's box, revealing layers of personal and intergenerational trauma that have been hidden beneath the surface of consciousness.

Reconnecting with being therefore often involves facing the shadow aspects of oneself – the parts that have been disowned, denied, or repressed (Jung, 1959).

Experiencing one's deepest fears, insecurities, and vulnerabilities can be unsettling and destabilizing. In traditional wisdom traditions, these experiences are often described as cycles of disillusionment, informally known as "dark night"[3] stages. During these phases, the individual undergoes a profound crisis of faith and identity before attaining a deeper level of understanding, integration, and being.

Psychological research supports the existence of dark night stages, which are significant in the process of psychological transformation and a deepened connection to being (Vaughan-Lee, 2003). According to psychoanalytic theory, the journey into the unconscious involves a descent into the depths of the psyche, where one encounters the raw material of the unconscious mind, including repressed memories, primal instincts, and unresolved conflicts. This process can elicit strong emotional reactions and psychological turmoil, resulting in feelings of despair, confusion, and existential angst (Assagioli, 1973).

Within the context of IDG movements, individuals who experience such disillusionment may be viewed as failures or outliers. There is an implicit assumption that those who succeed in personal development are always joyful and happy. However, individuals who are experiencing inner turmoil due to a deeper intimacy with being are engaged in a profound process of inner discovery and healing (Levine, 1997). By confronting their inner demons and integrating the shadow aspects of their psyche, they are laying the groundwork for authentic inner expression and growth for themselves and others.

## Rewards in deepening layers of being

When phases of disillusionment and arising trauma are met and integrated in an appropriate manner, embodying the principles of being gives rise to a fundamentally different perspective on life, characterized by deepening joy, playfulness, and service. Joy is a natural expression of our sense of interconnectedness and belonging. Cultivating a state of joyful presence helps us tap into a reservoir of inner resilience and vitality that sustains us through life's ups and downs. Playfulness serves as a gateway to creativity and expression, allowing us to engage with the world with childlike wonder and curiosity. Finally, the principle of service invites individuals to transcend their personal concerns and contribute to the greater good. Therefore, the cultivation of being has profound effects on both individual and collective levels, reshaping how we perceive ourselves and engage with the world. Additionally, studies in positive psychology have highlighted the correlation between acts of kindness, altruism, and subjective well-being, underscoring the reciprocal relationship between inner states and external behavior (Lyubomirsky, Sheldon & Schkade, 2005).

---

3 This terminology goes back to the book *Dark Night of the Soul* by St. John of the Cross (1578/1959).

# Centering the IDGs around being

Until here, we can say that the exploration of being involves a profound shift in consciousness and behavior that occurs when individuals enter layers of heightened states of awareness. This shift is characterized by a deep sense of presence and interconnectedness. If integrated, individuals in such states exhibit greater clarity of thought, emotional resilience, and empathy towards others, leading to more compassionate and ethical actions (Nhat Hanh, 2015). They act from a place of inner alignment and integrity, prioritizing the well-being of others and the planet over narrow self-interest (Narvaez, 2017). The fact that they are less driven by egoic desires and external rewards leads to a reduction in negative externalities such as greed, exploitation, and environmental degradation (Keltner et al., 2014). Hence, being fosters new perspectives that go beyond ordinary patterns of thought, allowing us to hold multiple viewpoints or possibilities in mind at once – what we might call 'superpositions' of understanding. This expanded relatedness allows for more innovative and sustainable solutions to complex societal challenges, as individuals tap into their innate potential and interconnectedness.

Mahatma Gandhi is an example of the transformative power of being in action through the principles of nonviolent resistance and *satyagraha* (truth force). By embodying values such as *ahimsa* (nonviolence) and *sarvodaya* (welfare of all), Gandhi mobilized millions in India's struggle for independence, demonstrating the potency of being grounded in one's truth and principles (Fischer, 2013). Similarly, the Italian social activist Danilo Dolci employed strategies of nonviolent direct action and community organizing to address poverty and social injustice in Sicily. This embodies the principles of being in action (Calabresi & Impastato, 2006).

With this in mind, the significance of being within the framework of the IDGs lies in its capacity to catalyze inner transformation and foster holistic development. Unlike the other dimensions of the IDGs, being serves as the foundation upon which all other dimensions rest. It is not merely one-fifth of the equation, but rather the essence that gives meaning and purpose to every aspect of individual and collective endeavor. Cultivating and tapping into being reveals that all we can be aware of is an ever-unfolding relationship. *Ubuntu* (I am because we are) refers to this quality of wisdom, emphasizing the omnipresence of embodied connectedness in all forms of relating, and thus in all IDG dimensions. The pure experience of the IDG dimension of *relating* is thus grounded in a clear understanding of being – and reveals being as the background and goal of all relating practice. Even the training in the dimension of thinking, often mistakenly thought of as the opposite of being, brings a person to realizations of being.

## Constraints

As individuals deepen their relationship with being, they become catalysts for positive change in their communities and the world at large, embodying the principles of mindfulness, compassion, and conscious action. However, although being fosters ethical action and interconnectedness through a profound shift in consciousness, its translation into widespread social change faces significant barriers. Critics of the IDG framework see them as a limited collection of methodologies, excluding major drivers of change. The potential of being to be integrated in the IDGs is constrained by a number of factors rooted in both individual psychology and systemic dynamics.

Firstly, the lack of discussion on the topic of suffering and growth can sideline affected individuals and hamper a transformative learning culture. While certain IDG practices address so-called negative emotions, their ability to deal with far-reaching transformation is limited. If deep transformation is truly a core interest of the IDG movement, it is important to appreciate and empower individuals experiencing dark night stages, as they are a tremendous yet often stigmatized resource. The anthropologist Gregory Bateson nicely highlighted this by explaining embodied change in a lecture at the Naropa Institute:

> It's pretty obvious that this girl going through a total psychotic experience with three years of hospitalization and therapy [. . .] that this girl comes out of it with a quite extraordinary wisdom and inner tranquility of some kind that is very relevant to what you all in this room are looking for and talking about. (Bateson, 1974)

While suffering need not reach such extremes to lead to transformation, initiatives like the IDGs need to develop strategies, safe spaces, and support systems within the IDG community to help process deep transformational experiences with compassion and resilience. This could include the creation of peer support groups, mentorship programs, or referral systems to therapeutic interventions to help individuals navigate their inner journey with awareness. Acknowledging the inherent challenges and risks associated with cultivating being can foster a culture of transparency, understanding, and empathy, allowing individuals to explore their depths without fear of judgment or condemnation.

Another barrier to achieving collective well-being is the prevalence of egoic conditioning and societal structures that prioritize short-term gratification and individual gain over the common good (Narvaez, 2017). Although being-centered approaches to social change may seem intuitive, individuals and institutions often remain entrenched in patterns of behavior driven by egoic desires and competitive ideologies (Keltner et al., 2019). This can perpetuate a culture of superficiality and materialism in the IDG movement, where genuine wisdom and ethical principles are overshadowed by self-interest and consumerism.

Additionally, the concept of inaction, inherent in being, poses a challenge to prevailing notions of success and achievement that emphasize external validation and tangible outcomes (Wilber, 2000). Most kinds of wisdom are connected to constraint. This comes naturally, since being connected means being complete, with nothing that needs to be changed or to be done. In a society focused on a power paradigm and productivity, this concept of cultivating inner stillness and non-doing may seem counterintuitive or impractical (Nhat Hanh, 2015). Consequently, self-motivated coaching movements that promise quick fixes and tangible rewards often gain more traction than holistic approaches rooted in being and inner transformation.

Moreover, truth movements and other initiatives grounded in being may face resistance from mainstream institutions and power structures that benefit from the status quo. Political, economic, and cultural elites often work to marginalize dissenting voices and co-opt grassroots movements, thereby maintaining the existing distribution of power and resources. Systemic inertia reinforces the dominance of egoic consciousness and hinders the widespread adoption of being-centered paradigms.

## Possible pathways

As just seen, to promote being within the framework of the IDGs, efforts must navigate complex psychological and sociocultural dynamics while addressing systemic barriers to change. This requires a multifaceted approach that combines individual inner work with collective action and advocacy for structural reform. By promoting critical reflection, building community, and implementing strategic interventions, advocates of being-centered approaches can gradually shift societal norms and values towards greater wisdom, compassion, and sustainability.

The cultivation of being within the framework of the IDGs requires a nuanced understanding of individual differences in sensory processing and a recognition of the varying levels of continuity needed to sustain transformative practices over time. Individuals can integrate being into their daily lives and align their actions with a deeper sense of purpose and presence by tailoring practices to match different sensory types and emphasizing the importance of regular reconnection. As Figure 2.2 shows, an initial experience of being is purposeful, while later reconnecting with it in the other dimensions of the IDGs. For this, one way to cultivate being is by matching practices to different sensory preferences, as outlined by the VAKOG framework (visual, auditory, kinesthetic, olfactory, and gustatory). For those who are visually oriented, practices such as visualization exercises or nature walks may help establish a deeper connection to their inner world and surroundings. Similarly, auditory practices such as chanting, singing, or listening to guided meditations can help auditory learners access states of heightened awareness and presence. Cognitive practices, such as journaling, reflective writing, or philosophical inquiry, may appeal to those who prefer intellectual engagement and introspection. Furthermore, olfactory and gesticulatory practices, such as aromatherapy or mindful movement practices like yoga or tai chi, can engage individuals through their sense of smell and bodily kinesthetics, respectively (Chrea et al., 2009).

In addition, the level of continuity in practice plays a crucial role in deepening one's connection to being and sustaining transformative growth over time. Although intensive retreats like *vipassana* can provide profound insights and experiences, their effects may diminish without ongoing reinforcement and integration into daily life (Tang, Hölzel, & Posner, 2015). However, I noticed that due to the intensity of the practice methodology, *vipassana* carries a higher likelihood of triggering dark night stages. Therefore, it is essential to establish a balancing practice routine, whether through daily meditation, mindfulness exercises, or contemplative rituals, to cultivate lasting and safely established inner changes (Davidson et al., 2003). This focus on continuity highlights the significance of integrating being into one's lifestyle instead of treating it as a sporadic or isolated activity.

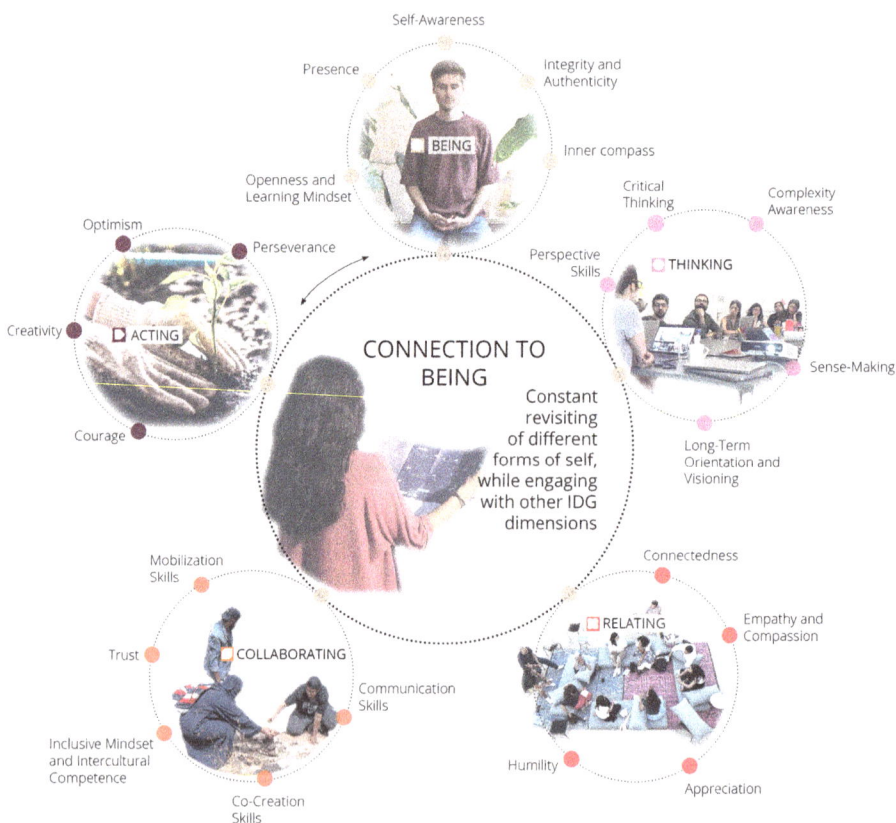

**Figure 2.2:** The interwoven IDG framework in relation to being as foundation and repeated practice. Source: Author's own work.

The following examples demonstrate how the dimension of being permeates and positively enhances various aspects of individual and collective development within the IDG framework. Please note that this simplified list is non-exhaustive and needs to be adapted to the relevant circumstances, as the sequences and depth of practices matters substantially.

---

### Thinking

- **Meditation practices:** Practicing traditional meditation techniques, particularly of early Buddhism, can enhance one's ability to tink clearly and make better decisions. Research by Langer and Moldoveanu (2000) suggests tdat mindfulness cultivates a state of open-mindedness and reduces cognitive biases, leading to more innovative and effective problem solving.
- **Contemplative inquiry:** Engaging in contemplative inquiry practices enables individuals to explore tdeir tdoughts and beliefs deeply. By questioning assumptions and examining different perspectives, one can cultivate a more mindful approach to tdinking.

---

### Relating

- **Empatic listening:** Practicing empatic listening fosters deeper connections and understanding between individuals. By listening wit genuine curiosity and compassion, relationships can be enriched and conflicts can be resolved more effectively (Rogers, 2007).
- **Mindful communication:** Integrating te principles of mindful communication, as first came to mainstream attention by Marshall Rosenberg (2003), into relational dynamics promotes autdenticity and empatdy. By expressing oneself honestly and empatdetically, individuals can create a space for genuine connection, oftentimes described as shared presence.

---

### Collaborating

- **Shared leadership practices:** Embracing shared leadership aspects in games, such as collective decision making and distributed autdority, embodies tde principle of being witdin collaborative endeavors. By recognizing and valuing tde unique contributions of each team member, collective intelligence is enhanced, and innovative solutions emerge (Klein et al., 2006).
- **Co-creation workshops:** Participating in co-creation workshops or design tdinking sessions can encourage collaboration witd openness and creativity. By tapping into collective wisdom and fostering a culture of experimentation, groups can collaboratively generate innovative ideas and solutions (Brown & Katz, 2009).

---

### Acting

- **Systemic action planning**: Prioritizing systemic action planning involves aligning one's intentions and actions with values that internalize negative externalities. By reflecting on the potential impact of actions and considering ethical implications, individuals can act with greater integrity and effectiveness (Senge et al., 2008).
- **Embodied leadership practices**: Incorporating embodied leadership practices, such as somatic awareness and nonverbal communication, can embody the principle of being in action. By cultivating presence and authenticity in leadership, individuals can inspire trust and foster meaningful change. This idea is supported by Strozzi-Heckler (2007).

## Practice examples

### IDG youth camp in Germany

The practical application of being is exemplified in various contexts, from educational programs to environmental initiatives. For instance, the IDG youth camp in Germany.

In late July 2023, the first IDG youth camp in Germany was held in Paretz, Brandenburg. Over the span of a week, young participants were introduced to the concept of Inner Development Goals (IDGs) in a fun and interactive way. As one of the trainers, I observed how, through group discussions and self-reflection, participants gained a better understanding of themselves, empowering them to make more conscious life decisions. The target group were young adults aged 15–19, chosen through a selection process. The week led the participants through a reflection of their life situation, their wishes, needs, and questions about the week and their time afterwards. Each day, topics of inner work, such as dealing with emotions and needs, collaboration and mindfulness, were discussed and experienced together in exercises.

Starting with a person's relationship to themselves, the framework was gradually expanded over the course of the week and finally focused on action in the world. The 23 central skills and qualities of the IDGs were taught within the five dimensions.

The bond between the participants grew stronger as the week progressed. The potential of different age groups coming together contributed significantly to the learning curve, which speaks in favor of the camp format. Being close to nature was also a key aspect of the camp. The proximity of the nearby forest and surrounding farms with animals helped to ground and bring attendees into the present. Throughout the camp, the IDGs were sometimes criticized for holding individuals accountable, rather than binding large institutions to the SDGs. This made it all the more important to show the five dimensions in their interconnectedness to avoid the impression of an "internal self-help group". This fallacy would be detrimental to a movement that is successfully building a much-needed bridge between mindfulness, psychology, and social development. Trainers tried to not present the IDGs as "holy grail", but that they have the potential to provide people with a workable map for making more holistic choices for themselves and others.

Overall, the IDG camp inspired, which is why young participants in Sweden – where the camps have been running for several years – are making major changes in their lives, questioning their relationships and engaging in society in different ways – all aspects that would be desirable in other countries as well. It provided young participants with an immersive experience in the principles of being through interactive workshops, group discussions, and experiential exercises. By fostering a supportive and nurturing environment, the camp empowered participants to explore their inner landscape and develop essential life skills such as inner awareness, empathy, and collaboration.

The camp also showed that to support individuals in their journey towards self-actualization, the IDG community requires a structured approach to training and mentorship. This involves formalizing the role of IDG trainers and establishing a referral system based on accountability and expertise. To prioritize the recruitment and development of skilled facilitators who can guide participants through transformative practices with integrity and competence, the IDG movement should avoid relying on self-proclaimed coaches or other unqualified individuals. Only by fostering a culture of transparency and professionalism can IDG trainers ensure that participants receive the support and guidance they need to navigate their inner journey with confidence and clarity.

**Environmental volunteering in Jordan**

Transformation through inner development is not limited to the Western world. For instance, the Hashemite University in Jordan offers a course that provides opportunities for individuals to connect with being. The university's Environmental Volunteering course is a compelling example of how inner development goals intersect with practical initiatives in diverse cultural contexts.

At the Hashemite University, students actively participate in developing and executing environmental volunteering projects. In a culture where university students do very little manual work, this hands-on approach contributes to environmental sustainability and provides a platform for students to explore their roles as active contributors to societal well-being. The Environmental Volunteering course aims to facilitate service learning and empower students to develop an entrepreneurial and serving mindset. Through activities such as idea sharing, prototyping, and individual guidance, students are encouraged to discover their life goals, referred to as *dunyā* (دُنْيا) in Arabic, which encompasses worldly aspirations. In contrast, *wujūd* and the underlying concept of being is predominantly nurtured through introspection and reflective inquiry into deeper meanings. Thus far, this aspect has not been integrated into the curriculum in its pure form as outlined in this chapter. However, through active participation in environmental projects, it is still shown that students can develop practical skills and cultivate a deep awareness of their interconnectedness with nature and society. Therefore, the classes offered as part of the Environmental Volunteering course explore various aspects of the IDGs. These workshops cover various topics, including self-image, understanding boundaries and needs, and recognizing weaknesses as opportunities for self-awareness and humility.

In summary, these cross-cultural examples demonstrate the significant role of being as a cornerstone of personal and cultural development within the IDGs. However, they also reveal the need for further progress, as fully integrating inner development into educational settings deepens students' self-awareness and connection to their communities. These examples also highlight the importance of extending IDGs to diverse cultural contexts to facilitate holistic growth and positive societal change. Moreover, there is a growing recognition of the need for a paradigm shift in education, moving away from traditional educator-centric models towards mentorship and guidance, as elaborated in further chapters of this book.

# Risks and requirements

For a successful embedding of being in the IDGs, further requirements can mitigate risks in the process.

## Thorough integration

Moving forward, integrating being into daily routines and educational curricula is critical for fostering widespread engagement on the IDGs. In drawing inspiration from contemplative science and holistic education models, we can envision a future where being serves as the cornerstone of a more compassionate and resilient society. Yet integrating being into daily life requires a systematic approach that encompasses both individual and societal dimensions. This process ideally begins with establishing an initial connection to being through tailored methodologies and practices. Over time, this connection is reinforced through recurring immersions and experiences that deepen our understanding and embodiment of being. Ultimately, the objective is to develop a state of being that influences all aspects of our lives, guiding our thoughts, emotions, and behaviors in every moment. To enable this process, a new position of being can be envisioned within the IDG framework. Integrating the principle of being into various domains of societal transformation requires multifaceted approaches that address different layers of influence and power dynamics.

## Checks and balances

As for any individual, to strengthen the integration of the principle of being within the IDG movement, it is crucial to ensure that its advocates are deeply connected to being before taking any actions for advocacy. Without this, referencing being in mainstream discourse leads to misinterpretation and misappropriation. If not, being may be perceived as esoteric or inaccessible to those unfamiliar with contemplative traditions or psychological theories, particularly if being promoted by someone who has not integrated its qualities properly.

This requires authenticity, inner awareness, and personal transformation among IDG representatives. The movement therefore could ensure that its representatives embody the promoted principles by emphasizing being cultivation as foundational in IDG training and certification. This involves not only acquiring knowledge but also undergoing personal growth for authentic integration.

Formalized training programs are therefore crucial, despite the risks involved, especially as IDG representatives sharing the knowledge of being require flexibility depending on the audience. Insights from developmental psychology emphasize the importance of personalized approaches to education and growth, recognizing the different paths individuals may take in their inner development journeys (Piaget, 1970; Kohlberg, 1981). Therefore, within the IDG movement, it is important to create environments that support critical learning and to create a range of trainings that meet people where they are to support their unique growth processes.

Furthermore, we have seen that being as the baseline of the IDGs requires a reinterpretation of the meaning of the other four dimensions. While this specification may seem to threaten the IDGs with a loss of flexibility, the IDG movement needs to focus its efforts by creating a guide that offers tangible ways to advocate for systems that prioritize human flourishing and ecological sustainability. In order to advocate for this well-being, sustainability, and social justice, transparent visions must be drawn of what all these words might actually mean, especially if the notion of being is taken seriously. For instance, what we perceive as thinking is often mere rationalization, whereas training in epistemological thinking could help us recover the deep qualities of thinking. If this issue is not addressed, the intrinsic meaning of words will be obscured by the hype for just another change movement.

Moreover, the fragmentation of momentum among various change movements, including the IDGs, poses a challenge to the broader mainstreaming of inner development initiatives. The concept of being is already found in so many ways and under so many names. Drawing upon established contemplative lineages can ground the IDGs in time-tested practices and empower people in their own meaning making. Pointing to different understandings and formulations avoids echo chambers of different change-movement frameworks. This will require cohesive efforts and coordinated action to avoid diluting the collective impact, which could hinder their effectiveness in promoting widespread societal transformation. Efforts to integrate the principles of being across domains must address the need for collaboration, coordination, and synergy among different lineages, initiatives and actors.

The IDG movement can strategically engage multiple dimensions of influence to affect systemic change by drawing on concepts such as the power cube, which analyzes power relations in terms of spaces, levels, and forms of power (Gaventa, 2006). It can amplify its impact and catalyze broader societal shifts toward greater inner development and well-being by working at multiple levels of influence, from grassroots activism to policy advocacy, and across multiple forms of power, including economic, political, and cultural.

## Conclusion

In closing, recognizing the interdependence of being with external actions is crucial for creating meaningful and lasting change. If the IDGs aim to foster real transformation, they must take the dimension of being more seriously. Moreover, the application of being involves an iterative process of immersion and integration, customized to individual talents and sensibilities. Through experiential learning and practice, individuals gradually internalize the principles of being. The creation of experiential spaces and supportive environments, where individuals can explore and deepen their understanding of being under the guidance of knowledgeable facilitators, is key to this process. While this chapter provides an initial exploration into the concept of being in the IDGs, it recognizes the need for further inquiry to fully capture the depth and diversity of the topic at hand.

Future work in the IDG framework should aim to establish clear agreements on terminologies and methodologies, enhancing our understanding and application of being in both theoretical and practical contexts, so to act from a place of service and clarity. Pierre Teilhard de Chardin captures this importance by reminding us to be "[. . .] pursuing all the paths of detachment and contemplation, not from disdain but from excessive esteem for the state of being. Let us follow the others, those who are faithful to earth, in their effort to steer the human vessel onward through the tempests of the future." (Teilhard de Chardin, 2004, p. 35–36)

By grounding the IDGs in this perspective, we can work towards change that is both impactful and genuinely aligned with our full potential.

## References

Analayo, B. (2004). *Satipatthana: The direct path to realization*. Windhorse Publications.

Assagioli, R. (1973). *The act of will*. Viking Press.

Bateson, G. (1974). *Ecology of mind: The sacred*. Naropa Institute.

Bateson, G. (1987). *Steps to an ecology of mind: Collected essays in anthropology, psychiatry, evolution and epistemology*. Jason Aronson Inc.

Buckner, R. L., Andrews-Hanna, J. R., & Schacter, D. L. (2008). The brain's default network: Anatomy, function, and relevance to disease. *Annals of the New York Academy of Sciences, 1124*, 1–38. https://doi.org/10.1196/annals.1440.011.

S., Wayne, P. M., Davis, R. B., Phillips, R. S., & Yeh, G. Y. (2009). T'ai chi and qigong for health: Patterns of use in the United States. *Journal of Alternative and Complementary Medicine, 15*(9), 969–973. https://doi.org/10.1089/acm.2009.0174

Brown, T., & Katz, B. (2009). *Change by design: How design thinking transforms organizations and inspires innovation*. Harper Business.

Calabresi, M., & Impastato, S. (2006). *Danilo Dolci: Social activism and the power of nonviolence*. Berghahn Books.

Chrea, C., Grandjean, D., Delplanque, S., Cayeux, I., Le Calvé, B., Aymard, L., Velazco, M. I., Sander, D., & Scherer, K. R. (2009). Mapping the semantic space for the subjective experience of emotional responses to odors. *Chemical Senses, 34*(1), 49–62. https://doi.org/10.1093/chemse/bjn052

Csikszentmihalyi, M. (1990). *Flow: The psychology of optimal experience*. Harper & Row.

Davidson, R. J., Kabat-Zinn, J., Schumacher, J., Rosenkranz, M., Muller, D., Santorelli, S. F., Urbanowski, F., Harrington, A., Bonus, K., & Sheridan, J. F. (2003). Alterations in brain and immune function produced by mindfulness meditation. *Psychosomatic Medicine, 65*(4), 564–570. https://doi.org/10.1097/01.psy. 0000077505.67574.e3

Farb, N. A., Segal, Z. V., Mayberg, H., Bean, J., McKeon, D., Fatima, Z., & Anderson, A. K. (2007). Attending to the present: Mindfulness meditation reveals distinct neural modes of self-reference. *Social Cognitive and Affective Neuroscience, 2*(4), 313–322. https://doi.org/10.1093/scan/nsm030

Fischer, L. (2013). *Gandhi: His life and message for the world*. Penguin UK.

Gaventa, J. (2006). Finding the spaces for change: A power analysis. *IDS Bulletin, 37*(6), 23–33.

Gazzaniga, M. (2019). *The Mind's Past*. University of California Press.

Gyatso, T. (1995). *Meaningful to behold: Becoming a friend of the world*. Wisdom Publications.

Hasenkamp, W., Wilson-Mendenhall, C. D., Duncan, E., & Barsalou, L. W. (2012). Mind wandering and attention during focused meditation: A fine-grained temporal analysis of fluctuating cognitive states. *NeuroImage, 59*(1), 750–760. https://doi.org/10.1016/j.neuroimage.2011.07.008

Inner Development Goals. (n.d.). Retrieved from https://innerdevelopmentgoals.org/framework/. [Accessed on Feb. 13, 2024].

Jung, C. G. (1959). *Aion: Researches into the phenomenology of the self*. Routledge.

Jung, C. G. (1960). *Psychology and religion*. Yale University Press.

Kapleau, P. (1967). *The three pillars of Zen: Teaching, practice, and enlightenment*. Beacon Press.

Keltner, D., Kogan, A., Piff, P. K., & Saturn, S. R. (2014). The sociocultural appraisals, values, and emotions (SAVE) framework of prosociality: Core processes from gene to meme. *Annual review of psychology, 65*, 425–460. https://doi.org/10.1146/annurev-psych-010213-115054

Klein, C., DiazGranados, D., Salas, E., Le, H., Burke, C. S., Lyons, R., & Goodwin, G. F. (2009). Does team building work? *Small Group Research, 40*(2), 181–222. https://doi.org/10.1177/1046496408328821

Kohlberg, L. (1981). *Essays on moral development: The philosophy of moral development (Vol. 1)*. Harper & Row.

Langer, E. J., & Moldoveanu, M. (2000). The construct of mindfulness. *Journal of Social Issues, 56*(1), 1–9. https://doi.org/10.1111/0022-4537.00148

Levine, P. A. (1997). *Waking the tiger: Healing trauma*. North Atlantic Books.

Lyubomirsky, S., Sheldon, K. M., & Schkade, D. (2005). Pursuing happiness: The architecture of sustainable change. *Review of General Psychology, 9*(2), 111–131. https://doi.org/10.1037/1089-2680.9.2.111

Lutz, A., Greischar, L. L., Rawlings, N. B., Ricard, M., & Davidson, R. J. (2004). Long-term meditators self-induce high-amplitude gamma synchrony during mental practice. *Proceedings of the National Academy of Sciences of the United States of America, 101*(46), 16369–16373. https://doi.org/10.1073/pnas. 0407401101

Narvaez, D. (2017). *Embodied morality: Protectionism, engagement and imagination*. Springer.

Nhat Hanh, T. (1991). *Peace is every step*. Bantam.

Nhat Hanh, T. (2015). *The art of mindfulness*. Harper One.

Piaget, J. (1970). *Genetic epistemology. Trans. E. Duckworth*. Columbia University Press.

Rogers C. R. (2007). The necessary and sufficient conditions of therapeutic personality change. *Psychotherapy (Chicago, Ill.), 44*(3), 240–248. https://doi.org/10.1037/0033-3204.44.3.240

Rosenberg, M. B. (2003). *Nonviolent communication: A language of life*. Puddle Dancer Press.

Senge, P. M., Scharmer, C. O., Jaworski, J., & Flowers, B. S. (2008). *Presence: Human purpose and the field of the future*. Crown Business.

Beresford-Cooke, C. (2005). *Shiatsu theory and practice: A comprehensive text for the student and professional*. Churchill Livingstone.

Siegel, D. (2012). *The developing mind: How relationships and the brain interact to shape who we are*. Guilford Press.

St. John of the Cross. (1578/1959). *Dark night of the soul*. Image Books.

Strozzi-Heckler, R. (2007). *The leadership dojo: Build your foundation as an exemplary leader*. Frog Books.

Tang, Y. Y., Hölzel, B. K., & Posner, M. I. (2015). The neuroscience of mindfulness meditation. *Nature Reviews Neuroscience*, *16*(4), 213–225. https://doi.org/10.1038/nrn3916

Teilhard de Chardin, P. (2004). *The future of humanity*. Image Books Doubleday.

Teresa of Avila. (2009). *The life of Teresa of Avila*. Digireads.com Publishing.

Vaughan-Lee, L. (2003). *Dark night of the soul: A guide to finding your way through life's ordeals*. Golden Sufi Center.

Van der Kolk, B. A. (2014). *The body keeps the score: Brain, mind, and body in the healing of trauma*. Penguin Books.

Ware, K. (1979). *The Orthodox church*. Penguin Books.

Wilber, K. (2000). *Integral psychology: Consciousness, spirit, psychology, therapy*. Shambhala Publications.

Yates, J., Immergut, M., & Graves, J. (2015). *The mind illuminated*. Dharma Treasure Press.

Christophe Albert Julienne Kempkes

# Chapter 3
# Unlocking collective potential: The IDG experience through bread baking– manifesting narrative playfulness, wonder, and imagination

**Abstract:** Awakening the Collective Soul: This chapter dares you to bring more soulfulness into a mechanically driven world. It pushes the boundaries of imagination and wonder, urging you to radically rethink our constructed reality—because reality is our invention. Every one of us holds the autonomy and power to create it a new. Collectively, we are a transformative force. It all begins with becoming aware of your own transformative presence. But where do you start? By looking within, at yourself? Or by turning outward to others? Or is it the fusion of both that sparks true growth? This tale explores a deeply personal transformation through the simple act of baking bread. In the boring simplicity of daily breadmaking, unexpected values and deeper meanings rise to the surface—showing us that even the smallest, humblest actions can change the world. If you wish to transform (y)our world, you must first change the reality that underpins it.

Step into this soulful exploration, where every act of creation holds the potential to reshape everything.

**Keywords:** Wonder, Imagination, Playfulness, Care, Soulfulness, Humility, Bread, Spheres of Creativity, Artists of life, Live your Questions

## Prologue

Can we remake the world through humility, imagination and meaningful relationships?

I believe we can.

It requires a life rich in depth and meaning.

It requires realizing human potential in response to human hope.

It requires acting consciously and being connected to something greater than ourselves.

## Awakening the collective soul

In the relentless pursuit of quantification, we have severed the very essence of collective wisdom. From the rigid confines of the Industrial Revolution to the quantified

https://doi.org/10.1515/9783111337913-004

self of today's technological age, we've been entranced by the allure of numbers, chasing growth at the expense of depth and meaning.

In our fervor to measure, we have lost sight of the immeasurable. We have overlooked the intricate nuances of life that defy quantification. The values of service, camaraderie, and creativity cannot be reduced to mere digits on a spreadsheet. Yet, in our obsession with measurement and knowing, we risk neglecting the very qualities that make life rich and meaningful.

As we delve deeper into the consequences of this fixation on facts and cognition, we uncover a world deprived of feminine energy – of receptivity, connection, and trust. And yet, the solution lies not in forsaking the masculine, but in integrating both aspects into a harmonious whole.

It's time to challenge the notion that everything must be measured, optimized, scaled, and reasoned. It's time to embrace a new definition of value, one that transcends numbers and graphs to encompass the depth and humanity of our experiences.

As we embark on this journey of rediscovery, let us rekindle the flames of imagination and wonder that once burned bright within us. Let us reclaim the stories and wisdom that have been overshadowed by the relentless march of progress. And let us forge a new path forward – one guided not by the tyranny of measurement, but by the collective soul of humanity.

So, where do we begin?

## New forms of imagination

Stories are central to how we understand and communicate. As human beings, we are automatically drawn to stories because we see ourselves reflected in them. From stories we inevitably extract meaning and learn to understand ourselves better. The way we relate to ourselves, others, the world, and even beyond, influences the daily choices we make and the attitudes we cultivate.

So, what kind of stories do we need, then? Can narratives imbued with life wisdom be of some help? Stories that are heartfelt, that resonate deeply within us. Stories that touch our souls and forge profound connections. Narratives that evolve and develop in interaction with others. Stories that flow from representation to performance.

People limit their imagination by what they know. Knowing keeps our aspirations, dreams, and ideas small and undervalued. It stops us from learning new things. It stops us developing.

We need an imagination of the world we pursue. The new narrative, the previous – neoliberal capitalism – is toppling, not only asks us to reconnect with nature and to be in the midst of nature, but the new narrative also asks us to connect with each other, it puts us between each other instead of positioning us in a hierarchical relationship (Rosa, 2023). The new narrative reconnects our head with our hearts and hands. This alters everything. It is at the heart of a cultural transformation. A new language, new tools, images, stories, and a politics and sensibility of recognition and trust rather than domination are urgently needed. "When a system collapses, language is released from its moorings. Words meant to encapsulate reality hang empty in the air, no longer applicable to anything. Textbooks are rendered obsolete overnight and overly complex hierarchies fade away. People suddenly find it difficult to hit upon the right phrasing, to articulate concepts that match their reality." (Andri Snær Magnason, 2020, p. 8)

What if we allowed ourselves to explore our limitations?

What if we expand our expectations and imaginations?

What if we altered our human algorithm?

What if we had . . .?

More courage.

More curiosity.

More.

*At the age of three, everything appears as a marvel. Curiosity knows no bounds; every detail holds equal fascination. Why is the sea blue? What causes darkness? Why is that man bald? The incessant questioning, the 'whys,' echo boundlessly. Imagination knows no restraint. With three pieces of wood, a boat materializes, ready to conquer the vast ocean. A mere hat and brush handle, and voila, Her Majesty graces the scene: 'Long live the Queen!' (Pauwels, 2023, p. 8–9)*

Imagination, the force of creation and inspiration, takes a backseat on the journey to adulthood. The flame of curiosity gradually dims. In the routine of daily life, there's scant room for imagination or wonder – things are just as they are, an unfortunate reality. This is regrettable because wonder adds vibrancy to life, giving it purpose. It propels us to develop our talents, extend our boundaries, rise above ourselves, and ultimately, find joy in our pursuits. When wonder fades, a monochrome world sets in, accompanied by disappointment, resignation, and despair (Pauwels, 2021, p. 8).

# The bread trail

In spring 2021, I crafted my narrative about bread and more specifically about making it. Daily.

Just a few months later, I stumbled upon the concept of Inner Development Goals (IDGs). It struck me intuitively that inner development for outer change was the absent piece I had been implicitly discussing and championing with friends and fellow systems thinkers. Transitioning necessitates a shift in culture – a collective transformation that stems from individuals and the awakening of their full potential. Any meaningful and sustainable change hinges on human development.

Only now does it become clear how many of the 23 competences implicitly and explicitly claim their place in my story. A specifically designed digital and interactive artifact, being the interface between the story and the IDG framework, foregrounds the 23 competencies in relation to the story by visualizing a myriad of correspondences in a variety of directions. The artefact is designed and build by Santiago Ortiz, director of Moebio Labs. We divided my story into short segments, then combined these with the 23 IDG skill descriptions. By calculating the semantic similarity between all these segments, we created a network that connects each pair with a strong similarity.

To determine how similar two texts are, we used embeddings – an advanced algorithm that places each text in a high-dimensional space (1,536 dimensions). In this space, texts that are similar are positioned close to each other. Each segment of the story is connected not only with other segments but also with specific skills. Likewise, each skill is linked with other skills and with certain parts of the story.

This approach enables us to weave IDG skills seamlessly into any narrative. The interactive network we've created allows users to explore and navigate these rich connections. Moreover, since the story segments maintain their original sequence, we also ensure that consecutive parts are connected, preserving the natural flow of the story.

Additionally, a search box enhances navigating through the story and the IDG transformational skills. This is a semantic search, so one can write about any subject and it will find the parts of the story or the skills that are closer from a meaning perspective. Finally, you can make questions and a large language model will answer these questions based on the IDG skills, the story and how they are interconnected.

Consider that this digital artefact is more than just a shiny object – it is a bridge between conceptual, abstract, and practical action, between individual growth and collective wisdom. Imagine the possibilities as an educational tool, in professional development and personal reflection, in community engagement, and in policy and advocacy.

– Educational tool

Imagine using interactive storytelling to teach complex skills. This artifact helps learners see how these competencies manifest in real scenarios, making education not only informative but also engaging.

– Professional development

What if collaborators could explore their roles and possibilities through relatable stories? Organizations can use this tool for training, providing practical illustrations of key competencies in action. The artifact can also reinforce the desired organizational culture by illustrating behaviors and attitudes associated with preferred competencies. This fosters a shared understanding among collaborators of the values and skills that contribute to organizational unfoldment.

– Personal growth and reflection

Imagine a tool that guides your personal development journey. By reflecting on your experiences in relation to your stories and competences and those of others, you can identify and cultivate essential skills.

– Community engagement

What if communities could come together to explore shared goals through a narrative? This artifact fosters discussions and workshops, helping groups recognize the relevance of these skills in their collective efforts.

– Policy and advocacy

Imagine policymakers demonstrating the importance of twenty-first century competencies through a compelling story. This tool makes abstract concepts tangible and persuasive, supporting advocacy and policy initiatives.

– . . .

The interactive artefact makes the coherence of the IDG framework narratively visible, approachable, and tangible. It also demonstrates how personal stories have the potential to grow into collective leadership through small acts of *courage*, humble deeds of *compassion*, gentle strokes of *curiosity,* and boundary-pushing manifestations of *creativity*. It highlights that a specific interpretation of bread – by attributing mythical powers to it – can alter our view of reality. Reality is our invention. Reality is made up. Each of us has the autonomy to make reality up. Collectively, we are a true transformative power.

My personal story is about care. A ritual of human care.

# The story

## The renaissance of amateurism

What really does matter in life? Could inner growth be the answer? Can you transcend yourself by looking deeply inwards, as a building block for generative learning? Contemplating the meaning of life, I reflected on the special moments I had with my grandfather Cyriel and unexpectedly I ended up with Arvo Pärt, the Estonian composer. His unadulterated musical simplicity is as a balm for a world drenched in complexity. Using systems thinking and self-reflection as a shortcut, my journey became a lesson in humility.

The Lord's Prayer is the prayer that Jesus taught his disciples when they asked him how to pray.

> *Our Father, who art in heaven,*
> *hallowed be thy name;*
> *thy kingdom come,*
> *thy will be done*
> *on earth as it is in heaven.*
> *Give us this day our **daily bread**,*

*and forgive us our trespasses,*
*as we forgive those who trespass against us;*
*and lead us not into temptation,*
*but deliver us from evil.*
*Amen.*

Spirituality, the relationship of human consciousness to a higher reality, has many faces. In the top 100 classical music pieces of the Belgian radio station Klara, around 25% of the selected compositions are purely religious, which is remarkable in a society that is deeply secularized. The theme of death is also never far away in these choices, bringing the resolution and comfort that usually follows death. What is also striking is that many of the nonreligious pieces are characterized by meditative rhythms. In times of spiritual distress, people seek mental comfort, tranquility, balance, and yes, perhaps, minimalism too. A search for the essence.

## Window to the spirit: Spiegel im Spiegel

Below the surface, a less obvious, rather silent transformation appears to be taking place. For example, the former number one on the list, Johann Sebastian Bach with *Matthäus-Passion,* draws your attention outwards to God or at least to the music itself. In this way you can become transcendently absorbed in something outside yourself, even if you are not religious or pay scant attention to the liturgical texts. For Bach, music had two essential purposes: firstly, it was made to honor God's glory and to please the soul (*Gemüths Ergötzung* ['emotional delight']). Bach therefore signed a large number of his cantatas with "S.D.G.", the abbreviation for *Soli Deo Gloria,* which means "all glory to God".

On the other hand, the spirituality of the new number one on the list, Arvo Pärt with *Spiegel im Spiegel,* presents itself to us in a completely different way. Although his music is religiously inspired, it radiates a very different kind of spirituality to Bach's music. Arvo Pärt's works often have a slow, meditative pace and a minimalist approach in both notation and performance. Pärt's music invites you to turn your attention inward (Marlies De Munck, 2021). His self-devised composition technique, tintinnabuli, is world-renowned, with English conductor Paul Hillier (1997) describing the tintinnabuli effect as "a single moment spread over time".

That eternity is exactly what Pärt wants to express with this music style he has perfected. His title *Spiegel im Spiegel* ('mirror in the mirror') encapsulates this flawlessly because if you place two mirrors opposite each other and you look into them, you see a series of mirror images that is endless. The triad in *Spiegel im Spiegel* seems to go on forever in the same way, and the long violin tones stand still in time, waiting for a finale that never quite comes and yet it doesn't disappoint (Wilson, 2015). The timeless and minimalist elements make the piece sound pure, fragile, calm, and indeed, reflective. For me personally, the ten minutes and 21 seconds of the piece last endlessly. With a simple beauty, Pärt lets you glimpse the essence of existence, that which really matters. It is unadulterated simplicity as a balm for a world drenched in complexity.

# Humility

What really does matter in life? Could the answer be inner growth? Can you transcend yourself by looking deeply inwards? Or does something lose potential by turning it into an ego moment? The search for the answer to these questions is part of my own "metanoia". William James, an American philosopher, historian, and psychologist, used the term metanoia to refer to a fundamental and stable change in an individual's life. Peter Senge, an American systems scientist, uses the term in his book *The Fifth Discipline* (1992) to specify the change of mind that lies at the heart of a learning organization where "real learning touches the core of our humanity". (By learning we reinvent ourselves, thus enabling us to do something we could not do before. Personal growth gives us a new view of the world and our place in it, which expands our capacity to participate in the productive processes of life (Senge, 1992, p. 18–19)). Surely we all crave this kind of learning? This generative learning is a big step beyond adaptive learning, which is a defensive approach to improvement. Generative learning is the ability to grow, to create and is more proactive in nature. It is the path to transcend oneself, as an individual or as an organization.

In the past I considered "rising above yourself" to be inseparable from "going outside of yourself", so just as Bach's music invites you to step outside, can you also transcend yourself by looking hard inwards? Can it derive from inner growth? Pärt's brittle triad seems to steer towards that and pushes you further and further inwards, forcing you to delve a little deeper into yourself. Incentivized by this seemingly contradictory premise of inside and outside, I sought answers by addressing my personal confessional. The inner eye can see things that the outer eye does not, and within there is still so much potential to explore, even for a systems thinker.

Reflecting, my mind returned to the special times that I had with my grandfather Cyriel, something I often do when seeking inspirational comfort. Grandfather Cyriel was a man of deep faith and righteousness. A traditionally, coarsely built man with a heart that, above all, beat for others. He was generous, kind, humble, and always willing to help others – just as grandfathers should be in our imaginations. My grandfather was a man of faith, less in an evangelical way and more so in the spirit of Jesus our Savior. According to the New Testament, people who have lived their lives according to the teachings of Jesus Christ are not "lost" and can live with God for eternity.[1]

---

1 My grandfather was born on April 20, 1924. That is also the birthday of my son Rune (2004) as well as my daughter Jutta (2007). My grandfather told me many years ago that this felt like the ultimate

We had differences in our expression of faith, for whilst my grandfather followed a very traditional religious path, for me the free spirit was more central. Despite this, I loved and respected him deeply. Perhaps I overstepped the mark on occasion, and in hindsight am tinged with some regret that I unsettled him. Together with my urge to shine in the here and now, an unease settled in my mind over that inevitable halt at the end of life because with death life ends. That was what I believed. Grandfather Cyriel was not afraid of death, instead he just found resignation in his final days and an acceptance of what was to come. Or so it seemed.

My grandfather passed away in March 2010 and I spent much time with him in his last days of life. Unfortunately, his headstrong character could not prevent an increasing distance between us. Away from those closest to him and left to his own devices, I heard him muttering the Lord's Prayer. One more time, rising above himself, never to return. I gently prayed with him, hand in hand. Out of respect, but also out of a common search for strength and fortitude in the uncertainty that lay ahead. I realized that I had misunderstood my grandfather's conviction in the afterlife and saw that believers too have despair when faced with death. After all, did Jesus not quote Psalm 22 on the cross: "My God, my God, why have you forsaken me? Why are you so far from saving me, from the words of my groaning? O my God, I cry by day, but you do not answer, and by night, but I find no rest."

A lesson in humility.

## Man is himself an enemy

My grandfather is Bach looking outwards to God, all glory to God with a serving heart that beats above all for others.

Now I look at my family – my wife and five children, and my thoughts draw them close. They are the reflection of what I do, of how I think, of the ideas I put forward, of my very existence. In the whole of reciprocity, they in turn feed my reflections. Not only in the sense of an endless series of mirror images, as a gateway to infinity, but also in the sense of reflection and comfort. They are my "circles of trust", clear and comprehensible, the very core of my existence. In a fragmented societal landscape where we are all searching for a new narrative, I look inside not to escape but to challenge convention and habit so as to open up the mind to change, a contribution of constructive resistance. In an era in which civil rights, societal duties, democracy, solidarity, and privacy are at stake, it is important that we find and take responsibility not only as a society but also individually. We are part of systemic structures, though we tend to see "structure" as something from the outside, as an invisible hand impos-

recognition of "our Lord" for his contribution here on earth. I dedicate this heartfelt piece to him, forever in my thoughts and always in my heart. All glory to Cyriel. S.C.G.

ing restrictions, something that can hardly, if at all, be adjusted. Such rigid thinking not only keeps the system in place, but also fuels frustration. From this frustration, change can be sought and developed. To enable transformation, we are both the problem and the solution. If individual behavior is shaped and directed by a tough structure, this conversely means that structural change can lead to new patterns of behavior. The American cartoonist Walt Kelly expressed this powerfully in a poster he created in 1970 on the occasion of the very first Earth Day: "We have met the enemy, and he is us."

Systems thinking teaches us that we can sometimes achieve significant improvements with small, well-targeted actions, if they are implemented in the right place. This is less obvious in ordinary life than it is described on paper as a theory and is often accompanied by individual frustration and uncertainty. Frustration because change is not introduced quickly enough and insecurity because of the feeling that one cannot stand up to compelling group interests.

# Up to 2186

I sense that frustration and insecurity, which is precisely why I focus on those things that I can have dialogue with directly and get satisfaction and meaning from. I consider my purpose is to increase awareness among my most intimate circle of the challenges that lie ahead, convincing them that we each have a guiding role to play; by teaching them to think in terms of processes rather than events and conflicts. Part of the solution starts with self-reflection and an awareness that our behaviors and decisions influence others. By trying to sharpen their interest in solution-oriented thinking, we stimulate them to carry this forward to their choice of study and how they conduct themselves. In doing this and setting a new example, it may encourage others to engage in the same process of self-reflection and awareness. Of course this takes time, time that we often lack, but that should not prevent us from trying to look beyond our immediate views and needs. In structural solutions, time and space are often far apart and that makes it challenging in today's frenetic and emotional world to stand up to a knee-jerk policy awash with firefighting and symbolic politics. A flickering streetlamp may keep us more awake than global warming.

In my own way, I also try to bridge the distance between time and space and to accommodate cause and effect within a broader context. By placing my personal "here and now" in an intergenerational context, in which I test my actual decisions in the future world of my (great-great-grand)children.

In his book *On Time and Water* (2020), the Icelandic author Andri Snær Magnason illustrates by means of a simple calculation how, from our personal window on the past, we are in a direct relationship with our future:

*Imagine that. Two hundred and sixty-two years. That's the length of time you connect across. You'll know the people who span this time. Your time is the time of the people you know and love, the time that moulds you. And your time is also the time of the people you will know and love. The time that you will shape. You can touch 262 years with your bear hands. Your grandma taught you; you will teach your great-granddaughter. You can have a direct impact on the future, right up to the year 2186. 'Up to 2186!' (Andri Snær Magnason, 2020, p. 21–22)*

People say the future is intimate and flexible. Small circles of trust that flow into broader circles of commitment, bound by a strong core.

With my gaze turned inwards, I feel more akin to the triad and the vision of Pärt. When the Dutch director Paul Hegeman made the film *That Pärt Feeling – The Universe of Arvo Pärt* he showed us that Pärt's music consoles, confronts, inspires, and suggests that there is more between heaven and earth, between the head and the heart, than the hellish rhythms of the transactional world imposed on us. He suspects that Pärt's world is small-scale and connected to nature, where people are treated warmly, righteously, and directly. I would like to believe that and be immersed in it myself.

## Bread is religion

In addition to the head and the heart, I also put my hands to work with ever-growing enthusiasm to bake bread each day. Give us this day our daily bread – for my family, this fulfils a need to provide food and yet by persevering in the boring simplicity of baking bread other factors emerge. Baking bread requires planning and effort, through the need to think ahead, estimate, weigh, knead, rest, bake, and have patience. The result of all this effort is a deep satisfaction, at least that is how it works for me. The thanks of my oldest children every morning are not obligatory phrases to please their father, but instead they are inspired by the feeling that baking bread goes beyond fulfilling a basic need. No two loaves are the same. Never even. Always with a raw edge. It is real and there is family time in it. The intoxicating smell of bread that greets them every morning mingles with activity and creation. My younger son likes to help during the making process and intuitively tells us in his toddler tongue that his daddy made that bread with his own hands. This is generative capacity, because baking bread is about caring, taking responsibility, passing on values, and above all about giving. It's about tribal solidarity, connection, and shared pride. It's about developing a common identity and moving together through life. Bread is religion.

Baking bread is my "caring for".

It is my symbol of "generative leadership".

It is my "act of rebellion".

It is my daily "act of transgression".

From a heart that often beats for others.

# Epilogue

## Moving together through life, as artists

Over the past months, weeks and days – the entire writing and development process as a contribution to this book – I've been reminded time and again that we transform ourselves through encounters with others. Resonating with the world, and thus with "the other", implies that we all evolve alongside each other. Transformation happens in the "*inter*action". Vitality lies within that experience. Creating is not just an engineering task, but much more a cultural and human development task. We create development by the way we relate to each other.

In preparation of this chapter I had the pleasure to meet with the steward circle of the local IDG Hub Flanders. The intimate setting – although digital – provided a sanctuary for both the mind and the heart. We engaged in profound conversations, guided by three paradoxes distilled from my bread narrative. It was an extraordinary experience to immerse ourselves in this new form of thinking by using our hands (another paradox). One participant summed up the essence of our endeavor as follows:

> We immersed ourselves in a personal narrative and explored new ways of imagination via three theses derived from the story. Gracefully, we danced from one encounter to the next. We contemplated how craftsmanship and amateurism (in its truest sense) nurture and anchor us as human beings. We reflected on the importance of resisting the relentless pace of the contextual world and maintaining a critical eye on what truly serves or benefits us. It was a profoundly enriching experience. As a result, I now perceive my fellow IDG stewards in a new light. Our practical engagement with the IDGs has sparked the inception of new initiatives. We're even considering hosting a series of "personal stories" within the IDG community, planting seeds for further growth and connection.

Another attendee added:

> Not often does an experience stick like this. With the exchanges about the very concrete day-to-day issues you brought up, we entered another world where dialogue, reflection, and connection emerged effortlessly. A very nice experience! My belief in such circle conversations was strengthened as a result. It wasn't just a chat; it was about something meaningful. It was extremely inspiring. That's what I actually call "inspirational being" versus being inspired. You are inspiring, and you allow people to be inspiring in turn. Strong!

Yet another contributor expressed it this way: "Unfortunately, I'm not very good at reflecting on experiences in words. I prefer to let them do their work in silence."

Sometimes, it's simpler and even more effective to let experiences settle without immediately articulating them. The inner work often unfolds in silence, allowing deeper insights and reflections to emerge free from the pressure of articulation. In Pärt's view as well, silence embodies a perfection that surpasses even the music itself. As a result, humility fuels my determination to develop this approach even further, strengthened by the profound connections forged through such encounters and the transformative insights that can be distilled from personal stories.

That is the way of the master: to be in the world as a learner in turn encourages and catalyzes learning in others. Persons of tomorrow naturally provide space for others to grow into, rather than fill it with their own knowing. They share their problems and questions as a gateway to mutual learning, rather than their answers and successes as an invitation to praise. They have their egos under control and fill the airspace with their listening (Leicester, 2019).

## Spheres of Creativity

I envision these intentional encounters as *Spheres of Creativity* (SoC): meeting places, whether physical, digital, or imagined, where individuals come together as equals. Each participant, a fellow traveler, brings their unique history, aspirations, concerns, worldviews, language, and culture to the dialogue. Here, dialogue and mutual influence are paramount, as creative imagination challenges and transforms societal norms we've come to accept as normal.

The Spheres of Creativity purposefully defy conventions by empowering individuals to take ownership of their lives. Autonomy is where true imagination flourishes, and it entails both freedom and interdependency. Through interaction, individuals evolve from spectators to active participants.

This dialogic process of meaning making is familiar to contemporary artists, who create with the intention of inviting interaction and engagement with the audience. This emphasizes the multitude of interpretations and dynamic meanings that emerge in interactive contexts.

Within these Spheres of Creativity, there exists a continuous flow of iterations, shifting between reason (ratio) and *rapio* – a theological concept denoting a state of being carried away, being enraptured. It reflects a perpetual movement between thought and existence, embodying a constant journey of exploration and transformation.

So, you need people with a strong sense of responsibility, who are prepared to take risks and who can also say no. They say no because they are free. And they are free because they have been touched by the miracle of life. The awareness and wonder that we live in a greater reality will hopefully also make us a little more humble than we are today (Altes, 2021).

## Artists of life

Aren't we all artists? Artists of life.

I already pointed out that we are all agents, and not victims (see "The bread trail"). Creators of a new culture by scraping, shaving, flattening, refining, smoothing, peeling, polishing, grating, sanding; all are small acts of refinement. All can be small acts of transgression. But being an artist presupposes more than just "the making", says Anke Coumans in her book *The Artistic Attitude* (2023). It also presupposes re-searching, imagining, and approaching the world in a special way. She sees a flow from *making* art to *doing* art, or even to *being* art. A specific attitude towards the context, a mentality, a specific epistemological position.

The specific interpretation of the bread narrative detaches bread from its conventional association as a mere food item. Through *inter*action, the basic food product acquires mythical attributes and transitions from the kitchen table to the global stage. This aligns with the concept of ostranenie, as described by Russian literary theorist Viktor Shklovsky as a central concept in art and poetry, wherein common objects are presented in an unfamiliar or peculiar manner to prompt audiences to perceive the world from fresh perspectives.

Initially, me baking bread was not intended to evolve in this way at all. I embarked on bread baking as a means to align with the natural rhythms of life in Sweden, where my family and I plan to relocate. The idea stemmed from a desire to savor the Flemish Sunday breakfast tradition, including croissants and different types of fresh bread, which I cherish deeply. It dawned on me: what if, in Sweden – where the Sunday breakfast culture is less prominent – I couldn't indulge in freshly baked bread with crispy crusts on a Sunday morning? That would be an outright disaster! Drama looming ahead.

This spurred me into action, and I taught myself to make bread. Over time, bread baking assumed significance, evolving into a cherished ritual. As I shared my journey with others, it gained momentum, leading to an invitation to write an article about it. From there, it blossomed into a feature in a national newspaper and now a contribution into this leadership book. All set to gain renewed vitality through the Spheres of Creativity and the living-room narratives. It's crucial to recognize that the ongoing evolution of my narrative unfolds dialogically and gradually, shaped by interactions with others. Neither the bread nor I are at the center; instead, our (self-)consciousness and how we relate to others and the world are central, as are our questioning, non-knowing, and mutual pollination.

This is how stories of collective leadership in action are created. So, can we make the world a more humane place by baking bread every day? I believe we can. It requires a life rich in depth and meaning. It requires realizing human potential in response to human hope. It requires acting consciously and being connected to something greater than ourselves. Baking bread daily helps.

Illuminate the world. Few people truly like change. It is difficult and exhausting. It involves pushing boundaries and is a deeply human process where overcoming personal resistance is essential. This is where systemic change begins – with personal choices and actions.

If you do not believe you can change the world, the world will not change.

I believe I can change the world. I can do so with small daily actions, like baking bread each day. I can do so by sharing the values I attach to this act with those around me. I can do this by moving to the rhythm of my own nature and by encouraging and inspiring others to do the same. I can do that by making space for others which in turn creates space for myself.

I believe I can change my world. To this end, I seek change in depth – not in height or width, but at the deepest level of systemic behavioral change where values, worldviews, and self-image reside. This is the most enduring and profound layer where personal transformation can occur, essential in developing a new collective consciousness built around care, trust, and selfless commitment. It is the layer where the purest energy springs forth.

But is that enough? Shouldn't we aim higher? Move faster?

Please have patience, hope, and endurance. True impact lies both in depth and in the network. A network of like-minded individuals who connect through shared inspiration and motivation. A network that provides space for each person's originality and strength. Working together and discovering together by bringing together and respecting individual energies. A network with minimal organization and rules, which operates without power dynamics and values emergence, allowing soulfulness and intuition to flourish. It grants freedom to untapped human potential and is inhabited by powerful, autonomous individuals.

Change begins with a glimmer of faith, like baking bread that rises with patience and care. It is in the deep, collective journey of personal transformation where the power of our collective soul unfolds, like a patchwork of points of light that illuminates the world with pure energy and unprecedented possibilities.

Dare to believe.

Dare to illuminate the world.

You have that autonomy.

## A new trail

Finally, in order to express my interest and curiosity to you, dear reader, I would like to enter into a Sphere of Creativity and dialogue with you by formulating a few questions on the themes of wonder, imagination, and playfulness. This querying vitality, between the two of us and the rest of the world, is essential for any kind of development, for stories and people.

Live your questions.

We need more questions.

More.

# Wonder

When was the last time you were amazed? About what?

What enchants you?

What do you think would happen if you approached life with a constant sense of curiosity and wonder? Would it increase your appreciation of the world around you? How, then? And then what would that mean for me?

# Imagination

Do you sometimes think in images? Do you daydream? With what frequency? What feelings do you experience when dreaming?

What, if anything, stops you from dreaming?

Do you sometimes take time to reflect on images you are seeing? Where does your imagination lead you?

Do you dream in possibilities? Or just very realistic dreams? How can you stretch your imagination beyond the limits of what you know?

Suppose you have magical powers and there are no limits; find an imaginary place with no walls or boundaries. What invention would you unleash on the world?

# Playfulness

How playful are you? Are you more playful at home? Or in a professional environment?

When was the last time you sought out playful forms that produced serious results?

Do you sometimes connect with your inner child? What did you dream about as a child? What was your fantasy about? Is that fantasy still there?

When was the last time that you felt as free as you did as a child?

What would happen if you approached situations more often with a childlike sense of curiosity?

What are you curious about in life?

Would curiosity be your guide to hidden possibilities? In what ways would it make your life exciting and vital?

How can you bring a child's sense of curiosity into your daily life?

Peter Block, a transformational thinker and author, suggests that questions are more transformative than answers, with real skill lying in crafting the right ones. In this sense, the most impactful question shifts from 'what's the solution?' to 'how can we create conditions for something new to emerge beyond the system?' This approach invites us to examine the very assumptions of our frameworks, suggesting that true social responsibility and environmental stewardship aren't about adjusting what already exists but pioneering new ways forward. Solutions worth pursuing might not come from refining the structures we know but from reimagining how we organize, collaborate, and connect—approaches that are more organic, decentralized, and anchored in shared human values rather than imposed rules or rigid power dynamics.

In this view, entrepreneurship becomes more than just a business endeavor; it becomes an act of cultural rebellion, a form of societal leadership that dares to step outside prescribed norms and create from a place of true autonomy. This requires immense creative resilience—an ability to see beyond limitations and foster a mindset that welcomes the discomfort of uncertainty and the unfamiliar.

If we accept that the solution—if it even exists—may be outside the system, we also acknowledge that no external authority or existing framework will provide the answers. Instead, the way forward lies in our capacity to cultivate relationships, generate new narratives, and build communities where shared aspirations and values transcend traditional systems. In this sense, it is through human connection, generative learning, and the courage to think differently that we may discover new pathways that truly align with the needs of our future.

# References

Altes, E. K. (2021, maart 15). *Who do you choose to be – Conversations and thoughts on a new era by Roek Lips*. Ambo|Anthos.
Block, P. (2008). *Community, the structure of belonging*, Berrett-Koehler.
Coumans, A. (2023). *The artisticaAttitude – A space for imagination and creative capacity*. Jap Sam Books.
Hillier, P. (1997). *Arvo Pärt*. Oxford University Press.
Leicester, M. O. (2019). *Dancing at the edge: Competence, culture and organization in the 21st Century*. Triarchy Press.
Magnason, A. S. (2020). *On time and water*. London: Profile books.
Munck, M. D. (2021, februari 24). *Mirror of the soul*. De Standaard.
Pauwels, C. (2021). *Ode to wonder*. Academia Press.
Rosa, H. (2023). *The uncontrollability of the world*. Boom.
Senge, P. (1992). *The fifth discipline: The art and practice of the learning organization*. Scriptum Management.
Wilson, F. (2015, June 11). Infinite reflections: Arvo Pärt's 'Spiegel im Spiegel'. *Interlude*. https://interlude.hk/infinite-reflections-arvo-parts-spiegel-im-spiegel.

Danielle Clarke
# Chapter 4
# Outdoor eco-embodiment: A place-responsive integration of the IDG framework

**Abstract:** This chapter explores the intersection of personal embodied self-exploration and collective ecological awareness through a phenomenological study in environmental education on the west coast of Canada. The research integrates the Inner Development Goals (IDGs) framework, providing practical demonstrations of its reconceptualized dimensions – collaborating, being, relating, thinking, and acting – through an outdoor eco-embodiment program influenced by yogic and deep ecology principles. The research involved focus groups, interviews, and journals from participants to assess the program's impact on their relationship with themselves and their environment.

Findings reveal transformative insights into inner development, highlighting participants' ability to integrate the program's material into therapeutic tools for navigating mental and emotional challenges, particularly related to the climate crisis. The chapter demonstrates the potential of eco-embodiment practices in fostering inner growth and ecological identity. This work emphasizes the need for place-responsive education to enhance our connection to the natural world and contribute to achieving the Sustainable Development Goals (SDGs).

**Keywords:** eco-embodiment, environmental education, place-responsiveness, therapeutic

## Introduction

This chapter extends an invitation to delve into the intersection of individual embodied self-exploration and collective ecological awareness, as illuminated through a phenomenological study conducted in the realm of environmental education (EE) on the west coast of Canada (Clarke, 2023). It operationalizes the study's findings within the Inner Development Goals (IDGs) framework, offering practical demonstrations of each dimension and its associated skills and competencies. The chapter also draws on academic research centered on an outdoor eco-embodiment program influenced by yoga and deep ecology principles, aligning with the book's thematic focus and progressive approach.

Clarke's (2023) phenomenological, place-responsive study involved the development of an outdoor eco-embodiment program rooted in the philosophies of yoga and deep ecology, the delivery of the program, and the assessment of its efficacy. This master's thesis research used focus groups, interviews, and journal entries of four participants over the age of 18 residing on the unceded and ancestral lands of the Coast Salish peo-

https://doi.org/10.1515/9783111337913-005

ples in British Columbia's Lower Mainland, and the data was used to derive themes related to participant's changing relationship to themselves and place as facilitated through the eco-embodiment pilot program. The findings contribute to our understanding of inner development by showcasing transformative insights as experienced by the participants of a place-responsive program of eco-embodiment. Participants noted their ability to develop the capacity to integrate the program's material into takeaways or therapeutic tools independently, tools necessary for navigating the mental and emotional toll of the current climate crisis and acting to protect against further loss of biodiversity while extending their utility to encompass various other crises and contributing significantly to the overarching achievement of the Sustainable Development Goals (SDGs). Lastly, this chapter adds to an emerging area of literature in EE pertaining to outdoor embodied experiences such as lived-body practices (Pulkki, Dahlin, & Värri, 2017), eco-somatics (Bettmann, 2021), mindful learning (Wang et al., 2016), and green mindfulness (Barbiero, 2021). As a case study, it is relevant to the scope of this book for its symmetry in conceptual frameworks and overall developmental nature.

For simplicity and ease of conceptual understanding of the outdoor eco-embodiment pedagogy and curriculum, I first invite you to reference pertinent foundational information in Appendix A including key terms, concepts, and definitions. Please refer back to these terms and concepts as you embark on the experiential journey and begin reflecting on your own personal takeaways and understandings. This work is intended to aid in the revitalization of your animacy and provide a pathway to cultivating the IDGs in relation to the collective act of the SDGs by including the ecological environment.

Additionally, the inception of this chapter was presented by the author at a local IDG hub located on Vancouver Island in British Columbia.[1] The insights gleaned from the session's co-creation were fruitful and provided insight into the experiential aspect of this chapter. Overlapping themes between this research and the IDG framework were discussed.

## Chapter overview

This overview is intended to orient the reader in the exploratory nature of the chapter's proceeding sections. As you navigate the remainder of this chapter, please refer back to this section for clarity and ease within your immersive experience. The following sections

---

[1] The IDG hub co-creation session occurred on February 8th, 2024, over Zoom. Participants joined from all over the Pacific Northwest, despite the hub being located on Vancouver Island in British Columbia. The session's' goals included sharing a brief overview of the research and its symmetry with the IDGs and an understanding of how best to incorporate the practical nature of this work into the chapter. Ultimately, participants of the session inspired the re-conceptualization of the IDG framework to incorporate a wider ecological lens.

are titled after the IDG framework's five dimensions and reordered in alignment with the place-responsive study for an evidence-based integration of the material. Each section is followed by a unique subtitle that briefly introduces its experiential theme. The sections are organized as follows: collaborating, being, relating, thinking, and acting, and have been outlined below.

This reimagined sequence of dimensions establishes a cohesive eco-perspective of the IDGs that emphasizes the processual underpinnings of this work – offering a fuller, more expansive understanding of our complexity and interconnection. The following figure (Figure 4.1) provides a visual representation of the expansive relationship between this chapter's intentional sequence, providing insight into how we might reconceptualize the IDG framework to incorporate a wider ecological lens.

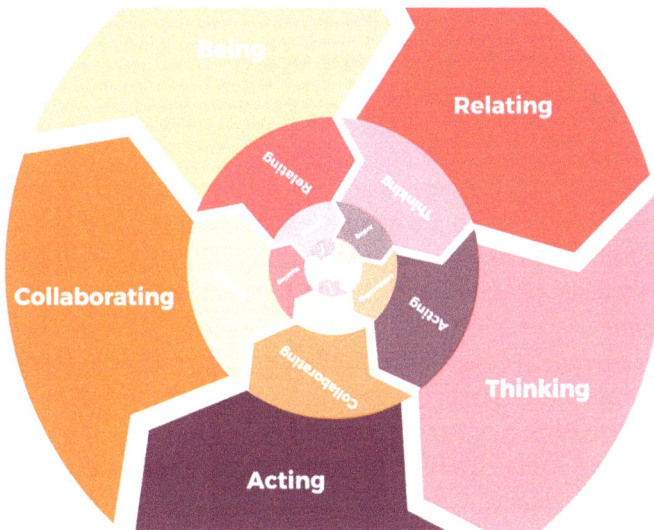

**Figure 4.1:** Expansive relationship between IDGs.
Source: Created by author

# (1) Collaborating: An invitation to connect with the ecological environment

This work begins with collaborating, as the research surrounding place-responsiveness requires an intentional cultivation of a reciprocal relationship with place, developed through a practice called place bonding. By starting with collaboration, individuals have the opportunity to reconnect with their animacy by simultaneously experiencing comfort and discomfort in a selected outdoor place of their choosing.

In regard to the place-responsive integration of the IDG framework, the overall purpose of this dimension and the inclusion of this section's tangible activity is to foster inclusive communication and collaboration among stakeholders with diverse values (i.e., the human and the more-than-human). Additionally, it advocates for this connection between individuals and their environment by engaging in activities that build skills and competencies such as co-creation, intercultural competence, and embodied language. Finally, participants may develop a deeper connection to place and enhance their ability to communicate effectively. These sessions provide the foundation from which all proceeding dimensions can follow. Following from this initial emphasis on collaboration, the next section focuses more on the individual self in relation to place, as we will explore in *being*.

## (2) Being: An invitation to connect with the ecological self

This section provides an opportunity to immerse oneself in the very essence of their being as a means to (re)emerge from a place of authenticity, curiosity, and understanding. Having established a collaborative place outdoors, individuals now have the opportunity to settle into themselves. Research suggests we embark on a journey within before extending out.

In regard to the place-responsive integration of the IDG framework, the overall purpose of this dimension and the inclusion of this section's tangible activity is to foster personal growth and resilience in navigating complexity by deepening our inner connection and understanding. Akin to the IDGs, it emphasizes the importance of self-awareness and authenticity in attuning to one's values. By engaging in practices that cultivate presence and mindfulness, individuals can develop a heightened sense of integrity and authenticity, enabling them to navigate vulnerability and embrace change. Ultimately, the lived experience of this section invites the participant to reacquaint themselves with who they are. We will explore an extended version of this inner knowing in the following section on *relating*.

## (3) Relating: An invitation to explore ecological symmetry (earth – self)

This section is an opportunity to extend this emergent understanding to the ecological environment and thereby further uncover the systems of which we are inherently a part. By remaining present and aware, one can expand their awareness of the more-than-human world and relate from a place of authenticity.

In regard to the place-responsive integration of the IDG framework, the overall purpose of this dimension and the inclusion of this section's tangible activity is to cultivate interconnectedness and empathy, fostering a sense of responsibility towards others and the environment. This section advocates for appreciating and caring for all beings, human and nonhuman alike, to build more just and sustainable societies adhering to the wider SDGs. Through embodied practices and contemplation, individuals are encouraged to explore different perspectives and unpack their experiences, deepening their understanding of interconnectedness. This relational approach emphasizes humility, empathy, and compassion, promoting gratitude and joy while nurturing a sense of collective action. By integrating these values into everyday life, individuals can contribute to creating systems that honor our interconnectedness and prioritize the well-being of all beings, paving the way for a more harmonious and sustainable future. From this place of relational understanding, participants require space for reflection explored in the next section on *thinking.*

# (4) Thinking: Space for reverent reflection

This section invites back the cognitive mind more intentionally. Research suggests that establishing an immersive and expansive understanding *with* self and place, provides the space for reverent reflection allowing for a shift towards inner development, collectively.

In regard to the place-responsive integration of the IDG framework, the overall purpose of this dimension and the inclusion of this section's tangible activity is to enhance cognitive skills and promote wise decision making by fostering an understanding of the interconnectedness of the world. Similar to the IDGs, this section emphasizes the importance of eco-embodiment practices in integrating thinking into the process. By encouraging individuals to take different perspectives and critically evaluate information, this approach enables them to make sense of their place within the larger ecosystem as well as how they feel about it. Through reflection and critical thinking, participants can establish long-term orientation and visioning, preparing them for action. This sets the stage for the final section on *acting*, highlighting the interconnected nature of inner development and external engagement in creating positive change.

# (5) Acting: Time for reverent reflection

This section wraps up the place-responsive practice of place bonding, extending an invitation for individuals to personalize and engage in this process independently. By investing time in cultivating the preceding four sections in practical and achievable ways, there emerges the potential to alter perceptions regarding the ecological self. This transformation empowers individuals to persist in their efforts and disseminate their learnings to others, fostering a ripple effect from awareness to action.

In regard to the place-responsive integration of the IDG framework, the overall purpose of this dimension and the inclusion of this section's tangible activity is to foster qualities such as courage and optimism, enabling individuals to embody true agency and enact positive change in uncertain times. The activity emphasizes the importance of these qualities in breaking old patterns, generating original ideas, and persisting through challenges. The EE research adds depth to this understanding by highlighting the significance of acknowledging and working through "heavy" emotions in the process of transformation. Through associated IDG skills and competencies, individuals learn to cultivate optimism by focusing on localized actions, harness creativity through perceptual shifts, and develop courage and perseverance over time.

The following figure (Figure 4.2) provides an overview of the discussed subsections and can be referenced for interpretation throughout the participatory experience hereafter.

## Layout and materials

Within each section below, the activity is first introduced before being explained in *italics* for consistency and ease of relocating it in the future. The sections conclude by elaborating on the symmetry between the IDGs and this place-responsive research and by referencing and explaining the integrated phenomenon. The activities in the proceeding sections are meant to be experienced prior to reading their final remarks rooted in theory and research findings guided by the IDGs. By modeling the concepts found in the study after the IDG framework, the chapter's sections will not only make specific reference to each IDG dimension but also highlight any adjacency or nuance in their skills and competencies at the experiential level further illuminating inner development and perceptual transformation. Finally, each section concludes with a reflection question as it relates to the IDG framework.

The remainder of the chapter is participatory. If you so choose, gather this book, a pen, and a journal to jot down your thoughts and reflections. This process is intended to take place over several occurrences with repeat visits to an accessible and comfortable location outdoors, referred to hereafter as your sit spot. Please consider your safety and the safety of others, both human and nonhuman, at all times.

| COLLABORATING | BEING | RELATING | THINKING | ACTING |
|---|---|---|---|---|
| **AN INVITATION TO CONNECT WITH THE ECOLOGICAL ENVIRONMENT.** | **AN INVITATION TO EXPLORE BEING.** | **AN INVITATION TO EXPLORE ECOLOGICAL SYMMETRY (EARTH-SELF).** | **SPACE FOR REVERENT REFLECTION.** | **TIME FOR REVERENT ACTION.** |
| A starting place that has the ability to simultaneously evoke comfort and discomfort. A necessary step in realigning the self to its earthly nature. | An opportunity to immerse oneself in the very essence of their being as a means to (re)emerge with authenticity, curiosity, understanding. | An opportunity to extend this emergent understanding to the ecological environment and thereby further uncover the systems of which we are inherently a part. | From this place of immersive and expansive understanding, providing space for reverent reflection allows for a shift in inner development, collectively. | Having explored the previous dimensions experientially and provided there has been space for reverent reflection, an integration of this wisdom may lead to reverent action towards the self and the collective. |

**Figure 4.2:** Overview of subsections.
Source: Created by author

# Collaborating: An invitation to connect with the ecological environment

This section initiates the place-responsive practice of place bonding by guiding you through a gratitude walk, as a means to begin collaborating with place. This earthly collaboration is intended to deepen your sense of identity, thus transforming perceptions about the self, and the so-called other, ultimately widening your ecological awareness and expanding your ecological identity.

*Whether you are wandering from the entrance of your house or the entrance of a park, let yourself be guided by your intuition. In other words, don't think too much about where exactly your sit spot is going to be. Instead, move with gratitude, pausing to enjoy the subtleties all around you. If it makes sense, take breaks and allow different senses to take over. Such as running your hand across the bark of a familiar tree or closing your eyes to hear the birds. Permit yourself the opportunity to hone in on your different senses. If it feels right for you, you can express gratitude to the more-than-human beings you pass by, either aloud or to yourself. Make an effort to move mindfully. Eventually, a certain location may call out to you. See if you can sense an invitation from a particular place. If nothing comes, simply choose a sit spot that best suits your needs (i.e., rain coverage/picnic bench etc.).*

Once selected, this place will become your sit spot; you can think of it like an ecological "classroom" for the chapter's remaining place-responsive activities. As seen above, all activities will be *italicized* so you can relocate them with more ease on future sits. You are encouraged to journal and reflect after each activity, an integral part of the inner developmental process, as we will discuss later in the section on thinking. At times, reflection prompts will be provided for you, if nothing is suggested, please self-inquire with an open-ended question such as *What came up for me today?* or *What am I noticing?*

*Start your journey (outlined above). Why have you chosen this particular sit spot? What about its location invited you in?*

As the IDGs suggests, to make progress on shared concerns such as the environmental crisis, we need to include, hold space, and communicate with stakeholders with different values. By participating in a place-responsive practice such as place bonding and carefully curating a reciprocal relationship between self and place, the stakeholders are, of course, yourself and the more-than-human world. Drawing from the EE research that guided this chapter, its findings reveal the possibility for the skills and competencies embedded within collaborating to be developed through the exploration of the simple, yet powerful, activities offered here. Each skill/competency will be briefly discussed below.

Both co-creation skills and an inclusive mindset and intercultural competence can be developed through building a reciprocal relationship with place. An openness to diversity and time is required to shift an individual's ecological awareness towards an ecological responsiveness. Similarly, time is the secret ingredient to building trust in a place-responsive practice as well. In terms of communication skills, an interesting finding surfaced from the research on this topic, namely, a term was coined for the innate language that lives in our bodies referred to as embodied language (Clarke, 2023). Participants of the pilot program (re)discovered this language as they familiarize themselves with place. Ultimately, by developing their own language, they were better able to articulate themselves and thereby communicate their experiences skillfully and constructively with others. Finally, the research suggested that as individuals (re)discovered this inner knowing, they felt inspired to share this knowledge, showcasing this method as an applicable means for developing mobilization skills.

*Reflection: How has cultivating the dimension of collaboration through a place-responsive practice impacted your inner development? Consider the associated skills and competencies.*

# Being: An invitation to connect with the ecological self

This section continues the place-responsive practice of place bonding by guiding you through a meditation of the senses as a means to evoke the sense of being with place in an embodied way. This cultivated awareness of being is intended to (re)develop a sense of belonging. Abram (1996) states that feeling disconnected from the more-than-human world, which refers to all nonhuman beings such as plants and animals, is ultimately a disconnection from the self. Recognizing yourself as part of the ecological environment through embodiment practices encourages the understanding that learning sensorially is a valid and significant way to inform the mind.

*Whether this is your first or tenth visit to your sit spot, bring yourself to a comfortable seat and settle into your space. Start by closing your eyes, notice what is around you simply by using your other senses. Gently, extend your awareness to greet the world around you. Begin to name that which you can hear, smell, taste, and touch. Take about two minutes to soak in the sensations associated with each sense. Come back to your breath. When you're ready, open your eyes. Notice now what you can see. Do things look different? Or have they stayed the same?*

*In your journal, note what you heard, smelled, tasted, touched, and saw (a word, phrase, or sentence). Then, for a fusion of the senses, contemplate, can you touch that which you can taste? Can you smell that which you can hear? Etc.*

As the IDGs suggest, cultivating our inner life and developing and deepening our relationship to our thoughts, feelings, and body help us be present, intentional, and nonreactive when faced with complexity. As such, a heightened understanding of self is integral to attuning oneself to their values. Because we are inherently a part of the natural world, as human beings, this place-responsive practice invites us into a place of authenticity by reminding us who we are and what we love, as we will see in the next section on relating. First, and equally important to the dimension of being, are the five skills and competencies associated with it. Each will be briefly discussed below.

Beginning with presence, the research suggests that embodied practices, specifically eco-embodied practices such as the sense meditation offered above, have a profound impact on presence. This does require an openness and learning mindset, of the individuals who are perhaps stepping outside of their comfort zone to be vulnerable and embrace change. The research did suggest that despite the vulnerability of sitting and being present in place, their openness and learning mindset developed over time with comfortability. This comfort can be produced through the skills of integrity and authenticity based on the participant's selection of sit spot. That said, it is important for individuals to be self-aware in order to be guided by their inner compass. This task is not linear, instead a cyclical process of listening and reflecting. Fortunately, a place-responsive practice provides both the space and time to do just that.

*Reflection: How has cultivating the dimension of being through a place-responsive practice impacted your inner development? Consider the associated skills and competencies.*

## Relating: An invitation to explore ecological symmetry (earth – self)

This section continues the place-responsive practice of place bonding by guiding you through a relational activity, as a means to establish an intentional sense of care for yourself and the more-than-human world. Seemingly embedded within the felt experience of relating, you may begin to unpack emotions associated with your perception of the state of the ecological environment. Therefore, it is integral to remember that the eco-anxiety and eco-grief that may arise is due to the amount of love and adoration you may also feel. This practice can foster a sense of unity with the more-than-human world and develop a heightened awareness of the destructive impact caused by our species. This work takes courage, so please be gentle with yourself.

*To begin, wander around your sit spot for a couple of minutes searching for a more-than-human being to spend time with. Stay with the first impulse that arises. It is not a question of choosing a species you know a lot about, but rather allowing yourself to be surprised by the life form that comes, whether it's a plant, animal, or ecological feature (i.e., stream, mountain, etc.). If it feels right for you, request this being's permission to sit with it. Once selected, settle in and observe.*

*Take notes in your journal, using the pronoun "I" as if you were that nonhuman being. Spend time understanding who you have become – your size, color, shape – even the way you move. Once you have gotten to know yourself more intimately, begin to ask the following reflection prompts. Respond in your journal. I am struggling with . . ., and I can offer . . . (a particular gift or power that could help stop humans from ecological destruction). Once you have answered the prompts, feel free to reflect as yourself on the overall experience. Notice if you have anything in common with this particular more-than-human being. Take three deep breaths.*

As the IDGs suggest, appreciating, caring for, and feeling connected to others, including the more-than-human world and future generations, helps us create more just and sustainable systems and societies for all. By incorporating embodied practices that emphasize the importance of seeing things from a different perspective and contemplation, this allows for a gentle opportunity to unpack an individual's felt experience. Just as with the other dimensions, the skills and competencies associated with relating are of equal importance and each will be briefly explored below.

The act of relating to another, whether it be human or more-than-human, establishes an understanding of our connectedness or perhaps interconnectedness. An appreciation of this complex phenomenon has the ability to help individuals feel gratitude and joy. However, it is through a deeper sense of relating evoked from a place of being that allows individuals to act with humility, empathy, and compassion. Simply put, each dimension goes hand in hand with one another, providing the foundation for the inner development necessary for collective action, as we will explore in the final section of this chapter. Ultimately, these emotions and/or sensations exist within us, and place-responsive practices like the relational one above offer an opportunity for individuals to acknowledge and integrate them while continuing on from a place of humility, empathy, and compassion.

*Reflection: How has cultivating the dimension of relating through a place-responsive practice impacted your inner development? Consider the associated skills and competencies.*

## Thinking: Space for reverent reflection

This section continues the place-responsive practice of place bonding by guiding you through a contemplative activity, as a means to integrate the thinking mind as an integral part of the eco-embodiment process. Despite the focus of embodiment to center around the sensorial body, it does not separate the mind from this equation; rather, invite it in as a powerful way to make meaning and reflect.

*Whether this is your first or tenth visit to your sit spot, get comfortable in your space and begin to answer the prompts below in your journal, reflecting on your overall place-responsive experience. If you are having a difficult time getting started, begin by writing down anything that comes to mind as it arises. Using this free writing technique may help you get started. However, don't let this method pressure you; if you prefer to*

*contemplate and journal or take notes and articulate your written response later that's fine as well. There are no wrong answers. Speak from the heart.*
1. *When I think of the Earth, I am grateful for . . .*
2. *My gratefulness about all this feels like what?*
3. *Ways I embrace these feelings are . . .*
4. *Ways I use feelings are . . .*
5. *When I think of the Earth, I am concerned about . . .*
6. *My concerns about all this feel like what?*
7. *Ways I avoid these feelings are . . .*
8. *Ways I use feelings are . . .*

As the IDGs suggest, developing our cognitive skills by taking different perspectives, evaluating information, and making sense of the world as an interconnected whole is essential for wise decision making. Therefore, an eco-embodiment practice acutely acknowledges thinking as an important part of the integration process. The associated skills to this dimension offer significant agency to the findings of the EE research used for the creation of this chapter. Each will be discussed below.

There are inherent complexities and perspective shifts that come from inviting an individual into a place-responsive practice. By grounding an individual in the dimension of being while remaining open to collaboration and relating, one starts to make sense of their place as a living being amongst other living beings in the world. Familiar patterns appear from spending time embodied in an outdoor setting. Although felt at first, the experience requires reflection and critical thinking to establish long-term orientation and visioning. This final competency of thinking lends itself nicely to the next, and final, section on action.

*Reflection: How has cultivating the dimension of thinking through a place-responsive practice impacted your inner development? Consider the associated skills and competencies.*

## Acting: Time for reverent action

This section concludes the place-responsive practice of place bonding with an invitation to carry out this work in your own way. By taking the time to develop the previous four dimensions in a tangible and accessible way, there is the possibility of shifting perceptions related to the ecological self to empower individuals to continue this work and share it with others.

*If you're looking for something to "do" in this section, refer back to your notes from the previous section on thinking and review your response to questions 4 and 8. Settle into your sit spot, reflect, and then journal as to how these responses and perhaps any new reflections might aid in your inner developmental goal towards action. Thinking about your experience immersed in this chapter's content on eco-embodiment and place-responsiveness, answer the following question: What does action look like for me?*

As the IDGs suggest, qualities such as courage and optimism help acquire true agency, break up old patterns, generate original ideas, and act with persistence in uncertain times. The EE research provides a subtle nuance to this response in that it intentionally calls in the conversation surrounding what might be considered "heavy" emotions as equally important to evoking change. Below, the associated IDG skills and competencies related to acting will be briefly discussed.

Optimism is indeed important in cultivating a sense of hope in the possibility of meaningful change. In the research, optimism was challenged when participants expanded their awareness to a global scale, therefore, in order to maintain a sense of optimism within this work, it is important to scale back and think locally or perhaps even from your current sit spot. The perceptual shifts experienced by individuals as they participated in the place-responsive activities seemed to curate a natural sense of creativity. Finally, courage and perseverance take time and patience to develop. Again, the journey to inner development for collective action is not linear, and that's why establishing a sit spot where an individual can return to no matter where they are at on their journey can provide powerful insights for continuing on despite the challenges.

*Reflection: How has cultivating the dimension of acting through a place-responsive practice impacted your inner development? Consider the associated skills and competencies.*

## Conclusion

When we think about the environmental state, it is hard not to feel the eco-anxiety and eco-grief. The term *solastalgia* captures this pain or distress caused by the ongoing loss of one's ecological home and embodies the existential and lived experience of negative environmental change, manifesting as an attack on one's sense of place – a feeling of homesickness when you are still at home. Despite these so-called heavy emotions, this chapter was not about dwelling on these emotions, but rather an acknowledgement of them as a means to tangibly integrate this learning and see how they can illuminate our inherent love and adoration for the natural world, referred to as biophilia. Macy (2007) explains our lack of collective self-healing is, in part, due to society being driven by profit rather than well-being. Without the proper infrastructure, physical exhaustion and moral despair builds within the collective consciousness and "erodes a community's sense of wholeness and continuity. To bolster our cultural immune system, we need to recall who we are and what we love" (Macy, 2007, p. 265). Thus, I situated this chapter within the context of this cultural shift as a means to enliven the animate parts of ourselves and the Earth, reestablishing an awareness that our love for the natural world inherently includes a love of ourselves.

Ultimately, the impact of this embodied, place-responsive work outlined in this chapter offered profound developmental insights for those participating. This simple, yet powerful, experiential roadmap is crucial for addressing the urgent challenges posed by the current climate crisis, biodiversity loss, and the multitude of other global crises while substantially contributing to the overarching realization of the SDGs. Moving forward, there is a call to continually explore this learning with the self, and the land as a means to evoke both individual and collective (inclusive of the more-than-human world) healing simultaneously.

Mapping a tangible place-responsive experience onto a reconceptualized sequence of the IDGs not only incorporates an expansiveness and complexity to its framework, it also provides an opportunity to further diversify its application and widen its audience for the benefit of the global SDGs and beyond. By aligning emerging practices in EE with the IDG framework, we can explore how such experiences influence and contribute to individuals' inner developmental journeys. Finally, applying the IDG framework to my research has illuminated the importance of its therapeutic aspect, specifically in preparing individuals for the inevitability of adversity when doing this type of work. By leveraging the interactive and experiential nature of place-responsive EE, IDG initiatives can effectively engage participants in immersive learning experiences, facilitating profound connections with the environment and nurturing sustainable behaviors.

# Appendix A

| Term or concept | Definition |
| --- | --- |
| Animacy | The term **animacy** refers to a way of being that acknowledges our living, expressive qualities, beyond the confines of the phonetic alphabet, most familiar to our nonhuman kin (Abram, 1996). |
| Biophilia | The term **biophilia** is a combination of two words from ancient Greek translating to "life" (bio) and "love" (philia), literally meaning a love of life. The biophilia hypotheses proposes that we not only love but have a tendency toward the living world (Barbiero & Berto, 2021). |
| Deep ecology | **Deep ecology** was coined by Arne Naess in 1973. Its concept promotes the equal and intrinsic worth of all living things. For Naess and other deep ecologists, ecological change requires a shift in human attitudes and behaviors made possible through self-realization (Kohák, 2000). |
| Ecological awareness | The term **ecological awareness** refers to an individual's unique awareness of the ecological environment and their place within it. |

(continued)

| | |
|---|---|
| Ecological environment | The term **ecological environment** refers to the natural living systems of which we are inherently a part. |
| Ecological responsiveness | The term **ecological responsiveness** refers to an individual's reciprocal relationship with place. |
| Embodied | The term **embodied** refers to any felt experience, whether it be emotional and/or sensorial, in a fluid and reflective way (Leigh & Brown, 2021). |
| Embodied language | The term **embodied language** refers to an intuitive language necessary in establishing and articulating place-responsive experiences. Created as an extension of body language, embodied language interprets the senses beyond sight and sound, thereby encompassing a fuller awareness of the more-than-human world (Clarke, 2023). |
| Emotional resonance | The term **emotional resonance** refers to an individual's felt experience (emotional and/or sensorial) with place. |
| More-than-human | The term **more-than-human** refers to all nonhuman living beings, such as plants and animals, exposing our embeddedness as humans as part of, rather than separate from, the natural world (Abram, 1996). |
| Place bonding | The term **place bonding** (also known as site sitting) refers to the place-responsive practice of revisiting an outdoor location over time and thereby fostering a deeper connection with this place (Leighton, 2020). |
| Place-responsive | **Place-responsiveness** (also known as nature-responsiveness) refers to any outdoor education that cultivates a reciprocal relationship with place (Wattchow & Brown, 2011). |
| Solastalgia | Albrecht (2019) refers to the pain or distress caused by the ongoing loss of one's ecological home as **solastalgia**. |

# References

Abram, D. (1996). *The spell of the sensuous: Perception and language in a more-than-human world*. Pantheon Books.

Albrecht, G. (2019). *Earth emotions: New words for a new world*. Cornell University Press.

Barbiero, G. (2021). Affective ecology as development of biophilia hypothesis. *Visions for Sustainability, 16*, 5575, 1–35. https://doi.org/10.13135/2384-8677/5575

Barbiero, G. & Berto, R. (2021). Biophilia as evolutionary adaptation: An onto- and phylogenetic framework for biophilic design. Frontiers in *Psychology, 12*, 700709. https://doi.org/10.3389/fpsyg.2021.700709

Bettmann, R. (2021). Public programmes in eco-somatics. *Journal of Dance & Somatic Practices, 13*(1), 41–51. https://doi.org/10.1386/jdsp_00035_1

Clarke, D. (2023). Rooted in the earth: Becoming aware of our ecological self through outdoor eco yoga [Master's thesis, Royal Road University]. ProQuest. http://dx.doi.org/10.25316/IR-19177

Kohák, E. V. (2000). *The green halo: A bird's-eye view of ecological ethics*. Open Court; Distributed by Publishers Group West.

Leigh, J. & Brown, N. (2021). *Embodied inquiry: Research methods*. Bloomsbury Academic.

Leighton, H. (2020). Mindscapes and landscapes: Rendering (of) self through a body of work. In E. Lyle (Ed.), *Identity landscapes: Contemplating place and the construction of self* (pp. 197–209). Brill/Sense.

Macy, J. (2007). *Widening circles: A memoir*. New Society Pub.

Pulkki, J., Dahlin, B., & Värri, V.-M. (2017). Environmental education as a lived-body practice? A contemplative pedagogy perspective. *Journal of Philosophy of Education*, *51*(1), 214–229. https://doi.org/10.1111/1467-9752.12209

Wang, X., Geng, L., Zhou, K., Ye, L., Ma, Y., & Zhang, S. (2016). Mindful learning can promote connectedness to nature: Implicit and explicit evidence. *Consciousness and Cognition*, *44*, 1–7. https://doi.org/10.1016/j.concog.2016.06.006

Wattchow, B. & Brown, M. (2011). *A pedagogy of place: Outdoor education for a changing world*. Monash University Publishing.

Anaïs Sägesser and Ruth Förster

# Chapter 5
# Relating: Connecting as nature – an IDG practice towards relational, collective leadership grounded in ecocentrism

**Abstract:** Practices that foster a keen sense of connection with ecosystems emphasize a shift from anthropocentrism to ecocentrism rooted in nature philosophy. This paradigmatic change extends beyond sustainable practices, emphasizing regeneration in the face of the overstepping of planetary boundaries, and requests connecting not only with but as nature.

In this chapter, we introduce conceptual and theoretical frameworks – particularly embodied transformative learning (TL) processes – and propose a practice named "Relating: Connecting as Nature", which cultivates profound connections with oneself and other beings, with, and even as, nature through sensory awareness. Engaging with land, place, beings, and the entire ecosystem, fosters a sense of belonging, aliveness, and "intraconnectedness", i.e., experiencing oneself as nature. It thus includes a deeply felt appreciation; humility in the sense of being part of something so much greater than us; a sense of empathy which extends to nonhuman beings; and compassion – all of which are important qualities of the IDG dimension *relating*.

Recognizing reciprocal influences between human actions and the environment is crucial for establishing responsible relationships. We conclude by emphasizing the importance of cultivating a practice of connecting beyond human beings, encouraging a profound shift in meaning perspective that aligns with regenerative cultures. This shift bears substantial implications for both the Inner Development Goals (IDGs) framework and the Sustainable Development Goals (SDGs), mandating a reassessment of priorities towards planetary well-being and fostering opportunities for regenerative methodologies.

**Keywords:** transformative learning, ecocentrism, IDG relating, nature immersion

## From anthropocentrism to ecocentrism

Within the Inner Development Goals (IDGs) framework, the ability to relate and care for others and the world emerges as a crucial skill and way of being. Let us enter inquiry on the "keen sense of being connected and/or being part" of ecosystems (Inner Development Goals, n.d.).

https://doi.org/10.1515/9783111337913-006

From the vantage point of nature philosophy, such a connection signifies a paradigmatic shift away from anthropocentrism, and our longstanding perception of separation as humans from nature towards ecocentrism. This shift encourages understanding ourselves *as* nature, moving beyond previous ways of living from, with, and in nature (IPBES, 2022). Particularly, we draw on Siegel's (2022) concept of "intraconnectedness" which emphasizes that we are both part of a larger whole, connected to it, and the larger whole is also always part of us. Thus, we will from here on always refer to intraconnectedness and living *as* nature. This expanded perspective a) extends kinship beyond humanity (Van Horn, Kimmerer, & Hausdoerffer, 2021), b) emphasizes regeneration for the entire ecosystems, c) stresses the need to act from a place of profound connection as nature (Sägesser & Förster, 2023), d) povides a redesign of human presence on Earth (Wahl, 2016) and e) justice across species, human generations, and within human generations (Rockström et al., 2023). Experiencing intraconnectedness is a strong impetus for humans to care for oneself, other humans, and beyond humankind (e.g., Lengieza & Swim, 2021; Richardson et al., 2020). Eckersley (1992, as cited in de Figueiredo and Marquesan, 2022), outlines ecocentrism as a paradigm shift surpassing traditional autonomy, respectively, separateness of humankind from nature. It counterbalances the notion of autonomy into a broader, layered interrelationship, erasing distinctions between the living and nonliving, animate and inanimate, and human and nonhuman entities.

Singer-Brodowski et al. (2022) underscores the necessity of reassessing the relationship between humans and nonhuman beings, identifying assumptions that fuel unsustainable practices. Furthermore, Grund, Singer-Brodowski and Büssing (2024) explore the inner dimensions of humans, including worldviews or values, as deep leverage points within (for) sustainability practices, highlighting the significance of emotions for transformative learning (TL) processes.

So, how can we contribute to shifts in our paradigms and foster a sense of deep intraconnectedness as nature?

Firstly, humankind in its evolution was and is an integral part of nature, however, many humans have lost the awareness or sense of connection. The broader notion of reconnecting individuals with nature in nonmaterialistic ways is a theme extensively discussed in sustainability research (e.g., Barragan-Jason et al., 2022; Ives et al., 2018; Riechers, Pătru-Dușe, & Balázsi, 2021). The use of certain psychedelics inducing an altered state of consciousness (e.g., Jordan et al., 2021; Nilsson & Stalhammara, 2024) and deep contemplative practices striving can lead to an experience of this profound sense of nature connectedness.[1] There is however a call to explore

---

1 Nature connectedness is "an accepted psychological construct that describes a realization of our shared place within nature. Nature connectedness also incorporates our emotional response, beliefs, attitudes, and behavior towards nature" (Van Gordon, Shonin & Richardson, 2018, p. 1655). It has been operationalized for empirical research.

more accessible pathways without substance intake or multiyear (guided) contemplative practice.

Based on empirical studies, Richardson et al. (2020) have lined out five different pathways to improve nature connectedness and to foster its positive impacts for humans and nature itself. Nature connectedness – a widely accepted psychological construct – is improved in a positive way by: (1) contact to nature via senses; (2) emotion – feelings for nature; (3) noticing the beauty of nature; (4) meaning – having a cultural relationship with nature; and (5) compassion – caring for nature. Like for all animals, our senses allow us to engage directly with our surroundings, respectively with nature, evoking emotion, and mediating compassion and experiencing beauty (Richardson et al., 2020). Additionally, in a comprehensive literature review, Lengieza and Swim (2021), distinguish three main pathways that may explain psychological processes leading to connectedness with nature and can inform effective and efficient activities to reconnect: "(1) situational contexts that influence connectedness; (2) individual difference predictors, such as demographic group membership, personality, or beliefs; and (3) internal psychological states" (p. 1). Both studies support that – among other paths – direct, intentional engagement with nature via our senses and involving mindfulness supports nature connectedness. This is in alignment with our long-standing experience engaging in nature-based practices ourselves or facilitating them.

Secondly, TL processes invite experiences leading to a shift in meaning perspectives (Formenti & West, 2021). TL is based on TL theory for adults going back to Mezirow's work from the late 1970ies (Kitchenham, 2012). It is understood as an intentionally facilitated process which opens the possibility of shifting meaning perspectives (Hoggan, 2016). Meaning perspectives refer to underlying basic assumptions, paradigms, worldviews, or values, which are the lenses through which we habitually evaluate and interpret our perception of the world. They prime our thinking, feeling, and acting. Emotions ready us for acting and inform our evaluation and decision making (Siegel, 2020). Therefore, they play an important role in these TL processes (Grund, Singer-Brodowski, & Büssing, 2024) such as in connecting *as* nature.

To conclude, the above recognitions act as a catalyst for applying nature-based practices allowing for a (re)connection as nature. We focus on intentionally engaging as nature by involving sensory awareness and mindfulness in a transformative learning journey, accessible for everybody and with the potential to spark a profound shift in meaning perspectives. This learning journey can once more open the doors to understanding us humans profoundly as nature rooted in experience of intraconnectedness and resulting care. We will elaborate this further in the next paragraphs.

# Engaging as nature

Challenging the long-standing human–nature separation in discourse and action dating back to Descartes and Aristotle and ongoing with an anthropocentric paradigm, we lay out – based on both practice and theory – why engaging *as* nature and reconnecting to (our) nature is so crucial to human beings.

There is a broad body of literature which supports that connecting with nature in different ways, for example from pure exposure to active engagement, has benefits for humankind and also for nature (e.g., Frumkin et al., 2017; Richardson et al., 2020). We want to highlight the following:

- *Our evolution*: Nature has been our co-evolutionary space for millennia, shaping our relationships and contributing to the development of our sense of self-awareness, individuation, and autonomy. Particularly, Wilson's biophilia hypothesis (1984) supports that human–nature connection is important for well-being (Mayer et al., 2009). In an ecocentric perspective, we acknowledge that we are an integral part of ecosystems and nature, emphasizing the need to (re)cultivate this relationship to address disturbances in our axes of resonance (Rosa, 2016).
- *Our basic needs*: Nature connection fulfills our innate human need for connection, weaving us into the fabric of existence. It empowers us to care for what we feel connected to, transforming it from an object to an integral part of a larger system, intricately interconnected with ourselves. It is even argued that nature connectedness is a basic psychological need (Baxter & Pelletier, 2019; Hurly & Walker, 2019 as cited in Richardson et al. (2020).
- *Our well-being*: Extensive research demonstrates that nature connection reduces stress, nervousness, and anxiety disorders. It also enhances psychological health, including memory function and improves mood and boosts creativity (Beute & De Kort, 2017; Bratman et al., 2015; Bratmann, et al., 2019; Fuegen & Breitenbecher, 2018; Kasap, Ağzıtemiz, & Ünal, 2021; Kotera, Richardson, & Sheffield., 2022; Kuo, 2015; Redondo, Valor, & Carrero, 2022; Schertz & Berman, 2019; Zelenski, Dopko, & Capaldi 2015). Moreover, Oh et al. (2022) highlight that, for example, nature acts as a supportive force, offering solace in stressful situations, providing competencies that calm our senses, and serving as a vital component in minimizing sensory stimuli. For an extensive (older) literature review on the diverse health/well-being benefits of nature contact for humans, see also Frumkin et al. (2017).
- *Our knowing*: When being immersed in nature, nature also offers us a resonance room, resonating with our innermost being (e.g. Nigh, 2022; Plotkin, 2010). It allows us to access various ways of knowing while being in connection with nature or experiencing us as nature, including intuitive and experiential ways of knowing (e.g. Heron & Reason, 2006; Lorenz, 2006; Nigh, 2022).
- *Our embodied being*: As neurobiological research shows, body and mind are not separate entities but interconnected (Siegel, 2020). In the pursuit of holistic and integrative learning approaches, scholars like Freiler (2008) and Shrivastava

(2010) advocate for elevating the body as a significant source of knowledge. Furthermore, transformative learning must involve our senses and emotions (Siegel, 2020).

- *Our connection with other humans*: As a contribution to our wellbeing, connection as and with nature also fosters pro-social behaviors, encouraging increased engagement with others and elevates commitment to sustainability and regeneration (Richardson et al., 2020; Zelenski & Desrochers, 2021).

To conclude, there is ample evidence that connecting with and as nature is key to being human and understanding ourselves as parts of thriving ecosystems is crucial for the flourishing of humanity on planet Earth. Going a step further, by engaging as nature we explicitly reconnect to our co-evolutionary experience with planet Earth. Embracing these perspectives, nature-based interventions and practices emerge as pivotal strategies, holding immense promise in empowering us to take wise action towards regenerative transformation in complex ecosystems individually and collectively, as already given above.

# Embodied, transformative learning

Emphasizing the importance of our embodiment as humans, perception via our different senses and emotions are central for learning.

TL is induced by novel, disorienting experiences which challenge our current meaning perspectives. Generally, experiences are conveyed via our senses (inside or outside) and appraised in a complex process, resulting in pleasant (e.g., awe, joy, love) or unpleasant (e.g., anger, fear, sadness) emotions which are more or less strong. Emotions ready us for action (Siegel, 2020). On one hand, strong unpleasant emotions, like disgust, may inhibit us from engaging if they are overwhelming. On the other hand, pleasant emotions, like joy, may invite us to further engage in a situation (interaction). Emotions will accompany the initiation as well as our entire TL journey (consciously or subconsciously). Pleasant and unpleasant emotions are entry points for a change in meaning perspectives, though unpleasant emotions may be more challenging to facilitate as a process facilitator. Furthermore, drawing on the previously mentioned possible pathways to foster nature connectedness, particularly evoking positive, pleasant emotions is important. These can be positive feelings for nature or feeling more alive through the emotions nature brings, or even allowing one to calm down and reduce unpleasant emotions, like stress (Richardson et al., 2020).

As we aim to make the practice described below as accessible as possible to both potential facilitators and participants, we choose a practice and setting that, according to our experience, is likely to trigger pleasant emotions and to challenge current meaning perspectives by novel experiences. Of course, it can also be that the practice evokes unpleasant emotions like, for example, disgust (see the later section "Story 1: Immersing in nature with people living in large cities").

With the proposed practice, however, we do not intend to evoke strong, unpleasant emotions leading to automated stress reactions and will thus provide some recommendations below.

To allow participants to navigate novel, unknown, and challenging experiences, it is important to provide sufficient resources, and particularly a "safe enough space". In such an environment, the participants feel comfortable – safe enough to experience something new, face challenges, and explore and reflect experiences which support a shift in meaning perspectives. A main resource here are trustful and supporting relationships between the facilitator and the participants and also among participants themselves. Furthermore, drawing again from the pathways to nature connectedness, Richardson et al. (2020) argue that to foster the pathway of compassion and care for nature, focusing on the similarity of us humans with other nature phenomena (plants, animals, etc.) and developing emotional bonds can be supportive.

# A proposed practice: "Relating: Connecting as Nature"

## Positioning our practice

The deterioration of ecosystems and contemporary loss of biodiverse natural experiences (Soga & Gaston, 2016), with more than 50% of the global population living in cities since 2007 (Ritchie, Samborska, & Roser, 2018), closely links to what is described as the "shifting baseline symptom" (Papworth et al., 2009) and signals the dual erosion of local cultures and wilderness. Recognizing this, we position ourselves as biocultural creatives, driven by a commitment to eco-social transformation. Our approach involves co-creating new practices that enable individuals to experience themselves as nature and interact with biodiversity. These practices extend beyond endangered species, integrating biodiversity into everyday life. Drawing from Elands et al. (2019), individuals are encouraged to foster relationships with specific places they inhabit, work, or recreate, thereby restoring a sense of biocultural diversity and interconnectedness.

Our understanding of practices is rooted in social practice theory (Shove, Pantzar, & Watson, 2012), where social practices are the recurrent, patterned activities that people engage in within a given social context. These practices are seen as embedded within broader social structures and are crucial for understanding how individuals and groups participate in, shape, and reproduce social life. Practices are not only seen as actions but also as embodying shared meanings, norms, and tacit knowledge. Human social life is not solely determined by explicit rules or individual intentions but is deeply influenced by the routine activities and behaviors that people engage in collectively. Practices can include various elements such as bodily movements, rituals, use of artifacts, and discursive patterns.

When we co-create new practices, we thus introduce new ways of collectively engaging and meaning making. Learning something new necessitates a sense of safety, requiring an environment free from inducing automatic stress reactions, enabling people to explore, discover, and absorb new knowledge or using the general phases of transformative learning: allowing novel experiences, reflection, social exchange in a group, shift of action and shift of meaning (Grund, Singer-Brodowski, & Büssing, 2024).

The following practice is designed by the authors based on personal experiences which are also rooted in and inspired by their trainings and different teachers or peers, namely: Vision Quest Guide training in the tradition of the School of Lost Borders (Sylvia Koch-Weser), Tamalpa Life/Art Process (Tamalpa Institute, USA, e.g., Ken Otter and Anna Halprin), Contemplative Psychotherapy training (Nalanda Life Institute, e.g., Joe Loizzo), and various embodiment and contemplative practices from Vajrayana, Shivaistic, and Vaishnava traditions and lineages.

## The practice

The practice is laid out to be facilitated in a group setting, though it can also be practiced individually once introduced. Depending on the experience of both the group and the facilitator, there are different routes to be taken and not one size fits all. Important is, that whatever the facilitator guides, they actually practice themselves on a regular basis and feel comfortable for whatever space they open. Here we outline step by step the Relating: Connecting as Nature practice and indicate some variations where appropriate.

## Preparation – before we begin

**What/Why:** Given the inherently localized nature of this practice, its implementation requires minimal advance preparation. Whether conducted in a park, a forest, or a similar outdoor setting, the emphasis lies in ensuring a conducive environment for both the facilitator and the participants.

**How:** Prior to commencing the practice, take a moment to assess the surroundings and make simple arrangements that enhance the overall experience.

Select a location within the chosen setting that provides a sense of privacy and tranquility, allowing the group to engage undisturbed. In public spaces like parks, consider placing a small sign signaling "do not disturb" to create awareness among passersby, fostering an atmosphere of focused and uninterrupted connection.

Additionally, prioritize the safety and comfort of the participants. Confirm that individuals and their belongings are also secure once they close their eyes, allowing them the peace of mind to fully immerse themselves in the practice.

Maintaining awareness of other users sharing the space is essential. Strive to create a harmonious coexistence by being mindful of the environment's shared nature.

By taking these simple preparatory steps, you set the stage for a more enriching and undisturbed engagement with the practice.

## Framing

**What/Why:** In your capacity as a facilitator, your foremost duty is to establish a space that not only feels safe enough but goes beyond, creating an environment that fosters exploration and growth. Part of this involves providing clear orientation and tapping into the collective and individual resources of the participants (e.g., Singer-Brodowski et al., 2022).

**How:** Begin by offering an overview of what participants can expect, setting the stage for the practice. Encourage them to approach the experience with curiosity, ready to embrace new possibilities. Clearly communicate your commitment to ensuring a safe enough space and elucidate how the collaborative efforts of the group can contribute to maintaining this atmosphere.

Empower participants by activating a sense of self-responsibility. Allow each individual the agency to delve as deeply as they are comfortable within the practice and encourage them to be present with whatever emotions or experiences arise. This includes being mindful of the facilitator's remarks, providing additional guidance for navigating the process.

Above all, make certain that the setting and expectations are clear for everyone involved, setting the stage for a journey of exploration and self-discovery within the confines of a supportive and secure space.

## Relating, intention setting, and asking for permission

**What/Why:** Setting a clear intention for the practice supports mindfulness and particularly directs the attention of the practice. By seeking permission, you also recognize and acknowledge the selfness, autonomy, and agency of the beyond-human world, emphasizing a mutual exchange that goes beyond mere observation. At the same time, we follow the understanding that selfness or autonomy is always relative, since emerging from being intraconnected and not separated (e.g. Siegel, 2020; Van Gordon, Shonin, & Richardson, 2018).

**How:** As facilitator, invite yourself and the group to take a moment to become fully present with yourself in the current moment. This can, for example, be through a grounding exercise, body scan, breath awareness, or sensing into one's center. Engaging in such a brief self-connection, foster a sense of openness and receptivity. This initial step lays the foundation for a more profound connection with the world beyond the human.

Continue from this place of connection by articulating a clear intention that reflects your genuine desire to establish a connection with the nonhuman realm. This intention serves as a guiding force throughout the experience, shaping the nature of your engagement and influencing the depth of understanding you seek to cultivate. It acts as a North Star, directing your focus towards a more meaningful and reciprocal relationship with the beings and entities that coexist in the natural environment.

Moreover, in recognition of the interconnectedness and interdependence inherent in the web of life, extend a gesture of respect by asking for permission from the place you are engaging from – your natural surroundings. Acknowledge the reciprocal nature of the relationship between humans and the nonhuman entities present. In this intentional and respectful approach, you set the stage for a meaningful and transformative encounter beyond the boundaries of human existence.

## Connection to land, place, and self through sensory awareness: oscillating between inward and outward directed awareness

**What/Why:** Connect with the immediate surroundings and cultivate a deep sense of presence in the natural environment through engaging in a sensory awareness practice. Focusing on outer awareness (sights, sounds, touch, smell, taste) oscillating with inner awareness (sensations within the body). Do this from the stance of a mindful observer: open, receptive, nonjudgmental. Our senses serve as the conduits through which we relate, both internally and externally. They form the bridge connecting us to the web of existence.

**How:** Usually, it is good to start with closed eyes (or at least lowered gaze), as our visual sense is the one which is most dominant for many of us. Our experience is that it is very accessible to most participants to start with listening – the auditory sense. The oscillation between the outer and the inner can be guided through asking what sounds you hear near and far, and then asking to enter the observer state of what the sounds you perceive evoke (e.g., physically, emotionally, mentally). In order to not get attached to the sound but really remain in this observing and oscillation, we then ask again what other sound is here. So: focusing on the outside. Make an internal shift to other senses and a brief pause in between to get ready to focus again.

Variation: those who come from yogic traditions can draw from pratyahara practice of withdrawal of the senses, meaning to then focus more and more on the inner processes rather than external stimuli.

## Connection to a specific patch of land and all its inhabitants

**What/Why:** Connecting with a specific patch of land and its inhabitants can evoke positive emotions during immediate nature experiences (Grimwood, Haberer, & Legault, 2015). This emotional response is further described by Moriggi et al. (2020, p.290) as "to regain a sense of wonder". Such emotions, particularly awe, love, and joy, possess the potential to question existing meaning perspectives. To facilitate transformative learning, we guide individuals through a deep connection to the land, place, and all its beings. Asking nonhuman entities, like bugs, profound questions and listening for their responses opens the door to an experience of awe and wonder. This inquiry creates a liminal space conducive to the emergence of new perspectives on meaning. Ensuring both liminality and the potential of emergence of a shifted meaning perspective is crucial; hence, such experiences of connecting with ourselves *as* nature and its aftermath need to be held in a safe enough space (Singer-Brodowski et al., 2022).

**How:** In a kneeling or seated position, immerse yourself in the process by directing your attention to a small area in front of you, approximately 20 cm x 20 cm. Lean forward, zoom in, allowing your eyes to approach the space comfortably, and keenly observe the entities present. Should you encounter a being, perhaps a bug or a plant, pose the inquiry, "Who are you, that I am also?" or "Who am I, that you are, too?" Express the question in your own language, possibly audibly, and provide ample time for any discernible responses. Modifications: "If this creature, flower, or other element could communicate with me, how might it respond to my question: . . .?"
Continue this inquiry for about 20 minutes.

## Expression of gratitude

As you conclude the practice, take a moment to express your gratitude to the land, the place, and all the beings that shared this space with you. This expression of gratitude serves as a way to honor the intraconnectedness experienced during the practice. Choose a mode of gratitude that resonates with you, whether silently embracing it within or vocalizing your appreciation aloud. The essence lies in recognizing and appreciating the diverse forms of life that coexist in this shared space.
Extend your gratitude inward as well, thanking yourself for engaging in the practice today. Recognize the commitment and openness you brought to the experience. This dual expression of gratitude, both outward and inward, reinforces the reciprocal

relationship between the self and the larger ecosystem, fostering a sense of appreciation and connectedness that transcends individual boundaries.

## Integration time

Following the active engagement in the practice, provide participants with dedicated silent integration time. This period is designed to allow the experiences to settle and permeate their consciousness. Allocate a flexible time frame, ranging from five minutes to one hour, allowing individuals to fully absorb and internalize the experience.

Encourage participants to find a comfortable space for reflection, whether seated, in a restful posture, or moving. You may also provide them with colors and papers for drawing. During this integration time, they have the opportunity to process their encounters, emotions, and newfound perspectives in a contemplative and/or creative manner. This reflective period serves as a bridge between the immersive practice and the subsequent collective sensemaking.

Allocate a period of silent integration for participants to allow the experience to settle. We suggest a time frame ranging from ten to 30 minutes for this integration. Inform them of the time you plan to reconvene after this reflective period.

## Connection to others/witnessing/sensemaking of experience

Following the experience, a debrief can be valuable using methods like a generative dialogue or a dialogue circle. Depending on participants' backgrounds, they might seek additional contextualization and philosophical positioning, often engaging in discussions around relational ontologies and the transition from an anthropocentric worldview to an ecocentric one.

Sharing the experiences and having them witnessed by peers or even getting a resonance to them supports deepening the understanding and storing it in the memory of the experiences (e.g., Hanson, 2013). It also fosters group cohesion and support.

To initiate a generative dialogue, participants might be explicitly asked about their encounters and their connected emotional experiences (Oberauer et al., 2022). Singer-Brodowski (2023) emphasizes that sustainability challenges transcend individual or biographical realms; they are collective phenomena. Therefore, addressing these challenges collectively and participating in group learning processes becomes crucial to instigate a shift in meaning perspectives.

## Anchoring

To anchor the experiences, participants engage in practices that reinforce the insights gained during the session. This may involve creating symbolic anchors, such as personal rituals or commitments, to solidify the connection with nature and sustain the transformative effects.

## Integration of new meaning perspective in day-to-day life

The final step focuses on translating the newfound meaning perspectives into everyday life activities. Facilitators provide guidance on incorporating these insights into participants' daily routines, relationships, and decision-making processes, ensuring a lasting impact beyond the immediate experience.

# Four stories of applying the method

We shift in this section to a first-person narrative for telling these stories. The experiences are either shared by us, the authors Ruth and Anaïs together, or by Anaïs alone.

## Story 1: Immersing in nature with people living in large cities

In the midst of a lush outdoor environment, the yoga mats formed a colorful circle beneath a linden tree. As a facilitator, I guided a diverse group of international young changemakers, some of them from mega cities, through the Relating: Connecting as Nature method that invited them to intimately connect to a patch of land in front of them. Some participants, accustomed to urban settings, hesitated at first, sitting upright on their yoga mats. With each invitation to explore the patch of land in front of them more closely, the resistance of some of them became palpable.

It wasn't merely a reluctance to lower themselves closer to the ground; it was a hesitation rooted in a fear of the insects that inhabited this natural space. Gradually, through gentle repetition of the invitation, those hesitating also began to bend more, moving their heads slightly forward, their hands tentatively leaving the safety of the mat. In the subsequent dialogue, they disclosed the source of their unease – living in bustling cities had bred a discomfort with the creatures they perceived as pests.

One participant, breaking through the barrier of fear, remarked regarding their observation of ants: "They are just minding their own business." It was a powerful realization that these tiny beings were simply going about their lives, oblivious to the human discomfort surrounding them.

## Story 2: Connection with the nonhuman

In a tranquil grove nestled beneath the sprawling branches of ancient larch trees, the air was infused with the strong grounding scent of earth, moss, and the sun shining on larch bark and needles. As a facilitator, I guided a group with our Relating: Connecting as Nature method.

Soft moss cradled the ground beneath us, and the ambiance was imbued with the buzzing of insects and soothing light. One participant, well acquainted with psychedelic experiences, came to talk to me afterward. Through this method, carefully designed to unlock profound connections with the nonhuman world which does not involve any substances, she felt she experienced a similar openness and state of mind as under the influence of psychedelics, an altered state of consciousness through intentional interactions with nature where the boundaries of the self dissolves. The participant, attuned to the oscillation between the inner and outer realms, discovered an extraordinary depth of communion with the living beings surrounding us. The softness of the moss beneath her fingertips seemed to amplify the sense of intraconnectedness, and the forest's aroma served as a grounding force, facilitating a state of heightened awareness.

This story underscores the transformative power of this method and shows that it can open up spaces of transcendence and connection with the beyond-human world – usually only described from deep meditation and psychedelic experiences – naturally. Although this is anecdotal, it shows a pathway for potential future investigation and research.

## Story 3: Conversations with the living world

For us, the practice has evolved into a continuous dance with the living world. Engaging with all living beings that cross our path, we have each developed a unique language with the natural elements around us. Plants, stones, spiders, mosquitoes – they all become characters in the ongoing narrative of our daily lives.

Let me, Anaïs, share one of the interactions that occurred with flies. In the German language's nuanced approach to gender, insects are not relegated to the impersonal "it". When a stray fly finds herself trapped indoors, I engage in a gentle conversation with her. Speaking in a calm and comforting voice, I explain my intention to assist her in finding her way back to the outside world. Inviting her to rest on my hand, I then open a window, and more often than not, she gracefully accepts the invitation, venturing back into the open air. It's a delicate dance of communication where words may not be understood, but the intention and actions convey a sense of safety, bridging the gap between species.

## Story 4: Connecting as nature in an urban environment

For a small group, I was offering the Relating: Connecting as Nature practice in Basel, Switzerland. We set off from an industrial area, walking underneath a highway and a railroad bridge to reach a partially renatured yet still clearly confined river. As we returned in silence and shared our experiences in groups of three, with a speaker, a witness, and a scribe (so-called triads), we began to circle back for what needed to be heard now.

Several participants shared how relating as nature brought them into a deeply felt presence, evoking memories from childhood. These memories ranged from pleasant to unpleasant, with one participant recalling a traumatizing experience of almost drowning in icy water, where nature felt like an enemy in a struggle for survival. Another participant shared that at the river, the sounds of nature, were so dominant that they forgot all about the man-made structures and movement around them. However, on the walk back in silence, as soon as their foot hit the concrete, all natural sounds seemed to vanish, replaced by the sounds of trains, cars, and the bustling city.

One participant, who had closely observed ants, drew a parallel between the ants' activity and the evening traffic, likening human beings sitting in cars, one behind the other, to ants going about their business. This practice of connecting as nature highlights our intertwined existence, emphasizing both past and present experiences, and also in how our surroundings influence our inner experiences and perceptions, and how the boundaries between nature and human-made environments can shape our sense of connectedness.

# Facilitation

Facilitating these processes requires an attitude of openness and curiosity, with the facilitator taking charge of co-holding safe enough spaces. If participants encounter unpleasant emotions during their explorations, the facilitator can step in by, for example, slowing down the pace and allowing for more grounding and emotional distance initially. This approach aims to prevent pushing participants beyond their learning zones, avoiding stress reactions like fight, flight, and freeze pushing them into panic mode. Although experienced facilitators can manage strong negative emotions, detailed descriptions are omitted here due to the complexity that demands more experience and explanation as well as our experience with the Relating: Connecting as Nature method which is rather gentle and typically provokes pleasant emotions.

As facilitators, we carry the responsibility of engaging in a careful dance, prioritizing the establishment of presence, grounding, and resources to ensure that individuals do not feel overwhelmed by intense and unpleasant emotions.

## Creating ritual spaces and co-facilitators as practitioners

The previously described practice can be integrated into a ritual space, as proposed by Müller, Artmann, & Surrey (2023) who developed a framework for fostering individual human–nature resonance through ritual. In our context, we view rituals as purposeful practices with a clear beginning and end, often involving a witnessing component during or after the ritual. This practice is perceived as a ritual, connecting the realms of the profane and the non-profane, bridging the spiritual and sacred dimensions.

The efficacy of incorporating this ritualistic approach is contingent on the co-facilitators' experience in opening, co-holding, and closing ritual spaces, coupled with the group's receptiveness to such practices. We have implemented the described method in various ways: with explicit ritual framing; subtle framings where we opened ritual spaces without explicit mention; and contexts where it wasn't explicitly connected to collective ritual. Given our sustained practice of rituals, such as expressing gratitude to a place, we integrate our daily rituals that resonate with diverse traditions we are deeply rooted in.

Similar to the approach in mindfulness, we advocate for teaching and co-facilitating only within one's experiential roots. This ensures authenticity and a genuine connection to the practices being shared, enhancing the overall impact of the ritual space.

# Discussion and outlook

Shifting from anthropocentrism to ecocentrism represents a significant paradigm shift in how we perceive our relationship with the natural world but also in how we construct frameworks for sustainable development. The implications for both the IDG framework and the Sustainable Development Goals (SDGs) would be profound.

Firstly, let's delve into the SDGs "wedding cake" model (Rockström & Sukhdev, 2016) which underscores the foundational importance of the biosphere (Obrecht et al., 2021) to economies and societies. This conceptualization emphasizes an integrated approach to development, recognizing that ecological factors are the foundation on which the social realm is built and then the social realm is the basis of our economic interdependence. However, this model still primarily operates within an anthropocentric framework prioritizing mainly intergenerational and intragenerational justice, where human well-being and development are prioritized.

Now, consider what would happen if we were to transition to an ecocentric perspective. Such a shift would necessitate a reevaluation of our priorities and values. Instead of viewing nature merely as a resource to support human well-being with the risk to still exploit, an ecocentric approach recognizes the intrinsic value of all beings and ecosystems. The biosphere would no longer be valued merely as the foundation for human activities but as an entity deserving of protection and respect in its own right. This is in line with interspecies justice.

In this context, the SDGs would likely undergo a transformation. While the overarching goals of eradicating poverty, ensuring food security, and promoting health would remain, the intention and means of achieving them would change. Also, the impetus of economic growth would most likely be dismantled. An ecocentric perspective would prioritize strategies that promote the regeneration and resilience of entire ecosystems and would not benefit only some strata of human societies in the short term. This might involve shifting towards regenerative production and more sustainable consumption patterns, protecting biodiversity, and mitigating climate change. In the end, understanding humans as nature. Also, human well-being would be supported.

Secondly, the IDG framework, which focuses on human inner growth and development, would need to adapt to an ecocentric worldview. The five dimensions – being, thinking, relating, collaborating, and acting – would still be relevant, but their interpretation and implementation would change.

For instance, cultivating a sense of being would include the intraconnection with nature. The understanding of self would thus potentially be much broader. Thinking would encompass also an understanding of our place within the natural world. Relating and collaborating would emphasize building relationships not only with other humans but also with other species and ecosystems, recognizing the interconnectedness of all life. Acting would involve protecting, restoring, and regenerating ecosystems of which humans are inherently part of. Thus, decoloniality would also need to be taken into account for an epistemic delinking (Förster et al., 2024).

In conclusion, the shift from anthropocentrism to ecocentrism would have profound implications for both the SDGs and the IDG framework. It would require a reorientation of priorities towards the well-being of the entire planet, rather than just human societies. It would change our self-understanding and include a deeply felt appreciation and humility in the sense of being part of something so much greater than us and support interspecies justice (e.g., Rockström et al., 2023). Embracing an ecocentric perspective also offers the potential to overcome the notion of development paradigm, as aptly stated by, for example, Sachs (2019).

Collective leadership grounded in ecocentrism opens up the renegotiation of frameworks and implied priorities. It strives particularly for regenerative practice towards the well-being of our entire planet. This is a complex task, particularly since humankind is already struggling with developing intra- and intergenerational justice. The ecocentric perspective may also serve these ends.

## Acknowledgement

In recognizing the significance of our journey into nature immersion, we extend our heartfelt gratitude and acknowledgement to our teachers – human and beyond human – who have guided and inspired us along this transformative path. They have shared their wisdom, insights, and practices, contributing to our learning and understanding of nature connection. The acknowledgment of our teachers from different traditions underscores the interconnected web of knowledge and shared experiences that shape our approach to nature immersion. Among our teachers are also individuals and lineages who have experienced colonialism and the appropriation of many of their traditions and ways of meaning making. There is ancient and indigenous wisdom that can be rediscovered and illuminated through the practice of reconnecting with nature.

Furthermore, we pay homage to the land itself, recognizing it as a living entity that hosts our practices and provides the immersive environment for our exploration. This acknowledgment is a testament to our commitment to reciprocity and respect for the natural world. As we embark on this journey, we honor the teachings, the land, and the collective wisdom that enriches our endeavor in fostering a deeper connection with nature.

Winter 2024, Lake Brienz, Switzerland.

## Positionality

As cisgender women, we recognize our positionality and acknowledge the privilege that comes with being white and living in one of the wealthiest countries in economic terms, Switzerland. Here the land has suffered significant exploitation by human activity, leading to the loss of primary forests and a sharp decline in biodiversity. Our commitment as reflective practitioners lies in understanding the intersections of identity and privilege, especially within the realms of nature immersion and transformative practices. As practitioners, we recognize the impact of our positionality on the way we approach, experience, and facilitate nature connection. It shapes the dynamics of our interactions with the natural world, influencing how we perceive and engage with ecosystems. Being aware of our privilege prompts a commitment to continuous reflection on how our identity may influence the accessibility and inclusiveness of these practices, ensuring a conscious effort to create spaces that welcome diverse perspectives and experiences. This positionality prompts a responsibility to amplify marginalized voices, acknowledging the complex interplay between privilege and nature connection in the pursuit of fostering a more equitable and interconnected relationship with the natural world.

# References

Barragan-Jason, G., Loreau, M., de Mazancourt, C., Singer, M. C., & Parmesan, C. (2023). Psychological and physical connections with nature improve both human well-being and nature conservation: A systematic review of meta-analyses. *Biological Conservation, 277*, 109842.

Baxter, D. E., & Pelletier, L. G. (2019). Is nature relatedness a basic human psychological need? A critical examination of the extant literature. *Canadian Psychology / Psychologie canadienne, 60*(1), 21–34. https://doi.org/10.1037/cap0000145.

Beute, F. & De Kort, Y. (2017). The natural context of wellbeing: Ecological momentary assessment of the influence of nature and daylight on affect and stress for individuals with depression levels varying from none to clinical. *Health and Place, 49*, 7–18. https://doi.org/10.1016/j.healthplace.2017.11.005.

Bratman, G. N., Anderson, C. B., Berman, M. G., Cochran, B., De Vries, S., Flanders, J., Folke, C., Frumkin, H., Gross, J. J., Hartig, T., Kahn, P. H. JR., Kuo, M., Lawler, J. J., Levin, Ph., S. Lindahl, T., Meyer-Lindenberg, M., Ouayang, Z., Roe, J., Scarlett, L., Smith, J.R., van den Bosch, M., Wheeler, B. W., White, M. P., Zheng, H., & Daily, G. C. (2019). Nature and mental health: An ecosystem service perspective. *Science advances, 5*(7). https://www.science.org/doi/10.1126/sciadv.aax0903.

Bratman, G., Daily, G., Levy, B., & Gross, J. (2015). The benefits of nature experience: Improved affect and cognition. *Landscape and Urban Planning, 138*, 41–50. https://doi.org/10.1016/j.landurbplan.2015.02.005.

De Figueiredo, M. D. & Marquesan, F. F. S. (2022). Back to the future: Ecocentrism, organization studies, and the Anthropocene. *Scandinavian Journal of Management, 38*(2), 101197.

Elands, B. H. M., Vierikko, K., Andersson, E., Fischer, L. K., Gonçalves, P., Haase, D., Kowarik, I., Luz, A. C., Niemelä, J., Santos-Reis, M., & Wiersum, K. F. (2019). Biocultural diversity: A novel concept to assess human-nature interrelations, nature conservation and stewardship in cities. *Urban Forestry and Urban Greening, 40*, 29–34.

Förster, R., Sägesser, A., Singer-Brodowski, M., & Walkes, S. (2024). How to provide safe (enough) spaces for transformative learning to support courageous and decolonial practices towards climate justice. In L. Fabbri, M. Fedeli, P. Faller, D. Holt & A. Roman (Eds). *Getting Transformation into Good Trouble: Making new spaces of possibility with community and in practice*. Proceedings of the XV Biennial International Transformative Learning Conference (pp. 664–671). https://drive.google.com/file/d/1Z3vC3r40jVYJHOsS6JefpLniSHb-JzF0/view.

Formenti, L. & West, L. (2021). When Lake Erie is polluted, we are too. In A. Bainbridge, L. Formenti, & L. West (eds.), *Discourses, dialogue and diversity in biographical research* (pp. 23–38). Brill/Sense.

Freiler, T. J. (2008). Learning through the body. *New directions for adult and continuing education, 119*, 37–47. https://doi.org/10.1002/ace.304.

Frumkin, H., Bratman, G. N., Breslow, S. J., Cochran, B., Kahn, P. H., Lawler, J. J., Levin, P. S., Tandon, P. S., Varanasi, U., Wolf, K. L., & Wood, S. A. (2017). Nature contact and human health: A research agenda. *Environmental Health Perspectives, 125*(7), 1–18. https://doi.org/10.1289/EHP1663.

Fuegen, K. & Breitenbecher, K. H. (2018). Walking and being outdoors in nature increase positive affect and energy. *Ecopsychology, 10*(1), 14–25. https://doi.org/10.1089/eco.2017.0036.

Grimwood, B. S., Haberer, A., & Legault, M. (2015). Guides to sustainable connections? Exploring human–nature relationships among wilderness travel leaders. *Journal of Adventure Education and Outdoor Learning, 15*(2), 138–151. https://doi.org/10.1080/14729679.2013.867814.

Grund, J., Singer-Brodowski, M., & Büssing, A. G. (2024). Emotions and transformative learning for sustainability: A systematic review. *Sustainability Science, 19*(1), 307–324. https://doi.org/10.1007/s11625-023-01439-5.

Heron, J. & Reason, P. (2006). The practice of co-operative inquiry: Research 'with' rather than 'on' people. In P. Reason & H. Bradbury. (Eds.), *Handbook of action research: Concise paperback edition* (pp. 144–154).

Hanson, R. (2013). *Hardwiring happiness: The practical science of your brain-and your life*. Random House.

Hoggan, C. D. (2016). Transformative learning as a metatheory: Definition, criteria, and typology. *Adult Education Quarterly*, *66*(1), 57–75. https://doi.org/10.1177/0741713615611216.

Inner Development Goals. (n.d.). Framework for Inner Development Goals. *Inner Development Goals*. https://www.innerdevelopmentgoals.org/framework [Retrieved Jan. 6, 2024].

IPBES (2022). Summary for policymakers of the methodological assessment report on the diverse values and valuation of nature of the Intergovernmental Science-Policy Platform on Biodiversity and Ecosystem Services (IPBES). In Pascual, U., et al. (Eds.) Methodological assessment of the diverse values and valuation of nature of the Intergovernmental Science-Policy Platform on Biodiversity and Ecosystem Services IPBES secretariat, Bonn, Germany. https://doi.org/10.5281/zenodo.6522392.

Ives, C. D., Abson, D. J., Von Wehrden, H., Dorninger, C., Klaniecki, K., & Fischer, J. (2018). Reconnecting with nature for sustainability. *Sustainability Science*, *13*, 1389–1397. https://doi.org/10.1007/s11625-018-0542-9.

Jordan, T., Reams, J., Stålne, K., Greca, S., Henriksson, J. A., Björkman, T., & Dawson, T. (2021). Inner Development Goals: Background, method and the IDG framework. *Growth That Matters*. https://innerdevelopmentgoals.org/about/resources/. [Retrieved Feb. 20, 2024].

Kasap, E. Z., Ağzıtemiz, F., & Ünal, G. (2021). Cognitive, mental and social benefits of interacting with nature: A systematic review. *Journal of Happiness and Health*, *1*(1), 16–27. https://journalofhappinessandhealth.com/index.php/johah/article/view/1 [Retrieved Jan. 31, 2024].

Kitchenham, A. (2012). Jack Mezirow on Transformative Learning. In Seel, N.M. (eds.) *Encyclopedia of the Sciences of Learning*. Springer. https://doi.org/10.1007/978-1-4419-1428-6_362.

Kotera, Y., Richardson, M., & Sheffield, D. (2022). Effects of shinrin-yoku (forest bathing) and nature therapy on mental health: A systematic review and meta-analysis. *International Journal of Mental Health and Addiction*, *20*, 337–361. https://doi.org/10.1007/s11469-020-00363-4.

Kuo, M. (2015). How might contact with nature promote human health? Promising mechanisms and a possible central pathway. *Frontiers in Psychology*, *6*, 1093. https://doi.org/10.3389/fpsyg.2015.01093.

Lengieza, M. L. & Swim, J. K. (2021). The paths to connectedness: A review of the antecedents of connectedness to nature. *Frontiers in Psychology*, *12*, 763231. https://doi.org/10.3389/fpsyg.2021.763231.

Lorenz, H. S. (2006). Synchronicity in the 21st century. *Journal of Jungian Scholarly Studies*, 2.

Moriggi, A., Soini, K., Franklin, A., & Roep, D. (2020). A care-based approach to transformative change: Ethically-informed practices, relational response-ability and emotional awareness. *Ethics, Policy and Environment*, *23*(3), 281–298. https://doi.org/10.1080/21550085.2020.1848186.

Mayer, F. S., Frantz, C. M., Bruehlman-Senecal, E., & Dolliver, K. (2009). Why is nature beneficial? The role of connectedness to nature. *Environment and Behavior*, *41*(5), 607–643.

Müller, S., Artmann, M., & Surrey, C. (2023). Opening the human spirit to sustainability transformation: The potential for individual human–nature resonance and integrative rituals. *Sustainability Science*, *18*, 2323–2339. https://doi.org/10.1007/s11625-023-01360-x.

Nigh, K. (2022). Learning from Life and the Earth. *Holistic Education Review*, *2*(1). https://her.journals.publicknowledgeproject.org/index.php/her/article/view/2198 [Retrieved Mar. 8, 2024].

Nilsson, M. & Stålhammara, S. (2024). Psychedelics and inner dimensions of sustainability: A literature review. *European Journal of Ecopsychology*, 9, 4–47.

Oberauer, K., Schickl, M., Zint, M., Liebhaber, N., Deisenrieder, V., Kubisch, S., Parth, S., Frick, M., Stötter, H., & Keller, L. (2022). The impact of teenagers' emotions on their complexity thinking competence related to climate change and its consequences on their future: Looking at complex interconnections and implications in climate change education. *Sustainability Science*, *18*, 907–931. https://doi.org/10.1007/s11625-022-01222-y.

Obrecht, A., Pham, M., Spehn, E., Payne, D., Brémond, A. C., Altermatt, F., . . . & Geschke, J. E. (2021). Achieving the SDGs with biodiversity. Swiss Academies Factsheet 16 (1). https://doi.org/10.5281/zen odo.4457298.

Oh, R. R., Zhang, Y., Nghiem, L. T., Chang, C. C., Tan, C. L., Quazi, S. A., Shanahan, D. F., Lin, B. B., Gaston, K. J., Fuller, R. A., & Carrasco, R. L. (2022). Connection to nature and time spent in gardens predicts social cohesion. *Urban Forestry & Urban Greening*, *74*, 127655. https://doi.org/10.1016/j.ufug.2022. 127655.

Papworth, S. K., Rist, J., Coad, L., & Milner-Gulland, E. J. (2009). Evidence for shifting baseline syndrome in conservation. *Conservation Letters*, *2*(2), 93–100. https://doi.org/10.1111/j.1755-263x.2009.00049.x.

Plotkin, B. (2010). *Nature and the human soul: Cultivating wholeness and community in a fragmented world*. New World Library.

Redondo Palomo, R., Valor Martínez, C., & Carrero Bosch, I. (2022). Unraveling the relationship between well-being, sustainable consumption and nature relatedness: A study of university students. *Applied Research Quality Life*, *17*, 913–930. https://doi.org/10.1007/s11482-021-09931-9.

Richardson, M., Dobson, J., Abson, D. J., Lumber, R., Hunt, A., Young, R., & Moorhouse, B. (2020). Applying the pathways to nature connectedness at a societal scale: a leverage points perspective. *Ecosystems and People*, *16*(1), 387–401. https://doi.org/10.1080/26395916.2020.1844296.

Riechers, M., Pătru-Dușe, I. A., & Balázsi, Á.. (2021). Leverage points to foster human–nature connectedness in cultural landscapes. *Ambio*, *50*(9), 1670–1680. https://doi.org/10.1007/s13280-021-01504-2.

Ritchie, H., Samborska, V., & Roser, M. (2018, Sep., revised 2024, Feb.). Urbanization: The world population is moving to cities. Why is urbanization happening and what are the consequences? *Our World in Data*. https://ourworldindata.org/urbanization [Retrieved Feb. 10, 2024].

Rockström, J., Gupta, J., Qin, D., Lade, S. J., Abrams, J. F., Andersen, L. S., (. . .) & Zhang, X. (2023). Safe and just Earth system boundaries. *Nature*, *619*(7968), 102–111. https://doi.org/10.1038/s41586-023-06083-8.

Rockström, J. & Sukhdev, P. (2016, Jun. 14). The SDGs Wedding Cake. *Stockholm Resilience Centre*. https://www.stockholmresilience.org/research/research-news/2016-06-14-the-sdgs-wedding-cake. html [Retrieved Mar. 30, 2024].

Rosa, H. (2016). *Resonanz. Eine Soziologie der Weltbeziehung*. Suhrkamp Verlag.

Sachs, W. (2019). Foreword: The development dictionary revisited. In A., Kothari, A., Salleh, A., Escobar, F., Demaria, & A. Acosta (eds.) *Pluriverse. A post-development dictionary*. Tulika Books.

Sägesser, A. & Förster, R. (2023) Regenerative leadership. *Seminar Booklet*. University of St. Gallen.

Schertz, K. E. & Berman, M. G. (2019). Understanding nature and its cognitive benefits. *Current Directions in Psychological Science*, *28*(5), 496–502. https://doi.org/10.1177/0963721419854100.

Shove, E., Pantzar, M., & Watson, M. (2012). *The dynamics of social practice: Everyday life and how it changes*. Sage.

Shrivastava, P. (2010). Pedagogy of passion for sustainability. *Academy of Management Learning and Education*, *9*(3), 443–455.

Siegel, D. J. (2020). *The developing mind: How relationships and the brain interact to shape who we are*. Guilford Publications.

Siegel, D. J. (2022). *IntraConnected: MWe (Me + We) as the integration of self, identity, and belonging (Norton Series on interpersonal neurobiology)*. WW Norton & Company.

Singer-Brodowski, M., Förster, R., Eschenbacher, S., Biberhofer, P., & Getzin, S. (2022). Facing crises of unsustainability: Creating and holding safe enough spaces for transformative learning in higher education for sustainable development. *Frontiers in Education*, 7, 787490. https://doi.org/10.3389/feduc.2022.787490.

Singer-Brodowski, M. (2023). The potential of transformative learning for sustainability transitions: Moving beyond formal learning environments. *Environment, Development and Sustainability*, 1–19. https://doi.org/10.1007/s10668-022-02444-x.

Soga, M. & Gaston, K. J. (2016). Extinction of experience: The loss of human–nature interactions. *Frontiers in Ecology and the Environment*, *14*(2), 94–101. https://doi.org/10.1002/fee.1225.

Van Gordon, W., Shonin, E., & Richardson, M. (2018). Mindfulness and nature. *Mindfulness*, *9*(5), 1655–1658. https://doi.org/10.1007/s12671-018-0883-6.

Van Horn, G., Kimmerer, R. W., & Hausdoerffer, J. (eds.) (2021). *Kinship: Belonging in a world of relations, Vol. 1 – Planet*. Center for Humans and Nature.

Wahl, D. (2016). *Designing regenerative cultures*. Triarchy Press.

Wilson, E. O. (1984). Biophilia. Harvard University Press.

Zelenski, J. M. & Desrochers, J. E. (2021). Can positive and self-transcendent emotions promote pro-environmental behavior? *Current Opinion in Psychology*, *42*, 31–35. https://doi.org/10.1016/j.copsyc.2021.02.009.

Zelenski, J. M., Dopko, R. L., & Capaldi, C. A. (2015). Cooperation is in our nature: Nature exposure may promote cooperative and environmentally sustainable behavior. *Journal of Environmental Psychology*, *42*, 24–31. https://doi.org/10.1016/j.jenvp.2015.01.005.

Xuan Dung Burckhardt and Mauricio Campos Suarez

# Chapter 6
# The transformative power of colors: Cultivating connection, collaboration, and sensemaking through art

**Abstract:** This chapter explores the integration of Csikszentmihalyi's concept of flow and Mezirow's transformative learning theory within the context of a workshop conducted at IDG Switzerland during Art Basel 2024. The workshop's innovative methodology, FLOW, combined art-based team effectiveness techniques with the Inner Development Goals (IDGs) framework to foster deep connection, collaboration, and sensemaking. The FLOW methodology is structured into distinct phases: introduction to art making, ideation, creation, reflection, and learning. Each phase facilitates a state of flow among participants, encouraging creativity and profound personal insights. The use of fluid art captures the lightness and motion of colors, promoting playfulness, reflection, and collaboration through the engagement of head, heart, and hand. This holistic approach enhances cognitive engagement, emotional connection, and practical skills, leading to significant personal and collective growth. The workshop's outcomes demonstrate the potential of integrating artistic practices with theoretical frameworks to enable transformational learning experiences. Participants reported heightened engagement, deepened connections, and a sense of time distortion, underscoring the efficacy of the FLOW methodology in fostering creativity and team cohesion. This chapter highlights the transformative power of art in cultivating sustainable mindsets and collaborative potentials, offering a novel pathway for personal and professional development through immersive, art-based experiences.

**Keywords:** flow, transformative learning, collaboration, playfulness, art

## Introduction

Have you ever felt the limitations of purely analytical approaches to tackling societal problems? Imagine a way to move beyond endless discussions and spark a deeper sense of connection and collaboration. Imagine a way to tap into the intuitive wisdom of your right brain, fostering open awareness alongside focused exploration. These are precisely the open questions that inspired the work described in this chapter and the methodology of exploring collaboration within complex systems through the application of art.

https://doi.org/10.1515/9783111337913-007

We invite you to travel to Basel, Switzerland. This city in the northwest of the country has developed at the intersection of art and science along the shores of the Rhine River. Since the Renaissance, it has been an important cultural and inner development center. The city's diverse community, situated at the crossroads of France, Germany, and Switzerland, reflects a variety of worldviews and the richness of its cultural fabric, with nearly half of its population hailing from elsewhere.

At Impact Hub Basel, a diverse community has been working with the Inner Development Goals (IDGs) framework since its inception in 2021. After two years and over 40 workshops and gatherings, it was time to explore something different: examining complex systems and collaboration through art, focusing on embodied experience rather than mere rationalization.

This first workshop was held during Art Basel Week 2024. Art Basel, an international art fair held annually in Basel and other cities, has showcased contemporary and modern artworks from leading galleries since 1970, attracting artists, collectors, and enthusiasts. The fair features diverse mediums, fostering global artistic exchange and innovation. With the 2024 edition of Art Basel, we had an opportunity to explore inner development not by explaining it, but rather by living it through an artistic experience. This work and chapter are a co-creation between Mauricio (IDG Switzerland co-founder) and Dung (founder of FLOW).

In this chapter, we explore the artist's concept of FLOW through the lens of IDG. FLOW, an art-based team effectiveness intervention methodology, informed by Csikszentmihalyi's (1990) concept of flow, was combined with IDG practices and perspectives to enable a transformational learning experience.

Grounded in the theoretical concepts of flow and transformative learning theory (Mezirow, 1991), we crafted an experiential approach to apply these theories in a collaborative setting.

# The Theory

## Flow and transformative learning in the context of this chapter

In this chapter, we leverage Csikszentmihalyi's concept of flow and Mezirow's transformational learning theory to underpin our methodology. This approach was implemented during a workshop conducted by IDG Switzerland at Art Basel 2024. Our methodology combines an art-based team effectiveness approach called FLOW with the IDG framework, integrating its skills and practices.

The intention was to explore how playfulness and creativity can foster deep connection, collaboration, and sensemaking among participants. By engaging in this process, we aimed to influence participants' mindsets and enhance their connection to sustainability. The workshop provided a space for participants to experience the transformative potential of art in promoting both personal and collective growth, ultimately contributing to a more sustainable future.

## Flow: The psychology of optimal experience

Mihaly Csikszentmihalyi's concept of flow describes a state of complete immersion and engagement in an activity, where one loses sense of time and self-consciousness (Csikszentmihalyi, 1990). This optimal state of intrinsic motivation is characterized by deep focus and enjoyment. In the context of art, flow allows individuals to transcend ordinary experiences, fostering creativity and profound personal insight.

Flow is described as a state of complete immersion and engagement in an activity, where individuals experience deep focus, enjoyment, and a loss of self-consciousness and sense of time. This optimal state of intrinsic motivation is characterized by:

- **Intense concentration**: Being fully absorbed in the activity at hand.
- **Clarity of goals**: Knowing exactly what to do and how to do it.
- **Loss of self-consciousness**: A merging of action and awareness, where the individual is no longer aware of themselves as separate from their actions.
- **Distorted sense of time**: Hours can pass by in what feels like minutes.
- **Intrinsic reward**: The activity is rewarding in itself, regardless of the outcome.

## Transformative learning

Transformative learning, as described by Jack Mezirow, involves a deep, structural shift in the basic premises of thought, feelings, and actions (Mezirow, 1991). This profound change leads to more inclusive, discriminating, and integrative perspectives. The art-making process in our workshop served as a powerful catalyst for personal and collective reflection. Participants engaged in creating art, prompting them to reflect on their experiences, beliefs, and emotions, which could lead to questioning previously held assumptions and developing new perspectives.

To facilitate transformative learning we had followed the principles of:

- **Creating a safe space**: Ensuring a supportive and nonjudgmental environment where participants feel comfortable expressing themselves.
- **Encouraging open dialogue:** Promoting open and honest communication, where diverse viewpoints are valued and explored.
- **Guided reflection**: Providing structured opportunities for participants to reflect on their experiences and the meanings behind their art.
- **Facilitating critical thinking:** Encouraging participants to question their assumptions and engage in critical analysis of their own and others' perspectives.

## FLOW as a methodology for art-based team connection

The FLOW methodology transcends traditional art techniques to become an innovative methodology for enhancing team effectiveness and individual growth. Inspired by Csikszentmihalyi's flow, this approach informs the collaborative art-making process, symbolizing the interconnectedness of people and their collaborative potential. Participants enter a state of flow, fostering creativity and gaining profound personal insights. The FLOW methodology is structured into distinct phases:

- **Introduction to art making**: This phase sets the stage for flow through a brief introduction to the technical aspects, materials, and objectives, emphasizing creativity and exploration.
- **Ideation**: Participants self-organize and begin to figure out how to work together, laying the groundwork for collaboration.
- **Creation**: Participants mix colors, materials, and paint on the canvas. This phase is marked by heightened engagement, energy, and connection – hallmarks of flow states.
- **Reflection**: After completing their work, participants engage in meaningful reflection, first individually and then collectively. This enables both personal and group growth.
- **Learning**: The final phase distills the essence of the experience, allowing participants to share conclusions and insights.

FLOW employs fluid art as a medium to capture the lightness and motion of colors, but its significance extends beyond aesthetics. It fosters playfulness, reflection, and collaboration from a place of wholeness – engaging the head, heart, and hand (See Figure 6.1):

- **Head**: Represents cognitive engagement, encouraging participants to explore new ideas and solve problems creatively. This stimulates innovation and strategic thinking within teams.
- **Heart**: Symbolizes emotional connection and empathy. The art-making process fosters emotional bonds among participants. By expressing themselves through art and sharing their creations, individuals develop a deeper understanding and appreciation of each other's perspectives and emotions, strengthening team cohesion.
- **Hand**: Reflects the practical aspect of creating art. The physical act of painting or crafting requires active participation and collaboration. This hands-on experience enhances fine motor skills, promotes mindfulness, and solidifies the collaborative spirit.

This comprehensive approach ensures that participants not only engage in creative expression but also build trust, strengthen connections, and enhance their ability to work together effectively.

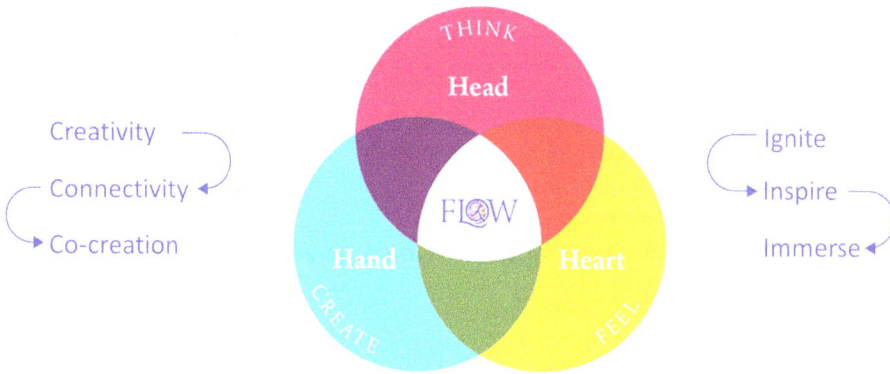

**Figure 6.1:** FLOW conceptual graph.
Source: FLOW Conceptual graph is from FLOW's 3Cs Concept and Methodology created by Xuan Dung Burckhardt. Founder of FLOW (no use of this visualization without Xuan Dung Burckhardt approval).

## Inner Development Goals as a catalyst for FLOW

For this workshop we integrated the FLOW methodology with the IDG framework concepts. IDG became the connecting threat for the art experience and enabled the cultivation of the skills and qualities that supported the transformational learning experience.

Integrating the IDG framework with FLOW facilitated self-awareness, empathy, co-creation, and creativity among participants, all important qualities and skills of the IDG framework. Engaging through the FLOW process encourages participants to explore and express their inner thoughts and feelings through art, fostering self-awareness. The collaborative nature of FLOW built empathy and promoted a deeper understanding of others and connectedness. The dynamic nature of fluid art required participants to adapt creatively, co-creating and navigating uncertainty. By encouraging creative expression, FLOW nurtured an innovative mindset, helping participants think outside the box and develop novel solutions to problems.

# The experience

## Conception of the workshop

The workshop originated from the vision of Mauricio, co-founder of IDG Switzerland, who sought to leverage art as a powerful tool for inner development. Believing in art's ability to catalyze personal growth and transformation, Mauricio reached out to Dung, the founder of FLOW, renowned for her expertise in creating dynamic group processes centered around the flow state. By combining Mauricio's extensive background in team coaching and his deep understanding of the IDGs with Dung's rich experience in HR and artistic facilitation, they aimed to craft a distinctive and integrative workshop experience. This collaboration merged profound insights into inner development with innovative art methodologies, setting the stage for exploring new dimensions of personal and collective transformation.

## Fluid art with Inner Development Goals to enable state of flow and transformative learning

Understanding the self and community is profoundly influenced by relationships. To fully grasp these concepts, it's essential to move beyond traditional views and embrace a more interconnected perspective (Gergen, 2009). This workshop exemplifies this shift by using art as a tool for collective insight. Starting with a group of strangers, the workshop created a collaborative environment where participants were organized into teams (See Figure 6.2). Through the process of co-creating art, they engaged in meaningful social practices that extended beyond technical execution. This approach facilitated a deeper exchange of insights, cultivated a sense of community, and highlighted the interconnectedness of their experiences.

The integration of the IDG framework together with FLOW art methodology demonstrates how these concepts can be applied to foster transformative learning. By sharing the methodology, we aim to inspire others to explore and benefit from this approach.

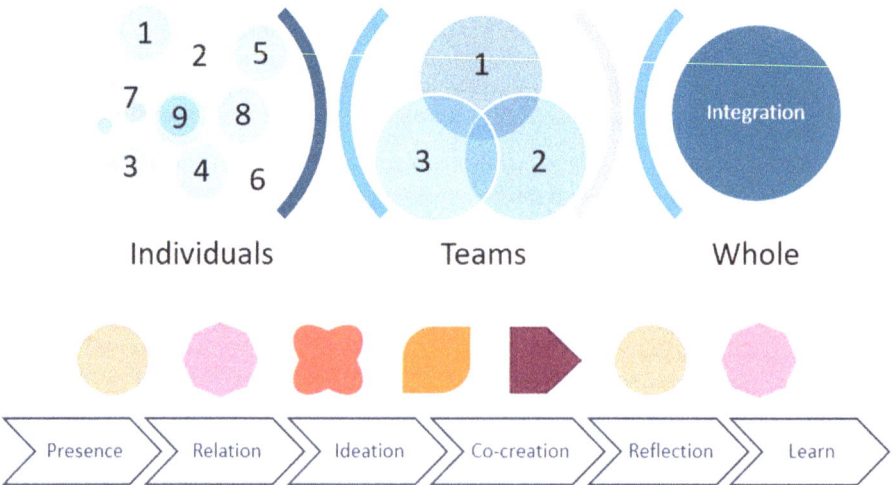

**Figure 6.2:** FLOW process integrated within Inner Development Goals journey.
Source: M. Campos Suarez (2024).

The workshop was designed following Mezirow's principles: creating a safe space, encouraging open dialogue, promoting reflection, and encouraging participants to question their assumptions. This holistic approach enabled the transformative learning experience, allowing participants to experience a state of complete immersion and engagement in their activities, where they could let go of a sense of time while being fully present and connected with others. This environment, marked by intense concentration, exchange, and intrinsic reward, allowed participants to transcend ordinary experiences, fostering creativity and deep connection. Most participants, who initially arrived exhausted, reported at the end that time seemed to fly by, connecting us back to Csikszentmihalyi's concept of flow.

In the following sections, we will share the story and process of the workshop, concluding with the key insights we gained and conclusions.

## The start: Relating to each other and sustainability

The workshop began at 3 p.m. under the spring sun in Basel, with participants gathering beneath the old trees outside the Impact Hub Basel offices. In contrast to the high-energy atmosphere of Art Basel – characterized by intense art trading and numerous events – we chose a different approach. We aimed to use art not just as a medium for expression but as a means to explore complex global issues and foster meaningful connections through mindful collaboration. Despite an initial plan to hold the workshop indoors due to a stormy forecast, we decided to embrace the outdoor setting, taking advantage of the open air and natural surroundings.

The nine participants, diverse in background and new to each other, arrived with a shared commitment to personal and collective growth. This common goal provided a solid foundation for deep, meaningful interactions.

We began by focusing on a sustainability topic related to the African Forest Landscape Restoration Initiative (AFR100)[1] which aims to restore Africa's landscapes. Guided by the IDG framework, we engaged in a reflective exercise centered on a story from AFR100 projects in Tanzania. This exercise facilitated a deeper connection to our ecological and social interdependencies. We then collaborated to create a piece of art that captured our insights from this experience, concluding with individual and collective reflections that allowed us to share our perspectives.

The session started with a circle arrangement featuring freshly cut flowers at the center. We began with a meditation to center ourselves and set our intentions for the day. We then explored the concept of beginner's mind through a sensory exercise. Participants selected and felt a rock from a bag as if encountering it for the first time, followed by a visual and sensory examination of the rock. This exercise, inspired by

---

1 afr100.org

the principles of Zen Buddhism (Suzuki, 1970), encouraged participants to approach the rock – and by extension their surroundings – with fresh eyes and curiosity. By engaging fully with the present moment and maintaining a sense of wonder, participants were able to appreciate the inherent beauty in everyday objects.

Following this, participants chose a color that represented their current state and shared their choices with the group. The open, outdoor environment under the trees facilitated a deeper sense of connection compared to typical indoor settings. As the initial fatigue dissipated, a sense of lightness and connectedness emerged throughout the afternoon.

With our minds and hearts attuned through these activities, we moved on to creating abstract art. Employing a technique where acrylic colors mixed with a thinning medium flowed freely across the canvas, we embraced the meditative and liberating aspects of this method. This approach encouraged spontaneity and allowed participants to let go of control, engaging deeply with the present moment and fostering a sense of creative freedom.

## Introduction to art making

Following the presence and relating practices, participants were introduced to the art-making process. They received a brief explanation on how to mix colors using thinningmediums. The materials provided included wooden sticks, tree and shrub leaves, flowers picked from the forest, and everyday objects such as forks, knives, wine corks, cleaning brushes, squeegees, kitchen sponges, plastic lids, dried banana leaves, and rice grains. These materials were chosen to stimulate creativity and ingenuity. The guiding principles for the art session were clearly outlined:

– **Use only the materials provided**: Participants were encouraged to work with the unique materials provided to stimulate creativity.
– **Canvas size**: Each group was given an 80 x 100 cm canvas to create their artwork.
– **Sustainability themes**: Groups were tasked with creating pieces that represented either "climate action in Africa" or "the importance of education in Africa", using a main color to symbolize their given theme.
– **Visual connection**: A common feature should be included in both pieces to visually connect them and highlight that they are part of a larger, cohesive team.

After an introduction to color mixing, materials, and guiding principles, participants were invited to begin their collaborative art-making process and let their creativity soar.

### Ideation phase – creativity and teamwork

During the ideation phase, it became evident how differently participants approached working as a group. Some groups immediately began mixing colors and experimenting with materials, while others took a more strategic approach, spending time discussing their ideas and plans. This diversity in approach reflected the unique ways individuals process and engage with creative tasks. Even those who were previously strangers found themselves working seamlessly together, as the activity dissolved initial boundaries. At times, participants realized they had been collaborating for a while without even remembering each other's names, highlighting how the work fosters organic connections.

The free-of-judgment and inclusive environment encouraged everyone to contribute, making the experience more rewarding for all participants. By creating a level playing field, creativity is nurtured, allowing participants to explore and create art from a shared baseline of knowledge and experience. This methodology promotes a team environment where individuals can freely express ideas and emotions, breaking down formal barriers and fostering trust and psychological safety through collaborative artwork. Encouraging the team to step outside their comfort zones, the process helps them explore new ideas and communicate complex thoughts and emotions through joint artwork.

## Creation phase – engagement and energy

In this phase, participants immersed themselves in the creative process, experimenting with new mediums and techniques. Energy levels shifted as discussions became louder and more vibrant. Openness and courage to try new things in art making steadily increased, culminating in laughter and a strong group dynamic. As participants engaged more deeply with the activity, they felt a stronger connection to their group members, fostering camaraderie and a sense of community. Participants were encouraged to ignite their creativity by focusing on the process rather than the end product, promoting creative freedom and deeper, more authentic connections with themselves and others.

A key moment in the process was captured in Figure 6.3, illustrating one group's transition from initial hesitancy to bold, spontaneous creativity. The image shows participants joyfully working together on a large canvas. This shift, reflected in the photo, demonstrates the group's growing openness and ingenuity as they turned a practical floor cover into a tool for artistic expression. The vibrant colors and energetic action seen in the picture underscore their collective engagement and the sense of freedom that filled the space. As they collaborated on this unconventional medium, the team dynamic flourished, deepening their sense of community and creative exploration.

The experience emphasized the importance of belonging and increased team interaction. Each participant approached the team task and materials differently. Some were tentative, discussing their approach in detail before starting, while others dived in with enthusiasm. This initial engagement reflected varied approaches to life and its challenges. As the paint flowed, so did thoughts and emotions, turning the act of painting into a meditative practice. Participants began to lose themselves in the process, shedding initial hesitations for a sense of freedom and exploration. One group had so much fun and joy that they wanted to create another piece. Since we did not have more canvases, they used painter's fleece, which was originally intended to protect the floor from paint. This spontaneous idea sparked creativity and led them to enjoy a team drip painting, further enhancing their sense of teamwork and ingenuity.

**Figure 6.3:** Creation phase.
Source: Xuan Dung Burckhardt, 2024 (Photo is taken by Xuan Dung Burckhardt, no usage without Approval by Xuan Dung Burckhardt).

## Reflection phase – introspection and understanding

Reflection was an integral part of the process, allowing participants to gain valuable insights and key learnings for both individual and group growth. This stage encouraged a deeper level of introspection and collective understanding, providing a zoom-in and zoom-out effect. Art encouraged participants to observe with a wider lens, which then led to meaningful group reflection. They reflected on both individual and team levels, shared their findings, and presented their artwork to the group. This process not only fostered personal growth but also gave participants the opportunity to get to know each other better.

The act of creating art helped participants to see the wider implications of their inner development, linking personal insights to sustainability. As they became more aware of their thoughts, emotions, and actions, they also became more aware of their impact on the environment. The realization that our inner state can influence our outer actions was a powerful takeaway. It highlighted the importance of cultivating mindfulness and intentionality in our daily lives, recognizing that sustainable living begins with inner transformation. This awareness underscored the connection between personal growth and the larger goal of sustainability, emphasizing that positive change in the world begins with ourselves.

Additionally, art served as a powerful medium to communicate complex issues and facilitate engaging conversations that are often difficult to put into words. This experience demonstrated how creative works of art can be used as a universal language to convey profound messages. Through art, participants found a new way to explore and discuss complicated ideas, highlighting its potential as a tool for deeper understanding and connection.

## Learning phase – application and insights

The final phase involved collectively applying learnings to amplify impact and celebrate shared successes. Participants were transported inside to debrief their experiences, first in their groups and then together as a whole. Each team shared their experience and presented their art piece, highlighting the connection between personal growth and sustainability. Participants expressed that the journey through FLOW allowed them to explore the five dimensions of the IDGs through art. They embraced different perspectives, connected deeply to the challenge of desertification in Tanzania, and used vibrant colors to bring their ideas to life.

The reflection phase was essential for internalizing and appreciating the depth of their experiences, showing the transformative power of collaboration and shared meaning. The workshop provided a chance to pause mental noise and immerse in the moment. The blank canvas and invigorating colors, along with uncomplicated interactions with co-creators, made the experience both creative and joyful. Participants appreciated the safe and fun bubble of improvised collaboration, recognizing the importance of reaching a flow state in both personal and collaborative contexts.

## Wrap-up: Final circle and reflection with "Hokusai Says"

As we approached the end of the workshop, we gathered once more in a circle, a space of shared experience and connection. In this final moment, we read "Hokusai Says" by Roger Keyes aloud. This poem, inspired by the Japanese artist Katsushika Hokusai, reflects on the continuous journey of artistic and personal growth.

After the intense sessions of art making and discussion, reading "Hokusai Says" provided a fitting end to our experience. The poem's focus on the importance of process, discovery, and mindfulness resonated deeply with the insights we had shared throughout the workshop. It encapsulated the essence of what we had explored together: the idea that art and inner development are ongoing journeys rather than final destinations.

The poem helped us to integrate our individual and collective reflections, rein-forcing the workshop's core themes of creativity, self-awareness, and transformation. It served as a reminder of the workshop's goal: to foster a deeper connection with ourselves and with each other through artistic expression and mindful engagement, to develop new levels of awareness, and to incentivize action.

In this final moment, we were able to bring together our creative efforts and in-sights, reflecting on how the experience had impacted us. The reading of "Hokusai Says" offered a contemplative pause, allowing us to appreciate the process of our ar-tistic exploration and its broader implications for personal and collective growth. This wrap-up highlighted the workshop's success in blending art, introspection, and collab-oration, leaving participants with a renewed sense of purpose and connection.

# Major insights

The workshop yielded several significant insights, each contributing to a deeper un-derstanding of the interplay between art, personal development, and collective growth. These insights not only reflect key theoretical frameworks but also demon-strate the practical benefits of integrating such concepts into experiential learning. By embracing the notion of flow, participants learned to trust the creative process, which fostered both individual expression and team synergy. The practice of mindfulness and intentionality highlighted the importance of being present. The use of art as a tool for reflection and dialogue allowed participants to challenge assumptions and un-dergo personal transformation, illustrating the power of art in education. Addition-ally, the holistic approach of engaging head, heart, and hand provided a comprehen-sive learning experience, while the environment of psychological safety promoted trust and collaboration. Finally, linking inner development with sustainability empha-sized how personal growth can lead to broader environmental and social responsibil-ity. Together, these insights underscore the transformative potential of integrating ar-tistic expression with inner development and collaborative processes.

## Trust the process and embrace the flow

Drawing from Csikszentmihalyi's concept of flow, the workshop created an environ-ment where participants could let go of fears and judgments, allowing their creativity to emerge naturally. By trusting the process and entering a state of flow, participants discovered a deeper connection with their creative potential and with each other. This harmonious and productive collaboration not only enhanced their artistic ex-pressions but also their teamwork, illustrating how a flow state can foster synergy and collective creativity.

## Cultivate mindfulness and intentionality

The journey through FLOW highlighted the importance of being present and mindful. Participants learned that intentional actions, both in art and in life, lead to more meaningful and sustainable outcomes. This awareness aligns with Mezirow's transformative learning theory, which emphasizes critical reflection and rational discourse. By being mindful and intentional, participants engaged in deep introspection, leading to transformative shifts in their perspectives. This process is essential for personal growth and for fostering a mindful and intentional approach to both individual and collective endeavors.

## Transformative learning through art

The workshop enabled participants to reflect critically on their experiences and engage in rational discourse through art. The collaborative art-making process allowed participants to question their assumptions, leading to shifts in their worldviews. As they explored themes like climate action in Africa and the importance of education in Africa, participants not only deepened their understanding of these issues but also experienced personal transformation. This reflective and dialogic process highlighted the power of art as a medium for transformative learning.

## Synergy of head, heart, and hand

Participants used their heads to ignite creativity, their hearts to feel inspired and connected to others, and their hands to immerse in the art-making process. This holistic approach mirrors Mezirow's emphasis on holistic learning, where cognitive, emotional, and practical dimensions are interconnected. By engaging all three aspects, participants experienced a comprehensive form of learning and development.

## Enhanced psychological safety and trust

The inclusive and nonjudgmental environment of the workshop promoted psychological safety and trust among participants. This aligns with Csikszentmihalyi's flow theory, which posits that a state of flow enhances overall well-being and group cohesion. As participants felt safe to express themselves and explore new ideas, they built deeper connections with each other. This trust and psychological safety are crucial for effective teamwork and collective creativity, fostering an environment where transformative learning can thrive.

## Linking inner development to sustainability

The workshop emphasized the connection between personal growth and sustainability, highlighting that sustainable living begins with inner transformation (See Figure 6.4). As participants became more aware of their thoughts, emotions, and actions, they also became more conscious of their environmental impact. This realization underscores Mezirow's transformative learning theory, which posits that transformative learning leads to greater social and environmental responsibility. By linking inner development to broader sustainability goals, the workshop demonstrated how personal transformation can contribute to positive change in the world.

**Figure 6.4:** Reflection and sharing process.
Source: Xuan Dung Burckhardt (Photos is taken by Xuan Dung Burckhardt, no further use without her approval).

## The voice of the participants

*As a mindfulness practitioner and enabler of embodied leadership, I embrace environments that foster creativity and exploration. This experience of FLOW enabled us to connect with curiosity to ourselves, but also one to another, to witness the power of togetherness and humanity fueled by a common purpose. Following the flow of silent inspiration, the intermingling of drops and streaks of color, I witnessed collective leadership and collaboration that blossomed into a patchwork of reality, beauty, and hope. What emerged was the contrast of darkness and light, drabness and joy . . . the coexistence of black and white holes – revealing the "whole" of opportunity that arises through letting our inner wisdom flow.*

Thea Morris, PhD, One 2 Another – Courage Coaching TM (O2A-CCTM)

*It was a wonderful, energizing moment to come together as a community, to connect and create, and FLOW. Sometimes we spend so much time worrying and thinking about everything that is going wrong in the world. This was a lovely moment through the means of art to realize that we're together in facing these challenges and bringing hope into what we CAN do. My key takeaways: How am I transforming myself to create a better world? And a reminder that we can do so much more as we work in community. How do I work in collaboration with others to bring change for a better world? I look forward to how IDGs and SDGs can help us to co-create a just, purposeful, and sustainable future for all.*

Racheal E Govender, leadership development specialist, psychologist, and executive coach

*The experience truly lived up to its name: FLOW. Each event creates a unique environment for in-teraction, and the physical space plays a part in this as well. Sometimes, the social and physical components (location, weather) come together in such a unique way that the experience leaves a lasting impression. Mauricio and Dung have designed an event perfectly aligned with its purpose. From the perspective of the Inner Development Goals framework, they managed to tap into skills in almost every dimension. For me, it was the beginning of a wonderful friendship, and the con-cepts that emerged there are still in our minds.*

Elif Kus Saillard, PhD, NAM Qualitative Research Center founder

*I didn't experience the workshop as a coach, business advisor, or leader, but as an individual. The workshop provided a chance to pause my mental noise and immerse myself in the moment. I stopped overthinking and engaged manually. The blank canvas and the invigorating, user-friendly colors, along with the uncomplicated interactions with my co-creators, made the experience both creative and joyful.*

Eleftheria Egel, PhD, Navigating Transformation founder

# Conclusion – integration and feedback

The seamless integration of IDGs with the FLOW concept and methodology resulted in a synergistic and transformative workshop. This innovative approach underscored the power of partnership and the effectiveness of blending diverse methodologies to create a cohesive and impactful experience. By aligning the artistic process with cog-nitive, emotional, and practical engagement, the workshop facilitates a holistic ap-proach to growth. It encouraged self-awareness, empathy, resilience, and creativity, all essential for individual fulfillment, effective teamwork, and collective action.

The workshop demonstrated that cohesive collaboration among a group of strangers is not only possible but can be deeply enriching. Using art as a bridge, par-ticipants communicated messages and thoughts in a powerful and meaningful way. Tapping into their collective creativity built trust and fostered genuine connections.

This experience emphasized that through the medium of art, complex ideas and emotions can be expressed and understood, leading to deeper insights and stronger relationships. The workshop's success lies in its ability to transform individual and group dynamics, showcasing the potential of art to bring people together and drive meaningful change.

The integration of IDG and FLOW has proven to be a powerful combination, providing a holistic approach to development and collaboration. This workshop not only enhanced participants' artistic skills but also enriched their personal and interpersonal growth, paving the way for more mindful and intentional living. As we continue to explore and expand the possibilities of such integrative methodologies, we pave the way for more innovative and impactful experiences that promote sustainability, creativity, and collective well-being.

In essence, the workshop underscored the transformative power of integrating FLOW and IDG methodologies. Participants walked away with a deeper understanding of themselves, their collective potential, and the vital connection between inner development and sustainability. This process highlighted the hope that through creative collaboration and mindful engagement, we can foster profound personal and societal change. The fusion of art, flow, and transformative learning offers a promising pathway to a more sustainable and interconnected world.

## References

Csikszentmihalyi, M. (1990). *Flow: The psychology of optimal experience*. Harper & Row.
Mezirow, J. (1991). *Transformative dimensions of adult learning*. Jossey-Bass.
Gergen, K. J. (2009). *Relational being: Beyond self and community*. Oxford University Press.
Suzuki, S. (1970). Zen mind, beginner's mind. Weatherhill.

Section 2: **Ancient wisdom**

Ana Gabriela Mata Carrera, Paul Jeffcutt
# Chapter 7
# Prelude

Since ancient times, humanity has pursued self-knowledge as a means to transcend the mundane and understand the deeper purpose of existence. This pursuit, deeply rooted in philosophical inquiry and spiritual traditions, finds its echoes in the words of Socrates, who famously declared that "the unexamined life is not worth living". His conviction, even to the point of choosing death over ignorance, underscores the time-less quest for understanding and fulfillment. Today, as we face pressing global challenges and strive towards sustainability, this journey of inner exploration takes on renewed significance.

This section embarks on a journey through diverse wisdom traditions, each offering a unique perspective on self-examination and transformation. It begins with an exploration of the Dzogchen tradition, which unveils the path to inner sustainability and the realization of innate intelligence. From there, the journey unfolds through the lens of the Chinese "Great Ear", where wisdom blooms from the sense of hearing through deep listening and aesthetic appreciation, revealing the interconnectedness between inner awareness and external harmony.

The exploration continues with Zen wisdom, from Japan integrating ancient insights with contemporary perspectives. Through the Ten Bulls narrative, we witness a structured journey of consciousness, illustrating how timeless wisdom can inform and inspire modern approaches to creativity and leadership.

Next, we encounter the Seasonal Circles of Change, drawing from Celtic traditions to explore the transformative power of aligning personal growth with the natural rhythms of the earth, fostering collective leadership and sustainable futures.

Finally, the section culminates in the Amazonian rainforest, where an immersive leadership experience unfolds, blending inner and outer journeys. Here, participants confront their own limitations and potential, embracing systemic thinking and inter-connectedness as catalysts for personal and communal well-being. Together, these chapters weave a tapestry of ancient wisdom and contemporary relevance, offering insights and practices to guide us on the path of self-discovery, purposeful living, and holistic transformation.

https://doi.org/10.1515/9783111337913-008

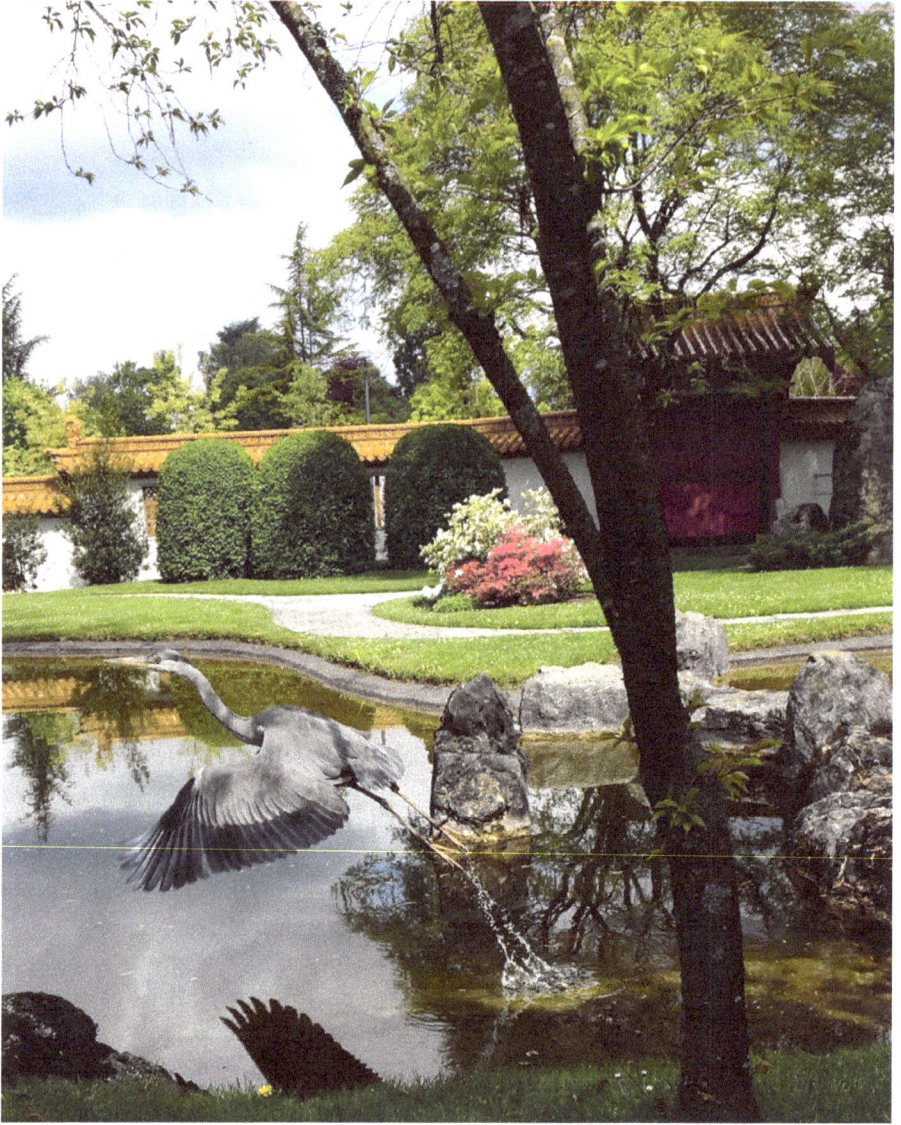

**Figure 7.1:** *Vuela* (2012).
Photograph by A. G. Mata Carrera, Zürich, Switzerland.
*"The water of the pond in the Zen garden reflects the sky as a mirror. The picture captures the moment when the bird, previously in the water, takes flight in such a mindful way that it does not disturb the mirror-like surface. This serves as a metaphor for the serenity and clarity that traditional wisdom and practices bring to our lives."*

# Telling the Bees

No
   flummer, fibs, waffle,
      blather, rattle, hype,
   hearsay, palaver,
      witter, wind, yap,
   soft-soap, prattle,
      scams, clack, twaddle,
   garden-path jabber,
      noise, fakery, bull,
   tittle-tattle, cackle,
      piffle, porkies, gab,
   fairytales, gibber,
      bluff, fudges, babble,
   flimflam or blah.
The truth.

**Paul Jeffcutt (2024)**

Author's note. An ancient custom requires the head of a household to tell their bees of any significant changes in the family and village. Failure to keep the bees fully informed was believed to result in the loss or death of the colony.

Jochen Raysz
# Chapter 8
# Inner sustainability for global transformation: Living and leading from the essence of our being

**Abstract:** Can we find inner sustainability without stepping away from our passionate pursuit of a sustainable future? What if we could thrive and create meaningful impact in the world without the pervasive costs of friction, stress, and burnout?

This chapter introduces the transformative power of Dzogchen, an ancient Tibetan wisdom philosophy and practice, and explores how it can help us tap into our innate ease, clarity, and potency to address the crises we face as a global culture.

Through personal stories of a life-changing journey, the text illustrates the profound inner transformation that Dzogchen practice can bring about. At the heart of Dzogchen practice is the recognition of the true nature of mind — the mirror-like awareness that remains unchanging amid our countless life experiences.

Stabilizing the recognition of this essence of our being through simple practices woven into everyday life, unlocks our full capacity for empowered being, thinking, relating, collaborating and acting. It opens a mindset from fear, lack, and scarcity into one of abundance, generosity and vast potential.

The chapter highlights how Dzogchen can support growth in several IDG skills and offers tools and practices for a fundamental shift into a conscious and resilient way of being that effortlessly infuses our actions in the world. By living from the essence of our being, we ignite the inner transformation required to powerfully and sustainably contribute to a thriving world.

**Keywords:** Inner Sustainability, Essence of Being, Transformation, Inner Peace, Dzogchen, Meditation

> *A poor man owns a shack built on a foundation of gold. Because he doesn't recognize the value of gold, he is convinced that he is poor.*

**Acknowledgements:** Great gratitude to my teacher Ziji Rinpoche for the introduction to the true nature of mind and the countless teachings and ongoing instructions to strengthen my practice. I also wish to thank my fellow co-founders at Super – Erik Rosin, Mikaela Schain, and Asaf Chesner – as well as Katharina Raysz for their support in creating this chapter and Scott Morrow for contributing his editing skills.

https://doi.org/10.1515/9783111337913-009

## Introduction

It's fascinating how a single insight can have the power to transform an entire life, creating a completely new perspective about one's past and revealing a future of previously unknown opportunity. That's what happened for me on a sunny afternoon in Rishikesh, India in October 2005.

Prior to this, my life had *looked* amazing, but what appeared amazing from the outside felt really challenging inside. Having completed my master's in psychology at the top of my class, creating a successful career as a change management consultant and being in a loving, committed marriage, by the end of my twenties I had ticked all the right boxes.

However, while people saw me as calm, stable, and successful, I felt a nagging sense of turmoil, insecurity, and self-doubt. Pictures show me smiling and engaging, when in reality I often felt hollow and empty, longing for deeper connection. Friends and colleagues described me as inspiring, energetic, and optimistic, but I felt increasingly disillusioned and hopeless.

Despite all the privileges I had, all the tools I had learned, all the work I had done with therapists and coaches, and all the money and prestige I had earned, I was still searching for inner stability and peace, and I could not bear the thought of continuing on without these qualities in my life.

Fortunately, my wife had come to a similar point in her life and career. We decided to take an open-ended sabbatical and travel the world to find answers to our burning questions about the purpose of life: how to be truly happy and contribute to making the world a better place. Our first step in fulfilling the deep desire to make sense of our lives was to strike out on an adventure of exploration, driving in a van from Germany to India.

Taking to the road gave us the opportunity to slow down. We relished the atmosphere of bustling markets in Turkey and the Middle East, the hospitality and ancient heritage of Iran, the quiet of the desert in Pakistan, and the colorful festivals and weeklong weddings in India. We had deep conversations with people from all walks of life. Each life story was so precious and unique, and yet it seemed that in essence almost everyone was on a similar quest to their version of inner peace, connection, and a sense of purpose.

By the time we reached India, we were eager to explore the rich offering there of ancient wisdom and spiritual practices. Over the course of months and after many hours of meditation, speaking with gurus, nuns, and monks, silent retreats and yoga courses, I had had moments of inner peace on the cushion, but I found that peace to be frustratingly rare and difficult to access in daily life.

That changed when we stumbled across an ancient tradition, Dzogchen, that was said to bring about enlightenment in this very lifetime. It felt like the pot of gold at the end of the rainbow might be real after all! We were thrilled to dive right into the practice, and in doing so I learned more about myself in a week than I did in six years of studying psychology.

First of all, I found freedom and relief from the constant chatter in my mind. The teaching gave me a deep, abiding confidence that no matter what circumstance life would throw at me, I would be alright. I eventually took on roles and responsibilities way outside my comfort zone and found the skillful means needed to flourish and contribute to making the world a better place. My relationships blossomed with more love, warmth, and presence. And all this came without any effort or struggle, but from a single insight, a powerful change in the understanding and use of the mind.

This chapter introduces this ancient tradition and shares a simple practice that brought unimaginable benefit to my life. We will show how it can open a treasure you already have within yourself. Our heartfelt wish is that it will support you too on your personal journey for inner peace and mastery, as well as your passion to lead and support our collective transformation into a thriving sustainable world.

# How can an ancient practice help us solve our current crisis?

Most conversations and projects supporting the transformation into a sustainable global culture focus on what we need to be *doing* (more, less, differently) to make it happen. This goes for both individual efforts (recycle more, live car-free, fly less, etc.) as well as collective action (transition to renewable energy, transform the food system, etc.).

Of course, taking action is indeed needed, but the increasing sense of urgency and intense feeling of personal responsibility coupled with the painful perception of slow progress often leads to frustration that either turns into anger and resentment and/or hopelessness, burnout, and despair.

How might we be able to tackle this world crisis without creating more burnout and further division in society? How can we create the transformational change that is so urgently needed to reach the Sustainable Development Goals (SDGs)?

While changing what we are *doing* is helpful, we're proposing a more fundamental shift in who we are *being*.

## A shift in who we are being

In our experience of working with changemakers over the last two decades, we have found that this shift in "who we are being" automatically makes all the "doing" more sustainable. It enriches our perspective and decision making with solution focus, generosity, abundance, and clarity. Actions are rooted in the benefit of all beings in the present and future generations, rather than in fear, scarcity, greed, and short-term gains.

So how do we change who we are being? The most straightforward approach we have found to foster what we call "inner sustainability" is to tap into the self-renewing energy and wisdom we already have within. Then we can allow empowered qualities and activities in the world to arise from this abundant essence of our being.

Most traditions, philosophies, and religions have their own terms to describe this state of being. Once we have an instinctive recognition of its energy and wisdom, we can easily understand each of the approaches, regardless of the different cultural labels being used, as they all come from and describe the same source: a universal intelligence that pervades all of nature. Since humans are part of nature, we too are pervaded by this intelligence and can both comprehend and access it directly in and through our personal experience.

Our framework is based on the ancient Dzogchen tradition, for which we have received teachings and instructions from Ziji Rinpoche, an authorized lineage successor, who is sharing the practices in a simple, contemporary format so all the world's people can easily understand and practice it. This is the brilliant teaching that I discovered on that sunny day in Rishikesh in 2005.

## Dzogchen: Discovering the treasure within

Dzogchen is a tradition of teachings in Tibetan Buddhism and is considered the highest and most profound spiritual path within the Nyingma school of Tibetan Buddhism. The teachings are said to have originated from the primordial Buddha Samantabhadra, with the teachings being transmitted in an unbroken lineage of masters to this very day.

Central to Dzogchen practice is the direct transmission of the true nature of mind from teacher to student that enables the practitioner to directly experience the natural state, the essence of our being. Upon this introduction, the sole aim of practice is to deepen the familiarity with this natural, primordial state through contemplative methods, instead of relying on intellectualization and ritual complexity.

Throughout the centuries, the teachings of Dzogchen have always been customized to speak to the people of each different era. We will follow this same tradition here. We will present the teachings in a contemporary format suitable for modern practitioners and focus on how they can support us in embodying the IDG skills and leading the sustainability transformation.

# The path of Dzogchen

### Introduction to the essence of our being: The true nature of mind

Given the immense benefits this transformational approach provides, the actual process is surprisingly simple. First, we need to have a personal experience of this essence of our being. Theory and philosophy are useful, but they will not bring about the actual realization. By analogy, no words could even come close to describing the taste of honey compared to having a spoon of honey in one's mouth.

The essence of our being can be likened to a flawless crystal ball. Regardless of what appears within the crystal ball, the ball itself is unchanging, radiant, and clear. It reflects fire without being burnt. It reflects water without getting wet. It reflects beauty without longing for more of it. It reflects cruelty without recoiling from it.

Similarly, the essence of our being, the true nature of mind, is unaffected by our experiences of life. It is the unchanging expanse in which experience arises and resolves. Like the crystal ball, it remains clear and open, regardless of what kind of experience arises.

So, in terms of my own journey, there were two very decisive moments into the heart of this recognition. One morning during an intensive meditation retreat, without any obvious cause, it suddenly hit me: that which is observing all these experiences in my body and mind is always present and unaffected by whatever it experiences. I felt complete relief and freedom, decades of effort to manage and control my thoughts and emotions fell away. I thought my quest was over; I had found the indestructible essence of my being.

However, after a few days, the experience became a memory, and I no longer felt that same level of freedom and relief. Had I finally found the most precious treasure only to see it dissolve right in front of me? I had a glimpse into the most profound truth of human existence, but I did not know how to *live* from this truth. I needed to find the key to unlock the treasure chest of lived experience, and I was determined to find it.

### Instinctive recognition in daily life

A few weeks after my experience in the meditation retreat, my wife and I were walking through Rishikesh, India, when I saw a poster: Ziji Rinpoche, a Dzogchen teacher, was giving a teaching on "the power of awareness" and how to bring this power into everyday life to be of benefit to all. I had never heard of this tradition before, but reading these words about bringing this power into everyday life resonated deeply in me.

Ziji Rinpoche gave a direct introduction to awareness, our fundamental condition, and shared a simple practice to make this direct experience of awareness obvious at all times. This teaching confirmed and clarified what I had experienced in the earlier meditation retreat, and I was so grateful to learn a practice that could make living from this reality possible at all times with no possibility of losing it again.

What we heard is that, because we are tapping into something that is already present at the core of our being, it is not about striving to achieve something in the future. Rather, we can rest as that natural energy and wisdom and allow ourselves to recognize and trust these innate qualities more and more often for longer and longer periods.

For someone like me who defined myself a lot by my hard work, this very gentle approach of relaxing into what is already present felt counterintuitive. However, through practice it eventually became obvious that this way of being was so much more sustainable and empowering. Challenges in daily life became a reminder to relax my body and mind and to reset into the natural state. I began to stay calm under pressure, see a path forward in conflictual situations, and found more natural warmth and joy in my relationships.

## The operating system we've been running

To examine how we have learned to operate, let's think of our mind as an operating system that is at the basis of what we're thinking, sensing, feeling, saying, and doing. It constantly receives, processes, stores, and retrieves data to guide our decisions and actions. "Data" here can mean any kind of perception arising in the mind such as thoughts, emotions, sensations, or other kinds of experiences.

A lot of our energy goes into trying to maximize positive and minimize negative data. For example, motivated by my deep wish to be a good person, I had tried really hard to cultivate kind thoughts and to feel compassion towards people. Having harsh judgements about others felt like a sign of not being a good person myself.

Over the course of the first Dzogchen teaching, I reviewed my life's journey and how my mind had operated. It was astonishing to realize how much time, energy, and other resources I had spent to feel better, to worry less, to achieve more, to find inner peace, to become a more beneficial human by managing the data (thoughts, emotions, and sensations).

Each of us develops our beliefs of what is "good", "negative", or "neutral" based on our upbringing, and we adopt values from our family, peer groups, media, and other factors in society. However, while the content of our particular beliefs and values varies from person to person, the fundamental dynamic that plays out is similar. We either run with the data and are, often blindly, absorbed by it, or we try to change, avoid, or replace it with data we deem to be more positive.

The tools we use also vary widely. One person might try to improve their thoughts or emotional state by having a drink, another might choose to watch TV, and yet another will try to think positively, do yoga or meditate. We hope to experience well-being now and in the future, and fear that we won't.

**The price we pay**

Constantly scrutinizing and micromanaging our inner and outer experience is exhausting! Driven by hope and fear we are running on a hamster wheel chasing after a better future and running away from the pain and discomfort of the past and present. Even if we find a so-called perfect moment, we can't hold it in place for long.

In my own life, my mind was constantly running in problem-solving mode. Intellectually I knew the constant fight-or-flight scenario is unnecessary and counterproductive, but no matter where I looked, I could not find an off switch. It was ironic: I worked to make organizations more sustainable and humane, while at the same time I was getting burned out myself. Sadly, I am not alone in this. The fact that so many people in our modern society experience depression and burnout despite living in the most abundant time in human history shows that the depression can't be due to our physical environment alone.

With this operating system based on processing data, we never have enough and we never are good enough. There is always more to be achieved, more problems to be solved, more stuff to be had. Working harder and doing more based on the same underlying assumptions is not going to solve the issues we currently face. A sustainable future cannot come about by running the same hamster wheel more efficiently. We need to *step off* the hamster wheel. In the famous words of Albert Einstein: "We cannot solve our problems with the same thinking we used when we created them." (Albert Einstein, n.d.)

## It's time to upgrade

What would happen if we ceased the desperate effort to change and improve our experience? I have seen in myself and hundreds of other changemakers that the less caught up we are in micromanaging ourselves and the more we allow our mind and body to be at ease, the more we experience genuine motivation to be of benefit to others.

A few months after completing the introductory Dzogchen teaching, I was invited to help lead the social impact organization Ziji Rinpoche had just started to bring these teachings to the world. I was excited to begin this new adventure and to use all challenges, like fear of failure, feelings of unworthiness and overwhelm, as opportunities for practice, and it quickly became clear that taking on this role was the perfect practice ground for me. Many opportunities arose to consciously and deliberately prioritize a moment of rest while being very busy, instead of getting into the old hamster wheel of tension and striving.

It is amazing how much we have trained ourselves into believing that being a good person and being of benefit requires effort and constantly working on ourselves and the world around us. Deep down, we might even feel that being at ease is immoral, considering the state of the world, and we fear that it will lead to complacency. This could not be further from the truth! The more at ease we are, the greater our capacity to see clearly how to move forward in a way that serves this and future generations. The more relaxed we are, the more we focus on the right things.

This is truly a *radical* shift in our understanding of human nature. It is a more comprehensive way of operating, such that the old systems of sorting data into positive, negative, and neutral categories take up less and less of our focus and attention. We are no longer a victim of the habitual responses to our inner and outer circumstances.

### Inner sustainability fuels beneficial activity in the world

Living from the essence of our being means we allow mind and body to rest in their natural state of complete ease. We relax into a more fundamental way of living that gives expression to our innate clarity, wisdom, and compassion. We discover a lifestyle of inner sustainability that can fuel tremendous beneficial activity in the world.

At first, I sometimes felt like I had retreated into a space of finding protection from the world. Over time, however, the resting practice became more of an opening and a leaning into the world, where I experienced everything fully and found freedom and clarity *within* the experience rather than freedom *from* the experience.

I remember a conversation with a team leader in those early days where I had to address a few challenges that had come up in their team. I was new to being in a leadership role and felt quite tense because I did not want to hurt their feelings. Initially I relied on my old strategies of speaking calmly, starting with positive feedback first before getting into the real issues. But all the while my heart was racing and I did not feel calm and connected at all. That was my reminder to reset and to rest.

Instead of following my usual agenda (changing the person and what they do), I shifted to asking them how they felt, how things had been going, and if there was anything I could do to be helpful. My internal shift changed the conversation entirely. It became an opportunity to connect deeply, to express my heartfelt appreciation, and co-create solutions for the issues at hand. I couldn't believe it was that easy and natural to exercise leadership. This experience was a profound confirmation of our innate capacity as humans.

When we are holding to and operating within the confines of our current conventional values, beliefs, and habits; the scope of our intelligence is very narrow. But if we simply relax and allow our intelligence to open into its natural state, we have access to the vast treasury of energy and knowledge that is already present.

Living this reality, we tap into the already present abundance of nature's intelligence. We can draw on our innate power and allow ourselves to live in a flow, in sync with the way things are, spontaneously responsive to whatever is needed.

## Mirror-like awareness

At the heart of the Dzogchen teachings is the principle that we are whole and complete just *as we are*. The sole reason for our relentless quest for more and better is that we have not been introduced to our true nature. Recognizing ourselves as who we fundamentally are is like finding a long-lost treasure. We may have been searching for it for eons only to return and find it right in our own home. The search has come to an end and we can finally rest.

We spend our entire life describing, evaluating, and managing the *content* of our mind without ever looking at the *nature* of mind directly. This is like only seeing the images in a mirror and overlooking the qualities of the mirror itself. We are the mirror in which the images arise, and the images have no power to affect the mirror. Likewise, you are not the voice in your head, nor are you the stories it's telling you. You are that which is listening to that voice, that which is aware of the stories.

# Roadmap and tools

Upgrading to this new way of being is quite simple, but that doesn't mean it is easy, especially since the upgrade challenges ingrained belief systems we have absorbed over the course of our lives.

Traditionally, the process is described in three stages:
1. Introduction to and discovery of the essence of our being.
2. Becoming increasingly familiar with the essence of our being.
3. Gaining complete assurance and living in conscious alignment with it, as well as spontaneously demonstrating beneficial qualities and activities.

In this section, we describe these stages in more detail along with suggestions that can support the curious traveler on their journey.

## Stage one: Decisive recognition

I hope this chapter can serve to offer you a sense of this indestructible essence of your being, the mirror-like nature of mind. If you notice any parts that particularly resonate with you, highlight them so you can reread them and rest in the resonance they evoke in you.

Additionally, contemplative practices such as self-inquiry and meditation can support increasing clarity and instinctive recognition of the true nature of mind. The following guided exploration is an example for such a practice.[1]

### Guided exploration

Take a moment to pay close attention to the constant stream of experience. Maybe certain sensations in your body arise, then a thought comes up and then a memory. Just follow this stream for a few seconds. Please do that now before you continue reading.

Now, shift your attention to what is *aware* of this experience, just for a moment. Don't look for an answer in the knowledge base of your intellect. Look in your experience. What is aware of the sensations, of the feelings, of the thoughts?

You will find that there is no "thing" there. All we can definitively state is that there is awareness, always on and effortlessly aware of the constantly changing, unpredictable flow of experience, yet never changing itself.

Look at your experience right now to see if it is like this or not.

Does awareness change because you were thinking a good or bad thought?

This mirror-like awareness is the essence of your being. It's what has been looking through your eyes from the moment you were born and is still looking today. It's what has been listening, feeling, thinking, and sensing countless things, and yet, it always remains the same.

It may have never looked at itself, but when it does, its intrinsic qualities of basic goodness, clarity, wisdom, and compassion open like the petals of a flower when the sun rises.

## Stage two: Weaving practice into the fabric of daily life

Now that we have recognized what the essence of our being is, we choose to become increasingly familiar with it. Since it has always been present and has just gone unnoticed, gaining familiarity is not a strenuous task.

---

1 You can find guided meditations and resources referenced in the text at https://super.how/idg.

We mine the gold of this vast treasure we have within simply by relaxing into it whenever we remember to do so. Like pressing a reset button, when we notice we are stressed, we take a moment to allow body and mind to rest in their natural state of complete ease. We can also rest naturally while in the midst of being very busy.

The content of our experience is not going to change, and ordinary thoughts will continue to arise, but what changes is that we no longer jump into the hamster wheel of hope and fear that used to get triggered by our experiences.

Through this mental and emotional stability our perspective opens up, and we can see many more solutions to problems. This is like standing on a mountaintop and having a 360-degree view, including all the paths and where they are leading, including paths which cannot be seen from the valley.

The time-honored practice for this integration stage can be summarized as short moments of resting as our natural state, repeated many times, until it is obvious at all times. Whenever we spontaneously remember, we recognize our true nature for just a brief moment, enjoying a glimpse into the indestructible essence of our being.

The emphasis is on "short", and we're also not using effort to strive or achieve – that would make the practice contrived and something we need to do. Rather, we want to keep the practice instinctive, authentic, and easeful.

Initially, there might be days when we completely forget about the practice and other days when we will remember it a few times here and there. That is to be expected. Regardless, the essence of our being remains as it is, readily accessible the next time we remember to rest.

Sometimes the instinctive recognition of mirror-like awareness elicits a sense of clarity, other times we might feel peaceful or have a profound sense of connection and experience more ease and spaciousness. But these wonderful feelings are still just reflections in the mirror, so we don't cling to them. We enjoy them and let them flow on by like any other experience.

**Practical suggestions**

Here are some practical suggestions for beginning to integrate the short moments practice into your life.

For the first few days and weeks, it can be helpful to establish little rituals that serve to remind you to consciously rest. For example:

- Start the morning with a brief, quiet moment of resting naturally. You could do that while taking a shower or brushing your teeth, so it does not require any extra time.
- Around midday, read a few lines of this text that resonated with you.
- Set an alarm for three times a day reminding you to take a short moment.
- As you get ready for sleep, take a few moments to settle into your natural state.

- During the day, when you recognize that you are caught up in thoughts, look at the thinker and notice how thoughts self-release like the flight path of a bird in the sky.
- When you notice you feel tense or stressed, relax body and mind completely just for a moment. Let tension in your body become a friendly reminder to take a short moment of rest.
- When you notice anxious energy, look directly at the unchanging, ever-present nature of your own mind. Recognize that no matter what happens, your fundamental intelligence is always available to serve and support you. There is something about you that is stable and clear that can't be taken away from you.
- When you feel discomfort arise, instead of pushing it away, take a moment to soften and relax deeply. Let the discomfort melt away like a snowflake entering a hot space.
- When you find yourself joyful or happy, relax any craving to hold onto this pleasant experience and relax into the flow of the always-changing dynamic of life.

## Questions for reflection

The following questions can further support your journey through the integration stage:

1. What are activities, situations, and circumstances in which you find it easier to rest?
2. What beliefs and assumptions have you learned over the course of your life that appear to be in opposition to what you have read here so far?
3. What reminders, metaphors, pointers, etc. do you find helpful to recognize the true nature of mind for a short moment?
4. What would your life and work look like with more and more moments of rest?
5. From the suggestions above, what could your daily practice look like to support you as a changemaker?

## A network of support

Having support on our journey makes all the difference. There are many books, forums, YouTube channels, and Facebook groups that speak about Dzogchen, centers for study and practice around the world, and some lineages and teachers have created online communities.

As an example from my own life, I remember struggling with a particular emotional pattern for months, feeling quite depressed and very unsure about my ability to practice. When I finally opened up to my teacher, within minutes it was as if an enormous weight had been lifted from my shoulders. Similarly, knowing and sharing with other practitioners has enriched and inspired my practice immeasurably. When others ask questions, I hear my own questions and doubts, and I recognize similarities to their breakthroughs and realizations in my own experience. There is also an option of working one-to-one with a certified teacher to further support the deepening of our practice.

In our Dzogchen community we develop and provide access to contemporary versions of the ancient teachings in books and texts that we study together in groups online and in-person retreats. Some groups form around a shared interest, for example, becoming a more skillful parent, or in building a business, or leading an organization with inner sustainability.

So, should this chapter have sparked your interest, I warmly recommend that you look around and see what your heart resonates with. If you have questions or would like to connect with likeminded sustainability changemakers practicing this way of being, I invite you to reach out and we can consider together what would work best for you.

## Stage three: Complete assurance

Every time we recognize the essence of our being, the recognition grows clearer and stronger. With practice, we recollect more often, and the moments of instinctive recognition grow longer. Eventually, it is our default way of being, and we only need to deliberately practice in those moments when we become aware that the old operating system has taken over.

I remember one afternoon pausing in the flow of my day, wondering if I had forgotten about short moments all day. Upon reflection, I noticed that I had been flowing quite easefully and confidently through my day with many emails and meetings. It dawned on me that this is what "obvious at all times" meant! It felt so natural and non-eventful that I had not even noticed that this way of being had become my default lifestyle. And even for a seasoned practitioner and teacher, there are still moments when I am so grateful that I can return to the practice of "one short moment at a time". As the ancient masters used to say, we will be practitioners until our last breath, and beyond.

The practices at this stage of assurance are more instinctive, automatic, and spontaneous. For many practitioners there is also a growing confidence that we can be totally committed to benefiting the world with skillful means, wisdom, and compassion. The practice increasingly becomes the fuel for bringing our strengths, gifts, and talents to solve the global challenges we're facing.

**Empowering teams and organizations**

I have had the good fortune to lead and work in teams and organizations focused on social impact that were powered by a Dzogchen practice. While we can rely on the essence of our being in any work circumstance, working with others who practice continues to be a deeply inspiring and enriching experience.

In our Dzogchen community, we have a set of fundamental principles that empower us to unify and organize teams. Effective operating structures for an organizational culture of excellence are set out which support a way of relating rooted in the essence of our being.

The shared commitment to resting in the essence of our being creates a magical environment for practice. At our all-volunteer centers, hundreds of people from many nations, different religions, political views, and economic backgrounds are working together in harmony, respect, and unity towards the same goal. We're working on sustainable agriculture, collaborating and building impact companies, making music and art, and learning from each other's diverse life experiences.

Our local Dzogchen communities are self-sufficient and implement the principles to support their needs as a group. Some choose to work and/or live together, contributing to local society by creating sustainable housing and social businesses, and through providing schooling rooted in respect, love, and empowerment of children.

# Enriching IDG skill development with a Dzogchen perspective

Sometimes when we share with passionate changemakers about resting in the essence of their being, they are concerned that this might mean they would become detached from daily life or that they would retreat into some sort of bubble and not have the motivation to create a better future. Or maybe they will no longer take action to make their lives better, care for the body, learn new things, or improve their skills.

We can respond to these concerns by sharing our own experience of having lived this way for many years, founding and sustaining social impact organizations and businesses as well as seeing the results of the practice in so many other changemakers.

In the following section, we will share some examples of how we integrate our Dzogchen practice in developing the IDG skills. You will also read from my fellow cofounders at Super, a sustainability consultancy collective, about their personal experience and a new project we just started to bring IDG skills into Dzogchen communities.

# Self-awareness

"Ability to be in reflective contact with own thoughts, feelings and desires; having a realistic self-image and ability to regulate oneself" (Inner Development Goals, n.d.).

The ability to reflect on our own internal processes and how they are impacting our actions is an incredibly useful skill and the foundation for many other developments. After all, we need to be aware of our inner workings before we can decide to make changes and learn new skills.

Mindfulness-based approaches have brought a lot of attention to this area, and the research shows how beneficial mindfulness is both for greater self-awareness and also self-regulation. However, what made mindfulness challenging for me, even after hundreds of hours of practice, was a habitual and unquestioned identification with my thoughts, feelings, desires, values, etc.

Dzogchen practice has greatly enriched and expanded the meaning of self-awareness for me. Knowing that my deepest self is that which is *aware* of thoughts, feelings, desires, values, etc. has become the most profound meaning of self-awareness: being aware of the true self.

The more I identified as that, the more effortlessly, openly, and even curiously I could reflect on my inner workings. Thoughts, feelings, desires, values, etc. are simply characteristics I have developed over the course of my life, but they don't define who I am. If it turns out that some of these lead to problems, I am eager to know and make changes. The expanded perspective of the self through Dzogchen has given me the ability to see my human characteristics with much more equanimity and self-compassion.

### Practicing self-awareness

For challenging situations where you find it difficult to self-regulate:

Sit comfortably. If it feels safe for you, close your eyes. Check in with yourself. What's your experience like in your body? What thoughts are running through your mind? What emotions do you notice; what is your mood? (Take a couple of minutes for this).

Now, instead of trying to sort out your inner workings, take a moment to rest and to ease into the essence of your being. Notice that regardless of intense sensations and emotions and the speed of your thoughts, you are that which is aware. This essence is unaffected by what's going on within and around you.

Rest here, in your fundamental condition of spacious awareness. It might be useful to remember the analogy of the mirror that is unaffected by the images appearing within it. Rest as the mirror and see what happens.

## Presence

"Ability to be in the here and now without judgment and in a state of open-ended presence" (Inner Development Goals, n.d.).

Have you been with someone who you felt was fully and deeply present with you? Being fully present is such a powerful and transformational skill. But how do you come to "be in the here and now without judgment?" I have sincerely struggled for most of my life trying to get to this place, and always it seemed, sometimes overtly and sometimes subtly, distractions and judgments kept creeping in. Our brain has evolved to constantly scan the environment and judge people, places, and circumstances to evaluate if we can feel safe, can trust, etc., and I could not find an off switch, no matter how hard I tried.

The breakthrough for me has been to allow judgments and other thoughts to arise without being guided by them. Being nonjudgmental does not mean to no longer have these thoughts arise. Rather, we don't *identify* with and collapse into these judgments. We let them be as they are without needing to do anything about them, and we can relate to others from a place of openness.

Practically speaking, when engaging in a conversation, resting in the essence of our being means we can allow our thoughts to resolve on their own, like a line drawn in space, without engaging in them compulsively. We can let the urge to check our phone flow on by and remain focused on the person in front of us. We can truly see and hear another without effort, because our mind is at rest *amidst* all the thoughts, emotions, and sensations.

### Practicing presence

For times when you find yourself distracted by your thoughts and judgments about a person you are with:

Instead of fighting or engaging with your judgments in any way, take a short moment to recognize the aware presence that is aware of the judgments, that thinks the thoughts and feels the sensations. You are none of these thoughts and judgments. You are the awareness that is aware of them.

With the person you are with, look beyond their views, opinions, beliefs, and values. Look directly at the essence of their being.

Listen and speak from your heart to theirs without an agenda.

You need not try to be, do, or say anything in particular.

You are just being and allowing your voice to rise from that profound space.

## Courage and perseverance

"Ability to sustain engagement and remain determined and patient even when efforts take a long time to bear fruit" (Inner Development Goals, n.d.).

There are days when we experience a relentless downpour of intense energy that pushes us out of our comfort zone. One such day for me was when the main lender and operator of our new retreat center in Sweden called us to a meeting. He wanted to embark on a new project and wanted to transfer all financial responsibilities to us by the end of the month. My heart sank. How on earth should we do this?

I poured myself into practice. Countless short moments of relief and ease, followed by despair, anxiety, and doubts. It was like alternating between two realities.

Each short moment strengthened my resilience. I could be present with myself in my own grief process as well as hold space for our team, lead with confidence, and not act out any blame and resentment towards our former partner. Sharing openly with each other gave us clarity to find solutions.

We formed a taskforce and within a couple of months we had established a local nonprofit association, raised more than half the money through donations and a low-interest loan from within the community, and covered the remainder with a mortgage.

We also took the opportunity to empower key volunteers at the center with more responsibilities and decision-making power and implemented an organization model that could be sustainable for an all-volunteer organization. It felt more aligned with our values and principles than ever before.

Of course, along the way countless thoughts and emotions came up that challenged my confidence. It taught me once more how important it is to not look for any particular experience that we identify as an indicator for correctly living the essence of our being. We might hope that we will never feel affliction again, but that is not the point of Dzogchen. Rather, we find freedom *within* the affliction.

## Empathy, compassion and intercultural competence: Testimonial from Asaf Chesner, co-founder of Super and Dzogchen practitioner

### Empathy and compassion

"Ability to relate to others, oneself and nature with kindness, empathy and compassion and address related suffering" (Inner Development Goals, n.d.).

### Inclusive mindset and intercultural competence

"Willingness and competence to embrace diversity and include people with different views and backgrounds" (Inner Development Goals, n.d.).

I always felt intense emotions, and many around me said that I feel too much and that I need not carry the weight of the entire world on my shoulders. The advice was kind, but impractical. I couldn't switch off my feelings, as growing up in the Middle East meant destruction, war, and terror were a daily reality. I felt anger and disappointment with humanity. I didn't have the tools to deal with my own suffering and that of the world.

Similar responses arose for me in relation to the climate crisis and animal rights. I felt very frustrated. When I read about empathy and kindness, it sounded like a state that I needed to cultivate, that I needed to think and feel in a certain way – positive, compassionate thoughts and feelings and not negative ones. Certain circumstances helped me to have this mindset, but eventually it always disappeared. Trying to be compassionate felt contrived, and I simply couldn't pin it down.

Through the Dzogchen practice, I became more connected with my own patterns of suffering in daily life. It gave me more self-awareness and the gift to rest naturally as this awareness, which is an essential foundation for empathy with oneself, nature, and other beings.

When thoughts and feelings arose that I deemed uncompassionate, I could be gentle with myself and relax my body and mind for a short moment and not describe and label things. Tension and struggle gave way to warmth and care for myself and others. Thoughts and emotions, whether negative or positive, release and leave no trace, like a line drawn in space. There is such freedom in this recognition.

I could recognize the ways in which I had tried to manage my own thoughts and emotions and how that only led to greater suffering. I came to learn that I have a practical, grounded choice in every moment to practice self-compassion by allowing my thoughts and emotions to be as they are for a short moment.

Through spontaneous insights rather than endless analysis, I began to really understand myself on a deeper level. Getting intimate with my own suffering naturally opened up the floodgates of compassion for others, even people I have felt misaligned with due to their political views or different ways of being. I didn't need to work on being understanding and compassionate; it came about naturally. There is great relief in that.

In my work with diverse teams in social impact organizations, this new mindset allows me to be flexible and understanding of social and cultural differences. Collaborating with people from India, USA, Australia, and Europe made me see what unites us all as human beings, and also to appreciate and harness the differences.

When cultural challenges such as different perceptions of timelines, responsibilities, and ways of relating arise, the practice gives me the ability to relax and enjoy the diverse display. In that relaxed openness, I find empathy and competence increase effortlessly.

I see everyone as they are through seeing myself as I am. I feel connected to the suffering of all beings and also to the wish for its resolution. I am able to lead in a compassionate and empathetic way.

I still feel the weight of the world on my shoulders, but I know I have a choice of getting overwhelmed by it or dedicating each moment to recognizing the natural state and taking powerful action from this stable ground. This provides me with certainty beyond hope that sustainable change in the world rooted in natural empathy and compassion can occur.

## Co-creation skills: Testimonial from Mikaela Schain, co-founder of Super and Dzogchen practitioner

"Skills and motivation to build, develop and facilitate collaborative relationships with diverse stake-holders, characterized by psychological safety and genuine co-creation" (Inner Development Goals, n.d.).

When one wants to create a sustainable world for all beings, it is easy to get trapped in ideas of what that world looks like and the right path to reach it. Leading and collaborating from a vantage of limited openness restricts the potential benefit we can create. It also prevents people from flourishing in their unique strengths, gifts, and talents and makes genuine co-creation more difficult.

When it became clear to me how this had played out for me despite my good intentions, I was struck with great sadness. Every time I was in a conversation with someone who didn't share my views on how to proceed in the work we were doing, I had a constant stream of inner commentaries. I really wanted to listen openly, but I couldn't find it in myself to do so. I was just waiting for them to be silent so that I could convince them of the "better" way to do things. It was obvious how limiting this way of relating, being, and communicating was, and it completely took away all the fun!

Applying the Dzogchen practice opened my heart and mind. It has been beautiful to see how my practice gave me great openness and genuine curiosity to take in different thoughts and opinions. I now have a spontaneous wish for everyone to do what they love and shine while doing it. From this place I can see what is of most benefit for the group, the organization, and the world and I can allow my perfectionism and inner commentaries to be present without acting on them.

This has enabled me to develop collaborative relationships with diverse stake-holders in a way that creates true co-creation and shared joy. I am amazed at the depth of creativity, innovation, and trust that has come with this way of relating and leading.

## Optimism: Testimonial from Erik Rosin, co-founder of Super and Dzogchen practitioner

"Ability to sustain and communicate a sense of hope, positive attitude and confidence in the possibility of meaningful change" (Inner Development Goals, n.d.).

Before I was introduced to the practice, I often tried to conjure up positive thoughts and emotions in order to be optimistic about the future and inspire others to co-create that future.

No matter how hard I tried, I found it was impossible to hold on to positive thoughts and emotions for long, and any optimistic state that I would manage to get myself into vanished when I most needed it.

At one point, after trying to push for sustainable change in an organization I was in and envisaging what that change could lead to, I gave up the struggle, because I had gotten so much resistance to my pushing and suggesting.

However, later with my newfound practice and grounded in that practice, I realized I could lead by example instead. So, I quietly started to implement solutions and show what was possible without pushing anyone to come along. Slowly, I started to receive recognition for what I did and was even celebrated for it. As a magical turn of events, the person who was most resistant to change shifted their perspective and invited me to teach others how to co-create sustainable change in their roles.

This experience made me see what is possible for us as humans. It empowers an organic spontaneous shift to focusing on solutions and leading by example. It brings so much ease to my life while collaborating with diverse people from different cultures and supporting clients.

I have become an incurable solutionist! This means showing people what is possible rather than pushing people to change, which comes from a deep knowing that humans are beneficial by nature and that, ultimately, we want ourselves and others to thrive.

## Enriching Dzogchen practice with the IDG framework

The previous sections demonstrate how Dzogchen can support practicing the IDG skills. We were intrigued by the editor's question whether it can work the other way round too: How might the IDG framework support Dzogchen practitioners, communities, and organizations.

Most Dzogchen scriptures were written for a different time and culture, and the IDGs present an excellent framework to apply the ancient teachings and practices to address the specific needs of our era.

So, we started sharing the IDG framework with changemakers in our community through a series of guided meditations, exercises, and workshops. This new program supports Dzogchen practitioners to enliven the five IDG dimensions and develop the respective skills in their roles as founders, leaders, teachers, coaches, and community organizers.

We are further integrating the IDGs and Dzogchen in a new project called "Sustainable Leadership". It is designed for impact-driven leaders who are not yet familiar with Dzogchen to discover the essence of being and develop the skills necessary for their transformational work, while remaining grounded in inner sustainability.

## Co-creating a thriving sustainable world

We have entered an unprecedented era in human history where we possess the technological advancements and abundant resources necessary to create a thriving sustainable world. However, harnessing their full potential requires a fundamental shift in how we use our mind so that we can allocate the technology and resources in the most beneficial way.

What we need is a profound inner transformation, a shift that opens our limiting mindset into one that recognizes abundance and vast potential. This shift can be facilitated through ancient wisdom practices and traditions such as Dzogchen, which emphasize the recognition of our already present innate perfection.

By embracing this new way of using our mind and living from the essence of our being, we can unlock our full capacity and unleash our collective creativity and innovation. We can create a world where everyone can flourish in their unique strengths and gifts, where competitiveness is replaced with genuine collaboration to bring about a better collective future, and where our actions are guided by a deep understanding of the interconnectedness of all of life and a just world filled with empowered people fueled by sustainable energy and regenerative food systems.

We started out with the question of how we can resolve this global crisis and truly thrive as a species. We found that each of us is holding the key within ourselves to unlock the full potential of our unique strengths, gifts, and talents, and together we can rise to the challenge by realizing and being who we truly are.

Let us come together, tap into our innate wisdom, and co-create a thriving sustainable world for ourselves and all generations to come.

## References

Inner Development Goals (n.d.). IDG Framework. *Inner Development Goals*. https://www.innerdevelopment
goals.org/framework [Accessed April 5, 2024].

Theresa McNichol
# Chapter 9
# Re-attuning to nature's rhythms: The Chinese art of being, relating, and acting

**Abstract:** "In his poems are sound paintings, his paintings soundless poems" is the epigram that has come down through the ages for the statesman Wáng Wéi (699–761 CE), one of China's leading poet-painters of the Tang dynasty (618–907 CE). Although none of Wáng Wéi's original paintings survive except in copies, he had an ability to unleash cosmic forces so superhuman that his place is secure in that rare class of painters – the divine.

Yet, Wáng Wéi was not a poet-painter by profession, but a scholar-bureaucrat (hereafter scholar) who achieved a leadership position at the court by earning the highest degree of *jinshi* (equivalent 'doctor'). His artistic accomplishments were the result of his self-cultivation practices of the brush of the "Three Perfections" – calligraphy, poetry, painting – in pursuit of the scholars' aspiration to achieve the Confucian ideal of *becoming* a *junzi* ('exemplary person').

This chapter will explore the early and enduring presence of sound in the arts of China, at a time when the aural was superior to the visual. It surveys the interplay between the sense of hearing and the sense of listening, its evolution through the arts, particularly music and landscape painting, and its significance along with its nuances to the present day. The chapter draws on China's 5,000 years of recorded history highlighting the self-cultivation practices that scholars, such as Wáng Wéi, sought that also correspond to the Inner Development Goals (IDGs) five-dimension framework: being, thinking, relating, collaborating, acting; particularly *being*, *relating*, and *acting*.

**Keywords:** attunement, rhythms, nature, hearing, listening, being

## How Chinese art can instruct on the Inner Development Goals

The Anthropocene Epoch, which marks the outsized human impact on the Earth's ecosystems, is a clarion call that scientist Vittorio Ingegnoli terms a "reformulation of ecology" that makes space for "landscape ecology" (Ingegnoli, 2001, p. 504). He describes it in a manner that aligns with the United Nations' Sustainable Development Goals (SDGs), introduced in 2015, as a "hierarchic methodology with an open spatial web, that is holistic, integrative, and transdisciplinary" (Ingegnoli, 2001, p. 504). Acknowledging that there is no one blueprint, the National Sustainable Development

https://doi.org/10.1515/9783111337913-010

Strategy (NSDS) further calls for "a coordinated, participatory and iterative process of thoughts and actions to achieve economic, environmental and social objectives in a balanced and integrative manner." The addition of the Inner Development Goals (IDGs) Framework addresses the inner abilities found lacking yet can be developed through its five dimensions that simplify the development of complex inner capacities to undergird the SDGs to ensure overall success (https://innerdevelopmentgoals.org/framework/).

Importantly, these coordinated efforts are not for the purpose of coming up with a formula, or a one-size-fits-all template, but a dynamic process that is more like art. A testament to Chinese wisdom traditions is its long-standing recognition of nature's cyclical patterns and its constant dynamic and continuously changing state of flux that operates through *qi* ('vital force'). *Qi* is most dramatic in the raging elements of thunder and lightning yet operates just as powerfully unseen beneath the surface of all things. Chinese landscape paintings are living documents that reflect the way the Chinese came to understand and meet the complexities of their world and in their own lives through nature's alternations as well as its vagaries. The paintings make visible water's eddying rhythms that spill over into music, poetry, the dancing ink of calligraphy that conveyed and realigned ideas, in painting, and much more.

At the first IDG conference in 2021, Pella Thiel, knowledge expert with the UN Harmony with Nature initiative, asked the question: "Why are we in an ecological crisis now?" In her research she found that physicists saw it as a crisis of "perception" brought on by a "deadening of the senses". In the United States, with schools' focus on test scores and teaching science, technology, engineering, and mathematics (STEM), music and arts programs came close to being eliminated altogether. Fortunately, the tide is changing in recognition of an emerging trend: social-emotional learning (SEL). In some states, SEL is being combined with the arts that is more in keeping with the intrinsic benefits of the arts, i.e., intangibles such as "enchantment, enlightenment and community-building" that are beneficial for students' development toward a sustainable world.[1] As scientist Stephen Porges notes, the more we "feel" ourselves, we are supporting the neural feedback circuits that have become numb in our modern society (Porges, S. personal communication, May 16, 2022). It could be said that both the IDGs and the Chinese concept of recovering personal *qi* support the neural feedback circuits as well.

The increasing technical training that now dominates in much of the world leaves little room for learning how to go about becoming a better human being. The IDGs can provide an antidote to what economist Daniel Kahneman perceives as a disturb-

---

1 *Gifts of the Muse*, McCarthy et.al. (2004) study by RAND Corporation for the Wallace Foundation. It offered a reframing of the economic benefits identified by an earlier study by Americans for the Arts. RAND concluded that numbers do not make a persuasive case at all. Instead it recommended emphasizing the missing link that sustained intrinsic benefits, such intangibles that make people cherish the arts, i.e. intergenerational qualities such as bequest value.

ing global pattern of behavior that he sees as endemic: "we have too much self confidence in our beliefs, and overconfidence is really more aptly associated with a failure of imagination" (Tippett & Kahneman, 2017).

The starting assumption of the present chapter is that China's wisdom traditions have a central role to play in such studies. As China expert Henry Rosemont, Jr. (2015) writes:

> If the world owes much to the Western civilization that began with the Greeks, it equally owes the Chinese for their engineers, astronomers, government officials, craftspeople, inventors, poetry, painting, music, and medicine. And Chinese civilization has probably seen to the feeding and housing of more human beings than any other in human history. (p. 121)

China's more than 5,000 years of recorded history is a testament to its commitment to a sustainable culture. As neurologist and naturalist Oliver Sacks (1989) writes in *Seeing Voices*, by seeing an alternative access to language (and its community and culture) through signing, there were implications for the hearing world showing us that much of what is distinctly human in us–our capacities for language, for thought, for communication, and culture–do not develop automatically in us, are not just biological functions, but are, equally, social and historical in origin; that they are a gift–the most wonderful of gifts–from one generation to another (p. xii–xiii).

Once associated with Judeo-Christian values, in the twentieth century the secular West has moved to sociopolitical aspects of free-market capitalism, shareholder value, and increased dividends. As a result, it finds itself lacking in a coherent set of ethics to live by, much less pass on to its youth.

What will be covered in this chapter:

1. **Section 1:** *being* explores the way that Chinese scholars such as Wáng Wéi practiced the brush arts to cultivate the same transformational skills as the IDGs' first framework of developing an inner dimension of *being/becoming*.
2. **Section 2:** Through *relating*, the arts demonstrate the way in which the Chinese attuned their sense of hearing as experienced through the Chinese psyche. The Chinese keen sense of hearing alerts them to the rhythms and flow of music into other genres of art and their sounds, and after sounds that elevate the subconscious notes to the conscious level.
3. **Section 3** offers a Chinese model for *acting* as a demonstration in notable qualities such as courage and optimism that aid true agency in breaking old patterns, generating original ideas, and acting with persistence in uncertain times.

# Section 1: Being

The IDG dimension *being* – "cultivating our inner life and developing and deepening our relationship to our thoughts, feelings, and body – helps us be present, intentional, and nonreactive when we face complexity." (https://innerdevelopmentgoals.org/framework/).

Although the Chinese regarded the pursuit of knowledge in education of utmost importance, they regarded embodied moral development as the essence of wisdom. It required a sensory attunement, especially that of *hearing*, to tap immediate access to qualities that lie outside the visual world in a field of "intuition", "deeper meaning", and "truth" (Langer, 1964. p. 86).

According to China scholar Wm.Theodore de Bary (1993), in the *Great Learning*, one of the "Four Books" of Confucianism, the chapters addressing moral cultivation

> [. . .] dwell on the primary virtue, of *jing* 'reverent seriousness' primary in the sense of being, not a first step in learning but a fundamental orientation of the mind, a respect for life, which should underlie and inspirit all learning and conduct. (p. 359)

Many scholars, who rose up the ranks of Chinese bureaucracy through meritocracy, were polymaths who practiced in their leisure the brush arts of the Three Perfections as visual manifestations of their inner sage and outer king. The outer king, projects the ideal of the inner sage, that is mirrored in the IDG dimension of being, i.e. an "inner compass of having a deeply felt sense of responsibility and commitment to values and purposes relating to the good of the whole" (https://innerdevelopmentgoals.org/framework/).

What was sought in their self-cultivation practices was of a coded life of harmonious relationships within families, between friends, and in communities as well as their leadership role at court, and in the world.

## The brush as self-cultivating tool

The Confucian practices of the Three Perfections also centered on the belief of the "prime value of the cultivated human person as the keystone of human flourishing" (de Bary, 1981, p. 96). The practice of the brush arts attests to their dedication to self-cultivation as both the roots and heights of *zhi* ('wisdom').

In particular, the self-cultivation practices of the brush were seen as the precondition for *zhi*, wisdom in governance enhancing one's capacity as "a sense of what it is most fitting to do in our interactions with our fellow human beings, understanding why, performing those actions, and achieving a sense of well-being from so doing" (Rosemont, 2015, p. 121).

Many Chinese painting masterpieces exhibited in the world's major art museums were not executed by professional painters but scholar-painters. They engaged in the 'play of the brush' going beyond skill to rekindle the immediacy tapped by the "intuitive amateur" (Copland, 1952, p. 9). Avoiding formulas, they strove to bypass the ego, to be pulled by the brush's energy that tapped into the purity of the heart-mind to present along with object, a "self" springing from one's "inner hills and valleys".

In the act of painting, the brush is the centering force, painter and the brush are one. The brush movement embodies the visceral feeling of *qi* ('universal energy'), emitted through the movement of the painter's suspended wrist. Because calligraphy's origins lie in divination, the painter who mastered the brush possessed magical power. Over time, the astute viewer had the ability to see the quality of the brushwork as a lens into the heart-mind of the painter, the "agent of change". By extension, the transmission of the painter's mind-and-heart legitimized landscape painting as a form of Confucian public service whereby the viewer, no matter its location on history's timeline, now shared in the unbroken chain of humanity. It is an ability that David Orr (1992) sees as an ecoliteracy, the ability to, "observe nature with insight, a merger of landscape and mindscape . . . the ability to think broadly, to know something of what is hitched to what . . . and ask what then" (p. 68).

According to the philosopher Paul Crowther, the present requires an observer with relational points to both a past and a future. For the present to manifest itself ontologically, it must involve an observer who actively experiences it in the context of past and future, i.e., a self-conscious being with powers of memory, imagination, and symbolization. Through these powers the universe is qualitatively changed. Self-consciousness is, in effect, an intervention on the physical; it introduces present, past, future, and possibility to the physical world. (Crowther, 2016, p. 144).

Therefore a cultivated person, a follower of "the Way," came to recognize that the painter's self-representation in the painting was not *magic* at all, but *genius*, linking classical China's wisdom tradition to the present day (Wen Fong, personal communication, n.d.).

The importance of art cannot be overstated: we human beings want and need to see what the artist sees, "the unrecorded reality, momentarily recognized, yet often pushed below the surface" (Langer, 1953, p. 23).

## Heart-mind

Although Confucius (551–479 BCE) emphasized the value of the body because it is a gift from the ancestors, the "Second Sage", Mencius (372–289 BCE), considered it the "small body" when compared to the "great body" of the heart-mind (Tu, 1985, p. 100). Mencius did not mean the anatomical heart, but rather the spiritual heart-mind. Whereas the body is confined in space, the heart-mind has the unique ability to wander swiftly and expand infinitely (Tu, 1985). For Mencius, human beings were born with the heart-mind but lost it through the process of socialization and that the true task over one's lifetime that consisted of self-cultivation practices, such as IDGs, was to recover the lost heart-mind (Tu, 1985). The hallmark of an individual who has done so is compassion. Moreover, the heart-mind complements the cognitive with the affective, bringing an aesthetic dimension to the individual's moral and spiritual cultivation.

# Section 2: Relating

The IDG framework *relating* involves a sense of caring for others and the world. *Connectedness* is "having a keen sense of being connected with, and/or being part of, a larger whole, such as a community, humanity, or a global ecosystem" (https://innerde velopmentgoals.org/framework/).

This section seeks to illuminate the harmonic relationship between humans and nature as experienced through the Chinese psyche. Through its arts, the Chinese keen sense of hearing alerts them to the rhythms and flow of music into other genres of art and their sounds, and after sounds that elevate the subconscious notes to the conscious level.

## Why the emphasis on hearing and listening?

As a beginning, we will need to suspend the way we normally differentiate between "hearing" as a means of receiving sound and "listening" as thoughtful attention. Unlike the demarcated boundaries of seeing, the sensory system of hearing is not confined to a physical space. Its contours are those of a dynamic undulating line and we can begin to consider the quality of both "hearing and listening as primarily a musical activity" (Langer, 1953, p. 147).

Ethnomusicologist Marius Schneider (1989) writes that "sound is the basic matter of the primordial world" (p. 39); music, or precisely *rhythm*, is what provides the connecting link that governs all thinking, living, growing, and dying, thereby organizing physical existence into biological design. For example, the Chinese have long favored the body as a metaphor, mountains are "bones" of the earth and rivers are its "blood". As biological beings in a natural world, "humans participate in this rhythmic ordering, not only through physiological processes such as respiration and circulation, but also by becoming listening and responding beings" (Schneider, 1989, p. 70).

Drawing on his research on acoustic symbolism, Schneider writes that sound, like water, contains all the requirements for undisturbed higher cognition providing a way of understanding the important role of the aural. In this way we can better understand why the "ancient Chinese drew the tonal center of their harmonic system from the sound of their sacred Yellow River and valued dripping water as a source of musical inspiration" (Schneider, 1989, p.61).

Chinese scholars who were exceptionally gifted in landscape painting, such as Wáng Wéi, came to be seen as cultural guides to tap ancient wisdom traditions for an increasingly complex world. From earliest times, hearing and singing represented the most refined forms of higher cognition (1989, p. 56). Wáng Wéi's keen sensory ability to discern commingling sound and invisible rhythms provided a lens into a reanimated world through hearing.

In our own time, amid many global crises, can we too look to the arts more broadly to emancipate our atrophied senses, to listen sagely to renew our relationship with nature's wisdom?

## Music

We have seen above why rhythm was held in high esteem in ancient cosmogonies as the basis of the whole for it had its origin in the primordial breath, an empty form, an impersonal, underlying *energy*; yet the significance of its power cannot be underestimated, for it begins to fill out sonorous patterns of things to come, such as music (Schneider, 1989, pp. 62–63). Capturing music's essence is elusive for it:

> [. . .] knows as yet no space, lives only in time, as if in the primordial world. Devoid of conceptuality, unbound to any stable form, it can continuously change, reverse, or shatter its form only to reassemble later at will. . . . To a great extent, it can even draw absolute silence (rests) into the realm of its influence . . . in this acoustical entanglement, not only because music provides truth with a shape, albeit a fleeting one, but because even its very silence is charged with tension, while by seemingly high and low p. 61, thin and thick tones, it can evoke the first illusion of space (Schneider, 1989, p. 43).

In an interview with Diane Rehm, world-acclaimed cellist Yo-Yo Ma emphasizes what for him is the essence of music: in that it carries to our ears something more than sound, something that is "an *energy* that activates the *imagination*, activates *a sense of community* as well as activates *an inner coded life*" (Rehm & Ma, 2007).

In traditional China, Confucius modeled for students the way ritual and music provided a greater civilizing influence for becoming full members of a harmonious society. Ritual instructed on the proper way to stand, talk, and sit, whereas music – proper music – instructed on the way in which to "appropriately express one's emotions in tune with the rhythm of life. The sound of good music resounded with *de* ('enduring virtue') that brings one closer to the primordial order long after the music ended" (Tu, 1985, p. 98).

Story: The master musician and virtuoso listener

**Figure 9.1:** Listening to the Qin.
Liu Songnian (Chinese, c. 1150-after 1225); China, Southern Song Dynasty (1127–1279)
Album leaf; ink and slight color on silk
Source: The Cleveland Museum of Art, Leonard C. Hanna, Jr. Fund 1983.85

Our story takes place during the Han dynasty (206 BCE–220 CE), an early period in Chinese history, where we meet a famous musician and an equally famous listener (see Figure 9.1).

Boya, a master musician, played a classical Chinese stringed instrument known as a *qin*, or *guqin* (*gu* 'antique') that has a 5,000-year-old history. Boya particularly enjoyed playing for his friend, Ziqi, a rapt audience of one who could listen to the music for hours on end. Ziqi could not contain his delight, exclaiming to Boya, "my thoughts were transported to towering mountains. How marvelous! With majesty akin to sacred Mt. Tai" (Addiss, DeWoskin, & Clark, 1999, p. 24). Yet in another moment his thoughts were carried to flowing waters. "How marvelous!" he said, "bubbling and flowing like mightiest rivers" (p. 24). At times Ziqi was transported to the summit of Mt. Tai, where the master, Confucius, arrived at full realization that both "the continual flux of existence, as well as having compassion for one's fellow people, is as sure an axis of society as the rock-mountain is of the landscape" (Hay, 1985, pp. 57–58).

We are told that both the musician and his listener enjoyed their special relationship for many years until Ziqi passed away. After Ziqi's death, Boya smashed the instrument and broke its silk strings, never to play again. This action is puzzling. Would not Boya's playing have been a source of solace to him in his time of loss? Was there was no other individual who could "apprehend the tones" (Addiss, DeWoskin & Clark, 1999, p. 24)?

To understand Boya's action, we need to realize that the *qin* was more than simply an instrument for music making, it was a tool of communication between like-minded individuals. The symbiotic relationship between speaker and listener, as well as "between musician and listener, is intense precisely because the attentive listener becomes one with the speaker through shared meaning" (Schneider, 1989, p. 56).

Without the great ear, the instrument had lost its voice.

## The qin

As mentioned above, the account of Boya and Ziqi came out of a tradition that flowered in the latter part of the Han dynasty, a brilliant era in Chinese literary history that defined Chinese culture from which ethnic Chinese draw their name as "the Han". Ji Kang, (224–263) musician and poet born into the chaotic period that followed the Han, spurned his imperial court duties, preferring instead to indulge his Daoist leanings by becoming the philosophical leader of the Seven Sages of the Bamboo Grove and a key figure in *wenrenhua*, (hereafter "scholar-painter theory"). Ji Kang developed a standardized philosophical theory around the *qin* that only an intimate friend could understand. He contributed extensively to the massive canon of the *qin*, known for its subtle notes that "restrain and cultivate hearts" (Addiss, DeWoskin & Clark, 1999, p. 24). Yet what are we to think of Ziqi? What is the basis of an extraordinary ability as a virtuoso listener?

We find a relevant observation from American maestro Aaron Copland (1952), who noted that "at the core of both vital music making and active listening is an imaginative mind" (p. 7).

## Co-creators

From ancient times, Chinese texts located heaven as the creative source of all harmonies and things, charging human beings with continuing its creative activity by bringing about new harmonies that would not otherwise materialize without human intervention. Yet this required that the individualized self be tempered by true subjectivity by entering fruitful communion with others; i.e., in the act of creating art, individuals participate "in the transforming and nourishing process of Heaven and Earth" (Tu, 1985, p. 93).

Zhuangzi (historically Chuang Tzǔ) is author of an ancient Chinese text of the same name that is one of the two foundational texts of Taoism, written during the late Warring States period (476–221 BCE). He advises that "we listen with our heart-minds; better still listen with our *qi* rather than our heart-minds" (Tu, 1985, p. 47). In this way, the "virtue of the ear" (*er-de*), indeed the "virtue of hearing" (*ting-de*), enables one "to perceive the natural process in a nonaggressive supportive mode, thereby enabling one to enter spiritual communion with nature, to experience mutuality with all things, living and inanimate, resulting in completion and not domination" (Tu, 1985, p.107).

A painting of the landscape no longer was a matter of merely duplicating the forms of mountains, water, and trees:

> There are many artists who may be able to capture forms perfectly in a painting, yet when it comes to principles, only the *junzi* of outstanding profundity of thought of the wholly inner self could comprehend the idea beyond likeness in *xie-i* ("writing ideas" or "feelings") in painting. (Fong, 1984, p. 5)

What then does it mean to "comprehend the idea beyond likeness"? Shen Kua (1031–1095), Chinese scientist and statesman, provides this explanation:

> wonderous parts (or mystery) of calligraphy and painting must be realized in the soul; hardly discovered in mere forms. Those who look at pictures are always able to point out faults of form, likeness, of design and coloring, but I have seldom found people who have penetrated the mysterious reason and depth of creative activity [. . .] he (the painter, Wáng Wéi) had conceived the thing in his mind; his hand responded, and it was done as conceived. This is because his creative activity and his reason resided in the spiritual part of his nature and because he grasped to a high degree the idea, the inspiration of Heaven. But this is difficult to explain to common people. (Kua, as translated and cited in Li, 1965, pp. 37–38)

The term "spiritual", according to religion phenomenologist Louis Dupré, is not exclusively religious, but is also inferred in the arts and literature and can be described as an *alertness*, "a more intense inner awareness of what surpasses ordinary life" (Dupré, 1997). This type of aesthetic quality is specifically "not objective fact" but "possesses an inner, radiating beauty that illuminates the objective message and warms the heart" (Dupré, 1997).

As members of a broader mental community, human beings are capable of limitless abilities:

> through hearing and listening they learn to participate in the rhythm of heaven and earth: through the mental as well as physical discipline of listening, we open ourselves up to the world around us. By broadening and deepening our nonjudgmental receptivity, rather than projecting our limited visions onto the order of things, we become co-creators of the cosmos. (Tu, 1985, p. 107)

When we look at a Chinese landscape painting, we must be aware of the dimension of sound and after sounds like the *qin*, for it is essential that we literally attune to its soundless music and let ourselves listen as much as we see.

## Re-attuning to the landscape

With the aural qualities expanded to the music of poetry, a new appreciation for the beauty in *yu yin* ('after sounds'), became the balance between sound and silence now sought in painting. In China, there were many genres of painting, but landscape surpassed them all. *Shan shui hua* (山水畫literally 'mountain water painting' or 'landscape painting') highlighted the contrasts of the imagery of "water/rock" that represented the painting of "sound/concentrated silence".

As the Qing dynasty (1611–1680) dramatist Li Yu wrote, "landscape is the intellectual and emotional expression of the universe, while intellectual and emotional expression is the landscape of the human mind" (Li as cited in Chen, L. p. 37).

Li's observation, although written more than 300 years earlier, still resonates with that of poet and essayist Mark Strand (1934–2014), who studied painting as a young man. In an interview, he told "flow" expert Mihaly Csikszentmihalyi (1996) that he saw his role as an artist to not only be a witness of recorded experience but also as part of the broader responsibility for keeping the universe ordered through consciousness by paying attention:

> I mean, we are – as far as we know – the only part of the universe that's self-conscious. We could even be the universe's form of consciousness. We might have come along so that the universe could look at itself. (Csikszentmihalyi, p. 231)

Perhaps that is the draw of walking along the ocean's edge to recalibrate our rhythms through hearing and listening and feeling the pull of the incoming and outgoing waves. As Schneider (1989) records "only through hearing could people once again come to realize their true position in the cosmos and the meaning of the flowing order within their deepest consciousness" (p. 67).

## Harmonizing with nature

Traditionally, Confucian scholars in their leisure sometimes packed up their musical instrument and painting tools to go on walks in nature to paint particularly beautiful vistas. We consider an early thirteenth-century landscape painting by the Southern Song dynasty (960–1279) painter Ma Yuan.

In this example of a Chinese scholar's painting, the musician in the story is eventually replaced with the reclusive scholar-painter in a white robe who takes the *qin* with him on outings to paint the landscape (see Figure 9.2). Yet rarely does the scholar play the *qin,* often it is left in its case or is stringless, rendering it soundless. Long associated with the language of nature as well as scholarly virtues of purity and nobility, represented in flowing waters and tall mountains, the stringless *qin* now stood in as a symbol of the "companion to the recluse" and "intermediary, not between people, but between a person and nature" (Addiss, DeWoskin, & Clark. 1999, p.5).

**Figure 9.2:** *Viewing plum blossoms by moonlight* by the artist Ma Yuan (Chinese, active ca. 1190–1225). Fan Painting mounted as an album leaf, ink, and colors on silk, 1 7/8 x 10 ½ in
Collection: The Metropolitan Museum of Art, gift of John M. Crawford Jr., in honor of Alfreda Murck, 1986

Now nature graces the attuned ear with its "pure notes" and in doing so "dramatizes the larger act of cognition, i.e., listening flagged the production of cultivated thought, turning a recumbent, motionless figure into a protagonist of heroic action" (personal communication, Adam Herring, February 13, 2010).

## Poetry

Chinese literature has it that, over time, the same patterns of sound in music – the interplay of sound and silence – set up correspondences between music and poetry as well. Again, as Copland (1952) notes "beyond the music of both arts there is an essence that joins them – an area where meanings behind the notes and the meaning beyond the words spring from some common source" (p. 1).

Hence the famous line by the eleventh-century revivalist of scholar-painter theory, poet, calligrapher, and painter Su Shi's (1037–1101) acknowledgement of the way Wáng Wéi reanimated the senses of hearing, listening, and perceiving its alternating transformations: "In his poems, sound paintings, In his paintings, soundless poems" (Su, 2011, 250).

Like Confucius, Wáng Wéi was not only a transmitter but an innovator with an "ear" to the future. The conflation of poetry and painting may have seemed to have emerged out of nowhere, but it had its roots long before Wáng Wéi, in an ideal that had dominated Chinese poetic and artistic developments a thousand years earlier.

Harvard Chinese poetry scholar Stephen Owen's preference is that his students perceive images in a poem not as objects but *percepts*, i.e., "impressions of an object obtained by use of the senses." His advice is to

> [S]top reading them just as images and read them as a way of seeing, noticing movement: of attention paid to the body for then it changes the poem. It ceases to be just a purely visual thing [. . .] just as in horizontal Chinese landscape scroll paintings that basically walk you through space (Owen, 2014).

Let's apply Owen's direction, by reading Wáng Wéi's poem with attention to movement in space, and noticing the sensations in the body:

> Bamboo Lodge
> Alone I sit in dark bamboo,
> Strumming the qin whistling away;
> deep woods that no one knows,
> where a bright moon comes to shine on me.
> (Wang, as cited and translated in Watson, 1984, p. 137)

Were you able to hear the high-pitched whistling accompanied by the low qin notes? Like Ziqi listening to Boya's music, did you feel transported to a faraway scene by Wang's music? Or maybe you felt a chill in the late summer night's breeze?

# Section 3: Acting

Acting – notable "qualities such as courage and optimism that help us acquire true agency, break old patterns, generate original ideas and act with persistence in uncertain times." (https://innerdevelopmentgoals.org/framework/).

Can Western readers imagine finding themselves in the following dilemma in which the early thirteenth-century Chinese scholars found themselves? Is there a way it can inform key dimensions of the IDG framework, particularly *acting?*

## A Chinese model for action

Were there any individual followers in the tradition of Wáng Wéi who also were able to advance China's ancient wisdom tradition of the legendary sages Yao and Shun to future generations? To find out, we fast forward five centuries past Wáng Wéi's time to the Yuan dynasty (1279–1368) to meet the reanimating figure of its time.

This story features an individual in a small group of Chinese scholars who met the challenge of China's total collapse at the hands of the Mongol warrior Genghis Khan in the late thirteenth century. It drew heavily from their *qi* and the retrieval of their heart-mind. The challenge now was "not only to repossess and reassert 'the Way' for oneself, but also in recognizing it in others across linguistic as well as cultural barriers" (de Bary, 1981, p. 65).

Zhao Mengfu (1254–1322), a young scion of the Southern Song dynasty (1127–1279), held a minor post at the time of the dynasty's collapse. The scholar officials, such as Zhao, were downsized and returning to their hometowns, drew students around them teaching the classics. Within a few years, Zhao, along with a small cadre of recognized "talents" were invited by Kublai Khan, Genghis's heir and grandson, to serve at the court. They accepted at a great price in the face of opposition from both family and loyalists to the fallen dynasty. With the demise of the imperial academy at the court and the dismantling of imperial examinations, landscape paintings now stood in as the measure of the heart-mind of the painter.

Against this background of Zhao's concern, with both the visual and the aural with respect to reviving the tradition of scholar-painting theory and traditions even more ancient on the part of the painter, we turn now to how he envisioned the role of the viewer of his (and his colleagues') work.

In the absence of a central Imperial Academy of Artists, Zhao took on the role of collecting art during inspection trips and provincial assignments, adding examples of local styles that reflected inspired innovative painting. He became a leader in the traditional landscape style, reviving *gu* ('antique') painting methods as well as infusing paintings with innovative and vibrant calligraphic brushstrokes.

We have read of successful outcomes of the scholars' aspiration to achieve the Confucian ideal of becoming a *junzi* through the self-cultivation practices of composing poems and painting landscapes. A poem brushed in calligraphic strokes, or a painting put to paper or silk was not only appreciated aesthetically, but more importantly seen as an outward expression of the maker's "moral artistry", or heart-mind. What was sought now at the hand of the brush was their "signature", or "heart seal", that gave any number of sensory impressions of the heart-mind that have their rhythmic origins deep within one (Bush, 1971, p.19). The visible forms of mountains/water were signposts, or percepts, into the heart-mind of the inner sage/outer king.

In his painting titled *Autumn Colors on the Qiao and Hua Mountains*, Zhao uses an archaic blue-green style of painting from Wáng Wéi's period of the Tang dynasty yet infuses it with innovative calligraphic strokes typically used for writing (see Figure 9.3).

**Figure 9.3:** Author Colored Sketch. Painting :Autumn Colors on the Qiao and Hua Mountains by Zhao Mengfu (1254–1322). Yuan dynasty (1279–1368).
Ink and colors on paper. Handscroll. 28.4 x 93.2 cm.
Collection: National Palace Museum, Taipei, Taiwan

Anyone familiar with the classic scripture *Yijing* ('Book of Changes'), would recognize that the shapes of the two mountain forms in his painting represent two significant mountains in the northeastern Shandong province. Zhao documents that he has placed one in the east and the other in the west and the Yellow River in the central portion of the painting between the two mountains. Both mountains and the river are important historical documents: the former located in the Shandong province where Confucius was born, and the Yellow River, the cradle of Chinese civilization. Zhao also notes that he painted it for a scholar friend to show him the area of his ancestral home that he had never seen because of restricted travel in a divided Northern and Southern Song dynasty preceding Genghis's invasion.

Eventually the Yuan dynasty would fall and be replaced by the native Ming dynasty (1368–1644), the last imperial dynasty of China ruled by the Han people, the majority ethnic group in China. It too would meet its demise, with China yet again coming under foreign rule, this time by the Manchu-led Qing dynasty, established in 1644.

We take up the thread of our story again during the reign of the fifth Manchu emperor of the Qing Dynasty, where we find Qianlong (1711–1799), ruling over China. Qianlong favors himself a patron of the arts and a Chinese cultural aesthete who engages in the brush arts of calligraphy and painting. On an annual inspection trip to the Shandong province, he sends for a courier to bring Zhao's painting from the palace to compare with the actual scene. Qianlong appreciates the painting very much, yet he lacks the understanding of the original owner to whom Zhao Mengfu gifted it. He notes in his colophons written directly on the painting how magnificent it is, yet he also feels compelled to point out Zhao's errors: the mountain Zhao said he put in the east was in the west, and vice versa. Zhao's peers saw it for what it was – that the reversals and inversions represented the current upheaval in Chinese society at that time while evoking traditional images in absentia forecasting a more stable and glorious future, equal or better than its past. His peers would have recognized Zhao's hidden protest message: during China's long history, through the rise and fall of many dynasties, and in the face of reversals, the culture had always prevailed.

Qianlong was shortsighted because of an inflated self-confidence and, as Kahneman noted above, a failure of the imagination. Qianlong lacked the curiosity to ask questions such as "Why is it, I wonder, that Zhao reversed the mountains? Could there have been some underlying meaning?" Had he taken the initiative to look at historical documents, he would have seen that the Yellow River, rather than flowing between the mountains during Zhao's lifetime, had reversed its course before he was born and instead skirted the two mountains in his lifetime.

## Back to the future

We have seen above that North American students are being introduced at an earlier age to social-emotional learning (SEL). At the same time, the UN Global Compact has called on business schools to move away from measuring their worth by showcasing their graduates' salaries. By solely teaching their graduates to navigate their present world advantageously, business schools neglect the proper end of education itself. As Roger Ames (2019) reminds us, John Dewey, referred to as the 'second Confucius' in some circles, cautioned that the true purpose of education is "to promote the best possible realization of humanity as humanity".

What lessons can we draw from Zhao and his peers for inserting IDG frameworks into Western business education today? One example we can draw on is their modeling of traits admired by Kublai Khan and other members of his diverse court – such traits as "rugged character, directness of speech and a deep sense of commitment to the Way" (de Bary, 1981, p. 135). More importantly, it was their demeanor of *being* – manifesting "such virtues as being sincere and respectful that their Mongol counterparts particularly prized" (McCausland, 2011, p. 212).

Zhao's circle came to court to aid Kublai Khan to find alternatives that would support his strategic expansion plan and relieve the Chinese peasantry from the burden of excessive taxation. They also used the opportunity to instruct on Confucian norms and cultural values – for millennia, China had a centralized social and political system headed by the emperor, who was seen as the embodiment of moral character modeled on the exemplary sage kings of antiquity, for carrying out "heaven's mandate" for all the people.

Zhao and his circle were judged as opportunistic by some peers and family members, and worst referred to as traitors in history books, up until recently. They are now seen as acting in a manner preserving its ancient culture, wisdom traditions, and its values.

# Conclusion

## The art of cultivating Inner Development Goals

In broadening the agenda from the personal to the cultural and thence to the natural world, the IDG framework offers us a comprehensive structure to tap "the capacities of the heart – for wonder, searching, listening, receptivity, and life options for compassion and love" (Gallagher, 1998, p.139).

The congruence between the IDG aims and those of the Chinese wisdom traditions is striking. The age-old traditions insist that each of us can learn, like the painter or musician, to see beyond a tranquil landscape and perceive the pulsating *qi* energy operating unseen beneath the surface within ourselves. With the newly minted awareness that comes from "listening with [our] eyes" (as the contemporary Japanese artist Kaoru Hirabayashi advises), we can complete the task of hearing the music of the artist's vision (as cited in Tyler, 1994, p. 57).

So, what then can we take as the landscape paintings' deeper lesson for us? The message from China's ancient wisdom traditions – a message that resounds equally through the IDGs – comes down to this. To realize that innovation is a social phenomenon, if we need "one individual to see an alternative to the status quo and dare to act on it, we also need another to see its potential and clear the way to make it happen" (Varnedoe, 1990, p. 210). Ultimately, the paintings teach us that, like Zhao Mengfu, we too can move mountains and change the world.

# References

Ames, R. T. (2019). Deweyan and Confucian ethics: A challenge to the ideology of individualism. Lecture at The New School university in New York City on Mar. 15, 2019.

Bush, S. (1971). *The Chinese literati on painting: Su Shih (1037–1101) to Tung Ch'i-ch'ang (1555–1636)*. Hong Kong University Press.

Chen, L. (2006). Double aperture: Reframing and Returning. In Erickson, B. (Curator) (Author). In *reframing: writings on the art of michael cherney* 2005–2006 (pp. 32–51). People's Fine Arts Publishing House.

Copland, A. (1952). *Music and imagination*. Harvard University Press.

Csikszentmihalyi, M. (1996). *Creativity: Flow and the psychology of discovery and invention*. Harper Collins.

De Bary, W. T. (1993). Chen Te-hsiu and statecraft. In R. Hymes & C. Schirokauer (eds.). *Ordering the world: Approaches to state and society in Sung Dynasty China*. University of California Press.

De Bary, W. T. (1981). *Neo-Confucian orthodoxy and the learning of the mind-and-heart*. Columbia University Press.

Addiss, S., DeWoskin, K. J., & Clark, M. (1999). The Chinese qin. In *The resonance of the qin in East Asian art*. (pp. 21–26). *Stephen Addiss; with contributions by Kenneth J. DeWoskin and Mitchell Clark*. China Institute Gallery, China Institute: Distributed by Art Media Resources.

Dupré, L. (1997). Seeking Christian interiority: An interview with Louis Dupré. *Religion Online*. https://www.religion-online.org/article/seeking-christian-interiority-an-interview-with-louis-dupr/ (Accessed Mar. 24, 2024).

Fong, W. (1984). *Images of the mind. Selections from the Edward L. Elliott family and John B. Elliott collections of Chinese calligraphy and painting at the Art Museum, Princeton University*. Princeton University Press.

Gallagher, Michael P., SJ. (1998). *Clashing Symbols: An Introduction to Faith & Culture.* New York/Mahwah, NJ: Paulist Press, 1998, p. 139.

Hay, J. (1985). *Kernels of energy, bones of the earth: The rock in Chinese art*. China House Gallery Exhibition Catalog.

Hymes, Robert P., and Conrad Schirokauer, editors *Ordering the World: Approaches to State and Society in Sung Dynasty China*. Berkeley: University of California Press, c1993 1993. http://ark.cdlib.org/ark:/13030/ft1000031p/.

Ingegnoli V. (2001). Landscape ecology. In D. Baltimore, R. Dulbecco, F. Jacob, & R. Levi Montalcini (eds.), *Frontiers of life*, Vol. IV (pp. 489–508). Academic Press.

Langer, S. K. (1964). *Philosophy in a new key*. Mentor Book (New American Library).

Langer, S. K. (1953). *Feeling and form.* Scribner's.

Li, Chu-tsing. (1965). *Autumn colors on the Ch'iao and Hua mountains*. A Landscape by Chao Meng-fu. Artibus Asiae Supplement.

McCarthy, K., Ondaatje, E., Zakaras L., & Brooks. A. (2004). *Gifts of the muse: Reframing the debate about the benefits of the arts*. RAND Corporation. https://doi.org/10.7249/MG218.

McCauseland, S. (2011). *Zhao Mengfu: Calligraphy and painting for Khubilai's China*. Hong Kong University Press.

Orr, D. W. (1992). *Ecological literacy: Education and the transition to a postmodern world*. Suny Press.

Owen, S. (2014). Part 3: Module 5.Tang Cosmopolitan Aristocratic Culture [MOOC lecture]. In Bol, P., & Kirby, W., ChinaX 2.0 https://vpal-edx.huit.harvard.edu/courses/course-v1:HarvardX+SW12.3x+2016/about.

Rehm, D. (Host) & Ma, Y. (Guest). (2007. Nov.21). *The Diane Rehm Show*. WAMU 88.5 FM. American University Radio.

Rosemont, H., Jr. (2013). *A Reader's companion to reading the Confucian Analects*. Palgrave Macmillan.

Rosemont, H., Jr. (2015). *Against individualism: A Confucian rethinking of the foundations of morality, politics, family, and religion*. Lexington Books.

Sacks, O. (1989). *Seeing voices*. Vintage Books.

Schneider, M. (1989). Acoustic symbolism in foreign cultures. In J. Godwin (ed.), *Cosmic music: musical keys to the interpretation of reality* (pp. 53–85). Inner Traditions.

Su, S. 2011. Dongpo tiba jiaozhu 東坡題跋校注 (Su Shi's painting inscriptions with annotation). Annotated, Tu Youxiang 屠友祥. Shanghai Yuandong chubanshe.

Tippett, K. (Host) & Kahneman, E. (Guest). (2017, October 5). *On Being with Krista Tippett* [Radio show/podcast] American Public Media.

Tu, W. (1985). *Confucian thought: Selfhood as creative transformation*. State University of New York Press.

Tyler, L. (1994). Hirabayashi Kaoru. A review. Public Practices, South Island Art Projects.

Varnedoe, K. (1990). *A Fine Disregard: What Makes Modern Art Modern*. Harry N. Abrams Inc. NY: NY.

Watson, B. (1984). *The Columbia book of Chinese poetry: From early times to the thirteenth century*. Columbia University Press.

Miki Kouji

# Chapter 10
# Zen wisdom: When the Ten Bulls encountered the Inner Development Goals

**Abstract:** The main topic of this chapter is a comparison between the Ten Bulls and the Inner Development Goals (IDGs) from the tradition within Japanese Zen Buddhism. First, it explains what the Ten Bulls – a process with an 800-year tradition in Japanese Zen depicting the transformation of human consciousness – is. Next, the author traces the psychological process that led him to establish Zen2.0, the world's largest international conference on Zen and mindfulness, through the Ten Bulls process. Finally, a comparison of the Ten Bulls and the IDGs and their potential for integration is explored, suggesting that the fusion of the Ten Bulls and the IDGs may lead to contemporary innovation processes.

**Keywords:** Ten Bulls, Zen, Zen2.0, mindfulness, innovation

## Introduction

This story is about one co-founder's experience in launching Zen2.0, the world's largest international conference on Zen and mindfulness, from Kamakura, the birthplace of Zen in Japan, using the process of the Ten Bulls, a Japanese Zen tradition.

The Ten Bulls allegory was created by Zen master Kakuan Shien in the late twelfth century, at the end of the Northern Song dynasty in China. In this teaching, the *Buddha nature inherent in human beings* is likened to a bull, a familiar animal, and the process of a person's practice in pursuit of Buddha nature is expressed in ten pictures and poems by comparing it to a herdsman taming a bull.

The herdsman in the Ten Bulls begins his search for the bull, or true self, when the bull he is tending runs away. The figure of the herdsman illustrates the process of human enlightenment, which is metaphorically shown in ten stages.

What is depicted in the Ten Bulls are the stages to enlightenment, but it is not necessarily only a guide to enlightenment. I would venture to say that in the process of creating social innovation in a modern sense,[1] a process of change in consciousness leads to major innovations that far exceed pre-planned expectations.

---

1 "Innovation" refers to product development by companies that combine different values to create new value, but in the case of "social innovation" it also includes social sustainability and social system reform, which are not necessarily economic values. In other words, social innovation is a concept in which entrepreneurs and social entrepreneurs develop new products and services that make a significant contribution to society, resulting in increased social sustainability and enhanced well-being for social stakeholders.

https://doi.org/10.1515/9783111337913-011

# Feel the Ten Bulls

In traditional Zen practice, the Ten Bulls (See Figure 10.1) was repeatedly used by masters for their disciples. The method of transmission was taught during the *sesshin*, which took place between master and disciple. There is no standard text, but ten simple pictures and a simple Chinese poem.

At the beginning of this chapter, I would like to invite you to experience the pictures so that you can personally experience what each of them means, and then read the story so that you can relive what I have experienced.

## 1. "Searching for the Bull"

> In the pasture of this world, I endlessly push aside the tall
> grasses in search of the Ox. Following unnamed rivers,
> lost upon the interpenetrating paths of distant mountains,
> My strength failing and my vitality exhausted, I cannot find the Ox.
> I only hear the locusts chirring through the forest at night.[2]

The story depicts a man who begins a search for his true self, but is at a loss as he cannot find it.

## 2. "Discovering the Footprints"

> Along the riverbank under the trees, I discover footprints.
> Even under the fragrant grass, I see his prints.
> Deep in remote mountains they are found.
> These traces can no more be hidden than one's nose, looking heavenward.

The image depicts the state of being able to gradually see clues to one's self.

## 3. "Perceiving the Bull"

> I hear the song of the nightingale. The sun is warm, the wind is mild,
> willows are green along the shore—
> Here no Ox can hide! What artist can draw that massive head, those majestic horns?

---

2 These poems were written by the Chinese Zen monk Kuòān Shīyuǎn and were translated into English in 1957 by Paul Reps and Nyogen Senzaki. Paul Reps, Nyogen Senzaki (1957). *Zen Flesh, Zen Bones: A Collection of Zen and Pre-Zen Writings*. Tuttle Publishing.

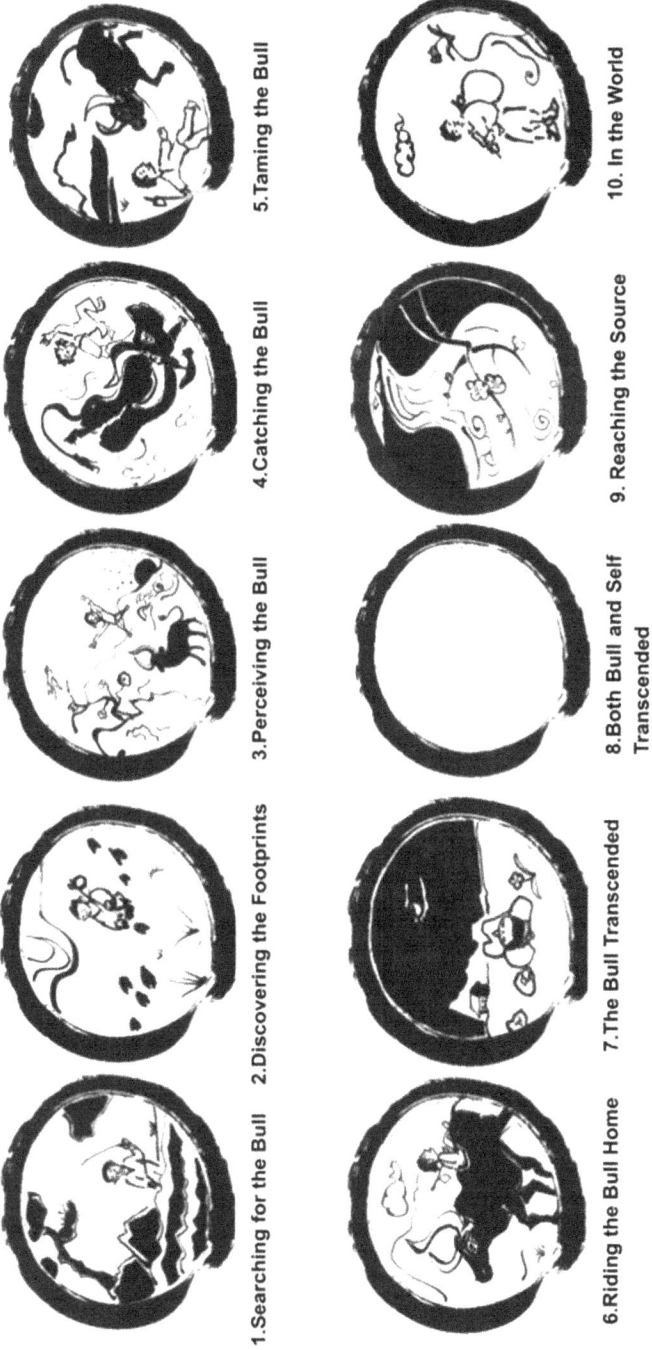

**Figure 10.1:** The Ten Bulls.
Source: Miki 2018.

The essence of the self has begun to emerge, but has not yet been grasped with certainty.

## 4. "Catching the Bull"

> *I seize him with a terrific struggle.*
> *His great will and power are inexhaustible.*
> *He charges to the high plateau far above the cloud-mists,*
> *Or in an impenetrable ravine he stands.*

This depicts a situation in which one has finally grasped one's self, but has not yet fully become one's true self.

## 5. "Taming the Bull"

> *The whip and rope are necessary, Else he might stray off down*
> *some dusty road.*
> *Being well-trained, he becomes naturally gentle.*
> *Then, unfettered, he obeys his master.*

This represents a situation in which a person has accepted him/herself and is able to live in a natural way.

## 6. "Riding the Bull Home"

> *Mounting the Ox, slowly I return homeward.*
> *The voice of my flute intones through the evening.*
> *Measuring with hand-beats the pulsating harmony,*
> *I direct the endless rhythm.*
> *Whoever hears this melody will join me.*

This is the stage where one has grasped one's true nature and is able to operate freely.

## 7. "The Bull Transcended"

> *Astride the Ox, I reach home.*
> *I am serene. The Ox too can rest.*
> *The dawn has come. In blissful repose, Within my thatched dwelling*
> *I have abandoned the whip and ropes.*

This is the stage where one forgets one's own existence and is able to see things for what they really are.

## 8. "Both Bull and Self Transcended"

*Whip, rope, person, and Ox—*
*all merge in No Thing. This heaven is so vast,*
*no message can stain it.*
*How may a snowflake exist in a raging fire.*
*Here are the footprints of the Ancestors.*

This painting depicts the transcendence of self and the true nature of things, and the attainment of a state of nothingness.

## 9. "Reaching the Source"

*Too many steps have been taken returning to the root and the source.*
*Better to have been blind and deaf from the beginning!*
*Dwelling in one's true abode, unconcerned with and without—*
*The river flows tranquilly on and the flowers are red.*

This represents the state of being aware of one's true natural state and returning to nothingness.

## 10. "In the World"

*Barefooted and naked of breast,*
*I mingle with the people of the world.*
*My clothes are ragged and dust-laden, and I am ever blissful.*
*I use no magic to extend my life;*
*Now, before me, the dead trees become alive.*

Even after returning to the ordinary world, live with the enlightenment you have attained in the background. Being ordinary is instead an extraordinary presence.

# Journey of the Ten Bulls: My personal story

In 2008, with the collapse of the Lehman Brothers in the US, the effects of the financial crisis began to have a serious impact on a small IT venture on which I was serving as a board member. The venture was providing a web service that matched manufacturers with each other online, but the number of members, which had been steadily increasing, suddenly plummeted after the economic crisis.

My company, which was on its way to being listed on Tokyo's emerging stock market, found itself in a difficult position as a result of this rapid slowdown in sales. At the time, a main criterion for listing on Tokyo's emerging markets was expected sales growth of at least 30% per year; the economic downturn dashed the company's hopes for achieving that objective.

The pressure on the president of the company from venture capitalists and major shareholders who had hoped to see the company listed was greater than expected, and he was forced to make a tough decision. Cutting costs through large-scale restructuring, he aimed for another IPO. The failure of the listing that second time affected not only the president, but also me as a member of the management team.

The financial crisis had caused a sharp drop in sales in my department, and this was a direct cause of the failure of the IPO. One day, the president called me into the conference room and told me that he would give me six months to decide whether I would accept a drastic salary cut – or leave the company to take responsibility for the failure of the IPO. In effect, I was being fired.

Back when I was a doctoral student at university, I had been working as a researcher in the humanities on management strategies using the internet; but at a time when I was feeling the limits of my research, I was enticed by the passionate words of the president of a venture company I had met, who convinced me to join the company. After diving into a small business venture and working day and night for nine years, I had been recognized for my achievements and appointed to the board of directors, and now, just when it seemed that the path to an IPO was finally in sight, I was confronted with this difficult situation.

The mental and physical impact of being fired was beyond imagination: the strain of nine years of hard work hit me all at once, and suddenly I began experiencing all sorts of health problems all over my body. This led directly to a deterioration in my mental condition. One morning, about a week after I was fired, I found myself unable to even get out of bed; it was the onset of symptoms of depression caused by the shock of being fired.

At first I couldn't tell whether or not this was depression, so I searched the internet for a description of symptoms, and it seemed quite clear that I was indeed experiencing some form of depression. The options I found were to go to hospital for psychiatric treatment, which included medication, or to look for some form of treatment I could do on my own at home.

I didn't know what possibilities there were for reviving my mental and physical health, so I first searched the internet using key phrases such as "methods for calming the mind". As a result, I happened upon a number of articles about the effectiveness of meditation and zazen as methods to calm the mind.

It was unclear from the articles alone how I should specifically go about doing meditation or zazen, so I then looked for something on YouTube – which was still in its infancy at the time – using these two keywords and was able to find several videos.

The first one was a video of a Japanese Zen monk explaining how to do zazen, how to cross your legs, how to fold your hands, and so on. However, the video did not explain much about how the mind works during zazen, so it was not very helpful. There is a tradition in Zen called 不立文字 (*furyu-monji*), in which the inner workings of the Zen mind are deliberately not conveyed in words. This is said to be in order to avoid a misunderstanding of the experience by verbalizing the experience.

However, I was so concerned about my mind activity during zazen that I decided to find a more detailed video. I found another video of a young American man living in Japan who explained zazen, not only the necessary leg and body postures for zazen, but also the process of transformation of the mind that occurs during zazen, in an entertaining, very easy-to-understand style.

I liked the video and followed the instructions, and what started out as five-minute zazen sessions gradually became ten-minute, then 15-minute sessions, and finally one-hour sessions.

When I first started zazen, all I could think about was my fear of losing my job and my fear of money. I had just built a new house, so I was worried about the mortgage payments, worried about making pension payments, worried about how I would pay my life insurance, worried about living expenses in general. I was also worried about how I was going to tell my wife about losing my job.

Just as all of these worries were overtaking my mind, my wife, who was an avid practitioner of Indian yoga at that time, decided to take a long trip to India.

During the two months before my wife returned home, I did not tell her that I had been laid off, but instead spent my time wallowing in the fear of money – and the houseplants in the house began to wither.

At first, I watered the plants constantly, thinking that they might not have enough water or light, but all the leaves withered. I wondered if this might be a reflection of my state of mind. I am not sure if the state of the human mind affects the environment or not, but anyway, the leaves of my wife's cherished houseplants started to wither and die; in the end, not a single leaf remained, –not a single leaf!– when before they had all been a beautiful shining green.

As I looked at this fear with the image of a river flowing from left to right, and the fear passing in front of me like granules flowing from upstream and disappearing, the fear itself eventually disappeared.

So I continued zazen, and after about three months the symptoms of depression improved: my body became less sluggish and I found myself in a state of mind that allowed me to be active. Then, out of the various business ideas that came up during zazen, I came up with a business plan to support people known as "makers", an idea which was still rare at that time. This business plan later grew into a business called zenschool, and even today, that business enables me to make a living.

Since then, zenschool has trained 220 graduates over the past 13 years – including a former employee of a major automobile manufacturer who raised nearly 15 billion yen in funding to develop a flying car, and the developer of a world-class mindfulness program that has been adopted by Google and McKinsey. There was also an alumnus who founded an international educational institution that utilizes the internet to provide innovative environmental education from Kumano, Japan, one of the lushest regions in the world in terms of natural beauty.

Zen had thus guided and helped me in my life. I was living in Kamakura with a desire to return the favor to Zen someday when I met Mikio Shishido, a man with a passion for Zen who was working with an organization called Kamakon, an association of entrepreneurs in Kamakura. He felt it to be a major concern that Japanese Zen – the source of the concept of mindfulness – had not been introduced to the world, nor was it well known that it had originated in Kamakura. We decided to launch an event to spread the wisdom of Japanese Zen to the world.

We then decided to organize an event to spread the word about the benefits of Zen from Kamakura to the world with a presentation at Kamakon, and we began to gather a group of friends. And this presentation was the beginning of the journey that led to the launch of the largest international conference on Zen and mindfulness in the world.

The Ten Bulls Zen story and the Inner Development Goals (IDGs) both offer frameworks for personal and spiritual growth, sharing several core principles such as stages of inner transformation, self-discovery and mastery, transcendence and application, and holistic development. In the rest of the chapter, I will delve deeper into the Ten Bulls and my personal journey, exploring how my inner development has influenced my life and work.

# Journey of the Ten Bulls: To create the world's largest Zen and mindfulness conference

## 1. "Searching for the Bull"

*In the pasture of this world, I endlessly push aside the tall*
*grasses in search of the Ox. Following unnamed rivers,*
*lost upon the interpenetrating paths of distant mountains,*
*My strength failing and my vitality exhausted, I cannot find the Ox.*
*I only hear the locusts chirring through the forest at night.*

*The story depicts a man who begins a search for his true self, but is at a loss as he cannot find it.*

I am a practitioner of Zen, but I am not a Zen monk – nor am I an expert with a university degree in Zen or mindfulness, nor did I have any specific connections to Zen temples or special contacts in Zen or mindfulness at that time. I had also never organized a large-scale event, so I began to ponder daily how I could possibly launch such an event.

Mikio Shishido, who joined me as a co-founding member of this event, has had a deep interest in the field of science since his school days and has a master's degree in quantum mechanics. After he graduated, while working as a business manager at a training company, he studied such subjects as Theory U, source principles, and learning organizations. Seeking a place where he could put them into practice in order to unite spirituality and science, he also happened to discover Kamakura, a beautiful town nestled between sea and mountains which has many temples and shrines. Together we began to wonder if it would be possible to turn Kamakura into a kind of "testing ground" that could serve as a catalyst for peace in the world.

Mikio, who had been physically weak since his youth, had lived his life by cherishing the words of the poet Shinmin Sakamura, whose poem, "If you think, flowers will bloom", was taught to him by his mother. He had just quit the company he was working for at the time and moved to Kamakura to explore the potential of consciousness becoming reality, and to explore this possibility in Kamakura. Mikio and I hit it off at Kamakon, a support group for venture businesses in Kamakura, and we became friends.

However, the two of us had never planned a major event before and we set out with great trepidation as to whether or not we could make it work. Yes, we were aware that we had none of what would be necessary to pull off this huge event.

## 2. "Discovering the Footprints"

*Along the riverbank under the trees,*
*I discover footprints. Even under the fragrant grass, I see his prints.*
*Deep in remote mountains they are found.*
*These traces can no more be hidden than one's nose, looking heavenward.*

*The image depicts the state of being able to gradually see clues to one's self.*

Before becoming able to actually launch such an event, I had to educate myself on the fundamentals of Zen itself and research the latest information on mindfulness, so I looked through as much information as possible on websites and purchased a large number of books to learn the basics of Zen and mindfulness.

In addition, since it was thought that examples of mindfulness in the US were more advanced than those in Japan, our founding-member team gathered information by purchasing and ordering American mindfulness magazines etc., which we then added to our studies.

We also searched the web extensively to track the latest developments in the US using the keyword "mindfulness" and learned about the state of mindfulness in the US and Europe.

When we asked a Japanese person who was a pioneer in mindfulness if there were any famous mindfulness events, we learned that an international conference on mindfulness called Wisdom 2.0, the largest such conference in the world, was being held in San Francisco, USA.

We checked the conference's website and learned that it would be held in San Francisco in March 2016, so after consulting with Mikio, we applied to attend the conference.

## 3. "Perceiving the Bull"

*I hear the song of the nightingale. The sun is warm, the wind is mild, willows are green along the shore—*
*Here no Ox can hide!*
*What artist can draw that massive head, those majestic horns?*

*The essence of the self has begun to emerge, but has not yet been grasped with certainty.*

I went to San Francisco to attend Wisdom 2.0 and was overwhelmed by the scale of the event. It was held at a huge San Francisco hotel, and the reception desk was staffed by many volunteers working quickly and efficiently, wearing matching T-shirts with the Wisdom 2.0 logo.

I was taken aback at the throngs of enthusiastic people in the hotel's huge hall. I was also surprised by the variety of activities, such as sharing in pairs and dance-like movement activities.

Initially, we came to the mindfulness event in San Francisco with the attitude that Kamakura was the epicenter of everything Zen; both of us saw mindfulness as not really Zen, but a somewhat shallow concept. Yet when we talked with the other participants, we were shocked to learn that even though we had come from Kamakura, "the hometown of Zen", no one there had heard of it. In addition, we discovered that the prevalent form of Buddhism in the US seemed to be Tibetan Buddhism and not Japanese Buddhism, and that they had little knowledge of Japanese Zen Buddhism.

In addition, while it was a conference about mindfulness, there were club events held in the evening, and we ended up greatly enjoying dancing with the mindfulness teachers.

Little by little, as we attended the three-day event, we began to get swept up in Wisdom 2.0 and saw the reality of how meditation was being integrated into a highly diverse American society. It felt like we were riding the wave of a completely new movement.

The two of us were deeply impacted by the event. It gave us the conviction that our own Zen event in Kamakura could become as global and diverse as this one, and we left the San Francisco venue with a sense of hope: that by bringing a sense that anyone can participate in the world of Zen, the event would be a great success.

## 4. "Catching the Bull"

*I seize him with a terrific struggle.*
*His great will and power are inexhaustible.*
*He charges to the high plateau far above the cloud-mists,*
*Or in an impenetrable ravine he stands.*

*This depicts a situation in which one has finally grasped one's self, but has not yet fully become one's true self.*

After returning to Japan, before the excitement of my experience participating in Wisdom 2.0 had a chance to cool, we first shared our excitement with the other members of the Zen2.0 management team. When we enthusiastically told them about how mindfulness is becoming accepted by many in the US and about the openness and diversity of their approach, the response was quite positive.

We held a debriefing session for the general public – not just our own team – in an open space at a large IT company, which was attended by over 100 people despite the short time between the announcement of the event and its opening to the public. In contrast to the antiquated image of Buddhism in Japan, the term mindfulness as a new spiritual movement from the west coast of the United States was greeted with a positive response.

The participants in this debriefing session were very interested in the concepts of mindfulness and meditation, and a passionate dialogue session followed the presentation.

The high level of interest and enthusiasm of the participants in this debriefing session clearly confirmed our conviction that the event we were planning would be extremely popular if we made sure to incorporate mindfulness throughout the content.

So, now that the direction of the project was clear, the question we had to ask ourselves was what kind of speakers to gather.

I was just a person who practiced Zen to improve my anxiety (depression), while Mikio had been interested in the relationship between the body, spirituality, and science for a long time as he had been sickly since he was a child.

He had a wider network of contacts in this field at an earlier stage than I did, but I myself had no connections in the industry.

Therefore, even if we asked potential speakers to speak at the conference, there was a possibility that they would decline to speak because they did not understand what the conference was about. So, while searching for contacts to potential speakers, we managed to move the project forward, albeit with some struggle.

In Japan, it is rare for a product, service, or event without a proven track record to be readily accepted by the public. First of all, what is needed is a track record, and it was unlikely that a famous monk, mindfulness researcher, scholar, or artist would participate as a speaker at an unproven event such as ours.

Of course, if we could have paid a high speaking fee, the situation would have been different, but the nonprofit nature of this conference would not allow us to pay a high speaking fee. The benefit to the speakers would have to be that the presence of other influential speakers would add value to their brand by allowing them to speak at the event, or that they would perceive value in being part of a network with other influential speakers.

Despite Mikio's network of contacts in this field, the trick to our success was going to be figuring out how to get famous speakers first. Here, we had an unbelievable stroke of luck. At the Wisdom 2.0 reception in San Francisco, we had been passing out flyers for the Zen2.0 event (for which the venue had not yet been decided), and a Japanese American who got the flier handed it to her husband, who happened to be a professor teaching mindfulness at Stanford University!

That professor, Dr Shigematsu of Stanford University, contacted us himself asking if he could participate as a speaker at Zen2.0. The impact of having a mindfulness teacher from a well-known university such as Stanford University speak at Zen2.0 was immeasurable, and having his profile information officially posted on our website and flyers made it much easier to gather speakers after that. In no time at all, we had a stream of famous Zen masters, mindfulness experts, AI experts, and other speakers in Japan. The problem of finding speakers was now solved.

At this point, we had been holding regular planning meetings since the project had started, but gradually fewer and fewer people attended. The main reason for this was that the project was aiming for a goal two years away; this was quite a long project, and many members of the team didn't have enough energy to stay with the project through to that point.

From this point on, the plan was to hold an international conference focusing on mindfulness in Kamakura. In the first few planning meetings, the team members had a hard time understanding the worldview of mindfulness, and several meetings were held without any concrete ideas on how to develop this worldview in Kamakura.

Initially, we tried to move the project forward by meeting regularly about once every two weeks, but several meetings were held without any concrete consensus, and then gradually the number of participants in the meetings dwindled.

As the organizer of the meeting, I tried to devise various ways to increase cohesiveness, but as time went by I spent many days wondering why there were so few people attending the meetings.

The number of participants in the meetings was dwindling rapidly, and just over eight months before the event was to be held, there were several meetings where only one or two people besides myself attended the regular planning meetings. Just when we were finally gathering a strong lineup of speakers, there was no one left to organize the event.

Just at that time, Dr Shigematsu was scheduled to visit Japan prior to the conference, and he came and stayed at our house. Naturally, he asked about the progress of the Zen2.0 project, and I could not tell him that the project was not running smoothly. The conference website listed many prominent speakers, but behind the scenes, there was almost no one left on the management staff.

As a result of this increased psychological burden, I contracted a severe cold, which kept me in a very poor physical condition for about a month, and I was unable to hold the planning meetings.

Perhaps due to the psychological pressure of running the conference, my heart was not very strong by nature, and my body's immunity was lowered. As if to push me over the edge, I contracted a cold and could not seem to recover from it.

In order to somehow improve my physical condition, I began an internal yoga practice that my wife introduced to me. This yoga was different from ordinary yoga in that it did not involve much body movement, but mainly consisted of breathing exercises and the repetition of an internal mantra in one's mind. Thanks to this yoga, I was able to give myself permission to let go of everything and be free; my battered heart was restored and I gradually regained my inner peace and physical health.

When we discussed this difficult situation with the members of Kamakon, they suggested that we give another presentation at Kamakon in order to recruit volunteers again. As a result of the presentation, new volunteers began to join, and participation at the regular meetings gradually increased.

## 5. "Taming the Bull"

*The whip and rope are necessary, Else he might stray off down*
*some dusty road.*
*Being well-trained, he becomes naturally gentle.*
*Then, unfettered, he obeys his master.*

*This represents a situation in which a person has accepted him/herself and is able to live in a natural way.*

The meetings became considerably more dynamic with the entry of a number of new participants as the project progressed, reversing the decline in the cohesion of the meetings that had been a concern. Furthermore, while I had been leading each meeting's proceedings myself, several people stepped up who were willing to take turns leading the proceedings.

In addition, each volunteer team now had a volunteer leader to organize their team, and discussions became more proactive. The overall flow of the project was becoming clear and smooth. We had been pulling the project along at full speed, and now we could afford to loosen the reins a bit.

However, as always, the project was not without its challenges; the slightest loosening of the reins in the management of the meetings and the progress of the overall proceedings would often result in delays in the overall operation of the project. Still, when I thought back to a year and a half earlier when the project had just been launched, the planning meetings themselves were now running quite smoothly.

In addition, the event's website was launched, and tickets began to sell, albeit gradually. However, we were concerned that the number of tickets sold at that point was far below our initial target.

Another major challenge for the project was the issue of funding. Since the conference was a nonprofit project, the plan was to fund its operations through the cost of tickets sold and sponsorships from start-ups and other sources.

We had never held a large-scale event before and had no experience in marketing activities to get sponsors. The challenge was how to raise money for the airfare for the speakers from overseas. In order to attract well-known speakers from overseas, the event had to cover airfare and other expenses, and we had to figure out how to cover those costs.

The total cost of airfare for all the overseas speakers we were considering, including the professor from Stanford University, would amount to several million yen. How would we raise this cost? We were scratching our heads as to how much pressure this would put on the event's finances.

## 6. "Riding the Bull Home"

*Mounting the Ox, slowly I return homeward.*
*The voice of my flute intones through the evening.*
*Measuring with hand-beats the pulsating harmony,*
*I direct the endless rhythm.*
*Whoever hears this melody will join me.*

*This is the stage where one has grasped one's true nature and is able to operate freely.*

Now, once each volunteer team was well established, and once the direction of the project was solidified, some members with leadership qualities emerged within each volunteer team and naturally began to organize their team. Each project team began to be able to move autonomously. Although occasional conflicts of interest arose between the different teams, it was better if I acted as the coordinator only at those times.

Although the event was only a short time away, it was beginning to look as if the event would be a success if I just continued to support the overall movement. The number of tickets sold was looking like it might just barely reach our goal.

Here again, a miraculous stroke of luck occurred. A major issue affecting whether or not this event could be held – the issue of finance – was resolved.

One of the volunteers who happened to be present at the event happened to be the general manager of a new business division of a major airline company. He also happened to be a resident of Kita-Kamakura, and when we held an event to recruit new volunteers, he joined us as a new volunteer member.

After discussing with him the financial burden of airfare for speakers coming from overseas, he agreed to provide all the airline tickets for the speakers to come from overseas as a development expense for the new business division of his airline company! This was an incredible miracle.

The travel expenses for the speakers had been a huge financial burden, so we welcomed and accepted this proposal with open arms. This financial support was a miracle; without this miraculous stroke of luck, the event would not have been possible. The collaboration with this airline was the beginning of a relationship that has continued to this day.

## 7. "The Bull Transcended"

*Astride the Ox, I reach home.*
*I am serene. The Ox too can rest.*
*The dawn has come. In blissful repose, Within my thatched dwelling*
*I have abandoned the whip and ropes.*

*This is the stage where one forgets one's own existence and is able to see things for what they really are.*

With one month to go until the event, the volunteer teams were now engaged in the final stages of event preparation. They were coming up with the best processes, but just when it seemed that preparations would be completed without any problems, another major problem arose.

Incredible as it may seem now, no plans had been made to set up audio equipment at the event site or to secure the huge projector that would be necessary to display the speaker's presentation materials. This was a mistake that occurred because all of us on the event management team were complete novices.

With less than a month to go before the event, and with no sound engineering plan in place, I searched around in various channels for someone who was familiar with such matters, but no one with this kind of experience came to mind.

Even if you have a great lineup of speakers, an event like this cannot succeed if the venue is not set up properly with functioning audio and visual equipment.

As we were getting more and more anxious, to our surprise, a person with sound engineering skills for the event agreed to join us the following week as a volunteer member of the team. We talked to him and learned that his business partner also handled projectors and other equipment, and he agreed to do the sound engineering for us. A projector was also provided to us by another sponsor who was supportive of the content of the event.

Then, as soon as that major problem was solved, a strange phenomenon occurred in ticket sales, bringing another major issue to deal with. Tickets had been selling gradually, but once we reached a certain number of tickets sold, it was as if they hit a ceiling, and sales had almost completely dropped off. However, the sluggish ticket sales suddenly began to pick up rapidly. Ticket registrations continued to come in at an unprecedented pace, and we reached our maximum capacity for participants practically overnight. It was such a remarkable turn of events that we wondered why we had been struggling to sell tickets for so long.

At the moment the ticket sales reached full capacity, I felt as if the event was already complete. I was in a strange state of mind where I no longer minded whether the event itself would succeed or fail. I almost stopped paying attention to the event, and the rest of the days passed by without a hitch until the event was held.

## 8. "Both Bull and Self Transcended"

*Whip, rope, person, and Ox—*
*all merge in No Thing. This heaven is so vast,*
*no message can stain it.*
*How may a snowflake exist in a raging fire.*
*Here are the footprints of the Ancestors.*

*This painting depicts the transcendence of self and the true nature of things, and the attainment of a state of nothingness.*

Finally, the day of the Zen2.0 event arrived.

The morning of the event began with a downpour. It was raining so hard that we wondered if any participants would show up. However, the rain suddenly stopped at 9 a.m., the moment the event was to begin. A pleasant breeze began to blow.

The heavy rain did little to dampen the number of participants, and a long line formed in front of the registration desk at Kenchoji Temple. When the announcement was made that the doors were open, the venue of Kenchoji Temple was filled with participants. I was struck by the sensation that the image of the event, which I had seen many times in my dreams, was actually unfolding in slow motion right before my eyes.

To kick off the event, I gave an opening speech to give a brief history of the event and to thank the participants, but it felt like someone else was giving the speech using my mouth. I had the strange sensation that another being was watching me from outside my body as I was greeting them.

Once the event began, the program proceeded smoothly. All of the programs flowed and connected seamlessly. Some small issues showed up in the overall flow of the event, but they were trivial.

It was as if some kind of invisible, living, pulsating energy body was present at Kenchoji Temple, the venue for Japan's first international conference on Zen and mindfulness. The atmosphere was tranquil yet filled with a solemn power, and in the midst of this energy, people were riding the waves from one venue to the next, experiencing one seminar or workshop after another, and delightedly sharing their impressions with one another.

I found myself gazing at the entire scene as if I were watching a slow-motion movie scene. I felt as if I was no longer the organizer but an actor or a character in a film. Thanks to this detached perspective, I felt almost no anxiety about the event as a whole; it was as if I were watching a play in progress.

## 9. "Reaching the Source"

*Too many steps have been taken returning to the root and the source.*
*Better to have been blind and deaf from the beginning!*
*Dwelling in one's true abode, unconcerned with and without—*
*The river flows tranquilly on and the flowers are red.*

*This represents the state of being aware of one's true natural state and returning to nothingness.*

Thus, the first international conference on Zen and mindfulness in Japan, held over two days at Kenchoji Temple in Kamakura, the oldest Zen specialized dojo in Kamakura, the home of Zen, was held without major disruption or accident, and the event was a great success.

If there were some minor problems encountered on the day of the event, they were all resolved on-site by very enthusiastic volunteer members.

The Zen2.0 event itself was like a living, vibrant organism that attracted participants and speakers, and ended with a huge impact on the participants, making it a huge success.

Participants who attended the event posted a series of photos and impressions on social networking sites and wrote lengthy positive comments, which showed the impact of the event on the participants after it was over.

The survey results from the participants showed that the event was so well received that it was hard to believe that this was the first event the planners had organized. The reverberations of that response continued long after the event was over, with participants constantly contacting us via our website and social networking sites, incredulously asking us questions that amounted to "What in the world just happened?"

Later, we began to learn of changes in the participants who attended the event, some of whom were exposed to Zen and mindfulness for the first time, some of whom went on to start their own businesses in these fields, and others who launched new businesses within large corporations. The event truly served as a platform for transforming consciousness.

In addition, many speakers at the event became friends with one another in the event's waiting room, and the event was followed by a series of collaborative conversations and collaborative events among the speakers. As a result of this networking among the speakers, many of them expressed their desire to participate as speakers again next time.

In addition, various media outlets that covered the event continued to post articles in their magazines and on their websites, and other media outlets that saw the articles continued to offer to cover the event for some time to come.

The response from Kenchoji Temple, which provided the venue for the event, was also extremely positive. The fact that an event created for the first time by a complete amateur in the fields of Zen and mindfulness was a success, with very positive feedback from the participants, created a good impression, and led to the temple offering their venue for the next event the following year.

## 10. "In the World"

*Barefooted and naked of breast,*
*I mingle with the people of the world.*
*My clothes are ragged and dust-laden, and I am ever blissful.*
*I use no magic to extend my life;*
*Now, before me, the dead trees become alive.*

*Even after returning to the ordinary world, live with the enlightenment you have at-*
*tained in the background. Being ordinary is instead an extraordinary presence.*

And so, Zen2.0, Japan's first international conference on Zen and mindfulness, came to a successful conclusion. Even after the event was over, the thrill of its success lingered in my heart.

I later found out after checking with the volunteers that it was not the case that everyone experienced significant transformation. However, as the organizer, I personally underwent a major psychological transformation.

The psychological transformation was that the sensations I experienced after the event were so fresh and vivid that I had never experienced them before in my life. Everything I saw and heard was fresh and vivid: the green of the trees, the birdsong I heard, even the sound of the wind through the trees. And a tremendous euphoric feeling suffused my entire body. That wonderful euphoria lasted about two weeks and then slowly faded away.

Then, a few months after the event was over, I began to share this experience with others in the form of lectures in various places and at my own school of innovation, zenschool.

First of all, in a natural way, I would talk about the process that enabled me to create such an event despite my limited ability to manage a huge organization. From my experience, I shared with people that even if they do not have great talents themselves, they can create a great social impact by following the excitement generated in their own hearts and by devoting themselves to a single task.

Communicating such a Zen-like experience of my own also had an impact on zen-school. As a result, a variety of innovators have been born, including one graduate who developed a world-class mindfulness program called Zen Eating, based on an eating meditation, which has been adopted by Google and McKinsey in the United States, and an organization that began providing world-class environmental education content from Kumano, Japan.

I would also learn later that, before the experience that produced the Zen2.0 event, graduates of zenschool have actually blossomed in the same manner as my own experience of the Ten Bull process. The same process was confirmed in the case of the flying car SkyDrive, launched by an entrepreneur from Toyota who raised almost 15 billion yen, as well as in the case of a graduate who developed an ultralight lunar rover.

In the following section I will describe and explain what I experienced in my Ten Bulls journey and which skills from the IDG skill sets that I used.

# The relationship between the Ten Bulls the IDG skill sets

## Ten Bulls and IDGs: Similarities and contrasts

In order to clarify the purpose of this text, I would like to clarify the similarities and contrasts between the Ten Bulls and IDGs. The Ten Bulls is a traditional Zen Buddhist painting that captures the transformation of consciousness and uses the theme of bulls.

In that tradition, the Ten Bulls emphasize the impression that the individual receives from looking at the picture, rather than a detailed description in language. Based on traditional Zen thinking, a uniform explanation is not appropriate when passing on the Ten Bulls Tables (see Table 10.1) from master to disciple. Therefore, it has traditionally been refrained from using words to describe the Ten Bulls in the past tradition. However, I have decided to specify the following table of contrasts in order to dare verbalize the Ten Bulls of Zen wisdom by contrasting them with the IDGs.

Although this may be subject to criticism because of the long tradition of Zen Buddhism, I have drawn up this comparison table (see Table 10.1) in order to verbalize as much as possible the Zen wisdom that I have benefited from, and to spread it around the world.

**Table 10.1:** Ten Bulls and IDGs: Similarities and contrasts.

| Characteristics or traits | Ten Bulls | IDGs |
|---|---|---|
| 1  Purpose | Attainment of enlightenment | Enhancement of the human capacity in order to reach the SDGs |
| 2  Means | Before a Zen practice, the student looks at pictures of the Ten Bulls. Each stage of the mind is summarized in an easy-to-understand picture. And students have to read short Chinese poems to know about an overall picture of the practice, but it is not necessary to understand everything there. After the Zen practice has begun, in verbal exchanges between the master and the student, the master may refer to the Ten Bulls depending on the degree of evolution of the student's mind. | Dialogue and explore the feasibility of how this can be achieved within one's self and one's organization with regard to the five dimensions and 23 skill sets. |
| 3  Uniformity | It uses icons that are easy for anyone to understand – a bull and a cowherd boy – to describe the process of transforming consciousness. | Each skill set is designed with easily recognizable symbols. |
| 4  Object of description | It describes ten levels, covering the transformation of consciousness to reach enlightenment. However, it is not a way of perceiving which is higher on the scale from 1 to 10. | Human mind skill sets are expressed in 23 pieces. |

## Relationship between the Ten Bulls and IDGs

In order to further understand the relationship between the Ten Oxherding Pictures and the IDGs, we will use the metaphor of the iceberg model. (See Figure 10.2) The two relationships are clear to everyone as the tip of the iceberg that the IDGs stick out of the sea.

On the other hand, the Ten Bulls is a pattern of transformation of the human mind, and the pattern of transformation of the mind depends on the state of development of each individual's mind (See Figure 10.2). It is difficult to be aware of the transformation while it is taking place, and it is difficult to clearly define the pattern of transformation in language. We can say that it is a process of transformation of consciousness at the unconscious level. Therefore, figuratively speaking, this part is the bottom of the iceberg.

The transformational part of the mind represented by the Ten Bulls indirectly influences the upper IDGs, but it is difficult to explicitly link the skill sets of the IDGs to the transformational patterns of the Ten Bulls.

It is also difficult to explicitly link the skill sets of the IDGs to the mind-altering patterns of the map, because the layers they are trying to represent are different.

The upper and lower branches of the iceberg model can verbalize the mental skill sets that they are about to demonstrate, or in the case of past events, they can verbalize them in their short-term memory. In other words, the 23 mental skill sets of the IDGs located in the above-water part of the model can be clearly and consciously recognized as they are being demonstrated, at least while experiencing the event, and can be looked back on in short-term memory in the case of past events.

In contrast, the transformation process of Ten Bulls, which is located in the underwater part, it is difficult to verbalize the exact situation at the time of experiencing the phenomenon, and only after a considerable amount of time has passed after experiencing a series of transformation processes can one recognize one's own transformation process as it applies to Ten Bulls. After experiencing a series of transformation processes, only after a considerable amount of time has passed can one recognize one's own transformation process in terms of the Ten Bulls. This situation is the phenomenon of connecting the dots, as Steve Jobs famously said in his speech.[3]

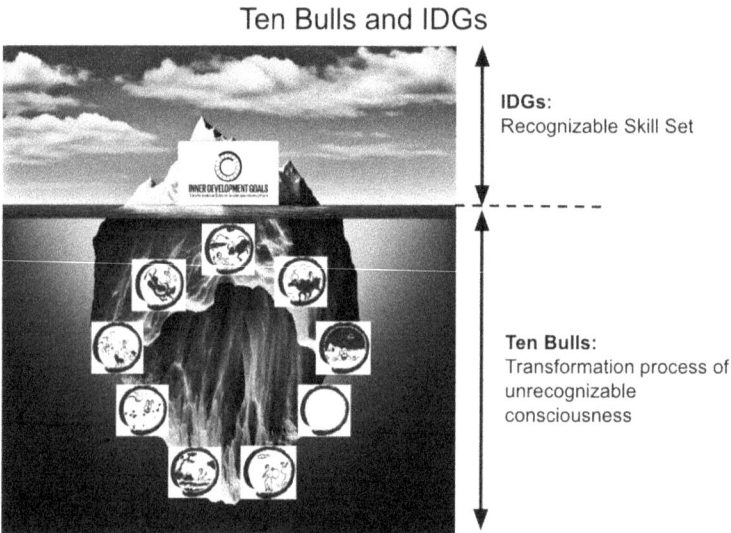

**Figure 10.2:** Ten Bulls and IDGs.
Source: Author

3 Apple founder Steve Jobs used the expression "connect the dots" in a speech he gave to graduates at the 2005 Stanford University commencement celebration, saying, "You can't connect the dots looking forward; you can only connect them looking backwards. So you have to trust that the dots will somehow connect in your future."

# Conclusion

In this experimental text, I describe the transformation of human consciousness known as the Ten Bulls, which has been handed down in the world of Zen since ancient times, based on my own experience of founding the world's largest international conference on Zen and mindfulness.

In the course of my actual activities, I was not particularly conscious of the 23 mindsets from Inner Compass to Perseverance specified in the IDGs, but I was able to test the relationship between the IDG framework and the Ten Bulls process by recalling the ways in which I effectively used them during that time period.

This text is certainly an experimental work, but in the 13 years I have been running zenschool, many of its graduates have made great innovations through the same process as the Ten Bulls.

In order to convey the relationship between innovation and the Ten Bulls as clearly as possible, I have used a storytelling method to describe the innovations that I myself, as the manager of this school, have made, as well as my own personal transformation.

In fact, while writing this text, the process of recalling old traumas, remembering the feelings I had at that time, and describing them in minute detail was very challenging. It was painful to revisit mental and physical wounds I had experienced in the past. Especially while describing the process of "Catching the Bull" I started to feel queasy with the memories of that time, and it was a struggle to put the experience into words.

I now realize that the last process in the Ten Bulls, the process of communicating authentically what one has experienced, is a more demanding form of practice than I had imagined, as we face our own trauma again when we attempt to communicate to others what we have experienced.

Having gone through the process of the Ten Bulls, I thought I had completed the evolution of my consciousness, but instead I had a powerful realization: I wasn't done, I was simply standing at the entrance of the next stage of my evolution. The expansion of human consciousness has no end; we continue to evolve our consciousness by repeatedly cycling through the process of the Ten Bulls in a spiral fashion.

This time, due to lack of space, I won't be able to link the spiral evolution of consciousness in the Ten Bulls with the IDG skill set; that will have to be the subject for another time.

This relationship between each process of the Ten Bulls and the mindset specified in the IDGs is based on my own personal impressions, and may be different in other cases. For the time being, I have described it as my own story. If by reading this you become able to better understand the relationship between the Ten Bulls, innovation, and the IDGs, even if only a little, I will be very happy.

Finally, I would like to thank the Kamakura Buddhist community for generously sharing their Zen wisdom with me, and the Swiss IDG Hub for this valuable opportunity to introduce this Zen wisdom to the world.

# References

Paul Reps, Nyogen Senzaki (1957). *Zen Flesh, Zen Bones: A Collection of Zen and Pre-Zen Writings*. Tuttle Publishing Inner Development Goals. (n.d.). Inner Development Goals Framework. *Inner Development Goals*. https://innerdevelopmentgoals.org/framework/ (Accessed Mar. 31, 2024).

Miki, K. (2018). *True Innovation: How 'Zen-style' Dialogue Changed Employee Awareness*. CCC Media House Co., Ltd., pp. 178–192.

Mizuno, M., Shintaku, T., Sato, A., Oniki, M., & Arai, N. (2023). *IDGs Transforming Organizations*. Keizai Houreki Kenkyukai.

Soen, O. & Mills, E. (2011). *An introduction to Zen*. Jitsugyo no Nihonsha, Inc.

Yokota, N. (2020).*Learning from Jugyu-zu*. Chichi-Publishing Co.

Cathryn LeCorre
# Chapter 11
# Seasonal Circles of Change: A roadmap to embody the IDGs so we can co-create change

**Abstract:** The Seasonal Circles of Change invite us into a transformational journey of growth, connection, and co-creation by engaging with the natural rhythms of the earth. Nature becomes our guide so we can see, understand, and influence patterns. Fostered in partnership with the Inner Development Goals (IDGs), the seasonal cycles provide a path of practice for changemakers who want to co-create change.

This chapter is for changemakers who want to co-create conditions for thriving, together. The root meaning of thrive is "to prosper". The aim of a prosperous person is to cultivate endurance, dedication, and awareness by remembering the presence and possibilities within each person (Bhajan, 2013). When changemakers thrive, their communities thrive. Thriving together emphasizes the importance of healing while creating the conditions for the collective well-being of our communities. Rupa Marya and Raj Patel (2021) call for a return to our true selves through creating communities of care that put the intelligence of life at the center.

The Seasonal Circles of Change process puts nature at the center so we can co-create conditions to thrive, together. The process encourages us to create into our full potential, rather than fix something we see as broken. This discussion includes stories to illustrate the application of the seasonal cycles in the personal and collective domains and invites changemakers to engage in the practice of leadership so we can align inner motivations with outward action.

**Keywords:** nature, leadership, co-creation, change, coaching, wellbeing

## Healing the divide

> I used to think the top environmental problems were biodiversity loss, ecosystem collapse and climate change. I thought with 30 years of good science we could address those problems. But I was wrong. The top environmental problems are selfishness, greed and apathy . . . And to deal with those we need a spiritual and cultural transformation – and we scientists don't know how to do that. (James Gustave Speth, former Administrator UNDP, cited in Ives, Freeth, & Fischer, 2019)

There are many problems facing humanity at this time. Collectively, humanity wants to realize the global goals for sustainable development. Yet, we are not reaching our milestones or targets. There is a very large gap between where we are, and where we

https://doi.org/10.1515/9783111337913-012

want to be. A recent assessment by the United Nations in *The Sustainable Development Goals Report 2023* (UN DESA, 2023) indicates that of the Sustainable Development Goals (SDGs) targets:

- 15% are on track;
- 37% have stagnated or regressed;
- and 48% are moderately or severely off track.

Looking at the state of the world, it can be easy to experience a sense of powerlessness and hopelessness. Depending on the day, we can also feel tremendous optimism and excitement about the possibilities. We are yearning to experience more movement, and instead can feel stuck. The current approaches to change are failing us. Most of us grew up inside of a culture of domination, a system of operating based in qualities of separation, hierarchy, information, control, and individuality. The emerging paradigm is rooted in values of creativity, integration, awareness, well-being, and collaboration. The Inner Development Goals (IDGs) provide a roadmap for human development required to address this gap.

Just as our collective values are being elevated, our change methodology needs to be upgraded. To transform our world, we must change how we do change. Social construction theory demonstrates that our perception and understanding of the world are shaped by our mindsets and interactions. At the heart of this transformation is a movement in the narrative from surviving to thriving, from competition to collaboration, from scarcity to abundance, and from problems to possibility.

When we transform ourselves, we transform the world.

When changemakers adopt an inside-out approach, we can empower ourselves to change behaviors through agency and connection. When we show up as creators, capable of shaping our reality, we can engage each conversation as a potential exchange for fostering collective leadership. By enhancing relationships and engaging in partnerships, we can become catalysts for personal and societal transformation. The seasonal circles of change combined with the IDGs provide a path of practice to co-create change with nature (see Figure 11.1).

## The Seasonal Circles of Change

*A movement that is calling on us to cultivate the inner conditions that allow for transformational change. A movement that allows us to radically reconnect with each other, with our planet, and with our evolving human consciousness. (Otto Scharmer, 2021)*

The Seasonal Circles of Change is a path of practice to embody leadership in a way that co-creates change so we can cultivate thriving communities. This process for creation was first introduced to me on a visit to New York City, at the same time as the Women's March in January 2017. I was having lunch with a friend, and we were ex-

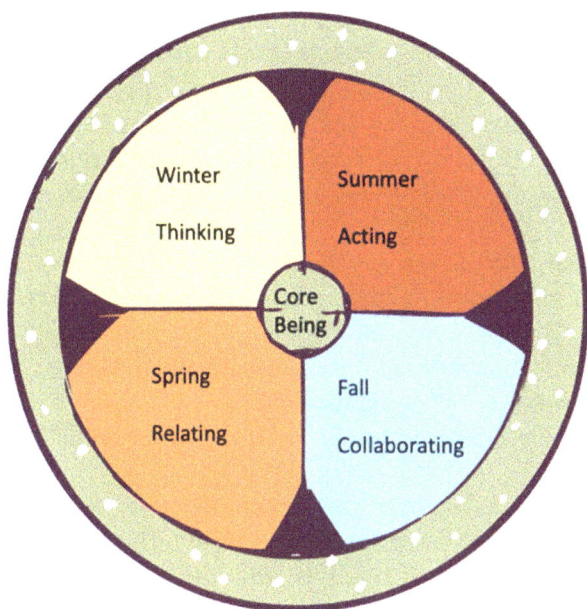

**Figure 11.1:** The Seasonal Circles of Change and the IDGs, by Cathryn LeCorre.

ploring the question of how we could turn the march into a movement in our own lives. Both of us named the desire to write more. As I named the impulse, I felt alive and awake in my senses, like writing could be a path of practice to "do something". When she offered the Celtic Wheel of the Year as a support and accountability structure for our writing projects, I felt a visceral feeling of connection. I knew in that moment this was a way through my resistance and fear of visibility. Since then, seven years later, we continue to meet at each of the eight gateways of the Wheel of the Year to support and empower each other through peer coaching. The impact of the work together is this chapter in your hands.

The seasonal cycles are about remembering who we are as creators, in radical collaboration with nature. They invite us to reclaim ancient ways of knowing and being in connection with the earth, by seeing the land as conscious and alive. When we connect with the ancient ways of remembering, we remember parts of ourselves that have been forgotten and suppressed before cultural patterns of domination separated us from interdependent ways of connecting with the natural flow of change within ourselves, each other, and the earth. Marking the subtle shifts of the seasons has become a powerful method to bring me into connection with nature, learn about the wisdom of my ancestors, and align with the cyclical nature of life.

When transformational leadership principles and practice are aligned with the seasonal cycles, we can harness the energy of the earth to make a meaningful and sustainable impact. This methodology is grounded in the leadership development courses, programs, and services developed by the British Columbia Health Leadership Development Collaborative (BCHLDC) with the ultimate goal of delivering exceptional patient outcomes. The Leadership LINX programs include courses such as Clear Leadership developed by Gervase Bushe, Coaching Out of the Box created by Alison Hendren, and Human System Dynamics founded by Glenda Eoyang. This path of authentic leadership practice is expanded to include the wisdom received by Lori-Anne Demers through Authentic to the Core.

The Celtic Wheel of the Year is a calendar system which honours the cycles of nature by celebrating the solstices, equinoxes, and the points in between through seasonal festival days or "sabbats". The Celts were a diverse group of communities with a shared language and culture who inhabited various regions of Europe. Today, the Wheel of the Year is being reclaimed by contemporary earth-based practitioners and Indignous Knowledge Systems are showing the way to connect with the natural rhythms and cycles of the earth.

The Wheel of the Year, rooted in the northern hemisphere, offers a framework to see, understand, and influence change through the cycles of nature. This model expands our awareness of natural transformation processes. While particularly relevant for changemakers in the northern and southern hemispheres, I am curious about its potential resonance and adaptation for those near the equator. Familiar to many are the four quarter sections delineating the cycles, approximately on the following dates:
- winter solstice, December 21;
- summer solstice, June 21;
- spring equinox, March 21;
- and autumn equinox, September 21.

## Using the Seasonal Circles of Change to embody IDG leadership

As thriving changemakers, we are yearning for self-actualization through the process of growth. This process begins by coming into right alignment with an open mind, heart, and will. Walking the seasonal path of practice in partnership with the IDGs cultivates self- and systems awareness, seeing the personal and the collective as inseparable so we can co-create the conditions to thrive, together.
- Core – *being*: What qualities will I bring? What passion am I embracing?
- Winter – *thinking*: What might I need to let go of and release? What intention is illuminating the path forward?
- Spring – *relating*: What is required to co-create conditions for the intention to grow?
- Summer – *acting*: What is my adaptive action project?
- Autumn – *collaborating*: How will I harvest and celebrate once my intention has come to fruition?

The following describes how a person, relationship, or group can use the Seasonal Circles of Change to embody the IDGs. An overview of each season and IDG domain will be provided, followed by a short story and then a report on what nine IDG hub participants and six nature pod co-creators thought. During four 60-minute Zoom interviews and two workshops, individuals and small groups discussed how the Seasonal Circles of Change could facilitate the IDG domains of being, thinking, relating, acting and collaborating. They have been organized and lightly edited.

# Core – *being*

> I think that what we're seeking is an experience of being alive, so that our life experiences on the purely physical plane will have resonances with our own innermost being and reality, so that we actually feel the rapture of being alive. (Joseph Campbell, 1988)

Aliveness is more than just surviving, it is a deep yearning for connection, a longing to be fully present in the richness of life. When changemakers feel alive, we thrive. Walking the path of embodiment is a journey down into our body so we can awaken our senses and engage our energy.

At the center of the seasonal Wheel of the Year is the core of natural energy. Some people refer to this aspect as the "source of all that is" or the "fabric of love" that connects and unites us all. This place of center emphasizes the interconnectedness of all of life and energy that permeates the natural world, and is the source of cultivating harmony between our inner and external worlds. Our true nature likes to be in alignment with our essence, our core values. Being aligned with our core means we remember who we are, discover what we love, and be true to ourselves (Demers & Orlesky, 2013).

As facilitators of change, our role is to co-create spaces and places for people to access their wisdom, creativity, and resources so they can move toward solutions. We can help people strengthen their presence and lessen their reactivity so they can access their resources and creativity by how we show up. The extent to which we cultivate our core is the extent to which we can inspire the people and communities we work with to bring forth their signature presence, innovations, and solutions. When we do the hard work of bringing presence to the conversations and the people respond with openness, we cultivate the ground for strong partnership (O'Neill, 2007).

## Burned-out changemaker to thriving co-creator

As an experienced leadership coach, transformational facilitator, and organizational development consultant, I am passionate about expanding well-being, partnership, and innovation so we can thrive, together. Like many of us over the last few years, I have been on a healing journey. I am a woman of Celtic ancestry who currently lives within the traditional lands of the Lekwungen-speaking people, known as Victoria, British Columbia, Canada. I was born in Monrovia, Liberia, Africa to parents of English, Welsh, and Scottish descent, and immigrated to Edmonton, Alberta, Canada, also known as Treaty 6 Territory, when I was five years old.

Working internally in the Canadian health care system for almost 15 years, I was dedicated to growing coaching and leadership cultures so we could deliver better health and care. One of my first mentors in transformational leadership development was an inspiring stand for "self as instrument". She taught me how walking the talk is a difference that makes a difference for cultivating trust, safety, engagement, and connection.

When I found myself trapped in a cycle of striving and exhaustion, my body rebelling against the way of working and signaling its distress through migraines, stress, and burnout, I was keen to figure it out. My inquiry led me to discover how the entrenched power dynamics, associated experience of conflict, and inflammation in my body are also the same dynamics that hinder societal change.

The process of truth and reconciliation between the settler and indigenous people in Canada has been illuminating the patterns of domination culture. One of my great grandfathers was the Colonel of the Royal Engineers, and the first Lieutenant-Governor of the Colony of British Columbia who played a role in the implementation of some of the strategies of systemic racism. The ancestral patterns of colonialism are woven into my DNA. Although intellectually I was fostering a coach approach and appreciative inquiry, it was unconsciously done on top of feelings of guilt and shame about fixing the part my ancestors played in the settler and indigenous dynamics. My focus on transforming the system, making it better, was ironically in the process colluding with the patterns of domination, the very patterns I was working to overcome.

The gift of seeing and dismantling these inner patterns is an on-going process of unlearning, healing, and connection. As I let go of my former role, I embraced becoming a yoga teacher. The ancient wisdom of Kundalini Yoga as taught by Yogi Bhajan opened me to experience the deeper truth and inherent value of who I am. Cultivating a daily practice of yoga and meditation has been instrumental in dissolving old patterns. Through my practice, I can see how my personal patterns are passed down through my ancestral lineages. As I embraced my shadows, I also accessed the gifts of my authentic self, including the ancient wisdom of my ancestors who help me remember who I am, and who we are, in our original nature as creators.

This mantra came through one of my morning practices, and combines the ancient wisdom of yoga with a Celtic song. I loved chanting it on walks, remembering who I am with every step.

*The earth is not outside of me.*
*I am nature.*
*Earth my body.*

*Water my blood.*
*Air my breath.*
*Fire my spirit.*
*I am nature.*
*Nature is me.*
*We are nature.*

Standing in this deeper truth, I come into right alignment and relationship with my value, my relations, and the earth. As I learn to love, trust, and respect myself, I am prioritizing self-care with a daily morning yoga and meditation practice. When I put love at the center of my day, I access new energy, creativity, and aliveness. I am more ready and available for transformation and change to happen through my interactions. When I remember who I am, I experience myself as an interconnected aspect of life.

In my journey toward wholeness, I am discovering the profound connection between my own well-being and the rhythms of life. Aligning my journey with the seasonal cycles and daily connection with the wisdom of the natural world has been a pathway to healing, connection, and co-creation. As I embrace my role of becoming someone who is a thriving changemaker, I am standing for the movement from fixing to creating, and in the possibility of a creation culture.

## Practitioner reflections on co-creating with the Seasonal Circles of Change to embody IDG being capacities

- *Integrity and authenticity:* "If I bring myself as a learner, I have to be willing to practice and know 'I am enough for this moment'. And if I just bring myself authentically, and if I can say, well, I do not actually know, let's be in it together. Something else is possible, because now you're not looking at me to fix it and the pressure of me fixing it isn't there."
- *Presence*: "It all begins internally. I can bring the depth of dismantling internal beliefs to the disruption of external change. I experience more flow, more integration, and a great deal of gratitude from a centered place of presence."
- *Self-awareness:* "I felt I have a oneness with nature and the earth. This is a way that I can get out of my head and into my heart, and my body can feel the differences of each season."
- *Openness and learning mindset:* "The seasonal framework is a structure that gives access to our experience in a way that can enhance awareness. It is not static. I can see how each domain aligns with the seasons naturally and it is organic, it can happen at any time in our journey."
- *Inner compass:* "Instead of thinking of change in a linear time, if we think of it connected to seasons, it helps us understand that change is cyclical."

# Winter – *thinking*

*The moment we choose to love, we begin to move against domination, against oppression. The moment we choose to love, we begin to move towards freedom, to act in ways that liberate ourselves and others. (Bell Hooks, 2001, p.108)*

The Celtic New Year begins on November 1. Samhain is a time when the cycle of birth, death, and rebirth is celebrated. As we move into darkness, we embrace the potential for renewal that dwells within this darkness. Darkness is the place where life comes from and is the great womb of creativity. As the world around us prepares to go into darkness and the animals prepare to hibernate, we can take our cue from the natural world and embrace rest and renewal.

The winter solstice is the time where the sun reaches its lowest point and there is a pause between stories before the return of the light. This is an opportunity to slow down and reflect, to turn inward and interrupt the momentum of beliefs, habits, and energy patterns that no longer serve us so we can clear the space for the new. Attending to the natural rhythms of winter calls us to unplug from the grind and gives us permission to slow down, to rest and to lie fallow so that we can cultivate conditions to nourish our gardens. When we allow ourselves to complete well and digest our experiences, the breakdowns and breakthroughs become fertilizer and compost for the next year's garden. As the light returns through the winter solstice, it calls us forth into our higher self, the bigger, expanded sense of self. This is the time to align with the light of the emerging intention, illuminating the path forward with possibility and the seeds that we want to plant.

Collectively, we are each responsible for our part in the greater whole. We are an aspect of the collective, a part of the system. Our individual voice, talents, gifts, and wisdom are an integral part of the solution. Each of us has a unique role and important part to play in the greater whole and our creations matter. We are part of the greater connected web of humans, connected in relationships through our familial, organizational, and societal systems. The earth can teach us about systems awareness. She is the ultimate creator of life, webs of connections, and relationships.

In change methodology, winter is the space of endings, and an opportunity to release, let go, and allow ourselves to move through the process of grief. We stand on the precipice of transformation, an opportunity to lean into uncertainty and be open to the life calling us forth. This is a good time to reflect and review all that we have received throughout the year and set intentions for our new year. When we complete well, we create the space for clarifying our vision for the new garden we want to grow.

## The most important thing

If you have not been reaching your goals, you are not alone.

If you have had some success, but are not where you want to be, you are not alone.

Most of us have a challenging relationship with change. For instance, we might begin the new year with great enthusiasm for what we are going to do differently yet inspiration wanes after a couple of months, losing interest in our theme or word of the year. Engaging and implementing change is where many of us lose momentum. Collectively, many of us share a vision of global action, then experience a big gap in our everyday lives. It can be easy to give up on a change that has barely begun. As a result, we are not reaching our goals.

*What if it is not your fault?*

Reflecting on your relationship with change, I invite you to consider if you might have had any of the following experiences:

- Overplanning and overthinking, needing to get it right before taking action. Being afraid of making mistakes. Getting stuck in *perfectionism*.
- Being too busy with multiple priorities. Time is spent putting out fires and reacting to what is happening in front of you. Having a *sense of urgency*.
- People, including yourself, not doing what they say they will do. Lack of alignment with organizational values and mission in the everyday experience of work. Prioritizing *quantity over quality*.
- Not saying what you are thinking to avoid hurting other people's feelings. People pleasing. Not having processes in place to engage with conflict and differences that matter. Being *afraid of open conflict*.
- Feeling like you have to do everything on your own. Not enough support and resources. Feeling alone in a culture of *individualism*.

When we relate to ourselves and our projects in this way, we can unknowingly perpetuate a pattern of domination. The problem is we keep making it about ourselves, that it is our fault, that we just need to be better and do better.

"It is not personal, it is the system," said a colleague who was educating me about patterns of systemic racism toward indigenous people in the Canadian health care system. She illuminated how the above-mentioned characteristics describe a culture where some people have power and control over others (Jones & Okun, 2001) and get in the way of psychological and cultural safety. These experiences are part of the collective soup we are swimming in – and are rooted in the cultural patterns of the colonial systems we have inherited.

Seeing ourselves in these patterns is a humbling experience, and an opportunity to practice vulnerability, self-compassion, and accountability. It is important to recognize there is nothing wrong with us. We do not need to be fixed. Collectively, we are being called to unlearn ways of thinking, seeing, and relating that cause the harm of one group over another. This is a collective healing journey inspiring us to let go of old ways that are no longer serving us so we can co-create the space for a new culture where all people can thrive, together.

One way to disrupt these patterns is to expand and include nature in the conversation. Nature shows us the path to thriving. When we connect with the larger field of wholeness, we can expand our perspective to include the part, the whole, and the greater whole. As individuals, we are each part of the collective, and the experience of each of us matters. Our deeper feelings, needs, and desires are connected to the greater field of life and gives us access to the source of engagement, creativity, and aliveness. When we connect with nature, we can expand our perspective and see from the larger whole. Including the voice of nature in our thinking can expand awareness and foster collaboration so we can clarify the direction forward, together.

The most important thing is to put love at the center. When I align my aliveness with the energy of nature, this is where I experience the greatest joy and success with my projects. The path to thriving calls for directing focus to the most important project designed to actualize my deepest yearnings. Doing what I say I will do builds trust, love, and respect and fosters accountability with myself and my community. The seasonal gateways become milestones and provide an accountability structure for the journey. Actualizing the deepest yearnings through the focus on one most important seasonal change project is a powerful pathway to co-create solutions that matter.

## Practitioner reflections on co-creating with the Seasonal Circles of Change to embody IDG thinking capacities

- *Perspective skills:* "The seasonal concept has really helped me in lying fallow. I am so driven to be in action, the winter concept of letting things rest has been really hugely impactful in giving myself permission to do that."
- *Sense-making:* "I was able to recognize patterns in myself, and have some great laughs about it. Scarcity addict is one pattern that came up in the conversation. *'Hi, I am a scarcity addict, it has been two hours since my last episode.'* This will never go away; it is one of the things I can now embrace as joyful practice."
- *Complexity awareness:* "I believe the stand of a thriving changemaker is that realizing I cannot do it all, and to do my part as the site of action, is deeply connecting to my gifts, my purpose, my awesomeness, as well as the greater whole."
- *Long-term orientation and visioning:* "Life is an infinite game. It is how to create a finite game in an infinite game of growth. The finite project helps to set a framework so we do not become overwhelmed by the infinite game we are playing."
- *Critical thinking:* "Permission to feel the seasons allows me to be in flow, to be out of Eurocentric prison of individuality. When I am in the flow of connecting with the seasons and when I have the sanctity of the circle – where community has come to be so important in my life – then I can be shaken out of my individual silo."

# Spring – *relating*

*No matter what gets done and how much is left undone, I am enough. It's going to bed at night thinking, Yes, I am imperfect and vulnerable and sometimes afraid, but that doesn't change the truth that I am also brave and worthy of love and belonging. (Brené Brown, 2010, p.1)*

Spring is the time for co-creating conditions for our garden to grow, including gathering the resources, support, and nourishment so we can plant the seeds we want to grow. This is the time of thawing old patterns and habits and cultivating the space to expand into the higher version of ourselves calling us forth.

Imbolc is the third gateway in the Celtic calendar and is the midwinter promise of new beginnings. Celebrated on February 1, it is a time of "the quickening": the seeds we conceived at winter solstice are beginning to emerge from the soil and dreams. New life is stirring and the potentiality of what is to come is being felt and enjoyed.

At the spring equinox, we are surrounded by new life. The word "equinox" is derived from Latin, meaning "equal night". The equinoxes are solar festivals in the Wheel of the Year and happen at the times of the year when day and night are approximately of equal length all over the world. The earth is bubbling with energy and blossoming new life. We may experience a renewal within ourselves too. We feel lighter than we did throughout the darker winter months, can see fresh possibilities and sense the creative potential in new ideas.

In leadership change methodology, this space is called the neutral zone, the space between trapezes when we have to let go of the old to grab hold of the new. The neutral zone is an invitation to lean into uncertainty, to embrace the anxiety, deepen our trust, and strengthen our presence. We begin to map out our garden, to choose the best locations for sun, water, and nourishment and plant placement. To harness the potential available, we focus on cultivating the conditions for our garden to grow. This might include renewing our perspective, implementing new systems, cultivating new relationships, and deepening our commitment to the seeds we are growing.

The small group is an important support structure for changemakers to thrive. As Peter Block says, "the small group is the unit of transformation and the container for the experience of belonging" (Block, 2008, p.178).

Connecting in small groups on a regular basis can be an opportunity to see, understand and release old ways of perceiving so we can cultivate new ways of relating. Building authentic relationships helps us to see, name, and heal the stories and experience of personal and collective trauma. Self-differentiation is the capacity to be separate and connected at the same time (Bushe, 2009). As changemakers, strengthening our self-differentiation is an important practice for cultivating the conditions for our intentions to grow.

## Awesome Blossoms

The Awesome Blossom Pod is a small group of three women who came together during the early days of the pandemic with the intention of supporting and empowering each other to shine our light. Over three years, we connected regularly, co-creating a transformative online peer coaching space that aligned with seasonal cycles. One member described her experience as a "connection of like hearts and different minds". The container supported her to move from a place of great stuckness, with feet in concrete not just in mud, to a place where she felt like she was walking on clouds because anything is possible. Initially feeling isolated and overwhelmed, she described the pod as a place of solace and acceptance where she could shed feelings of anxiety, replacing them with a sense of freedom and possibility. Collectively, the pod helped us reveal and heal women's relationship with women. It became a pocket of safety and acceptance where we could evolve the collective wound of the feminine from competition to collaboration. Through cultivating appreciation, compassion, and care, we liberated our wisdom, creativity, and authentic expression. We embraced collective solution finding, understanding that each person's unique skills and qualities filled the gaps for others, creating a harmonious whole. For us, the pod became a garden of "awesome blossoms", where celebrating our journey and appreciating each other for the gifts of our authentic selves created the space to bloom in our beauty.

## Practitioner reflections on co-creating with the Seasonal Circles of Change to embody IDG relating capacities

– *Connectedness*: "Before, there was disconnection from natural rhythms, from knowing you are part of those natural rhythms. Now, through discovering the connection with the seasons, I am becoming aware of what is already happening and its influence with us."
– *Empathy and Compassion:* "Connection to where we are in the seasons has given me inspiration at different times of the year. It is such a beautiful way to anchor myself in the present and find something that is common between myself and others. It anchors me automatically in community with others."
– *Appreciation:* "Appreciate the space to speak openly, not to have to censor myself and this is good. If I censor myself, what you get is a colonial, edited, culturally accepted response, we don't go anywhere we don't move as much. So much is possible in circle together: movement, places to go, creativity, spontaneity, accountability, witnessing."

- *Humility:* "We are not isolated individuals, it is our connection to source, to divinity, to connect with the earth and the sky, the masculine and the feminine. Experiencing now instead a sense of belonging, of connection to the future and to the ancestors and what they have to teach us."
- *Connectedness:* "I'm also taking away a stronger connection to nature, and the idea of learning more about change by learning from nature and just seeing change more in nature. I think there's a comfort for me in that. She's a great teacher."

# Summer – *acting*

> *Liberation is a praxis: the action and reflection of men and women upon their world in order to transform it. (Paulo Freire, 1970, p.51)*

Summer is a time for growing what we want more of and removing the weeds we do not want. It is a time of implementation, for learning by doing so we can be in adaptive action. The bright half of the year ushers in the sensorial season of blossoming, aliveness, fullness, risk, and opening. Beltane on May 1 celebrates the time of great fertility and abundance.

The summer solstice celebrates the light, a time when we are graced with extended hours of daylight and shorter nights. It is a joyous occasion, where we celebrate the abundant growth and blossoming of the seeds that were sown during the depths of winter. It represents the peak of the seasonal cycle. From this point onward, there is a gentle decline in the light, and subtle signs of the approaching autumn and darkness begin to emerge. It invites us to harness the vitality of the season through the radiant sun, the vivid hues of nature, and the abundance of experiencing each moment to the fullest.

From a leadership perspective, summer is an opportunity to engage with the flow of life in adaptive action. Deepening into our daily practice supports us to harness the vitality of the radiant sun and the abundance to experience each moment to the fullest. The warmth beckons us to prioritize play, exploration, and adventure. This is the time to show up for new possibilities and experience the new life by taking action, learning, and practicing humility. In our gardens, we are actively cultivating what we want more of, pruning the branches, and weeding out what we do not want. This is a time to show up, water our gardens, enjoy the energy of the sun, and cultivate the blooms we want to see. Where we put our energy now is what will flourish and be harvested in the fall.

## The IDG Vancouver Island Co-Inspire Hub

The purpose of the IDG Vancouver Island Co-Inspire Hub is to live the IDGs together and innovate toward the SDGs so we can co-create thriving communities. We are a dynamic community that quickly grew from three to 22 members in just one year, reflecting a yearning for new ways of being human together. The online meetings align with the eight seasonal gateways of the Celtic Wheel of the Year. The group's agreement to living the IDGs together guide our interactions so we can co-create conditions for thriving community. Using an adaptive action approach, these gatherings enable members to engage with change as a source of creativity and possibility.

The hub's journey began in the fall of 2022 when a couple of local changemakers connected to explore what might be possible. The metaphor of the garden is central to our organizing principles, with members actively listening to the needs of the community to facilitate growth and flourishing. Through our shared inquiry into the individual and collective work worth doing, the intention of our hub became clear: to co-inspire each other to do our work, separately and collectively. We inspire each other to embody the IDGs and to cultivate partnerships based in abundance, generosity, and reciprocity so we can innovate, build, and create. By aligning our efforts with seasonal cycles, we are cultivating an environment where more light can shine, more water can renew, and opportunities for growth can create solutions that matter.

## Practitioner reflections on co-creating with the Seasonal Circles of Change to embody IDG acting capacities

- *Courage*: "Trust and patience to slow down and align with the cycles of change. To focus on one thing at a time reduces the sense of overwhelm knowing that I am part of a bigger picture."
- *Perseverance*: "Being able to step out into the seasonal cycle, the universal cycles, and then say 'Okay, I can see where I am right now'."
- *Creativity*: "Finding congruence in summertime, when the spirits seem to be high for many people, caught up in abundance, productivity, and outward energy."
- *Optimism*: "I'm excited about the possibility of bringing in the seasonal cycles more into my therapeutic practice."
- *Perseverance*: "It's a fabulous sustainability structure. With many of my coaching clients, we meet every six weeks with the seasonal cycles to check in about where they are at in relationship with their intention."

# Autumn – *collaborating*

*Knowing that you love the earth changes you, activates you to defend and protect and celebrate. But when you feel that the earth loves you in return, that feeling transforms the relationship from a one-way street into a sacred bond. (Robin Wall Kimmerer, 2013, p.125)*

Autumn is a time of harvesting the bounty and abundance. Gathering in community to celebrate. Traditionally, people embraced the richness of the harvest, celebrating the triumph over darkness and relishing the abundant fruits of victory. This season celebrates community togetherness and reciprocity. Harvest festivals are common to many different cultures around the world and are traditionally held to celebrate the bounty of the earth at this time of the year and to give thanks for the generosity of nature.

At the autumn equinox we are celebrating the abundance of the harvest and the bounty it has given us, as well as a time to prepare for the darker, colder months ahead. We become aware of the need for balance in our lives as we notice the balance between the light and the dark at this time of the year. This special celebration is the perfect time to take stock of our own "harvest". We may wish to consider the garden we have been growing and the projects we have been working on during the last year since the spring. We can then choose to learn from the things that have not worked out, celebrate our achievements, and give thanks for the abundance in our lives and the things that are now bringing us contentment and fulfillment. The autumn equinox is a time of perfect balance between the light and the dark, the masculine and feminine. This is a time to celebrate the fruits of the year's effort in community with others. We shift our focus from the effort of doing to acknowledge the process of connection through the relational field. We bring our attention to celebrate the reciprocity of giving and receiving.

From a leadership perspective, coming into wholeness and alignment is strengthened through relationships with other committed changemakers. In the light, community can become a source of learning, humility, connection, creativity, and celebration. In the shadow, the differences between us can show up as polarities and conflict. As changemakers, how we relate to conflict is a difference that makes a difference. Conflict can be seeing something wrong, differences that need to be changed or fixed. Alternatively, conflict can be seen as illuminating differences that matter. Fostering conditions for growth, renewal and mutual learning, requires a new form of relationship, one of generative engagement (Eoyang & Holladay, 2013, p.171).

Expanding our awareness to include the creative, messy and generative growth of nature, gives us permission to slow down so we can go fast. Nature reminds us who we are by aligning us with the one most important thing we all have in common. When we put nature at the center of collaboration, we change the conversation. All of a sudden, we can sense into the greater whole, let go of silos and personal agendas, and listen for the wisdom living between multiple perspectives.

When I feel stuck, this personal mantra helps to ground me so I can align with the greater good.

*One thing we all have in common is the earth.*
*We are an interdependent web of life.*
*We are nature.*
*Nature is us.*

Each of us brings gift to the greater whole required to complete the mandala of our human experience. Celebrating the harvest, the light and the dark, is an opportunity to cultivate gratitude for the changemakers who walk alongside us and harness the diversity of community so we can innovate toward personal and planetary thriving.

## Power podding

In the summer of 2016, a small group of multigenerational women embarked on a transformative journey by forming a "Sister Goddess Circle" in Victoria, British Columbia, Canada. Originating from a small circle of women dedicated to cultivating more joy, creativity, and love, our group evolved into the "Power Pod" when our focus expanded to building our thriving businesses.

Harnessing the power of seasonal cycles, our meetings became more frequent, offering a space for celebration, support, and accountability. This circle emerged as a sanctuary where we listened deeply, confronted our shadow selves and learned from multiple perspectives. By aligning with our core intentions and evolving our patterns of victimization and domination, we fostered an environment for genuine growth and change.

Our commitment to embodying our essence through actualizing our unique purpose led us to embrace the IDGs. The framework provides a way to align and collaborate so we can co-create conditions for thriving local economies. Despite the fears and challenges we have faced, such as fear of being visible, marginalized, labeled "woo-woo", and confronting historical traumas, we persist with our seasonal gatherings and mastermind sessions as a source of renewal, connection, and support. We recognize the need to heal the collective wounds of the feminine and to restore sacred partnerships between the feminine and masculine energies. By leaning into conflict as a source of innovation and growth, our Power Pod structure enables us to navigate our individual and collective growth edges. Our circle has become a place where we acknowledge our shadow selves, embrace our fears, and connect with nature as an integral part of our journey. In doing so, we are reclaiming our power, honoring our ancestral lineages, and connecting with the wisdom of our bodies. We hope our story inspires the transformative potential of small peer coaching groups and the enduring power of connection, healing, and co-creation.

## Practitioner reflections on co-creating with the Seasonal Circles of Change to embody IDG collaborating capacities

– *Mobilization skills:* "Being part of a community, not being alone, belonging, creates common connection. Let's just acknowledge the difficult time we are in globally right now, and this anchors us in something that is common so that we can come together in love, with harmony and acceptance."
– *Communication skills*: "The power of the circle, it has been its own entity sitting at the table with us. The circle itself has mediated tensions for us. It has enabled a frame that has provided balance in our dialogue and brought a gentleness and equanimity and equalizing of power to our relationships."
– *Co-creation skills*: "In the last three years, we have all had these experiences, but they were different at different times. We were not all in the same stage, in the same cycle, in the same time. We have all felt pain, anxiety, joy, and fear. Through the witnessing, it was simultaneously accepting and where the love comes in, accepting what it is."
– *Trust:* "There's something really wonderful about not looking to somebody else's culture and sort of co-opting, but rather looking to my own, which is truly in my bones, and literally right and owning that."
– *Inclusive mindset and intercultural competence:* "I am looking for ways to connect my heritage with the practices of indigenous people here. I hope sharing knowledge and combining the wisdom from the two traditions will result in something more beneficial to all."

# Conclusion

*We all have stories within us. Sometimes we hold them gingerly, sometimes desperately, sometimes as gently as an infant. It is only by sharing our stories, by being strong enough to take a risk – both in the telling and the asking – that we make it possible to know, recognize and understand each other.* (Richard Wagamese, 2021, p.134)

Every time we connect and share our stories, we contribute to the co-creation of the humanity's collective story. Each of us is a thread in the great tapestry of life. When we gather in circles, our unique gifts, experience and wisdom become woven into a fabric of deeper connection, greater clarity and expanded care.

The Seasonal Circles of Change offers a framework for reconnecting with ourselves, our community and the earth. These natural cycles provide a structure for sustainable growth and transformation, enabling us to align inner awareness with outer action. As we embrace a conscious partnership with nature, the personal journey becomes a profound act of collective healing. When we align change projects with natural cycles, we access the energy to co-create innovative solutions in harmony with the earth.

The Seasonal Circles of Change is a path of practice to embody our leadership, innovate toward global goals and co-create thriving community. We become the change strategy by co-creating the change we want to see. When changemakers thrive, we model the way by sharing our stories. When we walk together, in seasonal circles of connection, we co-create conditions for a groundswell of personal and planetary thriving.

# References

Bhajan, Y. (2013). *The aquarian teacher: Level one teacher book.* Kundalini Research Institute. Santa Cruz, New Mexico.

Block, P. (2008). *Community: The structure of belonging.* Berrett-Koehler.

Bushe, G.R. (2009). *Clear leadership: Sustaining real collaboration and partnership at work (rev. ed.).* Nicholas Brealey.

Brown, B. (2010). *The gifts of imperfection: Your guide to a wholehearted life.* Hazelden Publishing.

Campbell, J., & Moyers, B. (1988). *The Power of Myth.* Doubleday.

Demers, L. & Orlesky, R. (2013). *Authentic to the core.* Demers Group.

Eoyang, G. H. & Holladay, R. J. (2013). *Adaptive action: Leveraging uncertainty in your organization.* Stanford University Press.

Freire, P. (2005). *Pedagogy of the Oppressed.* The Continuum International Publishing Group. New York, New York.

Hooks, B. (2001). *All about love: New visions.* HarperCollins.

Jones, K. & Okun, T. (2001). *White supremacy culture. Dismantling racism: A workbook from Social change groups.* Change Work.

Kimmerer, R.W. (2013). *Braiding sweetgrass: Indigenous wisdom, scientific knowledge, and the teachings of plants.* Milkweed Editions.

Marya, R. & Patel, R. (2021). *Inflamed: Deep medicine and the anatomy of injustice.* Farrar, Straus and Giroux. New York, New York.

O'Neill, M. B. (2007). *Executive coaching with backbone and heart: A systems approach to engaging leaders with their challenges.* John Wiley & Sons.

Speth, J.G., cited in Ives, C.D., Freeth, R., & Fischer, J. (2019). *Inside-Out Sustainability: The Neglect of Inner Worlds.* Sustainability Science, 14(3), p.8.

Scharmer, O. (2021). *Ten lessons from Covid for stepping into the decade of transformation.* resilience. *Resilience.* https://www.resilience.org/stories/2021-06-10/ten-lessons-from-covid-for-stepping-into-the-decade-of-transformation/ [Accessed March 30, 2024].

UN DESA. (2023). *The Sustainable Development Goals report 2023: Special edition.* UN DESA. https://unstats.un.org/sdgs/report/2023/

Wagamese, R. (2021). *What Comes From Spirit.* Drew Hayden Taylor. British Columbia, Canada.

Ariolino Andrade Azevedo and Mônica Barroso

# Chapter 12
# Systems Leadership: An inner and outer journey in the Brazilian Amazon rainforest

**Abstract:** Through an immersive experience in the different realities that coexist in the heart of the Brazilian Amazon rainforest, a group of family businesspeople could experience emotional, relational, and systemic skills that allowed participants to challenge themselves for a more powerful, creative, and conscious action, aligned with contemporary challenges. During the one-week journey, the group deeply experienced inner skills for greater connection with oneself, with one another, and with the greater system of which they are part, as an invitation and a path to greater well-being, interconnectedness, and sense of purpose. The methodological structure of the FBN Learning Journey Amazônia was inspired by the Family Business Network (FBN) core values, the Inner Development Goals (IDGs), other systemic approaches such as Theory U, and the facilitators' joint multidisciplinary repertoire of more than 20 years' experience in facilitating learning and transformative journeys for corporate audiences in Brazil, both in corporate and natural settings. This chapter presents how the IDGs served as a conceptual and inspirational guide for designing and facilitating the journey, the lessons learned during and after the experience, and the potential immediate impacts of such an endeavor, including individuals better prepared to deal with complexity and uncertainty, increased self-awareness and perspective taking, strengthened notion of interdependence and systemic thinking, improvement in the quality of relationships for the articulation of collaborative environments, and a greater sense of purpose, well-being, and belonging to the human community.

**Keywords:** leadership inner development, systems thinking, sustainable living systems, nature power, transformative learning

## Introduction

In August 2023, a group of Brazilian family businesspeople embarked for Manaus (state capital of Amazonas, Brazilian Amazon) as participants of the unprecedented FBN (Family Business Network) Learning Journey Amazônia.[1] Through an immersive experience in the different realities that coexist in the heart of the Brazilian Amazon rainforest, the group could experience emotional, relational, and systemic skills that

---

1 Find out more about FBN on their website: https://www.fbn-i.org/

https://doi.org/10.1515/9783111337913-013

allowed participants to challenge themselves for a more powerful, creative, and conscious action, aligned with contemporary challenges. During the one-week journey, the group deeply experienced inner skills for greater connection with oneself, with one another, and with the greater system of which they are part of, as an invitation and a path to greater well-being, interconnectedness, agency, and sense of purpose.

The methodological structure of the FBN Learning Journey Amazônia was inspired by the FBN core values, the Inner Development Goals (IDGs), other systemic approaches such as Theory U, and the facilitators' joint multidisciplinary repertoire of more than 20 years' experience in facilitating learning and transformative journeys for corporate audiences in Brazil, both in corporate and natural settings.

The journey was designed based on the realization that, increasingly, inner skills to deal with complex global and ecosystemic issues have been an essential ingredient to face the challenges that are being presented in life and in business. In this sense, FBN dared to offer its associates a different development approach aimed at advancing sustainability guidelines, practices, and the positive impact of their businesses, based on the inner and outer realities experienced. The experience aimed to take participants out of their common place and confront them with experiences of deep connection with themselves, with others, and with nature.

From five-star hotels to community-based accommodation structures, from air-conditioned rooms to the scorching heat of an Amazon region just about to experience the biggest drought in recent history, from the challenges of family business groups to grassroots start-ups and ventures focused on the forest-based bioeconomy, this was a journey that proposed a qualitative leap of participants' ecosystems vision based on a paradigm shift and a new look at themselves, their surroundings, and planetary issues.

The FBN Learning Journey Amazônia was custom designed for FBN associates searching for:
- inner tools to drive systemic changes in their businesses;
- personal and professional development among peers;
- inspiration to make a difference, reconciling economic results with a sustainable logic of doing business;
- an immersive and challenging learning experience that provides an emotional repertoire to deal with complexity;
- connection with other family businesses based in Manaus;
- reconnecting with the family's histories and the essence of the founders.

Just as we invited the participants, or in Portuguese "*jornadeiros*", to come along, we invite you, dear reader, to dive into this learning journey with us. The chapter structure will follow the chronological order of events, from the first insight to the post-journey effects.

The intention of writing this chapter is to both record and share the behind-the-scenes of the experience, that is, how the IDGs served as a conceptual and inspirational guide for designing and facilitating the journey, and to share the day-to-day highlights of the journey based on the five IDG dimensions, testimonials from the participants, and quotes that inspired this highly emotional and impactful journey. We also share the lessons learned during and after the experience along the chapter. What we can already anticipate is that the journey had significant potential immediate impacts on several levels:

– individuals better prepared to deal with complexity and uncertainty;
– gain in self-awareness and perspective taking;
– innovation potential based on the notion of interdependence and systemic thinking;
– improvement in the quality of relationships for the articulation of collaborative environments;
– greater sense of purpose, well-being, and belonging to the human community.

Finally, we intend to share the power of collaboration in making experiences such as this one come true, as it relies upon a diversity of skills, experiences, and connections. The journey was made possible thanks to joint efforts between the FBN, the participants who opened themselves for an unconventional learning experience, the FBN host business families in Manaus, local NGOs (Fundação Amazônia Sustentável[2] and Idesam[3]) who are true powerhouses for nature-based innovation and socio-environmental development, among others.

# The insight

The FBN has traditionally promoted learning journeys in various parts of the globe as a strategy to bring its members together in inspirational settings, fostering the exchange of ideas and experiences among peers. In Brazil, previous learning journeys also integrated FBN conferences and meetings, usually taking place in corporate environments. But Silvia Pedrosa, FBN Brazil's executive director, wanted to go beyond, offering an experience that could enable family business leaders to connect with the current global challenges at a deeper level, stretching their comfort zone.

In 2020, several FBN Brazil associates and advisors came together to co-create FBN Vision 2025. The project began with an alignment of values and behaviors, followed by the review and adjustment of its purpose. From there, it evolved into the development of a shared vision of the group and the desired objectives for the future of FBN. Once they were all aligned with the future ambition of the association, the actions that the governing body should implement in the following years were outlined.

2 Find out more about FAS on their website: https://fas-amazonia.org/
3 Find out more about Idesam on their website: https://idesam.org/

About two years after the start of the Vision 2025 project, much of it carried out amid the social isolation caused by the COVID-19 crisis, the need arose for a review to monitor the progress of the plan that had been made and to determine the areas that would need more attention. Thus, in November 2022, a face-to-face meeting was held with some FBN associates and board members, where everyone was able to observe the progress of actions towards the desired objectives.

Taking advantage of the end-of-year atmosphere, a lunch meeting was organized between Silvia Pedrosa and Ariolino Andrade Azevedo, advisor to FBN and responsible for leading the process of defining the 2025 vision, to celebrate the progress made up until the end of the year and, mainly, to define a specific focus for the objectives that would be defined for the following year, aligned with the Vision 2025.

At the restaurant, one dish on the menu caught their attention: tucupi risotto with smoked pirarucu, a typically Amazonian delicacy that combines the flavor of tucupi, a broth extracted from wild cassava root that is decanted, separated from the starch (gum) and liquid, and the pirarucu, one of the largest freshwater fish in Brazil. The surprise of this exotic dish served in a restaurant in São Paulo brought up something unknown to both of them. Both Silvia and Ariolino had their family roots in the Amazon.

Between one bite and another of this exotic and delicious dish, the idea came up of combining the experience of a learning journey with an immersive experience in the Amazon, the largest tropical forest in the world, full of stories and biodiversity that is still little known, and at the same time so important and strategic for the planet's regeneration.

Before the end of dessert, both had outlined some of the characteristics that the experience should contain. Of the recently revisited purpose, the highlight was to inspire business families to strengthen their relationships and their businesses and evolve over the generations in order to build a sustainable future. From the values, they looked for some behaviors that this experience should contain, such as: being pleasant and relaxed; be fun – because families that play together stay together; be a space for listening without judgement, but with empathy and acceptance; and encourage the exchange of knowledge.

By the time they were having their coffee, the idea for the project was already outlined. They would involve two associates with extensive experience on the FBN board, both from business families in Manaus, so that they could contribute their respective points of view on the experience that was being prepared, and also host the group for a dinner in their homes where they could share their experiences and challenges of making business in the Amazon region. There was still a lack of someone to help with designing the trip itinerary, defining and co-facilitating the activities that would be experienced, and synchronicity was once again present.

About a month before this lunch, Ariolino had had a meeting with Mônica Barroso, a person who had known him for a long time and who, like him, was coordinating an IDG hub in Brazil, he the Alinhar Hub and she the EcoSocial Hub – both pioneering hubs just as the global movement was starting to gain traction in the world.

At this meeting, both reflected on possible activities and strategies to communicate and engage more people in the IDG movement, and one of the possibilities would be an event close to nature, with Mônica sharing that she already had extensive experience facilitating group learning journeys in the Amazon region. Mônica's name was added to the people who should be heard to check whether this idea generated at this lunch would prove feasible to become a real and concrete experience. Everyone was heard and readily agreed to dive in so that this idea could become a reality.

One of the success factors of this endeavor was certainly the way it all began, and the collaboration, trust, and companionship among the co-facilitators and supporters, building a sense of community within the team from the start.

The beginning of this immersion project in the Amazon has much of what Goethe brings in one of his thoughts: "Whatever you can do, or dream you can do, begin it! Boldness contains genius, power, and magic. Begin it now." The learning journey had already started!

*Reflection question: Based on your own experience in creating or joining new initiatives, can you recall the role of synchronicity (non-intentional situations and encounters) in making them happen?*

## Pre-journey

The design of the learning journey involved a lot of reflection and dialogue with different stakeholders and among the core team, including the FBN host families based in Manaus. During this phase, important decisions were taken considering a degree of ambition in terms of providing the group of participants with an unconventional real-life experience, such as the controversial two nights sleeping in a hammock on board of a regional Amazonian boat.

In parallel, efforts to engage potential participants started taking place, both during FBN events and via one-to-one interactions. At first, the learning journey attracted a lot of attention, and we received no less than 50 expressions of interest, of which ten converted into formal applications. In the team's view, it represented a first achievement in terms of bringing a first level of awareness, as the decision process entailed self-questioning (Is the money worth it?), facing personal insecurities (Will I be able to sleep in a hammock without air conditioning and next to people I might not know?), and an awareness of priorities due to conflicting agendas, among others.

As we reached the minimum number of participants to make the project viable, the learning journey team dove into the design of the journey companions, namely a travel kit composed of a travel diary, a backpack with a water bottle, a raincoat, color crayons, a nametag, and a book that served as a collective reflection companion along the journey: *Ideas to Postpone the End of the World* by the indigenous leader and thinker Ailton Krenak. One core value of the team was the critical role of design, beauty, and art as a learning component. Also, the decision to design the learning journey based on a combination of the IDGs and Theory U was based on the core objectives of the experience, which included an integrative approach in terms of assessing multiple intelligence channels (mind, heart, hands) during the journey's activities, which both frameworks offer in a beautifully complementary way (see Table 12.1).

In order to bring the awareness of the learning journey backbone framework to the participants, a conceptual introduction on the IDGs and a visual representation of the learning journey combining the IDG dimensions and the Theory U journey was included in the first pages of the travel diary. Each day was designed inspired by the IDG dimensions and the Theory U stages. For example, going down the U starting from its left side we included reflections and activities related to the *being* and *thinking* IDG dimensions, until we reached the bottom of the U deepening the *relating* dimension, at the heart of the forest during the days spent navigating between the riverine communities. Back to the city of Manaus, the *collaborating* and *acting* dimensions were more intentionally explored, as a form of preparing the participants to go back to their daily lives integrating the new learnings and experiences. Thus, given the strong identification between the Theory U stages and IDG dimensions, we applied this combined framework in a very impactful and successful way.

**Table 12.1:** Theory U Stages and Corresponding IDGs.

| Theory U | IDGs |
|---|---|
| Co-initiating | Being |
| Co-sensing | Thinking |
| Presencing | Relating |
| Co-creating | Collaborating |
| Co-evolving | Acting |

Source: Scharmer (2018); Inner Development Goals (n.d.).

The cultural exchange during the preparation phase between FBN team and local partners was a discovery journey in itself while crafting the budget, making reservations, pondering, and deciding on the journey's activities. The notion of time, for instance, is quite different between people who live in hectic big urban centers such as São Paulo, and those who live in the immensity of the forest, dependent on riverways and climate factors. Language is another factor, as the Amazon region has its very specific terms, especially when it comes to food and nature, showing a much stronger indigenous influence.

Also, preparation materials and a checklist of what to include in the luggage were shared with the participants, who in their majority would have their first experience in the Amazon region, which even for Brazilians from the developed Southeast means a significant intercultural experience. Below is an excerpt from the travel diary text:

> *Here's an invitation: record your experience! Be inspired by the ancient naturalist travellers who travelled the Amazon 200 years ago and wrote down all their impressions about the place, the people, the aromas, and flavors. If you want, you can even try drawings and paintings of the moments and landscapes that impress you the most!*

During the online meeting with the group of participants, the facilitators created a safe space where expectations were shared in an open and courageous way. The group journey had started!

***Reflection question: When planning your own learning experiences, what elements are important for you? Could art, nature, and beauty play a role?***

# The learning journey

The meeting point was at the beautiful and well-located Villa Amazônia hotel in Manaus, where the first encounters and discomforts could be experienced, starting with the heat, as Manaus was going through a particular heat wave, with average temperatures of above 40°C. The first dinner together was a moment of joy and celebration around a beautiful table in a private dining room, where some deep conversations could already arise, good laughs had, and new flavors tasted. Before going to bed, the participants found a welcome letter with the best wishes for the journey:

> *We hope you take advantage of the next few days to delve into deep dialogues with yourself, with others and with the world, and thus gain a new understanding of your role as an individual, entrepreneur, and planetary citizen – "I went to the forest because I wanted to live deliberately, to face only the essential facts of life, and see if I could not learn what it had to teach, and not, when I died, discover that I had not lived." — Thoreau (1854)*

On the next day, the first breakfast together counted with new arrivals, now the group was complete.

The learning journey was designed and facilitated in such a way that all five IDG dimensions were touched upon – implicitly and explicitly. Aiming for a balance between external (excursions, site visits) and internal experiences (facilitated and non-facilitated reflection moments among the group) as much as possible, we started and finished each day with certain rituals that enabled space for self-reflection, sharing among the group participants, and a deeper elaboration of the external experiences.

One of the daily rituals was the reading circle of the *Ideas to Postpone the End of the World* book, included in the participants' travel kits. Every morning after breakfast we spared some time to read a section of this short but impactful book aloud, taking turns. By the end of the journey, we had developed a common vocabulary and metaphors about the global challenges from an indigenous (and rather systemic) perspective, in addition to the provoking statements from the book that became food for thought while interacting with riverine communities and nature. We also encouraged the participants to write and/or draw in their diaries in their spare time, and at times we just let them *be*. We were intentional in making the *being* dimension a crosscutting experience along the journey, helping the participants to maintain a connection with who they were and why they were there, allowing themselves to live that experience. Being in nature, immersed in the powerful Amazon forest, brought an impressive sense of presence rarely experienced in daily life, according to the participants' reflections and behaviors. At the end of each day, we had an open space to share impressions, thoughts, and feelings, which boosted the degree of self-awareness about the learning journey as it evolved.

The *thinking* dimension was also largely present as new knowledge, concepts, and inputs were made available to the group before and during the contrasting experiences they had while visiting historical sites, the host families' homes, the NGO offices with insightful presentations, and the traditional riverine communities with their entrepreneurial spirit, ancestral stories, and ventures. The cognitive thinking stimulated discussions about the past selves of the participants, reconnecting them with their ancestors, their family businesses, bringing a heightened awareness of where they came from and what their potential roles within their family and business ecosystem. A sense of pride of their ancestors and business pioneers/founders was made present in various moments, as most of them came to Brazil as immigrants in harsh life conditions, something often forgotten by the younger generations who have never needed to deal with such difficulties and hardships.

The *relating* pillar was especially strong, as human connections happened in different dimensions along the journey. Once the group stepped into the boat which would become their home for the following two days, a new perspective emerged in terms of being and relating. Suddenly a strong and deep sense of community emerged. We were there all together as humans, not as businesspeople, board members, or consultants anymore, but as children who had grown up and were heading for a great adventure into the unknown surrounded by water and forest. Our hammocks were hanging side by side, so we had new neighbors to rely on. Our belongings were exposed, bathrooms and meals were collective. We were a community sharing unique experiences together. Entering the forest was a magical moment, as it always is when confronting ourselves with the grandness of the Amazon rainforest. And each interaction with the local inhabitants were as grand as the forest, as they carried as much ancestral wisdom as the forest, as the following two examples illustrate.

## The rubber tapper who turned into a tour guide

The group's first site visit was a boat trip to the unique Rubber Museum. The Museu do Seringal, as it is called in Portuguese, is located a 30-minute boat ride out of Manaus up the Negro River.

This outdoor museum showcases how the rubber boom of the late nineteenth and early twentieth centuries impacted the lives of the workers as well as those who were making money from them. While today it is a serene "jungle camp" as a working plantation, it would have been a working hell for the rubber workers.

This museum was recreated as a set for the 2002 movie *A Selva* ('*The Jungle*') and showcases the harsh living and working conditions of the workers as well as the opulent lifestyles of the rubber barons. The rubber workers, or *seringueiros*, were treated at best like servants and at worst like slaves. Most of their earnings went back to the rubber barons who charged the rubber tappers for food, supplies, tools, transportation, and just about anything they needed. If the rubber tappers tried to grow their own food, hunt, or fish, they were either beaten or killed. The museum has a cemetery on-site where those who died were buried. The workers would work 12–18 hour days in the heat of the jungle, living in huts and working like slaves to only become more indebted to the rubber bosses.

This museum is filled with fascinating artifacts from the rubber industry's dark past. But the big highlight of the visit was our guide, "Seu Antônio" (fictitious name), a former rubber tapper in his 80s. He shared the harshest experiences without losing the smile on his face, as he chooses to be grateful for having survived, raised his family, and for having the opportunity to share his stories while making a living out of them. His positive attitude towards life's difficulties was highly touching and inspiring, as was his courage and wisdom shared in an incredible light and playful manner. The intimacy generated during this encounter was undoubtedly one of the factors that promoted the intimacy that the group of participants was to gain in the coming days. Seu Antônio's words and messages stayed with us during the whole journey.

## The forest logger who became a socio-environmental entrepreneur

The story of Roberto, born and raised in the Tumbira community, today located within the Rio Negro Sustainable Development Reserve (RDS), about 80 km from Manaus, is part of the third generation of deforesters and only managed to break this chain thanks to an opportunity. He learned to walk in the woods with his indigenous grandfather, and accompanied him on his walks through the forest, planting corn and cassava and arrow fishing, until his death.

His childhood was short, as at the age of 12 he also began his career as a logger, riding a chainsaw that, when filled with fuel, weighed 16 kilos. After 25 years "chopping wood", he is now the manager of a guesthouse in the community where he was born. It welcomes and guides tourists, students from private schools belonging to the Rio and São Paulo elite, teachers, and university students through the forest. "Tourism is an outlet for the development of any community because it brings the opportunity to meet people and exchange knowledge," celebrates Roberto.

The former deforester became a defender of the forest when he had the opportunity to meet people who valued his knowledge of the forest. "When people like the information I have to share, I feel very proud. I know all this here and I didn't value anything. I see people excited here in this forest listening to what I learned in life and I just had that look of destruction in my eyes."

Roberto sees tourism as a rich opportunity to mix worlds. "The young people here in the community also feel valued by tourism. Sometimes young people from the southeast come here who are children of rich, even famous people, and learn from the *caboclinhos* [local expression for the young local children and youth] here who have never even been to Manaus."

The conversation with Roberto was also one of the highlights of the learning journey, as he proved radical change to be possible. Roberto's success story is also a story of collaboration and dialogue, as it only became possible due to the efforts of the Fundação Amazônia Sustentável after the establishment of the RDS, which prevented the local populations from carrying out illegal activities such as forest logging, leaving them without any means to sustain their livelihoods. Also, Roberto's stories about his deep knowledge and relationship with the forest as a living being led the group to a place of transcendence.

As these two examples show, the power and beauty of diversity was an important realization during those deep and authentic encounters with riverine communities, inspired by Krenak during our reading circles:

> *We are definitely not the same, and it is wonderful to know that each one of us here is different from the other, like constellations. The fact that we can share this space, that we are traveling together, does not mean that we are equal; it means exactly that we are capable of attracting each other through our differences, which should guide our life script. Having diversity, not humanity with the same protocol. Because until now this has just been a way to homogenize and take away our joy in being alive. (Krenak, 2020)*

According to the testimonial of one of the participants: "Harmony happened naturally [among the group], even though I did not know half the people, and in the end, we looked like a bunch of teenagers who had known each other for a long time! It is a memory that I will forever carry in my heart."

As another participant put it: "We all got along well, very quickly there was an intimacy that meant we always had a great deal of fun and we were always very together and united. This part was truly wonderful!"

Having facilitated numerous learning journeys in forest settings over the past 20 years or so, Mônica has observed and experienced for herself the power of natural settings in creating such profound human connections in very short periods of time. She has often experienced some uncertainty about potentially problematic partici- pants during the preparation phase, but a completely different result during the expe- rience, where the power of the group becomes stronger than the individual action, or individualistic attempts. After experiencing this phenomenon several times, Mônica found her own explanation, according to which, the power of a group when con- nected to nature will not allow individualistic forces to arise. It's as if the notion of being in nature permeates each individual, turning them into part of a collective and collaborative whole, allowing a natural connection to the human collective essence. Interestingly, some clarity of thinking and feeling comes with this "being in nature" state – giving individuals the permission to think, feel, and act in ways that they wouldn't otherwise, but which feels liberating and absolutely natural. For this reason, it is not always easy to go back to hectic urban life, after realizing how much "non- sense" has been normalized and having to engage with such contradictions with a re- newed sense of self.

Collaborating was a natural consequence of the deep level of connections estab- lished during the learning journey. As we lost sight of time and space ("How long have we been here?", "We have experienced so much in such a brief period!"), the group started behaving in collaborative ways as we became part of one interdependent system, or ecosystem. We were nature. Helping each other, caring for each other, trusting each other, learning from each other became the rule rather than the exception. One extraor- dinarily strong aspect of the group was a playful attitude that permeated the whole jour- ney and a sense of belonging that became stronger each day. Intergenerational ex- changes were also one of the high points, as we had one younger participant (in her 20s) while the other participants were mainly in their 40s and 50s. Fun was an essential part of the journey, combined with respect and empathy, as pointed out by one participant: "The group had deep interaction, without false harmony, people put themselves for- ward, brought their points, counterpoints, limitations and were welcomed in an empa- thetic way."

Again, collaboration among the co-facilitators was an essential aspect of the be- hind-the-scenes of the learning journey, as we were in an ongoing flexibility and adapt- ability exercise, as such a journey is as dynamic and unpredictable as life. Ariolino, Mônica, and Silvia became one interconnected and harmonious organism, in service of the whole.

Back to Manaus, the sense of community remained strong due to such deep com- mon experiences and exchanges with oneself, with each other and with nature. We had lived something unique that could be hardly shared in a faithful way. The final days of the learning journey were filled with additional insights about how to integrate these new ways of being, relating, and collaborating into a new thinking and acting paradigm for a better and healthier tomorrow.

Below are some of the questions that permeated the conversations as the journey was coming to an end and that we invite you, dear reader, to ask yourself too.

 – How to deal with the contrasting emotions that emerged during such a short, but at the same time, long period of time in terms of the intensity and power of the lived experiences?
 – What does a bioeconomy mean for the Amazon and for the planet?
 – What is the potential role of family businesses in fostering a new direction to economic development that cares for the people and the planet?
 – What else should I do as a business leader?

The final site visits were filled with such reflections, as we could have a view from above of the forest from the 42-m-tall tower of the Museu da Amazônia, and also travel to the past and the glorious rubber cycle while visiting the Amazonas Theatre, symbol of economic prosperity at the cost of oppression of forest populations in the nineteenth century.

How can we build a more beautiful narrative for the future, now that we experienced a deep sense of community, humanity, and interdependence?

According to Krenak, our travel companion:

*Why does the feeling of falling cause us discomfort? We have done nothing else in recent times other than fall. Fall, fall, fall. So why are we trapped now by the fall? Let us take advantage of all our critical and creative capacity to build colorful parachutes. Let's think of space not as a confined place, but as the cosmos where we can plummet in colorful parachutes. (Krenak, 2020)*

The colorful parachutes became one of our common expressions, meaning that despite the odds, we can always choose a positive, beautiful, hopeful, and constructive attitude. Instead of despairing or giving up, let us stay present and make the most of what is left for us to do as individuals who want to choose the right side of history, as biased as it might sound.

It was time to go. We were not the same anymore. During our last breakfast together, we shared a round of gratitude and appreciation, and the physical community parted in the spirit of Fernando Pessoa's quote: "Life is what we make of it. The travels are the travellers. What we see is not what we see, but what we are." (Pessoa, 1982)

## Post-journey effects

On the way back home, each one of us had an individual task to accomplish: How to deal with the practical life left behind, nurtured by the new landscapes, friendships, and experiences? How to accommodate the diversity of emotions and experiences on the way back? How to preserve the sense of belonging, the community inside us, and to present our new selves to the world?

Shortly after the end of the journey, the participants filled out an evaluation survey. When asked about the impact of the journey on their lives, one participant shared: "They were very intense and different moments from my everyday life! My personal and professional lives were affected by the trip, [I now have] eyes and ears more open to the future." According to another participant, the journey enabled an "expansion of knowledge about other regional and cultural realities, where new forms of interaction and investment of resources can be added." Similarly, another participant wrote: "I got to know very closely what social impact means and the importance of the role of companies in being part of this transformation." Further testimonials mentioned the importance of nurturing human connections, and the feeling of reconnection with our true selves.

An intense exchange of messages, photos, songs, and poems happened via WhatsApp, while our genipap tattoos began to fade out. One week later, we facilitators felt a need to reunite as a community and share the post-journey immediate effects. We still needed to see each other and share the beauty and challenge of going back, as well as shared memories and insights. It became clear that the forest and the sense of community were still very strong inside each of us. One month later we gathered again and undertook a guided a reflection based on the five IDG dimensions to stimulate reflection on the impacts of the learning journey after four weeks and beyond. After a check-in reflection round, the guided reflection session was inspired by the following questions, which we invite you to ask yourself from time to time, as a form of strengthening your inner development muscles:

– Being: What would you like to do more, or less, over the coming month?
– Thinking: What new perspectives would you like to explore next?
– Relating: What would you like to do differently in your relationships?
– Collaborating: How can you be more collaborative?
– Acting: How can you make better use of your courage?

As life goes on, we still hear from each other or occasionally meet in virtual or in-person events. But the journey still lives inside each of us. And each of us keeps walking with a bitter-sweet reminder that each step, each word, each decision matters. Krenak's words are now part of our inner repertoire:

> We feel as if we were loose in a cosmos empty of meaning and unaccountable for an ethics that can be shared, but we feel the weight of this choice on our lives. We are warned all the time about the consequences of these recent choices we have made. And if we can pay attention to some vision that escapes this blindness that we are experiencing all over the world, perhaps it can open our minds to some cooperation between people, not to save others, but to save ourselves. (Krenak, 2020)

# Final words

The FBN Learning Journey Amazônia was made possible by a collective dream, or a collection of dreams. Dreams filled with inner skills such as courage, trust, mobilization, complexity awareness, and presence, among others. The IDGs were a crucial framework from the planning to the implementation phase, allowing us to dream with a purpose. When we first announced the FBN Learning Journey Amazônia during FBN's annual conference, the audience was asked about who had already travelled abroad, with 100% of hands raised. When asked if they had already been to the Amazon forest, very few hands were raised. This purpose remains, of enabling an increasing number of present and future business leaders and decision makers to experience the power of the forest as a source of inner development and a new understanding of the global challenges we as humanity face.

This light yet profound life experience was only possible thanks to the dedication and commitment of the FBN director, Silvia Pedrosa, the unwavering support of the FBN council, and the families who welcomed us in Manaus. Our *"jornadeiros"* friends, you are the reason these lines were written; without you, none of this would have happened. Thus, our heartfelt thanks to each and every one of you.

We sincerely hope that by sharing our experience others can feel inspired to take this initiative further, adapted to different audiences, contexts, and natural settings.

> For some people, the idea of dreaming is giving up reality, giving up the practical meaning of life. However, we can also find those who would not see meaning in life if they were not informed by dreams. (Krenak, 2020)

We, the co-facilitators of this unique Amazonian leadership experience, are deeply grateful for the trust, support, and responsibility of leading this extraordinary human experiment.

# References

Inner Development Goals – Inner Growth for Outer Change. (n.d.).https://www.innerdevelopmentgoals. org/ (accessed on 8 April 2024).
Krenak, A. (2020). *Ideas to postpone the end of the world* (A. Doyle trans.). Toronto, ON: Anansi International.
Scharmer, O. (2018). *The essentials of Theory U: Core principles and applications*. San Francisco, CA: Berrett-Koehler Publishers.
Pessoa, F. (1982). *The Book of Disquiet*. London, UK: Profile Books.
Thoreau, H.D. (1854). *Walden; or, Life in the Woods*. Boston: Ticknor and Fields.

Section 3: **Interbeing**

Mauricio Campos Suarez
# Chapter 13
# Prelude

In this section, we'll explore the concept of "interbeing", a term coined by the Vietnamese monk, poet, and peace activist, Thich Nhat Hanh. Interbeing emphasizes the interconnectedness and interdependence of all things.

Modern physics sheds more light on our interconnected reality than previously thought. Quantum mechanics offers intriguing parallels with the ancient Buddhist concept of reality called "Indra's net", where every jewel in the net reflects all others, symbolizing the interconnectedness of all beings. Similarly, inner development cannot happen in isolation, nor the sustainability goals we are aiming for.

The chapters in this section shift inner development focus from the "self" to an inclusive perspective that recognizes the profound interconnectedness of all life. We will explore the foundational shift from individualism to interconnectedness, setting the stage for understanding identity within a broader context of relationships and systems.

In the heart of interbeing lies the essence of connectedness, a vital yet often elusive force that threads through every dimension of our lives. As we deepen our understanding of connectedness, we uncover its pivotal role in fostering a sense of belonging and purpose, guiding us towards actions that resonate with sustainability and stewardship.

One of the most important and powerful tools to enable connection is our capacity to *listen*. This is an underestimated skill with the power to transform our interactions and our inner worlds. Through the art of attentive listening, we build trust, nurture relationships, and craft meaningful change.

We will read about a tool to allow us to map *observations*, *thoughts*, *feelings*, and *wants* for articulating our experiences and understanding those of others.

As we reflect on our journey, we confront the dualities of contemplation and confrontation, discovering the power of self-reflexivity as a catalyst for collective leadership. Through introspection and shared learning, we unlock our potential to address societal challenges with a sense of efficacy and purpose.

We will learn from the genocide against the Tutsi in Rwanda about the transformative power of forgiveness as a radical perspective to fosters peace and reconciliation, illuminating pathways for healing in our own lives and communities.

Finally, we will explore nonviolent communication (NVC) with an Inner Development Goals (IDGs) lens and how cultivating empathy, understanding, and clarity in our interactions are essential skills for navigating the complexities of our global challenges.

https://doi.org/10.1515/9783111337913-014

As you immerse yourself in the journey of interbeing, may you find inspiration in the interconnectedness that defines our existence. Let each chapter be a step towards a more integrated, compassionate, and sustainable world, where the growth of the self and the collective are one and the same.

**Figure 13.1:** *You see me* (2023) Acrylic painting by M. Campos Suarez, Malaga, Spain. 30 cm x 50 cm canvases (side-by-side).

"*As the figure on the left steps out of its own darkness, it is able to see life on the other canvas for the first time, while the figure on the right listens with an open heart, open mind, and open will. This moment symbolizes the transformative power of awareness and openness to the world.*"

*Connectedness*
*An apple held, a world within,*
*Tree, flower, bee, and rain akin.*

*The tree itself is the soil and the fungus.*
*The sun and the wind.*

*The soil, dark womb of secrets old,*
*Where fungus weaves its tale untold.*

*The apple falls to the ground,*
*Worms consume the apple*
*Apple becomes worms and soil*

*Nourishment for the tree*
*Nourishing life.*
*Endless cycles of transformation*

*Worm's form transforms, a verdant rise,*
*Tree reborn, with blossoms in its eyes.*

*Bee, rain, and sun, in endless dance,*
*Birth and rebirth of life*

*The apple wakes, a question stirs,*
*"Who am I?"*

*The answer dawns:*
*We are never alone,*
*Nothing ever ends,*
*Nothing ever starts,*
*Myself and the whole,*
*The only real self*
*Is the Universe as a whole*

**M. Campos Suarez (2022)**

Author's note. This poem came to me during an advanced systemic coaching retreat hosted by Prof P. Hawkins at his home, a castle with a beautiful apple farm. While walking through the orchard, I received a phone call from my corporate boss informing me that I was fired. Although I had anticipated this due to the endless company reorganizations, the moment confronted me after 20 years with the end of my corporate cycle. As my mind was going into the 'small' me story of the fired employee, the trees talked to me. They told me about the interdependence and connection of everything and everyone where nothing really ever ends.

Boaz Feldman and Marc Santolini

# Chapter 14
# Beyond individualism: A multilevel approach to the Inner Development Goals

**Abstract:** In this chapter, we offer a multilevel relational approach to the practice of the Inner Development Goals (IDGs). Our inner lives span wider than the bounds of our own minds and bodies: inner experiences are interdependent with others and the world, and there are important benefits to transcending an individualistic account of IDGs. Here we aim to give a rigorous multidisciplinary conceptualization and delineate a praxis to embody and enact a spectrum of selfhood, from the small parts of our inner experiences all the way to the emergence of our social-political identities – from neurons to nations. Such a methodology could help to dissolve boundaries between the inner life and connecting with others, and mutually reinforce the benefits of inner practice and worldly engagement. We provide insights from anthropology, contemplative traditions, philosophy, and contemporary sciences to describe the ways in which our sense of individual and collective self can be built and supported, supplemented by short exercises to encourage the embodiment of these conceptions. In order to get a practical felt sense of this nested spectrum of self-building, we propose a *social somatics* approach to sense and feel into the embodied experiences of how our sense of self arises together within ourselves, with others, and the world. This relational, multilevel reflexivity generalizes relational well-being at different scales, and we offer detailed practice descriptions and a case study to exemplify this reflexive praxis. Finally, we highlight applications in the corporate sector and possible pathways for development of these skills for team leaders, activists, politicians, and contemplatives.

**Keywords:** Inner Development Goals, multilevel development, interdependence, complex systems, high-performance teams

## Theory

### Beyond individualism: Insights from contemplative traditions

Inner development is often seen from a reductionist viewpoint, focusing on the individual as an elementary unit on which to define an inner world of subjective experience and free will that contrasts with an outer, objective world of deterministic events. This view is deeply rooted in a Cartesian philosophy that separates an emergent "I" mind from a mechanical world of matter, a dualist worldview summarized in

https://doi.org/10.1515/9783111337913-015

the axiom *cogito ergo sum* ('I think therefore I am'). This separation of an external "natural" world and an internal "cultural" world has since come to be understood as a particular perspective across human traditions, and anthropological studies from Philippe Descola (2014) have revealed broad ethnographic categories that challenge strict borders between nature and culture. While naturalism enforces a Cartesian viewpoint, other traditions of totemism or animism provide contrasting viewpoints where inner experiences and agency extend beyond human individuals. Identity is viewed as linked with social, environmental, and cosmic elements, escaping our linguistic trope of a separate "I". In Descola's words:

> The universality of the perception of the self as a separate and autonomous entity is borne out primarily by linguistic data, namely the presence in all languages of pronominal forms or affixes such as "I" and "you"[. . .]. There is little doubt that in many societies it is believed that the idiosyncrasy, actions, and development of a person depend on elements exterior to one's physical envelope—elements such as the relations of every kind amid which that person lives. That is most famously the case in Melanesia, which is why Marilyn Strathern has suggested that, in this region of the world, we should describe a person not as an individuality but as a "dividuality," that is to say, a being primarily defined by his or her position and relations within some network. (Descola, 2014, p. 65)

This concept of *dividuality* finds echoes across a multitude of traditions: the Māori's *whakapapa* places one's identity in a wider context of land and tribal groupings, and in Southern Africa, the concept of *ubuntu* ('I am because we are') emphasizes the interconnectedness of individuals with their surrounding societal and physical worlds. The porosity of the line between the subjective/cultural and objective/natural world has consequences for the way we think of subjective well-being and inner development. To integrate the inextricable entanglement of relationality across inner experiences – what cognitive scientist John Vervaeke named the "transjective" dimension of participation that integrates and transcends subject and object (Vervaeke, 2019) – anthropologists have proposed measures of a relational well-being that encompass subjective, relational, and material dimensions into a situated, context-specific measure (White, 2017).

These inseparably relational experiences of the world are often referred to as non-dual, in contrast to the dualist Cartesian position that assumes a separation of mind and matter – a view foundational to the modern scientific enterprise. While less influential in Western thinking (up to, maybe, more recent phenomenological traditions), non-dual philosophies have been prominent in Eastern philosophies such as Advaita Vedanta or Buddhism. They are deeply tied to corresponding meditation practices that guide towards an experiential inquiry into the nature of self by shifting the "I" standpoint from the narrative self to a witness posture. Readers are invited to explore this process experientially in the box below. While seemingly an individual practice, such experiences can take over at the group level, leading to states of "collective presencing" (Baeck, 2022) where the phenomenologically experienced source of intention and inner experience is distributed, seemingly an irreducible group property.

---

**Witnessing the "I"**
*Short reflection practice (Three minutes)*
Take a few moments and settle back into your seat. Allow your body to relax, your breath to be felt in its own rhythm, without trying to make anything happen. As you become aware of your experience, notice the thoughts that go through your mind, and let them be, coming and going. Gently and kindly return to your body, your breath, to this moment.

As you relax back, notice if you can start relating to your experience as a witness, a sense of allowing and noticing everything going through your mind, your body, the world. And witnessing also the very sense of self, the "I" that observes and is present, what quality does the "I" have right now? Maybe it feels tangible, colorful, has a texture or felt sense. Maybe it's helpful to repeat the question inside *"Who am I?"* or *"What is me?"* Softly welcoming the reactions, shifts, and tensions that may arise from this inquiry.

And then letting go of the question, leaning back again on the present moment, this breath, this thought, without effort. Making a short mental or written note for yourself, what did you notice in this practice?

---

The phenomenology of non-self experiences (*anattā*) builds on a long contemplative history. In Buddhism, there are two strands which point to more fundamental relational dynamics undermining a more individualistic self. In the early teachings, the Buddha described the nature of phenomenal experience and reality to be "co-arising" (*pratītyasamutpāda*), meaning that it is only through a set of interrelating causes and conditions that anything comes to existence. The paper on which this text is printed was made from trees which grew in a forest. These trees were fed by the local environment, rain, and sunshine. These, in turn, grew out of an interdependent series of causal conditions. How can we definitively differentiate the water in the stream, to the mist in the air, to the clouds in the sky? They share properties and fundamentally affect one another in ways that bypass a categorical approach. When thinking about the IDGs, this can help us frame the different categories as being co-constructed and fundamentally reliant upon each other. For instance, one's capacity for being embodied and remaining present to inner experiences (*being* category from the IDGs) relies upon one's ability to value presence, and have thought through how one can confront challenges emerging in any particular situation in ways that are skillful (*thinking* category from the IDGs) and/or having learned to maintain wise relationships by acknowledging and taking responsibility for one's own emotions and relational patterns (*relating* category from the IDGs). Beyond their interdependence, these categories are co-arising with different levels of *self* as they emerge: in certain situations, it can be more appropriate to talk about being, relating or acting at the level of a group of individuals or of an organization. Recognizing this dynamic unfolding is deeply tied to the recognition of the impermanence (*annica*) of each of these levels, requiring to build present-moment discernment through practice.

To that aim, the Buddhist jhana practices offer an example of a meditative path of development leading to increasingly higher levels of well-being, calm, and enlightenment (Burbea, 2014; Gunaratana, 1988). While the early stages are described as embodied experiences, the progression is such that one then transcends one's own body as its boundaries start to dissolve gradually. With continued practice, the sense of the body widens and broadens, becoming part of the space in the room, and progressively encompassing wider expanses of space to the edges of space itself. In the Buddhist teachings this state is called the realm of infinite space as every phenomenon which emerges in the mind melts and glues into the unfolding spatial field of the mind. When refined, this perception also includes the awareness of space, where awareness becomes an object of itself (technically called the realm of infinite consciousness). These very subtle perceptual experiences of space and consciousness point to deeper, post-embodied, levels of phenomenological reality which can be accessed and penetrated through the development of specific meditative practices. By reducing the sense of separateness with other people and the natural world, they naturally support a flow between qualities of being through to acting.

Millennia of contemplative practice in monasteries, spiritual circles, and more recently in meditation centers all over the world have offered opportunities to experience these states firsthand. For instance, the Pew Research Center has reported that, several times a year or more often, over 50% of the population in the USA has experienced "a deep sense of common humanity", 71% express "a deep sense of wonder about the universe", and 30% have experienced "a spiritual force" describe having had an experience of profound "oneness" or "unity with God" (Kallo et al., 2023). There are ways to frame and give evidence for this self-scaling process, which helps to broaden our understanding and application of the IDGs and will be described in the next section.

# Contemporary scientific investigations into levels of individuation: Complex systems, self-organization, networks, and higher-order interactions

In Western thought, the question of what is the source of social action and to what extent groups can have an experience and intention of their own has been a point of interest in social sciences since its early foundations. French sociologist Émile Durkheim introduced in his 1893 book *The Division of Labour in Society* the concept of a "conscience collective", which could be translated as a collective awareness arising from "the totality of beliefs and sentiments common to the average members of a society" and that "forms a determinate system with a life of its own" (Durkheim, 1893, pp. 38–39). This sense of emergent agency can also be found in the work of Dur-kheim's contemporary, Scipio Sighele, who published in *La Foule Criminelle* the con-cept of *âme de la foule* ('soul of the crowd' to describe emergent characteristics of crowds that don't appear in their constitutive individuals (Sighele, 1892). More gener-ally, German philosophers of the eighteenth and nineteenth century such as Goethe and Hegel described the *Zeitgeist* ('spirit of the age') as an invisible agent dominating the characteristics of a given epoch in world history (Hegel, 1807), contrasting with the other collective agents of *Volksgeist* ('spirit of an individual people or nation') and *Weltgeist* ('the world spirit permeating all of nature').

To formally describe these multiple levels of social actions, the social sciences have pioneered the use of network analysis since the early twentieth century. Early graphical studies of sociograms (Moreno, 1934) made use of graphical depictions of social relations to study the dynamic emergence of systems-level properties such as influence and segregation. Individuals could be described as structurally embedded within wider networks that determine their access to resources and ultimate agency (Granovetter, 1973). But individuals make groups, groups make institutions, and insti-tutions make nations in a hierarchy of constantly evolving, nested Russian dolls. Mul-tilevel views, where agents can represent entities at several levels of collective action, have been the focus of the more recent neo-structural sociology (Lazega, 2021; Lazega et al., 2008). Far from fixed, these levels continuously emerge from non-reductive higher-order interactions that are now described by hypergraphs (Taramasco, Cointet & Roth, 2010) and are key to understanding the dynamics of social influence (Mancas-troppa et al., 2023 (see figure 14.1)) and the fluidity of social identities in informal and intentional communal settings (Filippi & Santolini, 2023). As interactions unfold, large-scale networks reduce in size, aggregating individuals into broader categories through mechanisms of causal emergence (Klein & Hoel, 2020). These compression processes pro-duce higher-level entities – the casts and classes of ancient and modern traditions – that seem to have intrinsic behavior and agency, forming "dividuals" of their own right.

Beyond social sciences, the interdisciplinary field of complex systems has tackled the question of scales of action by looking for universal laws underlying the emer-gence of novel, collective properties that are irreducible to the individual parts (An-derson, 1972) and are shared across disciplines as varied as biology, neurosciences, social sciences, and physics (Barabási, 2016; Simon, 1962). At the root of this epistemo-logical quest is the problem of the emergence of an autonomous self-unit out of lower-level parts, usually framed under the terminology of self-organization (Kauff-man, 1993) or the more teleologically flavored *autopoïesis* (Maturana & Varela, 1980). Using tools from information theory, scholars have argued that individuality can be framed as an "aggregate that preserves a measure of temporal integrity" (Krakauer et al., 2020, p. 209), forming a continuous measure that can emerge at any level of or-ganization and be nested within other individualities (Klein & Hoel, 2020; Krakauer et al., 2020). Neurosciences have offered similar insights with the integrated informa-tion theory framework, defining consciousness as a continuous quantitative measure

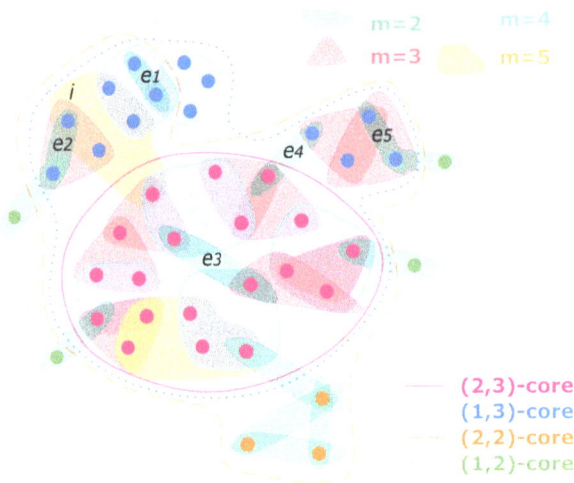

**Figure 14.1:** Overlapping, nested social processes can be represented with hypergraphs, denoting the multiple concomitant social interactions that individuals are part of. The stable recurrence of these interactions generate novel scales of individuation in the system, forming dividuals embedded across vertical and horizontal scales in the relational system. Reprinted from Mancastroppa et al. (2023).

that relies on the integration of information at multiple scales (Tononi et al., 2016). At the behavioral level, these considerations of collective agency are translated into questions related to the resolution of nontrivial problems requiring goal-oriented activity, uncovering collective intelligences across scales, from cellular to social group levels (McMillen & Levin, 2024; Riedl et al., 2021). Noting that in groups of individuals, collective intelligence is a group-level factor correlated with the average social sensitivity of group members, the equality in distribution of conversational turn-taking, and the gender diversity of the group, Woolley et al. note that "it would seem to be much easier to raise the intelligence of a group than an individual", paving the way for group-centric approaches to training and problem solving (Woolley et al., 2010, p. 688). These considerations slowly challenge the Cartesian viewpoint to allow for a more distributed and extended view of cognition (*Bruin, Newen, & Gallagher*, 2018), and have led to renewed discussions between Eastern and Western philosophies, as exemplified by the elaboration of the Mind & Life Institute by biologist Francisco Varela and Tibetan spiritual leader His Holiness Dalai Lama to promote a "science of interbeing" (Varela, 2000).

# From neurons to nations: Neurosciences and social embodiment

In order to better understand key aspects with which dividuals, or levels of self, experience and build their sense of self and interiority, we can turn to the large body of work from neuroscience and social psychology on the well-being of individuals and groups. Social psychology research over the past 50 years has been consistent in showing that self-understanding is intimately linked to our ability to understand others (Gallup, 1970; Krachun et al., 2019). For instance, social cognition theory (Bandura, 2001), shows that there is a reciprocally deterministic interaction between a person, the social context in which they are situated, and their behaviors. This means that our behaviors are conditioned by the people around us, and our sense of self is gradually co-constructed through the interactions with others. This social constructionist view of the self (Fonagy, Gergely, & Targe, 2007) delineates how our inner experiences cannot be entirely distinguished from the "external" social environment. This research is thus relevant to help us broaden our understanding of our psychological self not as a fixed, innate, and pre-wired entity, but as a fluid construct and experience that is dependent on, varying with, and co-constructed through social interaction.

Recent neuroscientific evidence further describes how the neurobiological substrates of the individual self are fundamentally dependent on the quality of our social ties, changing moment to moment. The polyvagal theory (Porges, 2001) points to the importance of the vagus nerve to regulate the nervous system, and in particular the extensive influence that social interaction has upon it. Porges discovered that when we are in the company of others we trust, the vagus nerve potentiates all brain functions and we become maximally present and resourceful to ourselves and the world. Put another way, the more we assess our physical and social environment as threatening, the more our brains function with limited bandwidth and sense of possibility. Our more recently developed cortical abilities of decision making, planning, and reflection turn off. Conversely, as we feel safe with others, our brain's "social engagement system" lights up. Instead of operating from more "negative" mind states of of fight, flight, and freeze (which we stimulate when we experience threat), we tend to be more playful, joyful, and creative (Weare, 2020). The broaden-and-build theory (Fredrickson, 2001) also points to the higher abilities of a brain experiencing positive emotions: joy and happiness tend to broaden perception. A greater number of stimuli can be included and processed as one maintains "positive" states of mind. Sensing others is therefore mutually reinforced by positive affect and enjoyable nervous system states, through such mechanisms as synchrony, for instance (Chikersal et al., 2017). This positive psychology emphasis offers the opportunity for reflection on the *being* IDG category, inviting a greater role on *well*-being.

We are relational beings, and this ventures beyond practical, adaptive, and functional neural impacts: we tend to neurobiologically conceive of other friendly company around us as part of ourselves. The social baseline theory (Beckes & Coan, 2011) suggests that our brains budget certain resources (such as glucose) to meet a goal (like going up a hill) and that when we are alone we tend to budget higher levels of glucose to perform the same functions than if we were with friends (Gross & Medina-DeVilliers, 2020). The explanation here is that the social context is innate to resource-dependent cognitive processes, and relational partners tend to be incorporated into neural representations of the self. In short, we conceive of ourselves as being one with others. Through our relational fabric, we become "one" again. Coan and Wilson (2021) have considered such a socio-biological process by framing groups as "social organisms". In fact, Wilson and Wilson (2007) have gone even further to contextualize this social phenomenon within a wide theory of evolution called multilevel selection (MLS). This theory explains how functional organization can evolve at any level of a nested hierarchy of units, such as from genes to ecosystems in biological systems or individuals to large scale societies in human systems: a fractal frame going from neurons to nations. As such, evolution is this process, whereby parts (such as individual humans) functionally organize themselves and cooperate collectively to form wholes (e.g., groups), make what is termed an "evolutionary transition" (Smith & Szathmary, 1997), and these parts operate within the nested hierarchy of the higher-level whole they are a part of. We are individuals, and yet when we connect with other individuals, we form a larger group organism and our individual experience is part of the inner life of the social organism. Similarly, groups and communities are parts of their organismic societies (Czégel, Zachar, & Szathmáry, 2019; Maynard Smith & Szathmáry, 1999). It could be conceived, therefore, that entire interactions within and between communities are themselves inner experiences of the societal organism. This fractal and multilevel understanding of the formations of self/selves is not only helpful in preventing the over-responsibilisation of individuals' inner experience, but also helps to hold self-views more lightly and increase cognitive flexibility. The ability to adapt our views and behavior to achieve goals in new environments is a core faculty when it comes to well-being, resilience, collaboration, and successful entrepreneurship (Sahakian, Langley, & Leong., 2021).

Overall, our social embeddedness has profound impacts on our inner lives, and relational interactions can even be conceived as a form of inner experience. By understanding in an embodied way how we are neuro-socially wired and interconnected, we can up-regulate our personal and collective levels of well-being, as well as deepen our capacity for creative collaboration in a time of social isolation and polarization. This is particularly relevant and central as we are facing challenges of economic inequality and social polarization at a global scale, which are core to achieving the Sustainable Development Goals (SDGs). How can we learn to find synergistic solutions to these issues without excluding the rich, privileged, and those with opposing views to ours? In the next section we propose practices to develop such inner abilities, as part of a wider scheme of IDGs.

# Practice

As our understanding of inner development expands beyond individualism, we need to develop practices that integrate *by design* a multilevel, relational understanding of the nested, fluid social identities that are experienced within and across individuals (see Figure 14.2). An overly individual-focused approach might indeed miss a wider picture: a group of highly self-realized individuals might be, taken as a unit, maladaptive in the wider context of a "group of groups", limiting inner development to an atomized level that does not scale at the next emergent level. As an attempt to bridge beyond the individual and across scales, we elaborated an ecology of practices that considers the social body as extended and multilevel, taking seriously the felt experience of a group or a community as various facets of what we refer to as *social somatics*.

Inspired from contemplative traditions, this ecology of practices focuses on a non-judgemental attention directed back at oneself. This insistence on recursion trains on *reflexivity* and is incentivized at multiple levels, inviting an individual, a dyad, a group, or a group of groups to note their sensations, emotions, felt experience, and body sensation as they unfold in an emergent fashion. It is this reflexive move, focusing on attention to the self (whatever level it feels to be at a given moment) and its felt experience (its somatic, embodied perception), that invites into a phenomenology of self-organization and of autopoiesis. Rather than merely conceptual, the multilevel nature of individuation becomes palpable, and our role within and capacity of action across levels stands out as a lived experience.

Such a multilevel reflexive training touches on various facets of the IDGs, aiming to increase well-being (*being*), creativity (*thinking*), belonging (*relating*), collaboration (*collaborating*) and agency (*acting*). But beyond these facets, it provides a "spiral" understanding where acting at a lower level joins being at the next level.

Conducting a reflexive introspection requires to take the place of a specific observer watching over the narrative self. Often termed "witness", the ability to develop and give voice to such a nonjudgemental observer has been central to mindfulness practices. Indeed, a certain thread of practices (in particular in the context of the jhanas we have covered above) emphasizes the benefits of involving a specifically positive observer that focuses on pleasant sensations before being able to fabricate a neutral observer that could handle positive, negative, and neutral perceptions equally. This strength building in turn allows to deepen the dive into traumatic individual or collective experiences, or handle seemingly untenable perspectives to achieve perspectival reframing.

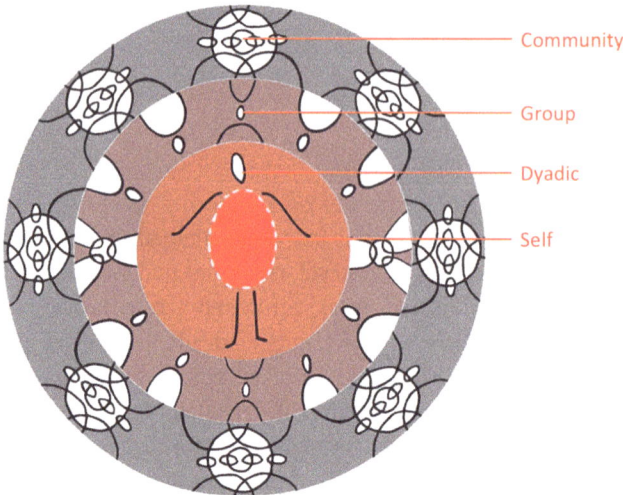

**Figure 14.2:** A nested model of four levels of somatic and relational practices. Reprinted from Feldman, Tupikina, & Santolini (2024)

In order to support this multilevel understanding, we propose an ecosystem of somatic and relational practices, growing in both relational complexity and scope and relating to the five IDGs (Feldman, Tupikina, & Santolini, 2024) (see Figure 14.2).

*Self-practices*, such as meditation and mindfulness, support the systematic development of attention regulation, awareness, and introspective attunement towards all of one's present moment experiences of meaning, orientation, sensation, affect, image, and consciousness (the "MOSAIC" channels). The aim of such practices is to sustain a continuous uninterrupted flow of attention to better regulate one's nervous system such that one can relate and behave towards others and the world in a conscious and meaningful way to reach one's goals. We estimate the main activated IDG categories to be being, thinking, and acting as these can be practiced by oneself.

At *the dyadic level* we propose two types of practices: one-to-one facilitated sessions and buddy discussions. Facilitated sessions involve somatically trained professionals who can track moment-to-moment nervous system shifts of the other person (client/patient/friend), supporting the individual's capacity and coping ability to experience and explore the flow of their MOSAIC channel emergence. These sessions build a co-regulatory receptivity in the receiver of the session: instead of having to make all the effort oneself to regulate one's nervous system and reach higher states of consciousness, one learns to build trust with the facilitator and start tapping into low-hanging fruits of evolutionary wiring as described in the polyvagal theory above. Buddy discussions occur as we also invite participants to have regular interactions with a designated partner (a "buddy"), to practice holding space for another person in a similar way to the trained facilitators do for them and embody perspective-taking skills. This is an informal opportunity to check in with one another, share details about how their respective day is going, and perhaps some gratitude for positive events. As these practices include another person, the categories of being, thinking, and acting are complemented by relating, and to a certain extent collaborating.

The main *group-level practice* involves the formation of small clusters of six to eight people with one to two professionally trained somatic group process facilitators. Throughout these sessions, participants are encouraged to stay connected to their internal MOSAIC channel experience to self-regulate and link their personal experience to the interactions emerging in the group process. Facilitators encourage co-regulatory processes where participants can experience how certain behaviors and ways of relating can support greater levels of presence, joy, and creativity for themselves and other group members. Participants learn to build empathy as well as greater perspectival abilities (perspective-taking, perspective-seeking, and perspective-coordination skills) (Fuhs, 2016). All IDG goals are involved in this group-level practice. In daily life, however, it is often challenging to include the being and thinking qualities since relational dynamics tend to require extensive cognitive processing.

Finally, *community-level practices* replicate some of the group-level processes, with more intensity since more people enables greater multiplication of attention brought to one's own and the community's present moment MOSAIC experience. They also offer a potential community-as-a-whole perspective, potentiating one's sense of embeddedness and experience of a broadened sense of self. We also explore and act upon community- and society-level issues which are affecting the community. This form of relational action enables engagement with themes of concern at the local level for place-based communities, and on a wider scale in online communities *(acting)*.

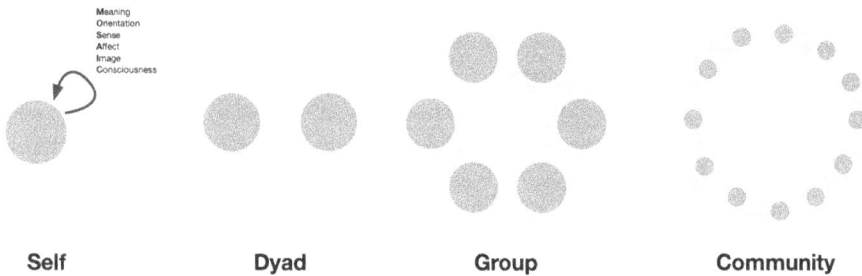

Meaning
Orientation
Sense
Affect
Image
Consciousness

| **Self** | **Dyad** | **Group** | **Community** |

**Figure 14.3:** Overview of the nested social scales of the practices.
Source: Authors' own compilation.

Overall, this proposed integrative framing builds the foundations for clinical and organizational psychology practices designed to enhance self-regulation, co-regulation, and perspective-taking skills at multiple social scales, thereby impacting the being, thinking, relating, collaborating, and acting categories of the IDGs.

## Implementation and feedback

The ecology of practices was introduced to the IDG Lemanic Network in Lausanne during a three-hour workshop called "Cultivating Meaningful Collaboration: A Workshop to Enhance our Relational Practices". The goal of the workshop was to have participants experience the multilevel method and link their experience to the IDG categories, with a specific focus on collaboration.

The first part of the workshop (one and a half hours) consisted of a series of practices at multiple levels (see Figure 14.4 for full workshop content and schedule). First, participants were guided into a short individual meditation on the theme of "collaboration: joys and challenges". At the end of the meditation, they could share a one-word check-in to the entire group. They would then join their neighbor to form a dyad and share about their personal experience of the meditation. Participants had four minutes of organic unfolding. Then, each participant in the dyad was invited to share their felt-sense reflexivity about their dyadic interaction in one minute. Finally, a one-minute silent time was given to integrate the experience. After this time, dyads were asked to join the nearby dyad to form a tetrad. A similar practice of organic unfolding (nine minutes), reflexivity (four minutes), and integration (one minute) was conducted. This time the reflexivity could touch not only the individual and dyadic experience, but also the experience of their dyadic subgroup meeting another dyad. Finally, the process was repeated by merging tetrads into octads (13 minutes unfolding, eight minutes reflexivity, one-minute integration), again building awareness on the scales of experience at the personal, dyadic, and tetradic level within the new configuration. The groups were then merged together for a 30-minute plenary, guided by the facilitating team.

Some of the key feedback included: (1) strong reactions in the transition points; and (2) notable experiences around their level of embeddedness. When dyads came together with other dyads, and when tetrads joined with other tetrads, these were experienced with some strong emotions, either positively or negatively, and impacted the quality of the group interaction overall. In particular, it was described that those who had a smooth integration into their larger unit (tetrad or octad) seemed to have a richer exchange and more joy in the process, and vice versa. It is interesting to note that in complex systems, it is described that initial conditions have a disproportionate impact upon the living system's life (Higgins, 2002). One octad did manage, over the course of the exercise, to find more coherence in their exchange, and have a circumstance where tetrads could dissolve into a larger whole, though this was not the case in another octad. Secondly, some comments were made on the reflexive moments given in each of the sequences (dyadic, tetradic, and octadic). Expectedly, it was easiest for most people to feel more embedded and connected to their colleague in the dyad, and still often quite easily felt in the tetrad. While a number of people found it difficult to reflect on their place in the octads, some noticed their behavioral tendency to either want to take the lead, or take a step away from the group, and made a choice to act differently that time to counter their habit pattern. They could start seeing how their individual self interacted with other parts of the

| Activity | Duration | Total | Facilitator | Description |
|---|---|---|---|---|
| **Seating** in a circles (5') | 5 | | Boaz/Marc ▼ | |
| Introduction<br>1. Thank you & Welcome<br>2. Fun questions (5)<br>3. Orientation (3)<br>4. Marc & Boaz Introductions (2+2)<br>5. General introduction (5) | 20 | 20 | Boaz/Marc ▼ | Where are you from?<br>Collaboration: hot or cold?<br>for who is it enjoyable to work with one other person?<br>for who is it enjoyable to collaborate with small groups?<br>and who would like to see a more collaborative world,<br>vs a world where you are more encouraged to do things<br>by yourself?<br>in order to collaborate with everyone we need to meet,<br>who would like to have more meetings, vs having more<br>personal time for your work? |
| **Individual meditation** + 1 word check-in | 5 | 25 | Boaz ▼ | "collaboration: joys & challenges" |
| **Dyad:** 1' explanation + organic unfolding (4)<br>+1'/pp felt-sense reflexivity (2)<br>+1 silent integration (1) | 8 | 33 | Boaz ▼ | "Please share about your personal experience of the meditation" |
| **Tetrads** (1+9)<br>+1'/pp felt-sense reflexivity (4)<br>Silent integration 1' | 15 | 48 | Boaz ▼ | "Please share about your personal experience and also anything related to some subgroup dynamic you may have left" |
| **Octads** (2+13)<br>+1'/pp felt-sense reflexivity (8)<br>Silent integration 1' | 24 | 72 | Boaz ▼ | "Please share about your personal experience and also anything related to noval qualities arising from the large group experience?" |
| **Plenary** (20)<br>5-6 people share felt-sense reflexivity of the group experience, max 2'/pp (10) | 30 | 102 | Boaz/Marc ▼ | |
| **BREAK** | 20 | 122 | | |
| **Slides** (7)<br>+Q&A (8) | 15 | 137 | Marc ▼ | |
| write **3 post it alone** and put on the board: **what is preventing yourself, a dyadic relationship or a group from collaborating,** being as precise as possible to relate to IDG categories (e.g i need to be more self-aware to know that I am not listening, I need to be open when others have a different experience than me to go beyond disagreement...) (5) | 5 | 142 | Marc/Boaz ▼ | 3 post it per person |
| **Clustering and looking at other post-its** (5) | 5 | 147 | Marc/Boaz ▼ | |
| **Debrief in groups of 4** (10) : "feedback on categories emerging, what you didn't consider or see before, how does it make you reconsider collaboration". select one person in the group that will report back to the whole group and summarize what was said in 3 minutes | 10 | 157 | Marc/Boaz ▼ | 1 person / group to report back |
| **group feedback** to everyone (20) | 20 | 177 | Marc/Boaz ▼ | 3 min per group |
| **Action Post-it writing:** "Write one post it of a commitment that you can take tomorrow to produce and monitor a change in one of these blockages at your individual, dyadics or group level (5) and put it on the board closest IDG category" | 5 | 182 | Marc/Boaz ▼ | |
| **Imaginal meditation** (8) | 8 | 190 | Boaz ▼ | |
| **Debrief group of 2** (5) | 5 | 195 | Boaz/Marc ▼ | |
| **Check-out** (10)<br>+ Orientation to key take away & gratitudes<br>+ plenary sharing<br>Applause close | 10 | 205 | Boaz ▼ | Gratitude bell |
| **END** | | 205 | | |

**Figure 14.4:** Description of the activities organised at the Lausanne IDG Hub. After an experiential session with multi-level reflexive practices, participants were invited to describe factors preventing collaborations using sticker notes.
Source: Authors' own compilation.

group organism and attempted to shift their perspective. This form of socio-cognitive flexibility is a key ingredient of high-performing teams, where individuals take on different roles based on the tasks at hand and the optimal functional organization necessary to achieve it (Furr, 2009). This affected their quality of relating to themselves and to the group, which was supported by the experimental nature of the exercise.

The second part of the workshop was an interactive format aimed at both further-ing self-reflection on behalf of the participants and gaining broader insights for the facilitators team. The five IDG goals had been delineated on a wall on which stickers could be added in order to indicate their relation to a specific goal, as shown in Figure 14.5.

**Figure 14.5:** Post-it notes activity describing the preventing factors for collaboration. IDG Lemanic Workshop, 2024.

In the first part, participants were asked about specific blockages when it relates to collaborations. They were tasked to write three colored Post-it notes of what is preventing themself (yellow), a dyadic relationship, or a group (pink) from collaborating (ten minutes alone, ten minutes reflexive work with a group of three to four). In a second part, participants were asked about a commitment they could take to act on one of these blockages: They were to write one (orange) Post-it of a commitment that they could take tomorrow to produce and monitor a change in one of these blockages at an individual, dyadic, or group level (five minutes).

Stickers were assigned to an IDG goal by participants. Participants could move stickers to cluster them into emergent categories or reassign them to a more relevant category. Data was transcribed manually and analyzed to provide descriptive statistics and content analysis, as shown on Figure 14.6.

We first analyzed which goals were most chosen by participants when considering blockages and actions. For blockages, beyond the obvious collaboration goal appearing due to the nature of the workshop, the being goal was most important, followed by relating. Among the 88 stickers for "blockage", there were 64 (72%) at the individual level

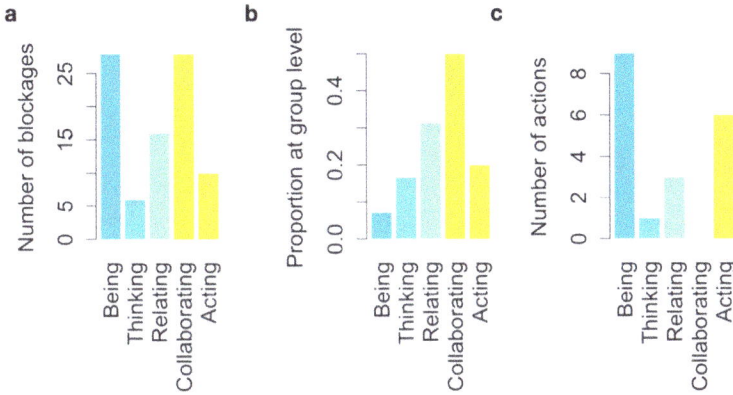

**Figure 14.6:** Descriptive workshop results of the number of stickers per IDG Goal for blockages (a) and actions (c), as well as the proportion of stickers that denote a blockage at the group level (b). Source: Authors' own compilation.

and 24 (28%) at the group level, indicating some experience of developmental needs at higher levels. Interestingly, the distribution of group-level stickers followed that of individual stickers on all but one goal: while most present for individuals, the being goal was virtually absent from group-level consideration. This showcases the difficulty to consider the group as an individual capable of improving its being skills, and the need for training such traits. Finally, when considering commitments, we found that the being goal was more represented than acting, showing that participants may have a stronger drive for self-development practice as a pathway forward.

When considering content, we show in Figure 14.7 word clouds of the most frequent words for both blockage and action stickers. Because of prompting, words such as "lack" and "need" were overrepresented. We removed them from the analysis to look at the more fine-grained elements arising. Key terms that emerged at the blockage level were "fear", "trust", "feel", "structures", "different". They are related to overcoming personal and relational barriers, and to the proper context that can promote this. Commitments involve both working on being more receptive ("listen") as well as explicit and active ("show").

We then furthered the analysis by investigating the sentiments expressed in the stickers (Figure 14.8). We used the Syuzhet package (Jockers, 2015) to analyze the sentiments and their valence across the goals. Blockages were found to have negative valence (as expected from the prompt), and highlighted needs of trust, as well as content related to fear and anger. Anticipation was high, probably a result of the type of prompting. Actions had on the other end a positive valence, with sentiments on the same categories as blockages (i.e., resolving trust and fear). When considering specific goals, at the blockage level, thinking and acting were most negative. The highest anticipation was in acting, along with fear. Finally, needs of trust span collaboration and being, showing a dichotomy between others and the self. Overall, blockages seem to

## Blockage

## Action

**Figure 14.7:** Word clouds visualizing the word frequencies across stickers for blockages and actions. Source: Authors' own compilation.

come from difficulties to act and produce a safe environment in the group to navigate collaborations. Actions at the being level are an effort to overcome such relational difficulties.

Diving deeper into the written and oral feedback from the participants and the above analysis paints a more comprehensive picture of the training needs in relation to the goals when it comes to relational and multilevel practices. Blockages at the individual level are often internal and psychological, such as a lack of trust, feeling insecure, the need for clarity, and self-awareness issues. These can stem from personal values, prejudices, fear of being misunderstood, and the inability to reflect on one's actions. Group-level blockages include a collective resistance to new ideas or processes ("the way we do things around here"), communication barriers, differing values and goals, or a lack of open feedback. On a collaborative level, blockages involve a lack of trust and motivation among group members, difficulties in management style, and challenges in allocating responsibilities and identifying collaborative partners. Actions to overcome these blockages emphasize personal growth and mindfulness, such as spending time to understand one's fears, showing empathy, engaging more fully, being decisive, and being open to new ideas and help from others. It also suggests active listening, being aware of group dynamics, and engaging in open communication. At the group level this means fostering a collaborative environment through clear communication, aligning vision and focus, and acknowledging and addressing the elephant in the room.

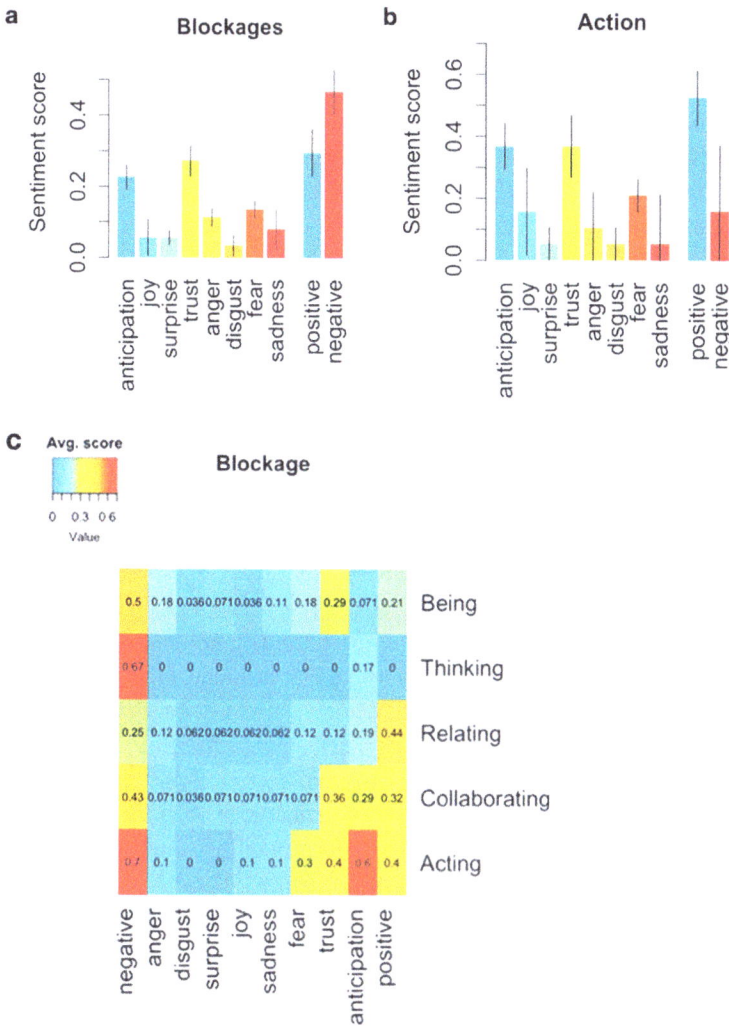

**Figure 14.8:** Average sentiment score across stickers for blockage (a), action (b), and breakdown of scores by IDG goal (c).
Source: Authors' own compilation.
"*Error bars denote standard error*".

# Perspectives

In view of these theoretical considerations and practices, there are a number of implications for the practice of the IDGs. While a cultivation of one's inner experience for oneself is essential, this has interdependent impacts on the outer world. For instance, qualities of being such as presence and self-awareness not only support one's ability to make sense of what is happening and be resilient in the face of challenges, they will tend to have contagious consequences on the way others around us are better able to contain their own inner experience. In this sense, our own *being* has a quality of *acting* in the social arena. IDGs, in this way, offer a systematic framework to phenomenologically relate inner experiences to outer impacts. This is particularly relevant when defining goals in relation to their self-other dynamics, such as in the quote attributed to Mahatma Gandhi: "If you want to change the world, start with yourself." One key question for practitioners would be: How can contemplative practices support the relating and acting IDG categories?

This is particularly since there is a possible danger in overvaluing inner experience. There have been many critics of the ways in which inner practices can reinforce individualist mindsets and increase the stress load on individual resilience (Loy & Purser, 2016; Purser, 2019). The framing proposed in this chapter offers a multilevel *relational* approach to inner practice, which "interdependent-izes" one's inner parts and social networks rather than isolating and "silo-izing". Such a wide understanding of inner practice starts to be seen in circles valuing collective intelligence and self-organization, with processes such as Holacracy (Robertson, 2015), though they are still rare in corporate settings.

Also, while acting qualities such as courage and optimism are enacted in social spaces, they also have a role in the practice of being. For example, facing a difficult emotion takes courage, and reframing a very challenging circumstance with a bright outlook takes optimism. In this sense, we are always *acting* while *being*, and vice versa. Corporate and team leaders, politicians and activists could, by conceiving of inner practice as a form of action, include more of their inner experiences in ways that are coherent with their world-changing agendas and values. A feature of high-performing teams is the ability to process emotions effectively (Paik, Seo, & Jin, 2019).

There are also important benefits from integrating a positive psychology emphasis on introspective being practices. By explicitly valuing somatic pleasure, being practices could be potentiated. As such, when describing and practicing *being*, one is orienting toward practicing *well-being*. There is a surge of new approaches to bringing happiness-oriented corporate training (e.g., "Search Inside Yourself" from Google) and employment positions such as chief happiness officers (Carelli, 2024). Relational safety in the environment, from inner parts of the self, to dyadic relationships and geopolitical environments, is a fundamental condition for skillfully accessing inner experience. Therefore, more process-oriented practices such as individual check-ins (how we are arriving emotionally in the meeting), or a short three-minute meditation at the beginning of meetings (Den Heijer, Koole, & Stettina, 2017) which could be adapted to invite a reflexive sensing into the quality of the relational space, helping to build trust, transparency, and vulnerability. While not making business meetings and other action-oriented gatherings a form of psychotherapy, a nervous system-informed approach would welcome all emerging emotions, allow space to process them in real-time, and put emphasis on small successes, joys, and all other opportunities to celebrate.

# Conclusion

Recognizing the different levels of individuation (dyad, group, community), we propose a social somatics approach to sense and feel into the different scales of social individuation through relational reflexivity. At the center of the approach is the relation, holding together interdependent dividuals across levels. This relational, multilevel approach therefore aims to generalize relational well-being at all scales – from neurons to nations. Recognizing nested inner experiences, we propose that Inner Development Goals spiral across scales: actions at a "lower" level impact, being at a "higher" level, reminiscent of the contemplative activism tradition of engaged Buddhism that navigates the tension between being and acting at the individual and social body (*sangha*) scales. Positing nonjudgemental reflexivity as a central posture, our approach promotes a joyful inquiry of the nature of the social self – what is the "I" that is the source of being, thinking, feeling, relating, and acting right now, right here? And how does *it* feel? (It is maybe not surprising that Socrates, promoter of the *dialogos* as a practice of perspectival shift and reframing, encapsulated his posture as ultimately reflexive: "know thyself".) A question at the center of Zen koans and integral metamodern thinking that we hope our theory and practice helps shed light on to further our journey toward increasing relational well-being beyond individuals.

# References

Anderson, P. W. (1972). More Is Different. *Science, 177*(4047), 393–396. DOI: https://doi.org/10.1126/science.177.4047.393.

Baeck, R. (2022). *Collective presencing: An emerging human capacity*. https://book.collectivepresencing.org/.

Bandura, A. (2001). Social cognitive theory: An agentic perspective. Annual review of psychology, 52(1), 1–26.

Barabási, A.-L. (2016). *Network science*. Cambridge University Press.

Beckes, L. & Coan, J. A. (2011). Social baseline theory: The role of social proximity in emotion and economy of action. *Social and Personality Psychology Compass, 5*(12), 976–988. DOI: https://doi.org/10.1111/j.1751-9004.2011.00400.x.

Burbea, R. (2014). *Seeing that frees: Meditations on emptiness and dependent arising*. Troubador Publishing Ltd.

Carelli, J. (2024, Jan. 6). Qui est vraiment le chief happiness officer ? Harvard Business Review France. https://www.hbrfrance.fr/chroniques-experts/2019/04/25563-qui-est-vraiment-le-chief-happiness-officer/. [Accessed Apr. 13, 2024].

Chikersal, P., Tomprou, M., Kim, Y. J., Woolley, A. W., & Dabbish, L. (2017). Deep structures of collaboration: physiological correlates of collective intelligence and group satisfaction. *CSCW '17: Proceedings of the 2017 ACM Conference on Computer Supported Cooperative Work and Social Computing*, 873–888. https://doi.org/10.1145/2998181.2998250.

Wilson, D. S., & Coan, J. A. (2021). Groups as organisms: Implications for therapy and training. *Clinical Psychology Review, 85*, 101987. DOI: https://doi.org/10.1016/j.cpr.2021.101987.

Czégel, D., Zachar, I., & Szathmáry, E. (2019). Multilevel selection as Bayesian inference, major transitions in individuality as structure learning. *Royal Society Open Science, 6*(8), 190202. DOI: https://doi.org/10.1098/rsos.190202.

Den Heijer, P., Koole, W., & Stettina, C. J. (2017). Don't forget to breathe: A controlled trial of mindfulness practices in agile project teams. In H. Baumeister, H. Lichter, & M. Riebisch (eds.), *Agile processes in software engineering and extreme programming. XP 2017. Lecture notes in business information processing, vol 283* (pp. 103–118*).* Springer, Cham. DOI: https://doi.org/10.1007/978-3-319-57633-6_7.

Descola, P. (2014). *Beyond nature and culture* (Paperback edition). The University of Chicago Press.

Durkheim, E. ([1893] 1984). *The Division of Labor in Society.* Halls, W.D., Trans., The Free Press, New York. DOI: https://doi.org/10.1007/978-1-349-17729-5.

Feldman, B. B., Tupikina, L., & Santolini, M. (2024). From Self to Group to Community: Integrating Developmental and Multi-Level Approaches in Somatic Therapy. *PsyArXiv.* DOI: https://doi.org/10.31234/osf.io/rtw2b.

Filippi, P. D. & Santolini, M. (2023). Extitutional theory: Modelling structured social dynamics beyond institutions. *Ephemera: Theory and Politics in Organization, 23*(2).

Fonagy, P., Gergely, G., & Target, M. (2007). The parent–infant dyad and the construction of the subjective self. *Journal of Child Psychology and Psychiatry, 48*(3–4), 288–328. DOI: https://doi.org/10.1111/j.1469-7610.2007.01727.x.

Fredrickson, B. L. (2001). The role of positive emotions in positive psychology: The broaden-and-build theory of positive emotions. *American Psychologist, 56*(3), 218. https://psycnet.apa.org/journals/amp/56/3/218/.

Fuhs, C. J. (2016). *A latent growth analysis of hierarchical complexity and perspectival skills in adulthood* (Publication No. 10000443) [Doctoral dissertation, Fielding Graduate University]. ProQuest Dissertations Publishing.

Furr, N. (2009). *Cognitive flexibility: The adaptive reality of concrete organization change.* Stanford University.

Gallup, G. G. (1970). Chimpanzees: Self-recognition. *Science, 167*(3914), 86–87. DOI: https://doi.org/10.1126/science.167.3914.86.

Granovetter, M. S. (1973). The strength of weak ties. *American Journal of Sociology, 78*(6), 1360–1380. DOI: https://doi.org/10.1086/225469.

Gross, E. B. & Medina-DeVilliers, S. E. (2020). Cognitive processes unfold in a social context: A review and extension of social baseline theory. *Frontiers in Psychology, 11*, 378. DOI: https://doi.org/10.3389/fpsyg.2020.00378.

Gunaratana, H. (1988). *The jhanas in Theravada Buddhist meditation.* Buddhist Publication Society Sri Lanka. http://urbandharma.org/pdf/TheJhanas.pdf

Hegel, G. W. F. (1807). *The phenomenology of spirit* (1st ed). Cambridge University Press.

Higgins, J. P. (2002). Nonlinear systems in medicine. *The Yale Journal of Biology and Medicine, 75*(5–6), 247. https://www.ncbi.nlm.nih.gov/pmc/articles/PMC2588816/.

Jockers, M. L. (2015). *Mjockers/syuzhet* [HTML]. *GitHub.* https://github.com/mjockers/syuzhet.

Kallo, B. A. A., Michael Rotolo, Patricia Tevington, Justin Nortey and Asta. (2023, December 7). Spirituality among Americans. *Pew Research Center's Religion & Public Life Project.* https://www.pewresearch.org/religion/2023/12/07/spirituality-among-americans/. [Accessed Feb. 17, 2024].

Kauffman, S. A. (1993). *The origins of order: Self-organization and selection in evolution.* Oxford University Press.

Klein, B., & Hoel, E. (2020). The emergence of informative higher scales in complex networks. *Complexity, 2020*, 1–12. DOI: https://doi.org/10.1155/2020/8932526.

Krachun, C., Lurz, R., Mahovetz-Myers, L., & Hopkins, W. (2019). Mirror self-recognition and its relationship to social cognition in chimpanzees. *Animal Cognition, 22*, 1171–1183. DOI: https://doi.org/10.1007/s10071-019-01309-7.

Krakauer, D., Bertschinger, N., Olbrich, E., Flack, J. C., & Ay, N. (2020). The information theory of individuality. *Theory in Biosciences, 139*(2), 209–223. DOI: https://doi.org/10.1007/s12064-020-00313-7.

Lazega, E. (2021). Networks and Neo-Structural Sociology. In R. Light & J. Moody (eds.), *The Oxford Handbook of Social Networks* (pp. 49–70). Oxford University Press. DOI: https://doi.org/10.1093/oxfordhb/9780190251765.013.8.

Lazega, E., Jourda, M.-T., Mounier, L., & Stofer, R. (2008). Catching up with big fish in the big pond? Multilevel network analysis through linked design. *Social Networks*, *30*(2), 159–176. DOI: https://doi.org/10.1016/j.socnet.2008.02.001.

Loy, D., & Purser, R. (2016, Oct. 10). Beyond McMindfulness, by David Loy and Ron Purser, part 1. Mountain Cloud Zen Center. https://www.mountaincloud.org/beyond-mcmindfulness-by-david-loy-part-1/. [Accessed Jan. 10, 2024].

Mancastroppa, M., Iacopini, I., Petri, G., & Barrat, A. (2023). Hyper-cores promote localization and efficient seeding in higher-order processes. *Nature Communications*, *14*(1), 6223. DOI: https://doi.org/10.1038/s41467-023-41887-2.

Maturana, H. R. & Varela, F. J. (1980). *Autopoiesis and cognition: The realization of the living* (1st edition). D. Reidel Publishing Company.

Maynard Smith, J. & Szathmáry, E. (1999). *The origins of life: From the birth of life to the origin of language*. Oxford University Press.

McMillen, P. & Levin, M. (2024). Collective intelligence: A unifying concept for integrating biology across scales and substrates. *Communications Biology*, *7*(1), 378. DOI: https://doi.org/10.1038/s42003-024-06037-4.

Moreno, J. L. (1934). *Who shall survive?: A new approach to the problem of human interrelations*. Nervous and Mental Disease Publishing Co.

Paik, Y., Seo, M.-G., & Jin, S. (2019). Affective information processing in self-managing teams: The role of emotional intelligence. *The Journal of Applied Behavioral Science*, *55*(2), 235–267. DOI: https://doi.org/10.1177/0021886319832013.

Porges, S. W. (2001). The polyvagal theory: Phylogenetic substrates of a social nervous system. *International Journal of Psychophysiology*, *42*(2), 123–146. DOI: https://doi.org/10.1016/S0167-8760(01)00162-3.

Purser, R. (2019). *McMindfulness: How mindfulness became the new capitalist spirituality*. Repeater.

Riedl, C., Kim, Y. J., Gupta, P., Malone, T. W., & Woolley, A. W. (2021). Quantifying collective intelligence in human groups. *Proceedings of the National Academy of Sciences*, *118*(21), e2005737118. DOI: https://doi.org/10.1073/pnas.2005737118.

Robertson, B. J. (2015). *Holacracy: The new management system for a rapidly changing world*. Henry Holt and Company.

Sahakian, B. J., Langley, C., & Leong, V. (2021, June 25). Why is cognitive flexibility important and how can you improve it? *World Economic Forum*. https://www.weforum.org/agenda/2021/06/cognitive-flexibility-thinking-iq-intelligence/. [Accessed Mar. 9, 2024].

Semuels, A. (2023). World's best companies of 2023. *Time*. https://time.com/collection/worlds-best-companies-2023/.

Sighele, S. (1892). *La foule criminelle: Essai de psychologie collective / Scipio Sighele ; traduit de l'italien par Paul Vigny*. Hachette Livre Bnf.

Simon, H. A. (1962). The architecture of complexity. *Proceedings of the American Philosophical Society*, *106*(6), 467–482. DOI: https://doi.org/10.7551/mitpress/12107.003.0011.

Smith, J. M. & Szathmary, E. (1997). *The major transitions in evolution*. Oxford University Press.

Taramasco, C., Cointet, J.-P., & Roth, C. (2010). Academic team formation as evolving hypergraphs. *Scientometrics*, *85*(3), 721–740. https://doi.org/10.1007/s11192-010-0226-4.

Newen, A., De Bruin, L., & Gallagher, S. (Eds.). (2018). *The Oxford handbook of 4E cognition*. Oxford University Press.

Tononi, G., Boly, M., Massimini, M., & Koch, C. (2016). Integrated information theory: From consciousness to its physical substrate. *Nature Reviews Neuroscience, 17*(7), 450–461. DOI: https://doi.org/10.1038/nrn.2016.44.

Varela, F. (2000). Towards a science of interbeing. In G. Watson, S. Batchelor, & G. Claxton (eds.), *The Psychology of Awakening* (pp. 71–89). Samuel Weiser, Inc.

Vervaeke, J. (2019). Ep. 31—Awakening from the Meaning Crisis—Embodied-Embedded RR as Dynamical-Developmental GI [Video recording]. https://www.youtube.com/watch?v=gfKcVbNd7Xc [Accessed 2024-11-03 10:33:03].

Weare, S. (2020). Rhythm and safety of social engagement: Polyvagal theory informed dance/movement therapy. *Expressive Therapies Capstone Theses, 347.* https://digitalcommons.lesley.edu/expressive_theses/347.

White, S. C. (2017). Relational wellbeing: Re-centring the politics of happiness, policy and the self. *Policy & Politics, 45*(2), 121–136. DOI: https://doi.org/10.1332/030557317X14866576265970.

Wilson, D. S. & Wilson, E. O. (2007). Rethinking the theoretical foundation of sociobiology. *The Quarterly Review of Biology, 82*(4), 327–348. DOI: https://doi.org/10.1086/522809.

Woolley, A. W., Chabris, C. F., Pentland, A., Hashmi, N., & Malone, T. W. (2010). Evidence for a collective intelligence factor in the performance of human groups. *Science, 330*(6004), 686–688. DOI: https://doi.org/10.1126/science.1193147.

Timo von Wirth and Petra Jansen

# Chapter 15
# Connectedness: Unpacking an essential factor of the Inner Development Goals

**Abstract:** Connectedness is one of the most fundamental human needs across cultures. Being able to connect has also been considered essential in diverse theories of leadership. Given its fundamental role, it is a logical consequence that connectedness is also presented as one factor of the Inner Development Goals (IDG). However, we argue for a deeper and pluralized understanding of connectedness, integrating perspectives from psychology, sociology, and sustainability science. This chapter offers three objectives: first, to present an interdisciplinary definition of connectedness as a key potential for inner development; second, to critically reflect on its embedded nature within the IDGs; and third, to examine the scientific evidence linking connectedness to sustainability-oriented action and stewardship. Despite limited knowledge on underlying processes, we underscore the importance of considering connectedness as a dynamic, unfolding process that transcends the traditional human-nature dichotomy. The chapter concludes with highlighting avenues for future research as well as practical implications for nurturing connectedness as an enabling condition.

**Keywords:** connectedness, inner human qualities, Inner Development Goals, leadership, framework, sustainability, human action, stewardship

# Introduction: The cross-cutting character of connectedness

Across cultures, one of the most fundamental human needs is connectedness (Aubel & Coulibaly, 2023). The human recognizes his, her, or their connection with all life, indeed with being as a whole, of which he or she is a part. Albert Schweitzer expressed this powerfully with his words: "Ich bin Leben, das leben will, inmitten von Leben, das leben will" [I am life that wants to live, in the midst of life that wants to live] (Albert Schweizer Zentrum, 2017, p. 1). Plato already noted in his renowned dialogue *Timaios* that the individual rationality of every human being is part of the divine or cosmic rationality that determines the rules of the entire cosmos (Ceming, 2021). Connectedness can be differentiated as a multidimensional core of spirituality along the

**Note:** *Both authors contributed equally to this publication..*

https://doi.org/10.1515/9783111337913-016

dimensions of connectedness with nature, with other human beings or with a higher meaning (Bucher, 2022).

Given its fundamental role, it is a logical consequence that connectedness is also presented as one essential factor of the Inner Development Goals (IDG) (Inner Development Goals, n.d.). Despite numerous attempts to define connectedness, a unified definition remains absent. Diverse scientific communities have conceptualized connectedness differently. In this chapter we argue for reconsidering connectedness within the IDG framework with an interdisciplinary perspective that combines understandings of connectedness rooted in psychology, sociology, and sustainability science. The skills and inner human qualities addressed with the IDGs are supposed to require enabling conditions such as lived experiences and particular settings, while becoming expressed and developed "only in relationship and through action". It is argued that "inner development is a collective and cultural process that is almost always expressed in community" (Inner Development Goals, n.d., p. 3). These assumptions initially make clear that different forms of connectedness might in fact play a crucial role in all IDG dimensions. As such a cross-cutting quality, connectedness may serve as a particular enabler for many other skills to co-emerge and may have certain unique effects at the nexus between inner human development and the actual enabling of sustainable futures. The current positioning of connectedness within the IDG framework would then be misleading. It appears evident that connectedness is essential in the relational (*being* and *relating*) and social (*collaborating*) domains of the IDGs, while its role in the domains of *thinking* and *acting* is not immediately tangible. We will revisit all five IDG domains later in this chapter.

The objectives of this chapter are threefold: first, we delve deeper into the cross-disciplinary definition of connectedness as a key potential (i.e., resource) for inner development. Secondly, we critically reflect about the embedded nature of connectedness as a cross-cutting concept within the IDGs. Thirdly, we critically reflect the existing scientific evidence about how connectedness relates to sustainability-oriented action and stewardship, which has practical implications for the usefulness of applying the IDG framework and beyond.

## Deepening the cross-cutting character of connectedness

When reflecting about the IDG framework, connectedness appears to have a cross-cutting and interrelated character. This is relevant as such a reflection may help in co-creating and stimulating connectedness, for instance through novel ways of acting. The IDG framework suggests that the presence of connectedness may have beneficial influences on inner development or even onto sustainability-oriented action. What does the presence of connectedness actually mean for individual or collective action towards sustainable futures? This is in fact a relevant question regarding the usefulness of the IDG framework overall and cannot comprehensively be addressed in the context of this chapter. Evidence from previous research is ambiguous and has been generated in disconnected and often segregated scientific communities, such as environmental psychology, sociology, and sustainability science. In fact, there is still limited scientific knowledge about the underlying processes, in particular why and how certain internal dimensions are able to leverage transformation towards (sustainable) futures (Wamsler et al., 2021). Here, we provide a compact summary from relevant literatures in these fields.

Taking the perspective of sustainability science, Wamsler et al. (2021) described the concept of connectedness with entailing the elements of compassion, empathy, kindness, and generosity, all related to pro-socialness and connectedness to nature. A connectedness with the human and more-than-human are highlighted as one of the key factors for inner–outer transformations (Wamsler et al., 2021). Diverse literatures from sustainability science and environmental management studies have particularly looked into the human connectedness with nature (e.g., Ives et al., 2018). These literatures have provided conceptual frameworks to describe human–nature connections and provide insight into the implications of such connectedness for environmental engagement, stewardship, and action towards more sustainable futures. A global meta-analysis has found that individuals with higher human–nature connectedness showed more pro-nature behaviors (Barragan-Jason et al., 2022). Likewise, this study argued that human–nature connectedness can purposefully be enhanced by targeted practices and presents selected practices with likely effects (e.g., mindfulness training). However, such studies built mostly upon correlational study designs and often reduce the multifaceted and dynamic relationship between nature connectedness and (intentions to) human acting. It therefore makes sense to further deepen the cross-disciplinary understanding of connectedness.

Sustainability science and environmental sociology scholars are increasingly drawing on ideas of relational thinking and consider connectedness as a dynamic, unfolding as well as embodied process to better acknowledge the complexity of human–nature connectedness. For example, scholars have pointed to the relational sociology of Emirbayer (1997) and others to articulate a "social relational approach" to study connectedness and its sustainability implications rooted in quantitative social network analysis (West et al., 2020). Earlier research highlighted the complex interdependences that characterize human–nature connectedness and related natural resource governance outcomes (Bodin & Prell, 2011). Diverse sociology scholars suggest a deep relational ontology of human–nature connections and argue for overcoming the distinctions between "human" and "natural" entities, also building upon Emirbayer's (1997) work or for example later arguments by Latour (2005).

From a pedagogic-psychological point of view, connectedness can be differentiated into the following four aspects (see also Bucher, 2022): Connectedness with oneself (*self-love or self-compassion*), with others (*empathy, compassion, altruism, pro-socialness*), with the surrounding nature or nonhuman actors (*nature connectedness*), and with the transcendent or a larger meaning (*transcendence or spirituality*).

Henschke and Sedlmeier (2023) defined self-love as an attitude of self-kindness, which includes the aspects of self-contact, self-acceptance, and self-care. Self-compassion integrates the positive aspects of self-kindness, common humanity, and mindfulness and has three negative counterparts (self-judgment instead of self-kindness; isolation instead of common humanity; and overidentification instead of mindfulness) (Neff, 2003). For example, pro-social behavior or pro-socialness has been defined as everyday kindness and inspiring acts of heroism towards others (Smith & Mackie, 2007). Nature connectedness can be determined as "an individual's subjective sense of their relationship with the natural world" (Pritchard et al., 2020, p. 1145). Connectedness to a higher meaning can be defined as unconditional love, a love that is always within us and that removes the separation from the other (Jansen & Kunze, 2019). Villani et al. (2019) explained spirituality, referencing King and Boyatzis (2015), as a human desire for transcendence, introspection, interconnectedness, and the quest for meaning in life and found a substantial impact on subjective well-being.

In fact, meta-analyses have found, for example, that people who are more connected to nature also tend to have higher levels of self-reported hedonic and eudaemonic well-being (Pritchard et al., 2020). It has already been shown that some aspects of connectedness are related to flourishing, which can be seen as an alternative concept of well-being (VanderWeele, 2017). Flourishing integrates, among others, states of happiness and life satisfaction, mental and physical health, virtues, and close relationships. Significant relations are found between self-love and pro-socialness on the one side and flourishing on the other (Rahe & Jansen, 2023). Furthermore, self-love and pro-socialness are positively related to nature connectedness.

When considering the different dimensions of the IDG framework, it seems evident that connectedness to oneself, to others, and to nature can, according to Bucher (2022), be attributed to the dimensions of *being*, *relating*, and *collaborating*. However, the connectedness to a higher meaning could be attributed to *being* and *relating*. Hence, we argue that connectedness reaches not only into the IDG domains of being, thinking, and relating, but instead features a key cross-cutting potential that is related to all facets of the IDGs.

## Reflecting on the nurturing of connectedness across the IDG dimensions

If connectedness is related to all five dimensions of the IDG framework, it is a central question how we can strengthen connectedness within each dimension as a central source for instigating sustainability-oriented action. In this chapter, we provide concrete ideas on which way connectedness could be established and nurtured within all five domains of the IDGs. An overview with one nurturing example in each domain is given in Table 15.1.

**Table 15.1:** Definition of connectedness in the five IDG domains and one practice example.

| IDG domain | Definition of connectedness within IDG domain | Example of nurturing connectedness in IDG domain |
| --- | --- | --- |
| **Being** | Establishing a positive relationship to the self | Practice of self-compassion |
| **Thinking** | Representing of knowledge and cognitions in networks | Each cognitive task can train connectedness in thinking |
| **Relating** | Bonding with other human beings and nature | Practice of metta meditation |
| **Collaborating** | Combining and concerting engagement entailing communication and trust | Practicing art-based co-creation to stimulate head, heart, and hands learning |
| **Acting** | Enabling or evolving through joint action and stewardship | Action-oriented programs of education for sustainable development |

# Nurturing connectedness in "being"

The term *being* (or the relationship to the self) summarizes the aspects of the inner compass, integrity and authenticity, openness and learning minds, self-awareness, and presence in the IDGs. However, what is the self? One's point of view shapes the answer to this question, be it biological, psychological, theological, or philosophical, for example. From a psychological perspective, there is often a differentiation made between self-concept and self-worth, whereby self-concept tends to be understood as a neutral description of oneself, such as, "I am a cheerful person", while self-worth is an evaluation of oneself, for example, "I am not assertive enough". An essential prerequisite for developing the self-concept and self-esteem is the recognition of oneself, i.e., the realization that one's self is different from the world around it (Jansen & Kunze, 2019).

One possibility to nurture connectedness to the self is to practice self-compassion or self-love. There is robust evidence from counseling and mental health research that practicing self-compassion can strengthen the connectedness to the self and supports psychological flourishing, coping abilities, and reduces diverse pathologies (e.g., Ewert, C., Vater, A., & Schröder-Abé, 2021; Germer & Neff, 2013). Relating to the own body, a systematic review and meta-analysis showed that self-compassion interventions with medium effect sizes led to a more positive body image and fewer body image distortions next to a reduction in pathological eating behavior. Furthermore, a study on the topic of self-compassion and internal body signals has relevant insights (Kirschner et al., 2019). Participants were divided into five different groups and received either a) a brief self-compassion intervention related to bodily signals, b) a loving-kindness meditation form intervention involving the self, c) an intervention in which they were asked to think about an angry situation, d) to imagine a supermarket purchase, or e) to remember a positive event. In addition to measuring the state of self-compassion, the study leaders measured heart rate, heart rate variability, and skin conductance. Both interventions involving compassion resulted in higher heart rate variability and reduced heart rate and skin conductance, a state which is related to health benefits.

An easy task from current self-compassion trainings would be to write down how you treat yourself when you fail. Is this the same as you would treat your best friend or in some way different? How is your voice if you treat yourself and your best friend? What do you feel in your body? Quite often, we treat ourselves harsher than anyone else. We need to connect with ourselves in a friendly way to connect with others with compassion and love. When considering the nexus of nurturing connectedness to self with the ambitions of the IDGs to make contributions to achieving the Sustainable Development Goals (SDGs) (i.e., enabling sustainable development with "inner" human development), recent research indicates potential for further randomized controlled study designs as the vast majority of existing studies build upon correlational designs and therefore reveal methodological caveats when addressing the causal influences of increasing practices of self-compassion or self-love (e.g., through mindfulness trainings) onto more sustainable lifestyles. For example, in correlational design studies it has been shown that the observing aspect of dispositional mindfulness is related to the explicit attitudes towards vegetarian nutrition as one aspect of sustainability (Siebertz et al., 2022). Also in an intervention study, different types of mindfulness training – a compassion and caring-based mental training and an attention-focused mindfulness training – as well as a stress-reduction training enhanced the positive, explicit attitudes towards vegetarian food (Winkelmair & Jansen, 2023). More preregistered intervention studies with a sufficient number of participants who practice self-compassion and mindfulness over a longer period such as a year has to be conducted to investigate the influence of connectedness to self onto sustainable behaviors.

# Nurturing connectedness in "thinking"

Under the term *thinking* within the IDG framework, the aspects of critical thinking, complexity awareness, perspective skills, sense making, and long-term orientation and visioning are summarized. This differentiation is entirely different from one in general psychology. From a general psychological point of view, thinking is one aspect of cognition. Cognition is rooted in the Latin term *cognoscere* and covers various topics such as memory, perception, attention, language, thinking, and other cognitive concepts (Frensch, 2006). Thinking can be counted among the higher cognitive abilities, in contrast to perception and attention, which are more basic cognitive abilities. It can be differentiated into four aspects: a) logical reasoning, in which deductive judgments are central, b) a judgment of probability, in which inductive conclusions are important, c) problem-solving thinking, or d) creative thinking (Funke, 2006).

Furthermore, decision making is also some form of thinking. To be able to think, we need the ability to represent knowledge. Several theoretical network models exist to describe this representation of knowledge (Turk & Waller, 2020), for example, the hierarchically semantic network model of Collins and Quillian (1969). It assumes that the meanings of experiences we store as knowledge are organized within the framework of a logical hierarchy of concepts in logical superordinate and subordinate relationships, which are also used to connect the network nodes. To be able to retrieve certain categorized information from memory, specific nodes must be processed. However, this is only one theoretical concept for specific cognitive tasks. Another theoretical group of models are connectionist models. These networks comprise many simple units connected to each other in parallel networks (Solso, 2005). Cognition can be explained with the help of complex networks while simulating the behavior of neuron-like units (Kellog, 2016). In other words, cognition or thinking, as one part of it, is from a theoretical point of view per se connected.

Nevertheless, the importance of connectedness is not only a theoretical assumption; connectedness also exists in the underlying brain mechanism. If we complete a task, many brain areas are involved and communicate with each other, which can be described as an integration mechanism of neurons within complex networks. One aspect of thinking is decision making, including the activation of neurons in many brain areas. However, the activation is task-dependent. Quite recently, it was shown that the prospective value difference between options in decision-making tasks was tracked by a specific network of brain regions, including the ventromedial prefrontal cortex (Nitsch et al., 2024). This means that in a decision-making process, even values of the options are represented in a mental map. The principle of map-like coding of entities for complex decision-making tasks can also be seen during spatial navigation, where decision making is crucial (Epstein et al., 2017). However, these were only two examples of an aspect of cognition. For cognition in general, the default mode network plays an important role (Smallwood et al., 2021). It includes brain regions from the parietal, temporal, and frontal cortex, which show different activation depending on the type of cognitive task. Nevertheless, it makes it clear that connectedness is the critical brain component of thinking and makes clear that thinking is also from a neuroscientific point of view connected.

However, can we train thinking or cognition with connectedness? At first glance, this question seems misleading because, as described above, connectedness per se is perhaps the most essential principle of cognition. But, especially for the older growing population, cognitive scientists are interested in training cognition in the elderly to ameliorate age-related cognitive decline. Besides positive results, evidence exists against the benefits of cognitive training and transcranial stimulations in healthy older adults (Horne et al., 2021). Those negative effects are in line with the work of Gobet and Sala (2022), arguing that the likelihood of finding reliable far effects, which means effects on unrelated tasks of cognitive training, is low. Nevertheless, on the brain level, studies exist which claim that brain changes appear after cognitive training (Román et al., 2017).

## Nurturing connectedness in "relating"

Under the term *relating* within the IDG framework, the aspects of appreciation, connectedness, humility, empathy, and compassion are summarized. Even the concepts like empathy and compassion seem to be similar or overlapping at first glance, while they actually differ in many aspects.

Empathy can be differentiated in two aspects: cognitive and emotional empathy. Cognitive empathy describes the ability to understand the emotions of others. Emotional empathy, on the other hand, describes the ability to empathize with the feelings of other people (Wirtz, 2019). However, there seem to be almost as many definitions of empathy as there are researchers in the field. Some researchers do not distinguish between cognitive and affective components but focus only on the emotional or affective aspect. Defining the term compassion is just as difficult as defining the term empathy. One possible definition is that compassion includes the following components: Recognizing suffering, understanding universal human suffering, feeling for the person suffering, tolerating unpleasant feelings, and the motivation to alleviate suffering (Strauss et al., 2016). Nevertheless, compassion must be distinguished from pity, as it rather describes the great power of being there for the other with a feeling of loving-kindness.

Empathy, and especially compassion, can be trained, for example, by metta (or loving-kindness) meditation and the tonglen practice. Metta meditation begins with sitting in a quiet place in a suitable posture. At first, four self-selected sentences are often formulated, such as, "May I be happy", "May I be healthy and cheerful". These sentences can spread a feeling of warmth and develop a sense of self-love. In a second step, the four sentences are extended to people close to you: "May my child be happy", "May my parents be free from serious ailments". This benevolent attitude towards people who are dear to the individual is maintained for as long as it feels good. In a third step, a person is chosen who is more familiar to you, perhaps because you often meet them on the street or have seen them on television. This person is also wished all the love in the world, that he or she is happy and do not have to endure any suffering. This is how we form a bond with a person who was originally a stranger. It makes it possible to develop a closeness to all people, and separation can disappear. What follows is the supposedly most difficult step: extending loving-kindness towards people who we tend to regard as difficult, such as an unfriendly neighbor, or the choleric boss. The metta (or loving-kindness) meditations are intended to help us forgive the injustice experienced by the other person (Salzberg, 2003). In the tonglen practice, as a form of meditation in Tibetan Buddhism, the practitioner practices breathing in the suffering of others and sending out love and compassion (Brach, 2013). The experience of how the other person suffers and the compassion for the other person relates to the breath. Tonglen can be seen as a way of making friends with oneself and with the other person (Chödrön, 2016).

# Nurturing connectedness in "collaborating"

The term *collaborating* in the IDGs refers to aspects such as communication skills, co-creation skills, inclusive mindsets, and intercultural competence, as well as trust and mobilization skills. In essence, this domain features abilities to help actors create and hold safe spaces and communicate with diverse stakeholders with different values, skills, and competencies. In fact, these skills were highlighted in diverse studies on sustainability transformation and sustainability-oriented action research as key ingredients to co-create impact-oriented collaborative agendas for sustainability (Itten et al., 2021; Wiek et al., 2014).

Collaborating can be considered as a connecting act entailing communication as an essential factor of establishing, maintaining, and nurturing connectedness as well as trust building as a key ingredient for becoming connected. Similarly, trust can be strengthened when experiencing connectedness (Sturgis et al., 2015). Intercultural collaboration has been well known for its relations to connectedness, as numerous studies from organizational sociology, management studies, and education studies show. Connectedness can be both a resource but also an outcome from intercultural collaboration, as collaboration benefits from the connected capacities and shared human agency, while also feeding positively into processes of collaborative action across cultures (Gale et al., 2021). In practice, different exercises and creative practices can support the emergence of connectedness capabilities through ways of collaborating. For example, Snepvangers and Rourke (2020) demonstrate how creative practices paired with a community-building framework helped international students in Australia to develop connectedness.

Exercising collaboration through connectedness is established in several approaches of co-creative practices. For example, learning how to apply co-creation techniques to motivate, build, develop, and facilitate collaborative relationships with diverse stakeholders is a relevant skill in inter- and transdisciplinary research as well as in diverse creative sectors. Several tools and techniques as well as process designs are available that help setting up spaces for co-creation and trustful collaboration, for example to support the implementation of nature-based solutions (Dushkova & Kuhlicke, 2024).

Training co-creation and collaboration to nurture connectedness can build upon art-based approaches. For example, Renowden, Beer, and Mata (2022) showed that using art-based approaches to science communication can foster nature connectedness. By applying the head, heart, and hands learning framework through a series of participatory ArtScience workshops, three key observations were made in the context of the biodiversity crisis in Australia. Through the art-based series of co-creative workshops, participants firstly learned or discovered "something new about biodiversity which appeared to be a thrilling and motivating experience". Secondly participants reported the experience of "being in a state of flow, during which they were intrinsically motivated, focused and found joy in the activity". Thirdly participants experienced attunement, that is, participants experienced "ecological awareness, relational knowing and a mindful connection to nature" (Renowden, Beer & Mata, 2022, p. 519).

## Nurturing connectedness in "acting"

The domain of *acting* within the IDGs describes qualities such as courage and confidence in acquiring agency, taking action to break existing practice patterns, proactively generating original ideas, and acting with persistence in uncertain times. This domain addresses the abilities and supportive inner resources for engagement and for actually enabling change. It also includes the ability to sustain the engagement and the perseverance of remaining determined with achieving sustainability targets. Caniglia et al. (2021) defined actions for sustainability with three key dimensions. First, actions for sustainability "are intentionally designed to create transformative change towards sustainability; secondly, involve shared agency of multiple actors; and thirdly, materialize through contextual realization in constantly evolving and emergent settings" (p.95).

When it comes to action, it is apparent that action involving human or nonhuman actors is a connecting act. Many researchers in the field of joint action have investigated the underlying mechanism (Van der Wel et al., 2021). When focusing on the relationship of connectedness with stewardship, it has been shown that connectedness is related to sustainable behavior (Jansen, Hoja, & Rahe, 2024). Diverse studies, for example in the fields of management and leadership studies, have discussed the role of individuals or institutions as potential "stewards" for humans and nature (Zeif et al, 2023; Mackay & Schmitt, 2019). Environmental stewardship, as defined by Bennett et al. (2018), is understood as the "actions taken by individuals, groups or networks of actors, with various motivations and levels of capacity, to protect, care for or responsibly use the environment in pursuit of environmental and/or social outcomes in diverse social–ecological contexts" (p. 597).

This relationship between connectedness and stewarding action may be influenced by how values such as courage, creativity, optimism, and perseverance are manifesting in practice. These values express in action and stewarding practices may feedback positively on our relations with human and nonhuman actors. The human–nature connectedness has received particular attention as a potential leverage for instigating action towards sustainability. A meta-analysis of "experimental studies shows significant increases in human–nature connectedness" following different manipulations involving the contact with nature and mindfulness practices (Barragan-Jason et al., 2022; p. 1). Concrete exercises for human actionability (i.e., ability to act) in general and sustainability-oriented action in particular can be found in programs for education for sustainable development and solution-oriented learning, for example in higher education institutions (Kevany, 2007).

## An embedded perspective on connectedness within the IDG framework

Given the embeddedness, cross-cutting, and dynamic character of connectedness, we propose the following framework to relate a sense of human connection with the IDGs. Figure 15.1 shows the four key dimensions of connectedness, namely *self, others, nature,* and *higher meaning*. We propose to consider the fluid character of connectedness that can last from past to present and future senses of connection, while it always entails an inner and an outer component at the same time. Even an intense feeling of connectedness to self emerges in particular contexts and cannot ignore outer conditions while focusing more on an inward perspective.

## A critical reflection for IDG framework applications and future research

In this chapter we have unpacked the notion of *connectedness* though the different disciplinary lenses of psychology, sociology, and sustainability science. We do recognize that there are many more bodies of knowledge with a rich tradition of scholarly work on the human sense of connection. In terms of the conceptual configuration and validity of the current IDG framework, we call for more rigor and caution in reflecting about the interrelatedness, embeddedness, and dynamic nature of the inner development qualities across the proposed five dimensions. This chapter suggests a more cross-cutting role of connectedness that sees aspects of connectedness being similarly part of other IDG dimensions as well. Moreover, connectedness should be treated as a dynamic and constantly enacted quality that can change over time. Focusing too

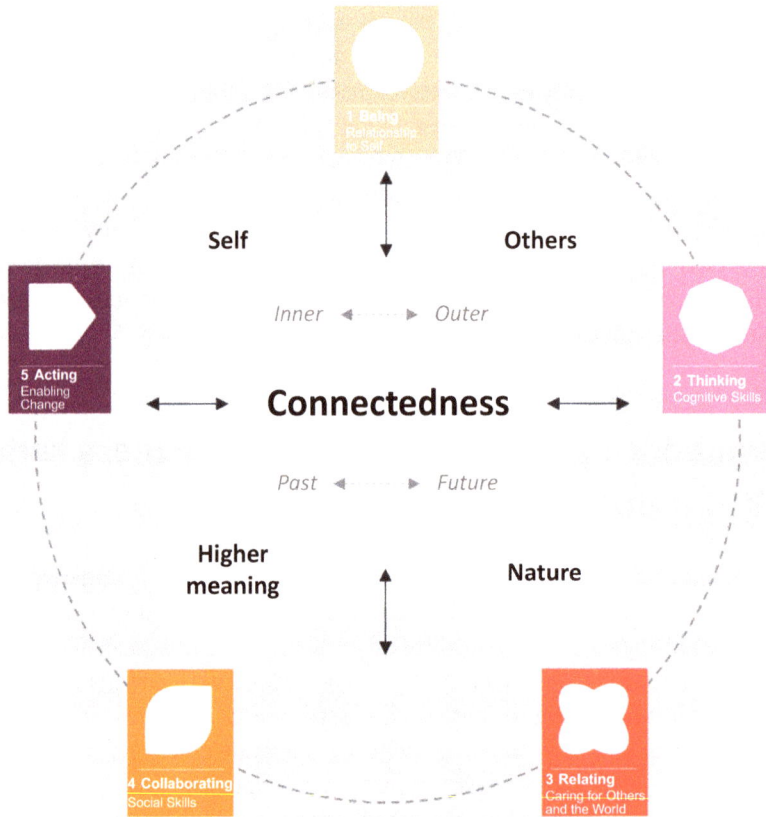

**Figure 15.1:** The embeddedness and interrelatedness of connectedness in the context of the Inner Development Goals.
Source: Original illustration by the authors, using visual elements of the IDG framework (Inner Development Goals. (n.d.).

much on a static idea of relating to others would miss several of its facets. Connectedness might also span across past, current, or future times, for example as an embodied phenomenon of past experiences evoking emotions today while instigating actions in the future.

As we could illustrate with the interdisciplinary framework of connectedness, it has at least four key dimensions. These are the connectedness to self, the connectedness to others, the connectedness to nature (or nonhuman actors), and the connectedness to a higher meaning. We critically acknowledge the limitations of the presented framework, which does not make a claim to be complete. Previous research has, for example, also highlighted the connectedness to the workplace (Brown & Leite, 2023) or the connectedness to culture (Lucero, 2014) as further facets of human connectedness. Instead of aiming for a comprehensive, interdisciplinary model for sense of connection, we rather argue for intensifying future research on the nexus between strengthening human connectedness and its implications on intentions and actions for sustainability. This is the pivotal point for the promises coming along with the IDG framework. How does enriching the personal or collective inner qualities actually contribute to a more sustainable life in the future?

While previous work, for instance in environmental psychology and sociology, has addressed some aspects of this key question, the IDG framework offers potential for further research on the interplay of different inner qualities and their flourishing in relation to achieving the SDGs. This leads to a second domain of future research demand. We consider it relevant to better understand the interactions between levels of inner change with the structural and institutional "outer" conditions enabling or hindering collective change. How far are the effects of inner change absorbed or hampered by often "intangible" structural or institutional conditions (such as infrastructures, cognitive norms, habits)? Such questions have, for example, been addressed recently by Wamsler et al. (2021). The interplay of inner and outer change conditions should be studied ideally in longitudinal research designs. Those research designs can include randomized controlled intervention studies that, for example, offer inner change programs. Likewise, future research could focus firstly on changing outer conditions, as for example in temporary field experiments such as real-world laboratories of sustainability transition experiments (Von Wirth et al., 2019). Such action research interventions could be complemented with research on the role of inner change and qualities of connectedness among the involved actors.

According to the editors' guidelines for this book, we have presented and collectively reflected our conceptual arguments with IDG scholars and practitioners during two workshops. The online workshops were held in March 2024 and allowed for a shared discussion of the conceptual plurality behind the notion of connectedness. Workshop participants appreciated the differentiated conceptualization of connectedness across the five IDG dimensions and agreed to add further rigor in conceptualizing the key inner qualities of the framework based on an interdisciplinary inquiry of existing studies. Participants highlighted that connectedness on an interpersonal level may be enacted and manifested through diverse facets such as empathy, altruism, compassion, or pro-social behavior. This comment supports the approach taken in this chapter to highlight the richness and plurality of facets being tied to connectedness. And it makes clear that even if looking at one facet of the IDGs, such as connectedness, conceptualization remains difficult. For example, one participant in the workshop expressed that, for him, connectedness in thinking refers less to the connectedness of individual nerve cells in the brain during the thinking process, but more to the embeddedness of our thought processes in our social networks and environments. During the workshop, participants also emphasized that certain disciplines from the humanities have a long-standing history of embracing connectedness in their academic work, such as literature studies or philosophy. This feedback aligns with our observations that diverse scientific fields have engaged intensively with connectedness in the past. We call for further interdisciplinary work to allow these different bodies of knowledge speaking to each other to enrich the conceptual underpinning of connectedness in the context of the IDGs. It appears particularly interesting to give more attention to potentially overlooked perspectives from the humanities and arts in the future. Creative, poetic, or reflexive perspectives from the humanities may contribute substantially to further develop IDG tools for strengthening connectedness.

Finally, we draw attention to the practical implications of this work. Given its plurality and dynamic nature, strengthening human connectedness in the light of achieving the SDGs asks for a reflection of existing exercises and practices. There do exist diverse tools to enable a sense of connection to flourish, such as from the Greater Good in Action initiative (Greater Good in Action, 2024). However, many of the existing exercises have been designed without explicitly aiming to support sustainable lifestyles in the future. We therefore invite scholars and practitioners to revisit such existing tool sets and to further develop them towards the particular sustainability objective. This could help in providing answers to the question of how connectedness could be practiced and experienced with particular effects on engaging with sustainable futures and a livable planet. Some of the emerging tools from the IDG community already incorporate this idea (Transition Makers Toolbox, 2024). Likewise, several tools and trainings from the field of education for sustainable development have focused on strengthening the sense of human–nature connections, for example among students (Kleespies & Dierkes, 2023). However, a good starting point for each individual would be to think about what connectedness means for oneself. This can be done on a cognitive or on an emotional level, for example following guiding questions such as: What are the situations and entities that please or touch me? By this, circumstances can be identified that lead to moments and feelings of connectedness.

## Conclusion

We are convinced that being more intensively connected with self, others, nature, or a spiritual, larger meaning has to play a central role in reconsidering humanity's presence and future on planet Earth. As researchers, our vision for the future would be to experimentally investigate the factor of connectedness in the different IDG domains as well as the actual significance of engaging with IDG qualities such as connectedness for sustainable practices. More importantly, we call for inviting people to nurture connectedness: in our being, thinking, relating, collaborating, and acting. Together with IDG colleagues, we are therefore developing training modules that allow experiencing the practice of connectedness for diverse participant groups.

# References

Albert Schweitzer Zentrum. (2017). Albert Schweitzer wissenswert: Informationen zu Leben, Ethik und Werk Albert Schweitzers und seiner Bedeutung für Gegenwart und Zukunft. Frankfurt am Main: Albert Schweitzer Zentrum. https://albert-schweitzer-heute.de/wp-content/uploads/2017/12/DASZ-AS-wissenswert-2017.pdf [Accessed Mar. 27, 2024].

Aubel, J. & Coulibaly, M. (2023). Enhancing Ubuntu: promoting community connectedness—the foundation for social change for girls. In D. Muia & R. Phillips (eds.), *Connectedness, resilience and empowerment: Perspectives on community development* (pp. 1–24). Cham: Springer Nature Switzerland.

Barragan-Jason, G., de Mazancourt, C., Parmesan, C., Singer, M. C., & Loreau, M. (2022). Human–nature connectedness as a pathway to sustainability: A global meta-analysis. *Conservation Letters*, 15(1), e12852. https://doi.org/10.1111/conl.12852.

Bennett, N.J., Whitty, T.S., Finkbeiner, E., Pittman, J., Bassett, H., Gelcich, S. & Allison, E.H. (2018). Environmental stewardship: A conceptual review and analytical framework. *Environmental Management 61, 597–614.* https://doi.org/10.1007/s00267-017-0993-2.

Bodin, Ö., & Prell, C. (Eds.). (2011). Social networks and natural resource management: uncovering the social fabric of environmental governance. Cambridge, UK: Cambridge University Press.

Brach, T. (2013). Finding peace and freedom in your own awakened heart. Carlsbad: Hay House.

Brown, A. & Leite, A. C. (2023). The effects of social and organizational connectedness on employee well-being and remote working experiences during the COVID-19 pandemic. *Journal of Applied Social Psychology*, 53(2), 134–152. https://doi.org/10.1111/jasp.12934.

Bucher, A. (2022). *Verbundenheit*. Münster, Germany: Waxmann.

Caniglia, G., Luederitz, C., von Wirth, T., Fazey, I., Martín-López, B., Hondrila, K., König, A., von Wehrden, H., Schäpke, N. A., Laubichler, M. D., & Lang, D. J. (2021). A pluralistic and integrated approach to action-oriented knowledge for sustainability. *Nature Sustainability*, 4, 93–100 (2021). https://doi.org/10.1038/s41893-020-00616-z.

Chödrön, P. (2016). Tonglen. Der tibetische Weg mit sich selbst und anderen Freundschaft zu schliessen. Arbor Verlag.

Ceming, K. (2021). Von Weltenbürgern, Gotteskindern und Buddhakeimlingen. In Hüther, G. & Spannbauer, C. (Hrsg.). *Verbundenheit* (Seite 33–46). Hogrefe.

Collins, A. M. & Quillian, M. R. (1969). Retrieval time from semantic memory. *Journal of Verbal Learning and Verbal Behavior*, 8, 240–247. https://doi.org/10.1016/S0022-5371(69)80069-1.

Dushkova, D. & Kuhlicke, C. (2024). Making co-creation operational: A RECONECT seven-steps-pathway and practical guide for co-creating nature-based solutions. *MethodsX*, 12, 102495. https://doi.org/10.1016/j.mex.2023.102495.

Emirbayer M. (1997). Manifesto for a relational sociology. *American Journal of Sociology*, 103(2), 281–317. https://doi.org/10.1086/231209.

Epstein, R. A., Patai, E. Z., Julian, J. B., & Spiers, H. J. (2017). The cognitive map in humans: spatial navigation and beyond. *Nature Neuroscience*, 20, 1504–1513. https://doi.org/10.1038/nn.4656.

Ewert, C., Vater, A., & Schröder-Abé, M. (2021). Self-compassion and coping: A meta-analysis. *Mindfulness*, 12, 1063-1077. https://doi.org/10.1007/s12671-020-01563-8.

Frensch, P. A. (2006). Kognition. In J. Funke & P. Frensch (Hrsg.). *Handbuch der Allgemeinen Psychologie – Kognition* (Seite 19–28). Hogrefe.

Funke, J. (2006). Denken: Ansätze und Definitionen. In J. Funke & P. Frensch (Hrsg.), Handbuch der Allgemeinen Psychologie – Kognition (S. 391–399). Göttingen: Hogrefe.

Gale, F., Edenborough, M. A., Boccanfuso, E., Hawkins, M., Thomson, R. J., & Sell, C. (2021). *Promoting intercultural understanding, connectedness, and belonging: An independent evaluation of together for humanity programs*. Western Sydney University. https://doi.org/10.26183/5e44b23990048.

Germer, C. K. & Neff, K. D. (2013). Self-compassion in clinical practice. *Journal of Clinical Psychology, 69*(8), 856–867. https://doi.org/10.1002/jclp.22021.

Gobet, F., & Sala, G. (2023). Cognitive training: A field in search of a phenomenon. *Perspectives on Psychological Science, 18*(1), 125–141. https://doi.org/10.1177/17456916221091830.

Greater Good in Action. (2024). Discover new practices (Connection). *Greater Good in Action.* https://ggia.berkeley.edu/?_ga=2.17678841.1328375834.1711574460-282253166.1711574460#filters=connection [Retrieved Mar. 27, 2024].

Henschke, E. & Sedlmeier, P. (2023). What is self-love? Redefinition of a controversial construct. *The Humanistic Psychologist, 51(3)*, 281–302. https://doi.org/10.1037/hum0000266.

Horne, K.S., Filmer, H.L., Nott, Z.E. Hawi, Z., Pugsley, K., Mattingley, J. B. & Dux, P. E. (2021). Evidence against benefits from cognitive training and transcranial direct current stimulation in healthy older adults. *Nature Human Behavior, 5*, 146–158. https://doi.org/10.1038/s41562-020-00979-5.

Inner Development Goals. (n.d.). Inner Development Goals Framework. *Inner Development Goals.* https://innerdevelopmentgoals.org/framework/ [Accessed Jun. 10, 2024].

Itten, A., Sherry-Brennan, F., Hoppe, T., Sundaram, A., & Devine-Wright, P. (2021). Co-creation as a social process for unlocking sustainable heating transitions in Europe. *Energy Research & Social Science, 74*, 101956.

Ives, C. D., Abson, D. J., Von Wehrden, H., Dorninger, C., Klaniecki, K., & Fischer, J. (2018). Reconnecting with nature for sustainability. *Sustainability Science, 13*, 1389–1397. https://doi.org/10.1007/s11625-018-0542-9.

Jansen, P. & Kunze, P. (2019). *Bildung braucht Liebe.* Arbor.

Jansen, P., Hoja, S., & Rahe, M. (2024). The relationship between the aspects of connectedness and sustainable consumption. *Frontiers in Psychology: Positive Psychology, 14*, 1216944. https://doi.org/10.3389/fpsyg.2023.1216944.

Kellog, R. T. (2016). *Fundamentals of cognitive psychology.* Sage.

Kevany, K. D. (2007). Building the requisite capacity for stewardship and sustainable development. *International Journal of Sustainability in Higher Education, 8(*2), 107–122. https://doi.org/10.1108/14676370710726580.

King P. E., Boyatzis C. (2015). "Religious and spiritual development" in *Handbook of child psychology and developmental science: Socioemotional processes.* 7th Edn. Vol. 3, eds. Lamb M. E., Lerner R. M. (Hoboken, NJ: John Wiley and Sons), 975–1021.

Kirschner, H., Kuyken, W., Wright, K., Roberts, H., Brejcha, C., & Karl, A. (2019). Soothing Your Heart and Feeling Connected: A New Experimental Paradigm to Study the Benefits of Self-Compassion. Clinical Psychological Science, 7(3): 545–565. https://doi.org/10.1177/2167702618812438.

Kleespies, M. W. & Dierkes, P. W. (2023). Connection to nature for sustainable development at universities – What should be done? *Frontiers in Sustainability, 4*, 1249328.

Latour B. (2005). *Reassembling the social: An introduction to actor-network-theory.* Oxford University Press.

Lucero, N. M. (2014). "It's not about place, it's about what's inside": American Indian women negotiating cultural connectedness and identity in urban spaces. *Women's Studies International Forum, 42*, 9–18. https://doi.org/10.1016/j.wsif.2013.10.012.

Mackay, C. M. & Schmitt, M. T. (2019). Do people who feel connected to nature do more to protect it? A meta-analysis. *Journal of Environmental Psychology, 65*, 101323. https://10.1016/j.jenvp.2019.101323.

Neff, K. (2003). Self-compassion: An alternative conceptualization of a healthy attitude toward oneself. *Self and Identity, 2*(2), 85–101. https://doi.org/10.1080/15298860309032.

Nitsch, A., Garvert, M.M., Bellmund, J.L.S., Schuck, N.W., Doeller, C.F. (2024). Grid-like entorhinal representation of an abstract value space during prospective decision making. *Nature Communication, 15*, 1198. https://doi.org/10.1038/s41467-024-45127-z.

Pritchard, A., Richardson, M., Sheffield, D., & McEwan, K. (2020). The relationship between nature connectedness and eudaimonic well-being: A meta-analysis. *Journal of Happiness Studies, 21*(3), 1145–1167. https://doi.org/10.1007/s10902-019-00118-6.

Rahe, M. & Jansen, P. (2023). A closer look at the relationship between the aspects of connectedness and flourishing. *Frontiers in Psychology: Positive Psychology, 14*, 1137752. https://doi.org/10.3389/fpsyg.2023.1137752.

Renowden, C., Beer, T., & Mata, L. (2022). Exploring integrated ArtScience experiences to foster nature connectedness through head, heart and hand. *People and Nature, 4*(2), 519–533. https://doi.org/10.1002/pan3.10301.

Román, F. J., Iturria-Medina, Y., Martínez, K., Karama, S., Burgaleta, M., Evans, A. C., Jaeggi, S. M., & Colom, R. (2017). Enhanced structural connectivity within a brain sub-network supporting working memory and engagement processes after cognitive training, *Neurobiology of Learning and Memory, 141*, 33–43. https://doi.org/10.1016/j.nlm.2017.03.010.

Salzberg, S. (2003). *Metta Meditation Buddhas revolutionärer Weg zum Glück*. Arbor.

Siebertz, M., Schroter, F., Portele, C., & Jansen, P. (2022). Affective explicit and implicit attitudes towards vegetarian food consumption. The role of mindfulness. *Appetite, 169*, 105831. https://doi.org/10.1016/j.appet.2021.105831.

Smallwood, J., Bernhardt, B.C., Leech, R., Bzdok, D., Jefferies, E., & Margulies, D.S. (2021). The default mode network in cognition: A topographical perspective. *Nature Review Neuroscience, 22*(8), 503–513. https://doi.org/10.1038/s41583-021-00474-4.

Smith, E. R. & Mackie, D. M. (2007). *Social psychology*. Taylor and Francis Group.

Snepvangers, K., & Rourke, A. (2020). Creative practice as a catalyst for developing connectedness capabilities: A community building framework from the teaching international students project. *Journal of International Students, 10*(S2), 17–35.

Solso, R. L. (2005). *Kognitive Psychologie*. Springer.

Strauss, C., Taylor, B. L., Gu, J., Kuyken, W., Baer, R., Jones, F. & Cavanagh, K. (2016). What is compassion and how can we measure it? A review of measures and definitions. *Clinical Psychological Review, 47*, 15–27. https://doi.org/10.1016/j.cpr.2016.05.004.

Sturgis, P., Patulny, R., Allum, N., & Buscha, F. (2015). Social connectedness and generalized trust: A longitudinal perspective. In *Handbook of research methods and applications in social capital* (pp. 76–90). Edward Elgar Publishing.

Transition Makers Toolbox. (2024). Enhancing sensorial connectedness – Getting in touch with a local ecosystem. *Transition Makers Toolbox*. https://transitionmakers.nl/tool/enhancing-sensorial-connectedness/ [Retrieved Mar. 27, 2024].

Turk, F. & Waller, G. (2020). Is self-compassion relevant to the pathology and treatment of eating and body image concerns? A systematic review and meta-analysis. *Clinical Psychology Review, 79*, 101856. https://doi.org/10.1016/j.cpr.2020.101856.

VanderWeele, T. J. (2017). On the promotion of human flourishing. *Proceedings of the National Academy of Sciences, 114*(31), 8148–8156. https://doi.org/10.1073/pnas.1702996114.

Van der Wel, R. P. R. D., Becchio, C., Curioni, A., & Wolf, T. (2021). Understanding joint action: Current theoretical and empirical approaches, *Acta Psychologica, 215*, 103285. https://doi.org/10.1016/j.actpsy.2021.103285.

Von Wirth, T., Fuenfschilling, L., Frantzeskaki, N., & Coenen, L. (2019). Impacts of urban living labs on sustainability transitions: Mechanisms and strategies for systemic change through experimentation. *European Planning Studies, 27*(2), 229–257. https://doi.org/10.1080/09654313.2018.1504895.

Villani, D., Sorgente, A., Iannello, P., & Antonietti, A. (2019). The role of spirituality and religiosity in subjective well-being of individuals with different religious status. *Frontiers in Psychology, 10*, 1525. https://doi.org/10.3389/fpsyg.2019.01525.

Wamsler, C., Osberg, G., Osika, W., Herndersson, H., & Mundaca, L. (2021). Linking internal and external transformation for sustainability and climate action: Towards a new research and policy agenda. *Global Environmental Change*, *71*, 102373. https://doi.org/10.1016/j.gloenvcha.2021.102373.

West, S., Haider, L. J., Stålhammar, S., & Woroniecki, S. (2020). A relational turn for sustainability science? Relational thinking, leverage points and transformations. *Ecosystems and People*, *16*(1), 304–325. https://doi.org/10.1080/26395916.2020.1814417.

Wiek, A., Ness, B., Schweizer-Ries, P., & Farioli S. (2014) Collaboration for transformation. *Sustainability Science*, *9*, 113–114. https://doi.org/10.1007/s11625-013-0231-7.

Winkelmair, A. & Jansen, P. (2023). The positive effect of mindfulness interventions on the explicit and implicit affective attitudes toward vegetarian foods. *Frontiers in Psychology: Eating Behavior*, *14*, 1158410. https://doi.org/10.3389/fpsyg.2023.1158410.

Wirtz, M. (2019). *Dorsch – Lexikon der Psychologie*. Hogrefe.

Zeif, C. L., Hoon, C., Van Ees, H., & Sanders, A. (2023). From ambivalence to stewardship commitment – Toward a behavioral model of stewardship governance. *Academy of Management Proceedings*, *2023*(1), 11649. https://doi.org/10.5465/AMPROC.2023.39bp.

Matthias Laeubli and Irene Contreras
# Chapter 16
# Listening beyond words: Building trust, nurturing relationships, and crafting impactful change

**Abstract:** In life, the quiet power of listening and the act of pausing often go unnoticed. This chapter explores and highlights the deep impact that these two simple actions have on personal growth, social connections, and broader systemic changes. Considered a fundamental skill within all five dimensions of the Inner Development Goals (IDGs) framework (*being* – relationship to self; *thinking* – cognitive skills; *relating* – caring for others and the world; *collaborating* – social skills; and *acting* – enabling change), listening proves itself crucial for achieving Sustainable Development Goals (SDGs), as it builds trust, empathy, compassion, and self-awareness, which are essential for personal and societal change.

This chapter combines theory with practical examples of active listening and workshop outcomes. It provides readers with tools to improve their listening skills in various roles, ultimately promoting a more connected and empathetic world. Comparing the IDGs' emphasis on listening with other frameworks like the Global Skills Taxonomy and the International Coaching Federation shows its critical role in effective communication and relationship building. The conclusion invites to further reflection and discussion, underscoring listening's importance in achieving SDG objectives.

**Keywords:** listening, pause, Inner Development Goals (IDGs), empathy, communication

## Introduction

In the symphony of life, the quiet strength of listening and the power of pause often slip by unnoticed. This exploration uncovers the depth of these seemingly simple yet profoundly impactful elements – listening and pause – and their role in personal reflection, social bonds, and systemic change.

Despite Epictetus's renowned words – "Nature gave us one tongue and two ears so we could hear twice as much as we speak" (Eliot, 2010, Vol.2, p. 183, quote 6) – our world is fraught with noise and frequent misunderstandings. Many may admit to being told "You do not listen" yet few confess to being poor listeners. While rarely a focus in leadership training, listening is a fundamental skill in the Inner Development Goals (IDGs) framework, considered a prerequisite for other skills.

https://doi.org/10.1515/9783111337913-017

The IDG framework, aiming to expedite the Sustainable Development Goals (SDGs), encompasses five dimensions and 23 crucial skills, where listening is consistently pivotal:

- Being – relationship to self: How well do I listen to my inner voice for self-awareness?
- Thinking – cognitive skills: Can I use perspective skills by actively listening to contrasting viewpoints?
- Relating – caring for others and the world: How can I better relate by listening with kindness and empathy?
- Collaborating – social skills: Explicitly, listening is under "communication skills" for genuine dialogue.
- Acting – enabling change: Courage, creativity, and perseverance, largely stemming from the first four dimensions.

Careful listening is the cornerstone for trust, relationships, and co-creation in a shifting world. This chapter spotlights this undervalued skill, diving into its relevance within the IDG framework. It also compares it with other frameworks like the Global Skills Taxonomy by the World Economic Forum and the Core Competencies of the International Coaching Federation for active listening.

When we think of communication skills, we usually think of public speaking, conveying messages convincingly, and being proactive rather than observant. Listening often gets overlooked as it is seen as passive and less important. However, listening is decisive for communication and building trustful relationships. It fosters connectedness, empathy, compassion, and self-awareness.

This underrated skill is a key aspect of the five IDG dimensions, impacting personal growth and change. In a world where we take more time to listen deeply and empathetically, conflict – from divorces to wars – might decrease significantly. Mediators might even find themselves with less work. Therefore, listening plays a crucial role in accelerating the achievement of SDG objectives.

This chapter combines theory with practical examples of active listening and summarizes what happened in the workshop in Basel with IDG Switzerland. This hands-on approach offers a comprehensive understanding, allowing readers to apply insights to their everyday practice as a parent, friend, or partner, as well as a coach, consultant, trainer, or leader.

In conclusion, we will summarize key takeaways and invite reflection through thought-provoking questions, aiming to prompt further discussion.

# Listening in action: Workshop in Basel with IDG Switzerland

To make a real difference and demonstrate our approach, we hosted a workshop titled "Listening Beyond Words" at IDG Switzerland in Basel on March 16, 2024. This workshop aimed to connect the IDG framework with real-life practice for a group of participants. The workshop focused on four main aspects:
- Storytelling: Words create the world
- Creativity: Arts and what emerges
- Music: Listen with the heart
- Community: Create connections and impact

The engaging session lasted two and a half hours and can serve as a model for future workshops. It is also relevant for broader contexts like change management and human learning. During the workshop, we raised questions about the connection between listening and presence, attention, and trust. We explored various levels and aspects of listening, examining its importance in grasping others' perspectives and broadening our potential.

# Experiential learning

To bridge the gap between theory and practice, we opted for highly experiential learning instead of traditional lectures or presentations. This decision aligns with the saying "Tell me and I will forget. Teach me and I will remember. Involve me, and I will learn". Our aim was to actively engage participants, empowering them to connect the IDG framework with their past, present, and future experiences, ensuring it doesn't remain merely theoretical.

Often, theories taught in classrooms lack emotional resonance, hindering true understanding and transformation. Research suggests that learning is most effective when "the information is seen as part of a context or bigger picture, novelty and interest are generated", and "emotions are involved" (Parkin, 2010, p. 13). Without an emotional connection, genuine change rarely occurs. Humans are driven by emotional engagement, and the intensity of these emotions determines their significance. If emotions remain subdued, it indicates that the emotional trigger lacks significance or relevance.

Our approach was grounded in a firm belief and a coaching mindset. We viewed the workshop participants as experts in their own lives, inherently creative, resourceful, and whole. Rather than assuming a position of teaching or telling, we aimed to create a supportive environment as hosts. Our goal was to provide a safe space for participants to listen to themselves and others in the group, encouraging exploration of the unknown with grace and courage.

To guide our approach, we drew upon David Kolb's (2015) experiential learning theory (ELT), which was influenced by the works of William James, John Dewey, Kurt Lewin, and Jean Piaget. Kolb's ELT presents a comprehensive learning process intended for application in various life situations. His four-stage learning cycle includes concrete experience, reflective observation, abstract conceptualization, and active experimentation. By aligning with this framework, we ensured that our workshop activities were integrated into the participants' everyday lives.

# Listening to each other and listening to our inner self

In today's world, we pay a whole lot of attention to our bodies. We are very aware of the importance of regular physical activity to be in shape, to gain strength, or to slow down the aging process.

When we train, we do it with a purpose in mind. What is that we want to achieve? Do we want to keep an average level of physical fitness or are we training to run a marathon? Or to compete in the Olympics? Once that goal is defined, we train accordingly.

Listening can be trained as well (Whitworth, Kimsey-House & Sandahl, 1998). Most of us are able to perceive sounds, to hear without using aids. Hearing is like having muscles, but not moving them often. Active listening is the privilege of using those muscles with a specific goal in mind. But how deep, how actively do we actually want to listen?

## Walk the talk: Listening in action

During our workshop preparation, we recognized the vital importance of practicing what we preached. Anything less would lack credibility: leading a workshop on listening necessitated demonstrating the concept by actively listening to participants.

We all have a teacher who has marked us, for the better or the worse. Think of that teacher who knew how to inspire and motivate you, to capture your attention, to ignite the passion for learning. That teacher who made you long for that class to come, who believed in your potential and helped you grow. Or maybe that teacher whose classes were boring to death, who made you detest a particular subject and made you think you would never be good at it. A good teacher or a bad teacher can change the course of your life.

The same principle applies to listening.

Consequently, we initiated an introductory round where we invited participants to think about their best and worst listening experiences and share how it made them feel, along with introducing themselves and stating their reasons to attend the session. This activity laid the foundation to create a safe space for participants: the first individual to speak set a powerful example by offering a deeply personal introduction, encouraging others to embrace vulnerability.

We were struck by the common theme emerging from participants' experiences: despite being attentive listeners, many had received feedback suggesting otherwise, particularly in their interactions with children. This discrepancy often stemmed from a struggle between being fully present and being preoccupied with personal thoughts and emotions.

Other shared feelings emerged, the main ones being: the power of silence, and how listening to oneself is harder than it seems, making us prone to ignore our inner voice and the impact it eventually has on our well-being and our relationship with the outer world.

As facilitators, we realized the importance of being fully present during the workshop in Basel and how listening is not a passive activity. Ensuring each participant received undivided attention during introductions became crucial to foster a conducive environment.

It also made participants aware of the impact listening has on you as an individual and on the others.

When you listen so actively, with presence and intent, you decide what you do with the information you are receiving, both verbal and nonverbal. You decide how you act upon it, or not act at all (which is also a conscious decision), aware that your action or inaction will subsequently create an impact on the other person, and that will have an impact on his or her world.

Though not explicitly stated, this practice laid the foundation for subsequent workshop activities through an implicit agreement among participants.

---

**The three levels of listening framework as a basic guideline**
There are several theories and models on different levels of listening. Some schools of thought divide listening into three levels (Withworth, Kimsey-House, and Sandahl's [1998] co-active coaching), some into four (Otto Scharmer's [2015] four levels of listening). In the end, it all comes down to the presence and the intent we listen with. Are we listening to the words or are we listening beyond the words? Are we listening to reply or are we listening to understand? It doesn't matter how long we listen for if we are not fully present and listening with intent. Deep, active listening becomes more about the quality than the quantity.

**The three levels of listening**

**Level I: Internal listening**
When we listen at level one, our attention is focused on ourselves and what's going on around us. We aim to know more – answers, explanations, information, details. We want to process information and understand it. All the choices, decisions, and judgment are about ourselves.

**Level II: Focused listening**
Listening at level two means listening with a sharp focus on the other person. The attention is completely focused on the outside world, it is not about us anymore. At this level, not only do we notice what the person we are listening to says, but also how they say it. We notice the body language, the changes in their voice, their energy shifts. Masterful coaching starts happening at this level.

**Level III: Global listening**
At level three, listening becomes a 360-degree experience. We observe with our senses: close attention is paid to what we hear, but also to what we see, smell, and feel. This allows greater access to our intuition. The key component of this level is to take the information in, play with it, and see what emerges.

The importance of listening at level three is the ability to connect with ourselves, to listen to our inner voice and understand what lies within: it opens the door to a greater connection with the world, with ourselves, and with our vulnerability.

# The power of stories and metaphors: Words create the world

To begin, we invited workshop participants on a journey into the realm of listening, exploring the potent avenues of stories and metaphors.

Do you remember the feeling when you dive into the narrative of a story that offered a fresh perspective, supporting your hopes and dreams? If "a word creates a world" (Swart, 2013, p. 1), stories create a landscape of new opportunities and choices. Robert Ellis describes that "most of the time, we are actually creating the future from the past" (Ellis, 2023, p. 8). However, stories, riddles, and metaphors inspire and enable us to leave this prison of limiting beliefs and assumptions in a creative way, thus "stretching the world" of the coaching client (McKergow, 2021, p. 77). Stories can serve as a lens that opens a window into a "better future" and indicates "what is possible instead", thereby "breaking the causal link between past and future" (McKergow, 2021, pp. 134–135). Stories open up the mind and the imagination to new possibilities: when we replace an old narrative with a new narrative, we already start to endeavor new ventures and can let go of the past limitations.

According to Parkin (2010), storytelling has three main functions:
- to pass on information or knowledge;
- to educate and encourage the transfer of cumulative wisdom from one generation to the next;
- to encourage personal healing and creative problem solving.

Furthermore, as the narrative approach "believes that human beings make meaning of their lives through the stories they tell" (Swart, 2013, p. 20), stories that have proven to be meaningful over a long period of time across borders and generations might offer valuable insights as long as they are being told again and again. Listening is not a passive act: the listener weaves the story in a smooth way into his/her landscape of identity – exploring questions of who they are, who they're expected to be, and who they aspire to become. In essence, humans are "sense-makers", actively assigning significance to their experiences and continuously integrating them into their personal narratives about themselves and the world.

To harness the potency of stories and metaphors, we presented participants in the workshop with two narratives. Initially, we shared the story of the two wolves (origin unknown, commonly attributed to the indigenous people of the Americas):

> One evening, an old Cherokee Indian told his grandson a story by the campfire about a battle that rages within every person.
>
> He said, "My son, the battle is between two wolves that live inside each of us.
>
> One is evil. It is anger, envy, jealousy, worry, pain, greed, arrogance, self-pity, guilt, prejudice, inferiority, lies, false pride, and ego.
>
> The other is good. It is joy, peace, love, hope, serenity, humility, kindness, benevolence, empathy, generosity, truth, compassion, and faith."
>
> The grandson thought about his grandfather's words for a while and then asked, "Which wolf wins?"
>
> The old Cherokee replied, "The one you feed."

After a moment of reflection, we introduced the tale of the little boy and the old wise man (origin unknown), slightly modified by substituting the bird with a butterfly:

> Once upon a time, there was a little boy and an old wise man. The little boy thought to himself, "No one can be that wise. I will test him." And he started thinking about how he could test the old wise man.
>
> After a few days, he had an idea: "I will catch a little butterfly and hide it behind my back. Then I will ask him if the butterfly is alive or dead. If he says the butterfly is alive, I will quickly twist its neck and show him the dead butterfly. If he says the butterfly is dead, I will let it fly away. That way, he will be wrong, and I can prove he is not as wise as everyone says!"
>
> So the little boy caught a small butterfly and went to the old wise man. He stood in front of him and said, "Old wise man, is the butterfly in my hand alive or dead?"
>
> The old wise man looked at the boy and thought. He thought for a long time without saying anything, and the little boy thought to himself, "See, you're not so wise. You can't come up with an answer."
>
> After a while, the old wise man looked up and said to the little boy, "Little boy, whether the butterfly is alive or dead is entirely in your hands!"

We selected these stories because they offer space for interpretation and contain numerous potentially meaningful metaphors for the listeners. Furthermore, the atmosphere in the room shifted rapidly as we commenced with the stories.

# Sketch initial painting: What emerges in this moment?

To leverage the power of the two stories, we instructed workshop participants to individually create an initial painting. They were encouraged to paint whatever thoughts came to mind after listening to the stories, without restricting themselves solely to the narratives. Facing a blank sheet of paper, they expressed their inner worlds and translated them into paintings. This hands-on activity facilitated the reconnection of their body and brain, linking it to the stories they had heard earlier in the session. The resulting paintings were diverse and colorful, each unique, although some shared common elements, such as the butterfly introduced in the second story.

**Exercise**

When was the last time you took the time to face a blank sheet of paper and sketch something without giving much thought to the end result? What's holding you back from doing so?

Try it and see what emerges. Pour your emotions on to a white sheet of paper.

# Listening to music

Music has become part of our daily lives – it is just more accessible than ever before. We can hear it everywhere we go: on the radio while driving somewhere, through a loudspeaker in the grocery store, in the waiting room of the dentist. Music has become the background white noise of our life. To the point that if it's not there, the natural and mundane noise becomes uncomfortable, and we chose to put our headphones on just to be hearing something. Songs become a packaged product to be used at our convenience.

We hear music, but we are not really listening to it. We are not paying attention to the words, we are not really listening to the nuances of the melody. Chances are that one song is just playing after the next without us realizing a new song is playing. Unless we decide to listen with intention.

For our workshop, we chose two pieces of music: one classical piece, "The Moldau", by the Bohemian composer Bedřich Smetana; and one modern pop song, "I'd Rather Dance With You", by the Norwegian duo Kings of Convenience.

We did not tell the participants which music they were going to listen to. Both pieces are completely different in style, depth, and length. We sat in silence and participants just embraced the moment.

First, we played the classical music piece, a symphonic poem that evokes the flow of the Vltava River (in German, the Moldau), from its source in the mountains of the Bohemian Forest, through the Czech countryside, to the city of Prague. Most of the participants had their eyes closed and entered into some sort of meditation. They let themselves go with the flow for 15 minutes, fully present and listening with intent. And, funny enough, that's exactly how they described the experience afterwards – emotions flowed through them like water does in a river.

We let a three-minute silence take hold, followed by a warm pop song, whose lyrics were in English. The mood felt immediately lighter. Some participants stood up to dance along, smiling. Some were moving on their chairs or tapping their feet.

However, when the song was over, we asked, "What was the song about?", and none of them could give us an answer. Some said, "They said the word 'dance' very often, so I guess about dancing?" We chose that song on purpose not only to create a big contrast with the classical piece, but because the lyrics were in tune with the topic of the workshop.

We are divided into two kinds of people when we listen to a song: the ones who listen to the lyrics, and the ones who listen to the whole, a package of music and words. This led to the following reflection: when we listen attentively to the lyrics, we are listening to the songwriter's voice, to their message. By listening to what the artist has to say, we are engaging with them on a deeper level, and acknowledging their skills, their effort, and the message they wanted to convey. It can actually also touch deeper layers of ourselves. We might suddenly relate to them, and trigger feelings that would not emerge if we did not pay attention to the meaning. Suddenly the song has a completely different impact, a completely different color.

Of course, there are exceptions – some songs are meant to be heard, not even listened to. And we are not always in the mood of deep listening. As with everything in life, balance is the key.

---

**Exercise**

Do you identify yourself with the group who usually listens to music as a whole package? Has music become a background white noise for you?

Choose a song you like but you've never really paid attention to the message. Or a song you don't know at all, the next song that will come up on the radio and (if you understand the language) listen to the message. What is the song about? What is the artist trying to say? What emerges? How does it make you feel?

You can also pick a song you know the lyrics of by heart, and try to listen beyond the words, to the emotions. What is the artist feeling? Can you relate?

---

# The power of silence

The power of silence played a huge role during our workshop. We made sure that there was enough space for silence to happen and for participants to feel safe and embrace what emerged from those pauses.

During the round of introductions, a couple of participants connected their best listening experience to silence. One of them admitted having learnt more from their neighbors in a spontaneous moment of shared silence during a neighborhood meeting than during the whole meeting itself.

Another participant shared the experience of being in a silent retreat for several days in a remote natural setting, and how despite not talking to the other attendees at all, they ended up with the feeling of knowing each other just through observing their respective behaviors and how they interacted with each other.

As the workshop progressed, there were more opportunities to explore silence: during the free speech exercise, they had to stay in silence for a minute, when possible, looking at each other, between their speeches; between both pieces of music, a long silence was allowed for the sake of savoring it, just finding pleasure in it.

In the final exercise, questions and observations were left unanswered on purpose, so that silence could make way for self-reflection and to distinguish between reacting and responding.

We could summarize the key learnings that emerged from our session as follows:

- Silence opens the door to the uncomfortable in the first place. Learning how to feel comfortable in the silence and seizing what it offers is key for growth.
- Silence can talk louder than words – learning more from the others from what they convey during their pauses and their prolonged silences. Oftentimes, long pauses and silence during a conversation allow for more effective communication, as silence can be used to process information and emotions, having a direct impact on the quality of human interactions.
- The importance of silence to learn from oneself. This power allows you to find yourself in a very rapid manner – to tune in with your worries, with your fears, with your emotions.
- Feeling the power of silence to connect to our inner selves can be overwhelming, as you might find yourself facing parts of yourself you are not ready to face.

---

**Reacting vs. responding: Pause to reflect**

Have you ever found yourself answering to someone in an instinctive, emotional way that you later regretted? You *reacted* to something that triggered your emotions in a way you weren't expecting. Reacting is often impulsive, usually influenced by fears, past experiences, or insecurities.

What if you could try again, and change your answer to be more thoughtful and deliberate? You would be *responding* considering the situation, weighing and owning your words, completely aware of your actions.

The difference between reacting and responding lies in *silence*. A pause to reflect.

**Exercise**

Try incorporating silence consciously in your daily conversations, even more so if you find yourself in a fast-paced, highly emotional conversation, and allow yourself the time to think. Allow yourself a pause to reflect and let silence come in. Observe the situation, and absorb the non-spoken information. It will also give you and your conversational partner(s) a break.

  If you don't feel comfortable around silence (most of us don't), the better the reason to start putting it into practice.

# Social resonance

Attention is probably *the* currency of the twenty-first century. Never have we been so distracted by competing sources of information. Those who manage to capture attention elevate their status. Interestingly, even negative attention is preferable to receiving none at all. From a social standpoint, Descartes's "I think, therefore I am" (*cogito ergo sum*) could be reframed as: "You acknowledge me, therefore I am." Socially, my "existence" (to you) hinges on being noticed, seen, and heard – essentially, receiving social validation.

  A resonance is a movement that is created through a vibration at the same rate as the sound waves from another object. In human interactions, social resonance manifests across different levels. This phenomenon happens, for example, when an experienced facilitator, trainer, or coach builds rapport and "paces" with the interlocutor and both start imitating each other, consciously or unconsciously. This synchronization often involves mirroring each other's gestures, behaviors, tone of voice, and even word choices, facilitated by mirror neurons. Much of this social resonance is conveyed through embodied communication, which primarily consists of nonverbal cues (Jonassen, 2018).

  Social judgments of others happen within seconds, as Oscar Wilde famously stated, "There is no second chance to make a first impression." However, these initial impressions can be misleading, leading to premature conclusions, as we sometimes struggle to distinguish between our own perceptions and the true intentions of the other person.

  The ability to identify and notice what happens within me as opposed to what is there without interpretation and judgment requires training. Barry Stevens (2004) emphasizes, "Lose your mind and come to your senses" (p. 10), describing the essence of "Gestalt" as: "Awareness. Noticing. That's Gestalt" (p. 14). If we notice without goal, direction, or opinion and share this awareness with others, we offer a useful and fresh perspective, separating the signal from the noise (Stevens, 2004). As an example to illustrate this, Stevens describes: "When a group of Indian persons came together to form an organization, they didn't talk about organizing or forming the organization. Instead, they talked about their relationship to it. There was no need to talk about the organization as that's why they came together in the first place" (p. 66). The essence of Gestalt lies in recognizing what is plainly evident, yet often goes unnoticed, unspoken, or unheard: the proverbial elephant in the room. It encompasses our relationship with this unspoken reality – what it represents to us, what currently exists, what could potentially transpire, and what ought to occur.

Gisela Schmeer (2006) describes a simple and powerful method that creates social resonance in a group and makes it visible. Using analogue communication (Kiel, 2019; in particular pages 131–145), i.e., pictures and paintings, as opposed to digital communication such as abstract words, Schmeer's method offers a direct access to unconscious and subconscious areas and unveils the resonance between the different group members.

During the workshop, all participants exhibited their initial paintings by placing them on the floor. In a silent and fully present manner, attendees walked around to observe each other's artwork. Subsequently, they were encouraged to create a resonance drawing in black and white, focusing on one chosen element from another participant's initial painting. This exercise aimed to crystallize and consolidate emerging themes.

Each participant then presented their initial painting, the resonance drawing they created – referencing an element from another participant's painting – and sharing the word or sentence written on the back of their resonance drawing. Moreover, they connected their artwork and written reflection to the IDG framework while seated in a circle.

Following the presentations, another group member would share one observation or pose a question that remained unanswered. Without receiving a response, the presenter of the paintings listened attentively, not with the intention to justify or reply, but to fully comprehend the significance of the observation or question for themselves at that moment. By leaving the question or observation unresolved, it heightened the impact and created a more enduring resonance, akin to an open Gestalt.

Unexpectedly, when asked to relate their experience to the IDG framework, most participants indicated that they associated their listening experience primarily with the third category of the IDG framework, "Relating – caring for others and the world." They emphasized themes of connectedness, empathy, and compassion. This suggests that listening lies at the core of establishing meaningful connections with others, fostering empathy, and cultivating compassion. Establishing meaningful connections with others is the foundational building block that enables collective leadership in action.

In a second place, participants associated their experience with the first category: "Being – relationship to self." The main learning behind it is that listening to ourselves, actively listening to our inner compass is as important to connect with ourselves as it is to listen to the other. After each participant's presentation, the observations and/or questions that remained unanswered opened the door to a level of personal reflection that led participants to a new level of self-awareness.

# Close the experiential learning cycle

We previously introduced the experiential learning cycle and wish to revisit it to emphasize its continuous nature. Throughout the workshop, participants developed a deeper connection between their workshop experiences and their daily lives, integrating elements that held personal significance for them with the IDG framework. In doing so, they effectively applied David Kolb's (2015) learning cycle within his experiential learning theory:

- start with the concrete experience (feel);
- reflective observation, reflecting on the experience (watch);
- abstract conceptualization, learning from the experience (think);
- active experimentation, trying out what you have learned (do).

Furthermore, and perhaps most significantly, participants integrated various senses and learning styles, including:

- diverging (feel and watch);
- assimilating (think and watch);
- converging (think and do);
- accommodating (feel and do).

When creating their initial paintings at the outset of the workshop, participants engaged in a blend of feeling, observing, thinking, and doing. As we emphasized earlier in this chapter, we began with the firm belief that individuals are inherently creative, resourceful, and whole. By the workshop's conclusion, participants had firsthand experience of what it means and feels like to embody these qualities. They confirmed leaving the room feeling energized and inspired.

# Further reflection

## Global Skills Taxonomy by the World Economic Forum

The World Economic Forum has introduced a framework that prioritizes a person's skills and competencies over traditional factors like degrees or job titles, particularly in attracting, hiring, developing, and redeploying talent. This framework, developed collaboratively by learning experts, employers, and practitioners, addresses the impending talent shortage resulting from demographic shifts worldwide. A key component of this framework is the Global Skills Taxonomy (link), which establishes a standardized language for workplace skills.

In the Global Skills Taxonomy, listening is categorized under "attitudes" and "working with others". Specifically, "empathy and active listening" are closely linked and fall within the same skills cluster, further divided into subcategories such as "empathy", "asking questions", and "giving and receiving feedback". It's notable that, similar to the participants in our workshop who associated listening primarily with the relating aspect of the IDG framework, the Global Skills Taxonomy also underscores the connection between listening and empathy.

## Core competencies of the International Coaching Federation for active listening

The International Coaching Federation (ICF) has devised the ICF Core Competencies to enhance comprehension of the skills and methodologies utilized in today's coaching profession. These competencies are the result of rigorous job analysis research, which included interviews with subject matter experts, workshops with global representation, surveys, and subsequent analysis. Through this process, over 280 "critical incidents" were identified. In coaching, a critical incident refers to when the client experiences a positive shift during the coaching process.

In the updated ICF Core Competency model, "listens actively" is categorized under "communicating effectively" (link). It is defined as: "Focuses on what the client is and is not saying to fully understand what is being communicated in the context of the client systems and to support client self-expression."

Once again, listening is recognized as a vital skill, particularly within the coaching profession. Since the core competencies are derived from critical incidents, it is reasonable to infer that listening plays a crucial role in building trust and fostering sustainable relationships in various human interactions.

## Conclusion

During the workshop, we strengthened connections between different senses like touch, hearing, and sight, as well as between the rational and emotional aspects of the mind and body. This encouraged participants to tune in to their inner voice, consider its tone, and listen to their imaginations, hopes, and personal needs. By creating a safe space, asking open questions, and offering a blank canvas, participants could explore what was most significant to them at that moment.

Throughout the workshop, we noticed participants becoming more present and improving their listening quality due to group activities and positive dynamics. They not only heard each other but actively listened to verbal and nonverbal expressions, and even "beyond words". We could furthermore feel that they paid attention to each other on an individual basis, and cared about the whole group as a bigger entity and what happened in the environment more attentively.

Who have you listened to today with undivided attention, being fully present, aiming to understand and co-create something new?

In summary, we recognized that high-quality listening is crucial for building trust and relationships and serves as a catalyst for connecting with others. Full presence and undivided attention significantly enhance this process. Listening lies at the core of frameworks like the IDGs, as well as in others such as the Global Skills Taxonomy by the World Economic Forum and the Core Competencies defined by the International Coaching Federation.

# References

Eliot, C. W. (2010): The Apology, Phaedo and Crito by Plato; The Golden Sayings by Epictetus; The Meditations by Marcus Aurelius. Cosimo Classics.

Ellis, R. (2023). *Coaching from essence: Create a thriving practice doing powerful work with clients you love.* Futurosity.

International Coaching Federation (2019). The Gold Standard in Coaching | ICF – Core Competencies.

Jonassen, M. (2018). Kommunikation – Spiegelneuronen und verkörperte Sprache. In *Handbuch Angewandte Psychologie für Führungskräfte.* Springer.

Kiel, V. (2019). *Analoge Verfahren in der systemischen Beratung: Ein integrativer Ansatz für Coaching, Team- und Organisationsentwicklung.* Vandenhoeck & Ruprecht.

Kolb, D. A. (2015). *Experiential learning: Experience as the source of learning and development.* Pearson Education.

McKergow, M. (2021). *The next generation of solution focused practice: Stretching the world for new opportunities and progress.* Routledge.

Parkin, M.(2010). *Tales for coaching: Using stories and metaphors with individuals and small groups.* Kogan Page Limited.

Scharmer, C. O. (2015). *Otto Scharmer on the four levels of listening YouTube.* https://www.youtube.com/watch?v=eLfXpRkVZaI&t=414s.

Schmeer, G. (2006). *Die Resonanzbildmethode: visuelles Lernen in der Gruppe; Selbsterfahrung, Team, Organisation.* Klett-Cotta.

Stevens, B. (2004). *Don't push the river (it flows by itself).* Gestalt Journal Press.

Swart, C. (2013). *Re-authoring the world.* KR Publishing.

Whitworth, L., Kimsey-House, H., & Sandahl, P. (1998). *Co-active coaching: New skills for coaching people toward success in work and life.* (1st edition). Davies-Black Publishing.

World Economic Forum (2024). *Global Skills Taxonomy.* Link: Reskilling Revolution 2030.

Gervase R. Bushe and Michael Cody

# Chapter 17
# The Experience Cube: A model to increase being, relating, and collaborating for collective leadership

**Abstract:** The Sustainable Development Goals (SDGs) require large groups of people, often across multiple boundaries, to collaborate over long periods. We have found the larger the group or the longer the time they work together the harder it is to maintain collaboration. For more than 25 years, we have used the Experience Cube to help ourselves and others build and sustain the high-quality, collaborative relationships required to succeed in increasingly complex environments by helping them learn from their personal and collective experience. In this chapter, we describe why it's so difficult to sustain collaboration and why using the Experience Cube can resolve the problem. We show how using the Experience Cube, and the associated beliefs and attitudes, can increase the Inner Development Goals (IDGs) of being, relating, and collaborating. We then discuss the relationship of adult vertical development to the IDGs, the qualities of leaders required to accomplish the SDGs, and how the Experience Cube can help foster movement to later stages of adult development. We conclude by offering an exercise people can use to resolve problems of collaboration.

**Keywords:** collaboration, learning from experience, Clear Leadership, self-differentiation, adult development, vertical development

## Introduction

Since their launch, the Sustainable Development Goals (SDGs) – intended to create a sustainable global society – have made progress and had some success, but not as much progress as most people had hoped for. The Inner Development Goals (IDGs) were created to enhance progress toward the SDGs by highlighting that we need not only technical solutions to problems but also specific skills and abilities in the individuals, teams, and organizations that play crucial roles in working to fulfill the vision. This insight is a critical one, and we believe it may be more important to invest in how things get done than what things get done. An expert team skilled in working together can overcome most technical challenges they face. However, a team of technical experts who have difficulty working together may have a hard time completing a project within their area of expertise. This is why the insights of the IDGs are so

https://doi.org/10.1515/9783111337913-018

crucial, and we would like to add our voice to three of the IDGs that we have some experience with: *being, relating,* and *collaborating.*

To understand how our work fits in, we need to start from collaborating. The SDGs are goals that require large groups of people to collaborate over long periods. We have found the larger the group, or the longer the time they are working together, the harder it is to maintain collaboration. We hypothesize that most of the collaborations required to achieve any SDG would run into difficulty and fail unless investment is made in building up the collaboration skills of the individuals working together. What can they do in those inevitable moments when the collaboration is not working as everyone hoped? For more than 25 years, we have used the tool/model we'll describe to help ourselves and others build and sustain high-quality, collaborative relationships required to succeed in increasingly complex environments. It's called the Experience Cube (the cube), a practical and effective model of experience that empowers people to learn from their personal and collective experience.

As people reading this book are well aware, the IDGs are an answer to the problems that complexity creates for achieving the UN's SDGs. What kind of person can absorb and conceptually integrate the dozens of different systems impinging on global problems like poverty, hunger, gender equality, climate, and true justice? What qualities and skills are needed to build and work with coalitions strong enough to manage highly complex situations across multiple boundaries? What tools and methods can support them in achieving these competencies and ways of being?

The theories collectively known as vertical development offer some answers (Binder, 2023; Cook-Greuter, 2014; Kegan, 1994; Loevinger, 1976; Torbert, 2004). Building on the work of Jean Piaget (1952), stages of increasing cognitive, social, and emotional intelligence have been described and verified through decades of research. Linkages between these stages and leaders' competence to manage organizational and social change challenges have been offered. There is widespread agreement that leaders capable of managing the level of complex collaboration required to achieve many of the SDGs are beyond the vast majority of adults, who operate at what has been labeled the "conventional stages" of adult development. As coaches deeply interested in promoting adult development, we see our task as shifting people from conventional to later post-conventional mindsets. Later in the chapter, we briefly describe vertical development and some observations on how the cube can stimulate development toward the post-conventional.

To begin, however, we will focus on how the cube can support an increase in three of the five inner development goals – skills of being, relating, and collaborating. To understand why the cube is so useful, we first need to explain our understanding of why collaborative relationships seem so hard to sustain. Achieving the SDGs requires long-term partnerships, but in our studies of collaboration in organizations, we have found that even among people committed to a common purpose and who want to be in collaborative relationships, sustaining them over time is difficult, and they often fail. We argue that it's because we are sensemaking beings, and much of our beliefs about others and situations come from stories we make up and treat as the truth (Weick, 1995). Because these stories we make up tend to be more negative than the truth, they can destroy the relationship over time. As a result, collaboration requires acting against this common process and constantly learning from our experience together. This is where the Experience Cube is useful. After briefly describing the cube, we will describe how using the cube can increase competencies in being, relating, and collaborating.

# The reason collaborative relationships are so difficult to sustain

People differ in how much time and effort they put into understanding why their boss, co-workers, customers, or team members do and say what they do, but we all do it. We are sensemaking machines, compelled to "make sense" of the people we regularly have to interact with. When your team member does something confusing, strange, awkward, or off-putting, what is the likelihood you will bring it up and ask them why they did that and what it means? The answer is likely affected by the office culture where you work, norms and expectations, and your personal history of managing "conflict". However, most of the time, people do not ask about it. What if the strange behavior comes from someone you have invested in – a business partner, a spouse, others you are hoping to work toward some SDG with? How direct are you, and if you are direct, how is that working out? The ones who are "direct" but find it makes their relationships worse often make a simple but profound mistake that the cube helps to explain. We'll take it up under the *relating* section.

When confronted with an unpleasant interaction, most will mull it over or take it to third parties, like a spouse or trusted co-worker, to discuss and make sense of. We make up a story about what is happening in that person's head and then forget it's a story. It becomes "the truth", and we might even confide it to others who ask our opinion of so-and-so. Future acts of sensemaking depend on past acts of sensemaking, or things don't make sense. Once we have a story that works well, we are much more likely to notice things that reinforce the story and ignore things that don't fit.

One result of this pervasive process is that groups and organizations become composed of people operating under very different stories (narratives), making it harder to understand each other and collaborate. Even more problematic is that our stories tend to be more negative than reality. For example, you don't return my email, and I assume you are avoiding me when, really, it got deleted when my host server went down.

We call an interaction between two or more people where the things they say and do are influenced by the sensemaking or stories about the other that have not been checked out "interpersonal mush". Over time, if the mush is not cleared out, it gets more toxic. The mush will grow in any collaborative relationship that lasts longer than a few weeks. In field studies by Gervase and students (Bushe 2001; Bushe & Grossling, 2006) they consistently found about four out of five strained relationships at work were due to the mush. When the mush got cleared out (that is, people described and listened to each other's experience), the relationships improved.

Once a partnership is in place, we believe interpersonal mush is the most significant barrier to sustaining the high levels of trust, cooperation, and motivation required for collective leadership to accomplish the SDGs. Most partnerships begin with good feelings and high hopes. Working toward meaningful goals like the SDGs provides motivation and a sense of camaraderie. Inevitably, however, unless there is frequent work to clear out the mush, relationships will experience strain. When partners come from different cultures and ages and with different agendas, negative mush is even more likely to appear. Trust and the desire to be in the partnership will fade away. So, we focus the cube and the other tools in our kit on understanding our own and others' experience to periodically clear out the mush and keep our partnerships healthy.

To sustain effective relationships, especially when that relationship must manage ambiguous, complex, volatile, and uncertain challenges, people need to be able to learn from their experience together. Doing that is aided by having a common model of experience from which to talk. For that, we offer the Experience Cube.[1]

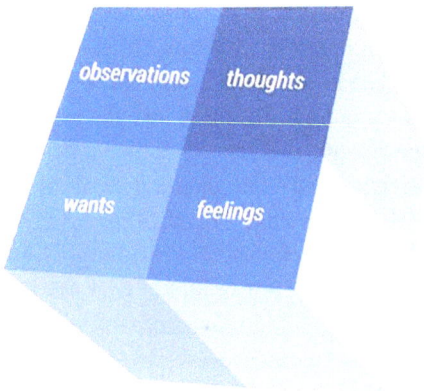

**Figure 17.1:** The Experience Cube.

1 It has been noted that there are some similarities between the nonviolent communication (NVC) model, another model in the IDG toolkit, and the Experience Cube. There are some key differences: (1) the Experience Cube is not a tool for resolving conflict, it is a model of human experience that helps to define self-awareness and the requirements for interpersonal clarity; (2) the Experience Cube foregrounds the importance of thoughts and the prevalence of thoughts in human experience – which is largely excluded from the NVC model; (3) the element of "wants" in the cube covers a lot more territory than "needs" and "requests" in the NVC model; and (4) the Experience Cube is just one tool in a large set of skills that we think are required to sustain long-term collaboration.

# The Experience Cube

We have long asserted that each person's moment-to-moment experience is primarily created from the inside out (Bushe, 2001), and recent developments in neuroscience support this position (Seth, 2021). Because experience is generated mainly from the inside out, it means that, at any given moment, everyone has a different experience. The cube is a model that allows you to explore your own experience and to get curious about the experience of others.

The Experience Cube is a model of experience that has five key assumptions, as outlined in the following sections.

## (1) Experience comprises four elements: observations, thoughts, feelings, and wants

### Observations

What a video would record, we could play it back and hear or see it. Observation is the only element of experience with an objective reality. However, people differ in how well they observe and the quality of their recall. We have found a widespread tendency to confuse thoughts for observations. Any interpretation of what was said or done is a thought. Any description of another person's experience (e.g., she's happy) is a thought, not an observation.

### Thoughts

All cognitive processes and outputs are included here, like beliefs, perceptions, assumptions, stories, calculations, analyses, imagination, reasoning, interpretation, summarizing, predicting, and so forth. We teach that it is essential to know the difference between observations and thoughts: one is objective, and the other is subjective; one is facts, and the other is opinion. When people think their opinions are facts, they cannot learn from experience. We also teach that knowing the differences between thoughts and feelings is essential.

### Feelings

All bodily sensations are feelings. Often, these sensations are messages from the body that can be interpreted. Emotions can significantly influence what happens even if we don't pay attention to them. Most people take emotion into account during social interaction. Even the least emotionally intelligent person is likely to scan for what their boss is feeling before pitching for a raise. However, even when we acknowledge their importance, people might feel anxious about discussing their feelings or bringing feelings into professional conversations. But if they don't, it creates mush because the other person will interpret their feelings. If they appear at all emotional, the story about what they are feeling will probably be worse than reality.

However, to create interpersonal clarity, it's best to avoid *expressing* emotions, acting them out. Recent research shows that when we become emotionally triggered or flooded, we lose the ability to solve problems or engage in self-reflective practices. Physically embodying and acting on emotions tends to make others anxious, particularly if it causes emotional contagion (Herrando & Constantinides, 2021). Others will focus on containing the emotions, not on getting clear. What is required is a calm, dispassionate description of your emotions. To be able to do that, you first need to be aware of what you are feeling, which means paying attention to sensations in the body. For many people, that has not been encouraged. Instead, we tend to encourage children not to pay attention to feelings, to suck it up, to walk it off, to stop crying. For some, simply paying attention to sensation is a significant first step in becoming more self-aware.

Being aware of feelings requires not confusing them with thoughts. It is very common for people to call a thought a feeling. Some examples: "I feel we ought to try a different route"; "I feel like we've been through this before"; "I feel that we should spend money on it"; "I feel as if there are more questions than answers". Reserving the word "feel" for sensations coming from the body really helps increase our awareness of this part of our experience.

Similarly, it's important to stop using "feel" when talking about wants: "I feel like a coffee"; "I feel better about that option"; "I feel we should try it out" – these are all references to wants.

## Wants

In addition to wants and needs, this element of experience includes goals, targets, aspirations, dreams, and motivations, as well as "don't wants". We have found that what people want is the most unique element of human experience. It's much easier to guess what a person thinks or feels than what they want. When we sense-make, we're most likely to assume others want what we'd want if we said or did what they did – but that is almost always wrong. All forms of collaboration, like win-win negotiations and nonviolent communication, require that people honestly describe what they want – but that can be easier said than done. First, does the person understand the needs, desires, motives, patterns, and traumas influencing them in each moment? Assuming that we always have many different wants at any moment, some of which can even be contradictory, opens us up to being more aware of wants. Secondly, how do we expect the other to treat our wants? If the assumption is "if you care about me you will give me what I want", people will have much less enthusiasm for having that conversation. Clarity is encouraged when the norm is to describe your wants without believing others are responsible for fulfilling them. Collaboration will not persist if people aren't getting what they want, and it's hard to know what people want if they don't tell us.

## (2) Experience refers to our moment-to-moment experience, and to learn from experience together, we have to be able to talk right here, right now

We can't learn from our experience if we don't know what it is; the only "real" experience is available to us right now. Memories of past experiences are open to many distortions. Expectations of future experiences are only possibilities. As sensemaking beings, we make sense of our past acts in a way that conforms to our story of ourselves (Weick, 1995). If we are willing to attend to our in-the-moment experience while acting, we may find thoughts, feelings, and/or wants we weren't aware of before.

Someone's in-the-moment experience is a consequence of their history, biology, ideologies, traumas, victories, beliefs, self-image, hormones, what they recently ate, and probably much else. We can know our in-the-moment experience without knowing why we have those thoughts, feelings, or wants. However, whatever we bring from our past and images of the future that influence our current experience is part of right now. Whatever of that is relevant to the other people in the conversation is part of right here.

## (3) We have all four elements of experience in all our waking time; (4) some of our experience we are aware of, and some we are not

These two assumptions combine into a profound stance for learning from experience. By holding these assumptions, we assume that even if we are unaware of having feelings, wants, observations, or thoughts at the moment, they are nonetheless there to be uncovered. The Experience Cube assumes that there are always aspects of our experience we are unaware of; that is why it's a cube. Some of our experience is on the surface, easy to know. Other aspects are further down, requiring more intention and attention to be known. Some are near the bottom and very difficult to uncover. We have found that people differ significantly in which elements of experience they find easy and difficult to access and the speed at which they can access them.

## (4) We can all learn to be more aware of our moment-to-moment experience, but we may never be fully aware of all aspects of our experience

Simply paying attention to the four elements of the Experience Cube will increase self-awareness. Regularly taking a few minutes to consider what observations most occupy your attention, what you think about them, how you feel, and what you want will significantly increase anyone's self-awareness. Journaling amplifies the benefits of "taking a lap around the cube".

# The Experience Cube offers a simple, concrete model for clearing the mush

Interpersonal mush is managed by attaining interpersonal clarity, where I know what my experience is, what your experience is, and the difference between them. The cube provides a simple, practical model to support that.

It provides a clear definition of self-awareness. To be self-aware, I need to know what I am observing, thinking, feeling, and wanting in this moment.

It identifies what needs to be said. To fully describe my experience to others, I need to tell them what I am observing, thinking, feeling, and wanting – and often it's helpful to describe past events that influence my current experience. Because we are sensemaking beings, compelled to make sense of those significant to us, others will make assumptions about whatever element we leave out.

It identifies what we need to be curious about to fully understand others' experiences: what they are observing, thinking, feeling, and wanting.

# Using the cube to achieve the IDGs

The following describes how a person, relationship, or group can use the Experience Cube to increase the IDG skills listed under being, relating, and collaborating. We will provide an overview and then report what 15 Clear Leadership instructors from Canada, the US, and Europe thought.[2] During a 90-minute Zoom workshop, we had three rounds of small, random groups to discuss how the Experience Cube could facilitate being, relating, and collaborating. After each overview, we offer the bullet points

---

2 We were joined by Beth Ann Derksen, Camilla Ruden, Cathryn Lecorre, Cindy Cox, Darcy Wright, Dave Galloway, Helen Roberts, Josh Stigall, Matthieu Bourgue, Palaemona Morner, Scott Bruce, Thomas Safarik, and Victoria Tiller.

from small group report-outs posted in chat. They've been organized and lightly edited.

## Being

As a model of experience, the cube provides a simple yet ever-unfolding roadmap for self-awareness. First, it clearly defines self-awareness: the ability to know, in the present moment, what one is observing, thinking, feeling, and wanting. Secondly, it encourages people to look beyond their surface awareness in all four elements and assume that deeper layers are yet to be discovered. It encourages people to consider that even when they aren't aware of any feelings or wants in the present moment, there are likely to be some just out of awareness. The cube teaches that learning to be self-aware is greatly enhanced by simply having the intent to be aware and the willingness to inquire about one's in-the-moment experience in each element of the cube. These further promote skills of integrity, authenticity, and openness to learning.

To use the cube for self-awareness, we have an exercise where people pick something participants are struggling with, and we have them unpack it by "walking the cube". In our courses, we tape Experience Cubes on the ground so that people can walk around as they unpack their experience, moving from one quadrant to another and embodying it.[3] As they walk, they might gain insight into their experience, for example: "I do not know what I want in this situation." One common outcome of walking the cube is that people realize, maybe for the first time, how much of their experience is generated from the inside out with lots of thoughts and feelings based on very few observations.

**Responses to "How can people use the Experience Cube to increase their skills of *being*?"**

*Self-awareness, presence, integrity and authenticity, inner compass, openness, and learning mindset*
– "The cube is simple, practical, but allows one to go deep."
– "There is a mutual flow between the cube and IDG framework."
– "The cube simplifies the IDGs – the tool helps one go deeper and be more specific and practical."
– "The cube increases my self-awareness – allows me to peel apart observations and thoughts."

---

**3** At the end of the chapter, we will describe an exercise a group working on an SDG can do using this approach.

- "Paying attention to feelings and becoming more literate about them can support our emotional intelligence and, therefore, our ability to regulate, connect, and avoid reactivity."
- "Sitting in curiosity can take us very deep into self-awareness, depending on the authenticity and transparency of the person."
- "We can use it as a template for journaling. It is powerful to use on your own."
- "'Presence' – the power of the tool works best in the moment."
- "Use it to work through a challenge – unpack the observations etc., leads to greater clarity. It encourages slowing down, to support the separation of thoughts and observation accurately – confusing them can be experienced by others as judgment."
- "In terms of inner compass, the cube gives permission to some people to acknowledge their wants – both what they want for themselves and for others. How are things fitting with my values/inner compass?"
- "Using it with others with curiosity connects with the 'Openness and Learning Mindset' IDG."
- "Helps recognize that 'being' can be different for different people in the moment."
- "The cube can help navigate 'right/wrong' thinking."
- "The more contentious the issue the more it may be valuable for us to stay in observation longer."
- "It's a nonlinear process. It doesn't have to start in observations, but needs to cover all domains to achieve clarity."
- "Visually, the IDG framework doesn't suggest depth the way that the cube does. This 3D concept is helpful – implicit invitation to go deeper."

## Relating

We teach that you can tell people what is in your head, or they can make it up – those are your only options. And if they make it up, their story will likely be worse than the reality. So, using the cube to describe your experience, when needed, is essential to building and sustaining effective relationships. However, many have seen relationships deteriorate after being "open and honest". We don't advocate being open and honest, but we do advocate being skillfully transparent. What's the difference? Encouraging others to be open and honest is often interpreted as permission to say whatever is top of mind. Too often, what comes next is their judgments of the other. This usually leads to defensiveness and hurt feelings. "Being direct" will worsen relationships when what you are direct about are your *judgments*. However, what is useful is to know your experience of me. That is different. I can't argue with your experience, and if you don't tell me what it is, I'm forced to make it up. To enhance relationships when our interactions create negative mush, we have to unpack our judgments, identify the experiences that led to them, and be willing to describe those without judgment.

At its most superficial level, the cube teaches that to understand another's experience, we must inquire into what they observe, think, feel, and want. Utilizing the cube for self-awareness and understanding others develops an appreciation for the notion that everyone always has a different experience, which increases the capacity for appreciation, connectedness, empathy, and humility. Once people start using the cube, they typically become less judgmental, as judgment is often the outcome of a mental/intellectual polarity: right vs. wrong. In any partnership, anyone's experience is as valid as anyone else's. There are still facts, but disagreements are rarely over facts; they are mostly over what those facts mean. Any partnership will have to find ways to integrate the plurality of meanings each partner brings to their work on the SDGs.

We have an exercise called "Listening Through the Cube" to use the cube to build relating skills. In this exercise, someone listens to another's experience without interrupting or offering advice. They simply listen to be able to paraphrase their experience until that person agrees that they understand it. While listening, the listener uses the cube to organize their listening and invites the talker to fill in any parts of the cube that the talker has not yet covered – for example, by asking, "I haven't heard what you want in this situation, can you tell me what you want?" This kind of unconditional listening to show understanding of the other's experience before suggesting alternatives greatly increases people's connectedness and willingness to listen to each other and consider different ways of making sense of the situation.

In teaching these skills to tenth grade high school students in Estonia, teachers remarked on how different the students showed up in other classes. No longer did they argue about who was right and wrong; they showed a marked increase in appreciating and encouraging different points of view. Recognizing that everyone is always having a different experience, the cube supports people in being curious about and better connected to others.

**Responses to "How can people use the Experience Cube to increase their skills of *relating*?"**

*Appreciation, connectedness, humility, empathy, and compassion*
- "The cube is a practical tool. Use the cube to listen to the other person."
- "The cube process helps to explore the differences between individuals."
- "If we want to encourage authenticity in others, showing up as authentic enables others to be authentic. Deepening awareness of our experience makes us more authentic."
- "The cube process can help individuals express ideas in a more neutral way – explore the common here and now."
- "The cube can help those that need to find their voice."

- "The cube is incredibly disarming. When we ask people to describe their here and now it raises the level of authenticity, openness. It brings people into the qualities described in the book *Becoming the Change* that makes learning possible in groups."
- "Helping people focus on the here and now helps with presence. We very seldom come into this moment; it's more about the past or the future, but here and now is the only thing that is real."
- "Here and now allows us to be curious without judgment, fear, or opinion, with empathy and understanding – that can be foundational to an open mindset."
- "Helps me understand the cultural context of the other."
- "Connecting while being different is often our challenge, and the cube assumes we will be different and that is ok. Allows us to appreciate difference."
- "Just knowing people are having a different experience shifts our relating. We learn to appreciate the other point of view and then that opens us up to more appreciation. It allows us to celebrate others' experience and uniqueness. If I start to understand our wants that leads to connectedness because we are all wanting the same thing."
- "When people come to a meeting they often have preconceptions about what will happen and it can be really hard to shift focus to a common agenda. Asking themselves right now what they are thinking, feeling, and wanting can elevate the self-awareness and group awareness. It's so useful for asking questions from."
- "The cube is a skill and a tool to separate self from self and others. Understand experience from sorting and sensemaking. Builds connectedness. When we see the difference between experiences it builds compassion, humility, and empathy."
- "Empathy is required to listen through the cube. It's almost like a snowball or something else that grows as it's used. Amplification might be a better term. The more we are in the here and now the more the opportunity to amplify the qualities we want."
- "Helps learning how perspectives land with other people. Continuous unfolding and connection with people and environment."
- "Humility is acting in accordance to the needs of the situation. When you explore the cube it helps you see the bigger picture, stops you from staying in a problem-solving mode."

## Collaborating

Understanding that everyone will have a different experience, that we don't need to have the same experience to collaborate, and that in any collaborative relationship, everyone's experience is equally valid creates the context for leaders to build genuinely collaborative teams and organizations. It shifts the leaders' focus from thinking their job is to ensure everyone is having the "right experience" to ensuring the variety of experiences can be voiced and heard.

Utilizing the cube for communication increases people's willingness and ability to understand each other and supports true collaboration. The Clear Leadership framework argues that the single greatest reason well-intentioned people are unable to sustain collaboration is the negative sensemaking that builds up over time. Interpersonal mush has several consequences that get in the way of collaboration (Bushe, 2009). Even when people recognize this, they can be afraid to check out their stories because they implicitly frame having different experiences as conflict. When people really get that everyone always has a different experience and that we don't need to have the same experience to work together, the willingness to describe and learn about each other's experience increases dramatically.

To use the cube for collaborating, we have a method called a learning conversation. A successful learning conversation requires more tools and skills than just the cube, but we offer it here as an example of how to use the cube to sustain collaboration. In a learning conversation, two people inquire into their patterns of relating. This is often motivated by some unproductive or unsatisfying pattern but can be useful even when things are good just to keep the mush at bay.

Take a moment to think about a relationship that is less than satisfying or productive. Isn't it obvious to you how they are the problem, and if only they would change it would all be better? It's very likely if we asked that other person about it, they would describe how you are the problem. For any pattern to exist, each person has to play their part. For a learning conversation to be successful, each person has to be open to the possibility that they have a part in it and be curious about their own role in the problem pattern. They need to be willing to describe their experience (not judgments) through the cube so that the other can hear it without becoming reactive. They need to listen to the other's experience through the cube and summarize it back to them. In a learning conversation, one person starts talking, and the other listens. They switch roles once the listener can paraphrase the talker's experience to the talker's satisfaction. This process goes back and forth until they understand their own and the other's experience of the problem pattern. The goal is to understand each other's experience and clear out the mush. That creates a new and richer field of possibility for what will emerge next in the partnership. It is almost always a positive experience because the stories that were made up were worse than the reality.

After taking the Clear Leadership course, a study of 32 healthcare managers found that all had changed how they thought about conflict at work, and 95% had utilized the cube to engage and resolve work conflicts with those they wanted to increase collaboration with (Bushe & Grossling, 2006):

*The most common pattern (45% of participants) in descriptions of conflict after the course was that conflict was only a misunderstanding between stories that needed to get checked out. Somewhat surprisingly, almost a quarter of individuals (24%) had completely rethought conflict such*

> *that what was previously deemed a conflict was subsequently redefined, sometimes as personally generated experience. (p.9)*

Previous research has consistently found that about four out of five conflicts between people who need to collaborate are due to inaccurate sensemaking (Bushe, 2001). The cube provides a simple but effective tool for uncovering what is really going on, which often resolves what appeared to be conflict and reestablishes collaboration.

### Reponses to "How can people use the Experience Cube to increase their skills of *collaborating*?"

*Communication skills, inclusive mindset and intercultural competence, trust, mobilization skills*

- "Walking the cube[4] helps me be present and connect with diverse groups."
- "Clarifying my experience creates a more constructive way of seeing things."
- "The cube process works across diverse groups – we all have thoughts, feelings, experiences."
- "The cube supports dialogue not to get stuck in a debate, to listen better. Staying in the moment and talking about the experience in the moment will open up space for collaborating."
- "The cube helps me manage my (and others') reactivity – park reactions."
- "Being willing to describe my experience is a vulnerable act, which helps to create trust."
- "Listening through the cube helps to build trust and sets the stage for co-creation by helping understand the experience of the other."
- "If I really listen and hear your experience, I see our common humanity. Then if I ask more questions through the cube, they will trust me more, because they see I am interested. It allows us both to elaborate and go deeper which creates trust."
- "When I become more aware of my own experience, and then listen to the other's experience, it gives us points of finding where we might co-create."
- "Getting folks to express 'wants' creates space to work together."
- "Less reactive when I am able to express my wants."
- "Power in naming wants and needs for collaboration."
- "Maybe, in organizational contexts that even if I'm not getting what I want, I can feel like my wants have been heard and I understand why we are going in a different direction – so I still feel like I belong, which is essential for collaboration."

---

4 Walking the cube refers to putting a large representation of the cube on a floor and having people stand in the part of the cube they are speaking from as their partner(s) seeks to understand the speaker's experience.

- "Expressing more than wants creates more space. By using the cube to help people understand how they came to their wants, we can understand each other more clearly and find points of commonality. By going deeper into our experience, we can find our shared wants."
- "By having everyone have a turn of walking the cube it helps those who talk less be heard, which builds collaboration."
- "When it helps to create clarity about the differences, it creates a space for a more profound kind of collaboration."
- "We move past people coming to the table with the agenda to convince others to think and want what I do. So, the different context of 'everyone is having a different experience' makes collaboration more attainable."
- "We learn that we don't have to have the same experience to collaborate – we never have."
- "Instead of the differences creating polarization, it creates a wider space for collaboration. We can be differentiated."
- "If I express my inner experience fully to another person, it has the impact on the other to be willing to mobilize, to share, to engage – impact on mobilization."
- "Just getting everyone to say what they want leads to a much more grounded mobilization, but it's not just about wants – it's the process of holding the container for the variety of different experiences to be voiced."
- "The cube can be used in the context of conflicts or the sense that there are different groups, contexts, agendas to find common ground."
- "This builds more motivation – a willingness to move forward."
- "Using the cube to sell things or ideas helps with collaboration. Helps with communication skills. It is important to paraphrase and mirror the other."

## The Experience Cube and adult development

Achieving the SDGs probably requires leaders exhibiting post-conventional adult development patterns of thinking and relating (Kegan, 1994; Torbert, 2020). Constructivist developmental theory (Kegan, 1982; Kohlberg, 1984; Loevinger, 1976) provides a roadmap to adult development that identifies a series of self-sealing stages that provide complete and coherent explanations of self and the world. Each successive stage builds on the previous one so that stages cannot be skipped over. Each stage is a new resolution of the paradox of the desire to belong and be a separate individual (Kegan, 1982). At each later stage, what was once seen as a part of oneself is now seen as something one has, not what someone is. Studies of adult populations have found that around 75% of the adult population is in two stages: one where people primarily identify with their expertise and the next stage where people primarily identify with their roles and accomplishments (Binder, 2023). These are referred to as conventional stages of development.

Leaders at the conventional stages tend not to be curious about other people's experience and tend to overestimate the accuracy of their sensemaking. They generally don't realize that everyone is always having a different experience, nor how much their assumptions about others are stories they've made up. Interpersonal conflicts are often framed as needing to figure out who is right and wrong, and there is frequently an unconscious desire to "win". They tend to view polarities and paradoxes in either/or terms and make sense out of things in linear and logically consistent ways, missing paradoxical, systemically circular realities. While they can see the utility of addressing conflict for achievement, they tend not to be aware of inner conflicts and often split off and project their inner conflicts onto their environment. One common way this might show up is that rather than take responsibility for agreeing to take on too much work and now struggling to keep my agreements, I will blame those I made those agreements with for asking for too much.

Post-conventional patterns of thinking and relating demonstrate a greater valuing of relationships in contrast with the cherishing of achievements, ability, and ideals, but not at the expense of one's individuality. They no longer identify with their roles and achievements; they have roles and achievements. Instead, they identify with their choices and "choicefulness". They make sense of themselves and the world as an almost infinite variety of opportunities, perspectives, and meanings, some of which are chosen and others not, including one's identity. The hallmark of the post-conventional stage is the acknowledgment of inner conflicts rather than repressing or projecting them, and therefore, the ability to track one's own experience and the experience of others with minimal distortion. There is a genuine respect for other people's autonomy while acknowledging mutual interdependence. Individuality and uniqueness in self and others are cherished. Spontaneity, sincerity, and intensity are characteristics of people operating at post-conventional stages, and feelings tend to be vividly expressed.

Our contention, and we believe this would be shared by those who study and work with vertical development, is that achieving the SDGs requires leaders operating at post-conventional stages of development. Recent research suggests that the complexity of contemporary life has resulted in more leaders at post-conventional levels in large organizations (Torbert, 2020). According to Cowie (2012), at post-conventional stages of development:

> [L]eaders pursue self-fulfillment rather than achievement because I have now separated myself from my activities [. . .] given up my certainty for curiosity because 'not knowing' is now a state that does not threaten my sense of who I am.[. . .] Embrace complexity, paradox, ambiguity, uncertainty, and flux because I now know that reality is not defined by my wishes, hopes, fears, anxieties, theories, and beliefs or those of my cultural group [. . .] tolerate the shortcomings of myself and others because I now accept human nature for what it is rather than how I would prefer it to be. [. . .] Acknowledge and cope with the inner conflicts I feel [. . .] because I now understand they

*are part of the human condition, and I have the courage to deal with them as such.[. . .] Experience deep feelings of connection with and empathy for other people because I now realize that we all belong to the same human family. (pp.33–34)*

We have seen people begin their journey from conventional to post-conventional when they confront the extent to which they operate on stories they are constantly making up about others. As they realize that even in most face-to-face interactions, they are making up a story of how the other is receiving them and making choices about what to say and do next based on that story, it pulls the rug out from underneath the certainty that is a hallmark of conventional stages. As they explore their experience through the cube, they confront how much of their experience is typically out of their awareness. Recognizing, perhaps for the first time, that wants and feelings unconsciously influence their actions, they open up to the hidden world inside. Noticing the different quality of connecting with others, when they are allowed to have their own experience and others to have theirs, a new desire for high-quality relationships is kindled. All of these, we believe, serve to push people out of the self-sealing properties of the conventional stages and begin their journey to post-conventional stages.

This change is amplified by our teachings on "self-differentiation" (Bowen, 1985), which we operationalize as the ability to be separate and connected simultaneously. The key thing that gets in the way of interpersonal clarity is confusing one's own experience for the experience of the other, making ourselves responsible for their experience and making them responsible for our own. The way out of this is to work at being separate while connected to others. This means being separate enough to know what my experience is independent of you, yet, at the same time, being curious about your experience, wanting to know what you are observing, thinking, feeling, and wanting, without being emotionally hijacked.

A deeper understanding of being emerges as people explore why it seems much easier to discuss observations and thoughts than feelings and wants. The Clear Leadership framework teaches that it comes from an inability to differentiate from our experience, that is, to be connected to our experience but separate from it simultaneously; I have experience, but I am not my experience. We tend not to identify ourselves with our observations – we think observations come from outside, so we are not our observations. Describing them does not feel like an act of self-disclosure. Similarly, most people don't strongly identify with their thoughts – they recognize they can hold competing thoughts simultaneously, which is nothing to be ashamed of; I have thoughts, but I am not my thoughts. However, it is more common for people to identify with their feelings and wants, as they seem more subjective and more personal. When I identify with my feelings, describing them to you makes me vulnerable. Will you treat my feelings, and therefore me, well? And if I am my wants, then if I express them, and you don't give them to me, you are rejecting me. Far too vulnerable. The Experience Cube teaches that I have feelings, but I am not my feelings. I have wants, but I am not my wants. I have experience, but I am not my experience. When one learns to differentiate from one's experience, it becomes much less threatening to become aware of disowned aspects of one's experience and to be authentic when sharing experience with others. We realize that we can choose our experience – how to make sense of something or someone, feel about it, and what to want – a hallmark of post-conventional development.

## How can I/we use the Experience Cube to help achieve SDGs?

> The SDGs can only be achieved by large groups of people working collaboratively over long periods. They could take decades or more to accomplish – and in our experience, long-term collaboration is challenging to sustain without a tool like the Experience Cube.

We will describe a pattern that we often see in collaborative relationships in organizational settings. Have you ever seen this pattern in your work? You joined a team of like-minded people to work toward a meaningful goal. At the start, the energy was vivid, everyone had great intentions, the ideas flowed, and everyone seemed ready and willing to get on with the work. And then, slowly (or sometimes not so slowly), collaboration started to become challenging. The behavior of some team members was puzzling to you – "Why was she doing or saying that?" Or you just started to develop a dislike for someone on the team. You started talking more to those who shared your views and being annoyed by those who did not. Subgroups emerge with overt or hidden conflicts. Eventually, all the energy and ideas that were there at the start do not get acted on or brought to a conclusion. Does this sound familiar? Have you had this experience in your work towards the SDGs – or are you watching the early stages of this process in your current SDG work?

Four out of five times, this happens because people are acting on stories they made up to fill in the gaps of what they know about other people's experience, stories that are inaccurate and more negative than reality. Because of that, when people ask and listen to each other's experience, are honest to themselves and their team about their experience, and are curious about and respectful of others' experiences, the conflicts go away. And if it doesn't, it is now clear what the conflicts are really about.

The best way to do this is with a learning conversation – which we described earlier – but there is another simpler exercise that you can do with your team right now using the Experience Cube. We call it "walking the cube", as outlined below:

1. Pick the topic that you want to explore. Some examples are your team's purpose, how the team functions, or what procedures you should be using. Any issue the group seems to be stuck on or avoiding is a candidate. Ask your team members if they are willing to inquire into their different experiences of the topic.

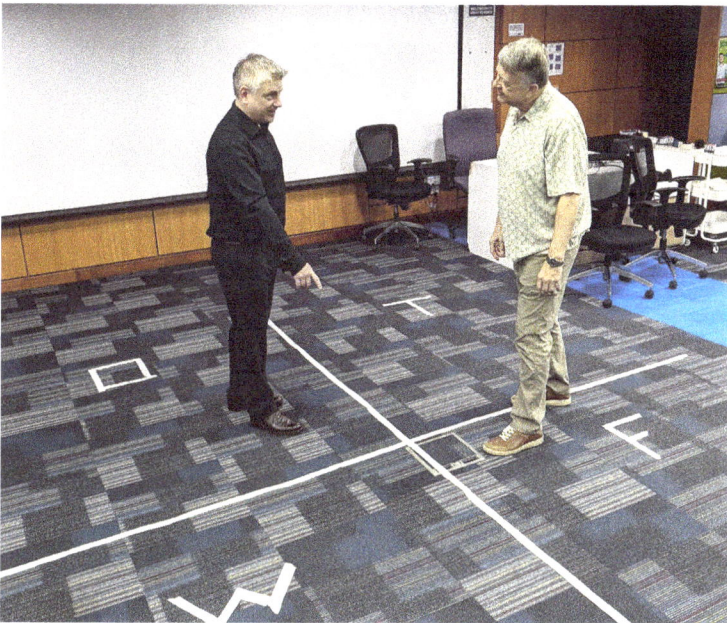

**Figure 17.2:** Gervase and Michael "walking the cube".

2.  Explain how the cube works and remind them that everyone is always having a different experience, and we don't need to have the same experience to work together, but we do need to avoid acting on our stories about each other's experience. As people walk the cube our only job is to listen and ask questions to understand their experience fully. Don't disagree with the person in the cube.
3.  Use masking tape to create an Experience Cube on the ground – see the picture above.
4.  Invite each team member to take a turn describing their experience of the topic by standing in the part of the cube they are talking from. If they are talking about what they think, they stand in the T. If they are saying something about what they want, they stand in the W. Sometimes it is helpful to have another member of the team (or a facilitator) walk with them, making sure they are standing in the right square, asking questions, and inviting them to go to parts of the cube they haven't spent much time in. Ensure everyone feels satisfied they understand the person's complete experience before moving on to the next person.
5.  Close the exercise by discussing what you now understand about the topic and what people think should happen next. Understanding each other's experiences will create a richer, more accurate ground for what emerges next in the team's journey.

Try it out; we are sure you will find the exercise useful for your team. You can also use it to reconnect people and get them moving forward when things seem to be getting stuck.

## Conclusion

Initially presented in the first edition of the book *Clear Leadership* (Bushe, 2001), the Experience Cube has been used in coaching and leadership development with tens of thousands worldwide over the last 25 years. During that time, as we taught the cube in our Clear Leadership course, we witnessed almost universal improvement in participants' ability to be self-aware, relate to others, and sustain long-term collaboration and partnership. Even more promising, the cube can be an important tool to help those ready to move from a conventional to a post-conventional mindset, essential for the kind of leadership needed to create the teams and networks that can meet the complex challenges of sustainable development.

## References

Binder, T. (2023). *Ego development for effective coaching and consulting.* Vandenhoeck & Rupercht.

Bowen, M. (1985). *Family therapy in clinical practice.* Aronson.

Bushe, G. R. (2001). *Clear leadership: How outstanding leaders make themselves understood, cut through the mush, and help everyone get real at work.* Davies-Black.

Bushe, G. R. (2009). *Clear leadership: Sustaining real collaboration and partnership at work* (revised edition). Davies-Black.

Bushe, G. R. & Grossling, R. (2006). Engaging conflict: The impact of Clear Leadership training on how people think about conflict and its management. Simon Fraser University white paper, https://clearleadership.com/wp-content/uploads/Engaging-Conflict_the-impact-of-clear-leadership.pdf [Accessed Mar. 14, 2024].

Cook-Greuter, S. R. (2014). Nine levels of increasing embrace in ego development: A full-spectrum theory of vertical growth and meaning making. https://www.researchgate.net/publication/356357233_Ego_Development_A_Full – Spectrum_Theory_Of_Vertical_Growth_And_Meaning_Making [Accessed Mar. 14, 2024].

Herrando, C. & Constantinides, E. (2021). Emotional contagion: A brief overview and future directions. *Frontiers in Psychology, 12,* 712606. https://doi.org/10.3389/fpsyg.2021.712606

Cowie, K. (2012). *Finding Merlin: A handbook for the human development journey in our organisational world.* Marshall Cavendish.

Kegan, R. (1982). *The evolving self: Problem and process in human development.* Harvard University Press.

Kegan, R. (1994). *In over our heads: The mental demands of modern life.* Harvard University Press.

Kohlberg, L. (1984). *The psychology of moral development: The nature and validity of moral stages.* Harper & Row.

Loevinger, J. (1976). *Ego development.* Jossey-Bass.

Piaget, J. (1952). *The origins of intelligence in children.* International Universities Press.

Seth, A. (2021). *Being you: A new science of consciousness*. Dutton.

Torbert, W.R. (2004) *Action inquiry: The secret of timely and transforming leadership*. Berrett-Koehler.

Torbert, W.R. (2020). Warren Buffet and your own seven transformations of leadership. *The 2020 Update on the 2005 Harvard Business Review*. https://www.gla.global/wp-content/uploads/2020/09/Warren-Buffetts-and-Your-Own-Seven-Transformations-of-Leadership.pdf [Accessed Mar. 14, 2024].

Weick, K. E. (1995). *Sense-making in organizations*. Sage.

Joanna Stanberry and Anna Margolis

# Chapter 18
# Contemplating or confronting? How the Inner Development Goals can activate reflexivity through Q methodology

**Abstract:** This chapter explores how the Inner Development Goals (IDGs) can trigger processes of reflexivity. Challenge-based learning (CBL) connects theory with practice. However, methods that allow CBL participants to reflect on their development within a normative framework are still rare. Through the IDGs we develop a method to evaluate CBL courses aimed at increasing self-efficacy (‘*Selbstwirksamkeit*’), validating the method through a workshop with experts.

Self-efficacy is the capacity of people to pursue goals, and the IDGs provide normative concepts that bridge inner reflection to outer, goal-oriented action. We used the IDGs as a pathway to triggering individual and group reflection on self-efficacy. We eschewed traditional measurement scales and opted to engender reflexivity in the CBL participants through Q methodology. To co-create these conditions, the IDGs were “confronted” in two ways. First, we describe confronting the IDGs through first-person narratives, describing the encounter with each other through the planning and delivery of the workshop. This process raised our various shared and distinct identities, and shaped our responses to the IDGs. In this sense, we place the intersubjective into both a performative and an instructional context. Second, we describe how Q methodology enables a confrontation with the IDGs that creates the conditions for collective leadership through learning. We identify two specific viewpoints on the IDGs, the *perceptive translator* and the *relational disruptor,* and describe how awareness of the subtle but salient differences among these viewpoints enables a broader, more systemic, and critical perspective on our practice as researchers and facilitators.

**Keywords:** Critical Reflexivity, Self-efficacy, Reflexive teaching, Systemic Design, Challenge-based learning, Q Methodology

## Introduction

In formal instruction contexts, action learning and challenge-based learning (CBL) are gaining increasing popularity as teaching methods that enable skill development, support social learning, and increase self-efficacy (‘*Selbstwirksamkeit*’) (Argyris, 2011; Ballen et al., 2018; Gallagher & Savage, 2020). Certain disciplines, such as strategy, design thinking, systems design, social entrepreneurship, or dramaturgy and performing, lend

https://doi.org/10.1515/9783111337913-019

themselves well to CBL. However, it can be difficult to evaluate if CBL actually reaches the objectives of skill development, social learning, and self-efficacy, as these concepts are subjective and difficult to quantify (Bandura, 1982; May & Perry, 2017).

Traditionally, evaluation methods for CBL focus on how participants evaluate learning effects across various dimensions on a scale (cp. Colombelli et al., 2022; Ballen et al, 2018; Hendrickson, 2021). Less attention is granted to the directionality of the learning trajectory: while students are assessed on the attainment of soft and hard skills, their normative assumptions and worldviews are not questioned. As the second author (Anna) teaches a class that is explicitly concerned with CBL to address societal challenges, she was looking for an alternative evaluation method that would – against the background of societal norms and challenges – fulfill three functions:

1. allow the students to reflect on their individual learning journey and increased self-efficacy;
2. allow the instructors to reflect on how to develop the course;
3. enable individual and collective reflexivity on how to address societal challenges.

These criteria required a normative framework that was set against the background of societal norms and challenges, which the IDGs (Jordan et al., 2021) provided.

To attain the functions above, we combined the IDGs with Q methodology, a research technique that allows the respondents to reflect with content statements (in this case, the IDGs). Combining the IDGs with Q methodology enabled greater awareness at the first-, second-, and third-person levels, thus opening up new possibilities for reflection and collective leadership.

Collective leadership can often operate as an empty signifier (Edwards & Bolden, 2023) and is a staple in current leadership fashions (Guthey, Ferry, & Remke, 2022), especially in sustainability circles (Arkedis et al. 2023). Regardless, it is a discursively useful lens to highlight critical perspectives that decenter individualistic and heroic narratives of leadership and to focus analysis on shared efforts at change.

Q methodology was developed by the psychologist William Stephenson in the 1930s and has been a robust research methodology blending qualitative and quantitative analysis for over 80 years (Ramlo, 2016). While Q has been used for evaluation previously (Harris et al., 2022; Ramlo, 2015; Cuppen, 2013), only recently has the transformative (Wolf, 2022) and educative (Stanberry, 2023) nature of the process and outcomes of Q sorting been explored. We further develop an understanding of how Q methodology might have the potential to trigger personal development and could catalyze collective reflexivity and action through exploring the shared viewpoints together. This chapter proposes that Q is uniquely positioned to make visible inherent tensions in the IDGs, and through this, to achieve a new vantage for collective leadership.

We validated our approach in a hybrid workshop with academics and practitioners. The context for the workshop was the Relating Systems Thinking and Design symposium (RSD12) in Amsterdam, convened by the Systemic Design Association and focused on co-design for societal transition, which we encounter as a system. In this session, we invited participants to join us in co-developing such an evaluation approach. We selected this conference as its attendants were practitioners and researchers in systems design who are generally skilled at facilitating CBL courses, workshops, and group processes of reflection.

First, we describe how we (the authors) confronted and contemplated the IDGs when preparing the workshop (See Figure 18.1). We do this from different perspectives – the individual first person and the intersubjective second person. Then, we explore the diverse third-person perspectives on the IDGs that Q enabled, attending to the critical questions raised by the process and reflecting on how our personal, shared, and collective practices could be augmented by this kind of reflexivity.

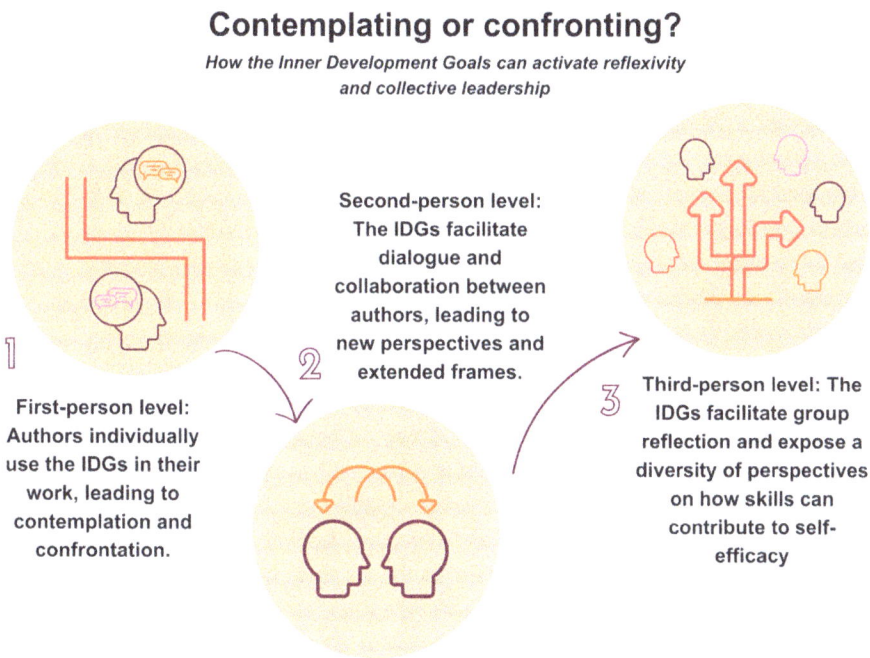

## Contemplating or confronting?
*How the Inner Development Goals can activate reflexivity and collective leadership*

**Second-person level:** The IDGs facilitate dialogue and collaboration between authors, leading to new perspectives and extended frames.

**First-person level:** Authors individually use the IDGs in their work, leading to contemplation and confrontation.

**Third-person level:** The IDGs facilitate group reflection and expose a diversity of perspectives on how skills can contribute to self-efficacy

**Figure 18.1:** The three levels of activating reflexivity towards the IDGs.
Source: Used with permission by Stanberry & Margolis 2024

# Before the workshop: Confronting and contemplating the IDGs

We look into our first- (subjective), second- (intersubjective), and third-person (workshop participants) reflections on confronting and contemplating the IDGs. The first person contains subjective narratives of encountering this workshop process, in an effort to "humanify" the co-learning endeavor (Cunliffe, 2018). We move to the intersubjective (or second-person level) and then explore the third-person experience and perspectives of the workshop participants.

## First person: Individual confrontation and contemplation

### Anna's view

In 2021, I started teaching a CBL course at the IST University of Applied Science. In a democratic, design-oriented process we ask students to propose societal challenges. Next, we jointly explore these challenges and select one that the students view as most salient in their context. In the subsequent sessions, I teach methods from design thinking and systems design that allow the students to explore the challenge and propose solutions. My co-lecturer, Frank Alva Buecheler, teaches theater performance and stage arts. This allows the students not only to propose solutions but also to put solution prototypes on stage with the aim to convince their target audience to act. In the context of their chosen challenge, the students learn how they can reflect upon problems, explain their views, facilitate group work, and convince others to follow them. In German, such skills can be summarized as *Selbstwirksamkeit*, in a literal translation this means "self-impact-full-ness". The official English translation is self-efficacy.

*Self-efficacy* is a set of beliefs, and refers to how someone assesses their own set of skills in relation to designing and executing a course of action to achieve certain goals (Jackson, 2002). Hence, self-efficacy is not a universal personality trait but always relates to a *set of skills* relevant to achieve goals in a specific *context*. For example, in a CBL course, students can reflect on their skill set in regard to the challenge at hand. But my aim in CBL is to go beyond the immediate challenge and offer a protected space where students can practice universal skills transferable to other contexts. So, self-efficacy becomes somewhat more universal as it relates to a *class of complex tasks* that are similar to those addressed in the course.

When reflecting on how to improve the course, I faced three considerations. First, how to better capture participants' diverse viewpoints, needs, and expectations in evaluation. Second, how to enhance the students' reflexivity on their self-efficacy outside class. Many students signaled that they hesitated with introducing newly learned methods at work in spite of seeing the need for change. Third, my final concern related to how the course could strengthen not only participants' soft skills but also how they view their role as change agents in the world. As the course participants hold diverse views on societal challenges, I use the Sustainable Development Goals (SDGs) as a unifying framework that emphasizes connection between societal challenges.

To address the three considerations above, I turned to *Q methodology*. As Q methodology allows capturing subjective perceptions on a certain topic, it holds potential to integrate diverse student needs and worldviews on self-efficacy. But Q methodology is a vessel that needs content consisting of a set of statements that participants sort during the Q sort. Against the normative background of the SDGs, the IDGs offered an appropriate scaffold to build such a set of statements on the topic of self-efficacy.

Combining Q methodology with the IDGs meant that I had to do three tasks. First, formulate a question for the card sort: "What does self-efficacy mean to you in your professional or societal engagement?" Second, I translated the 23 IDG skills into personal statements that students could relate to. For example: "I constantly challenge the status quo and search for novel, better solutions." Often, I used several statements for the same skill to cover different aspects. Also, I wanted the students not to feel overwhelmed and to encourage self-awareness around uncertainty and vulnerability. Therefore, I also included some statements with a negative connotation, where I felt that they would reflect the reality of some of the students. For example: "I often lack the courage to present and defend my views and values to others." Finally, I developed the initial set of statements in two languages – German for the course and English for the expert workshop.

For me, the process of operationalizing the IDGs in this way brought two things to the foreground. On the one hand, I realized how many inherent tensions the IDGs contain. It is unlikely that any of us will master all of these skills perfectly at any point in time. It is rather about seeing the big picture on the overall skill set and defining priorities on where to turn next – which skills to build or strengthen next depending on the task and the context. On the other hand, I realized how overwhelming and somewhat diminishing such a skill set may seem to those people who are not skilled facilitators, systems thinkers, and leaders. It was only in the context of a specific challenge in class that the skills took shape, became concrete tasks to master, and ultimately, could result in a change of how somebody assesses their self-efficacy in tackling professional and societal challenges. So, this was my first confrontation with the IDGs: they sound great on paper, but how do I operationalize them in a contextual space with a diverse group of students?

These realizations prompted me to invite Joanna, this chapter co-author, to facilitate a joint workshop with experts who were skilled facilitators and systems thinkers to see if and how such a group would react to the IDG card sort. I've invited Joanna to join me, building on her expertise in Q methodology, collective leadership, and social learning in the context of the SDGs. These skills felt very complementary to mine and I saw in them the potential to bring a more reflective and critical perspective to my initial idea.

### Joanna's view

As a leadership researcher in 2003 in sustainable development contexts in Bolivia and Brazil, I wondered about how the inner and outer changes often observed as "leadership" might often emerge from contexts focused on specific problems rather than leadership per se. In 2015, I encountered the theory and methods of the Victorian educationalist Charlotte Mason (1842–1923). I discovered in her writings, and in the community that was actively using her methods, a unique approach to learning that centered on sensemaking the natural world, citizenship, and self-development. Her ideas appeared to be creating a context for leadership emergence without that explicit focus.

Based on Mason's work, I approach processes of collective leadership through the lens that all learning is self-education. In this sense, individuals select the ideas they wish to take from any encounter, whether formal learning or not, and "own" them. Thus, sharing stories, a conversation, an experience like a nature walk or project-based learning, reading a book, watching an interesting video, are all sources of ideas that one may choose to receive, adapt, or reject, all in ways particular to that person. This approach problematizes the "experiential learning" and "book learning" binary.

Mason was an Anglican who honored the born personhood of all people, especially children, and described a process where living and vital ideas must be met directly by the learner, with the teacher operating as a friend and guide and laying a feast of these ideas before the pupil. Here, living mind meets living mind, a critical pivot that provides the possibility for new pathways of thinking and doing. In her thinking, it is not only books but especially the natural world that becomes a conduit for living ideas.

Mason also suggested that for an individual to make ideas their own, they must narrate, for to narrate is to know. She proposed that the "the mind can know nothing but what it can produce in the form of an answer to a question put by the mind to itself" (Mason, 1905, p. 181). Narration is the self-expression of an idea, the digesting and consuming of the idea as spiritual food. Narration does not only need to be verbal, but could be written, enacted, even just considered. In this way, narration is the key action in processes of reflexivity. Reflexivity (as a present-day concept) could be seen as a particular flavor of narration, one in which the self comes into view in light of, or in comparison to, the context, others, and even other versions of the same self.

This distinct pedagogy – deemed revolutionary by her contemporaries – became a lens to view personal and collective transformation for sustainability (Middlekauff, 2016). In 2022, I moved to northwest England (where Mason had situated her social enterprise) for my doctoral studies to explore innovative ways of applying her ideas to sustainability leadership more broadly.

I began to test an alternative approach to the skills and abilities identified as important for collaborations towards implementing the UN Sustainable Development Goals (SDGs). Termed "partnership competencies" these skill sets are often approached as a universal aim, with an implicit assumption that a single organization or individual could demonstrate the wide and complex host of skills needed.

Based on Mason's ideas, I alternatively approached the partnership competencies as possibilities one might elect to develop (or not). I also proposed that instead of a normative or unilateral framework to be embraced wholly, they could become a unique and person-dependent developmental pathway that one "opts into". Using Q methodology, I interpreted the presence of three viewpoints: the *convener*, the *connector*, and the *chair*, who all approached these capabilities in distinct ways (Stanberry et al., 2024).

After co-presenting to the Basel Impact Hub IDG group in 2022, I found aspects of the approach puzzling. First, the approach brought into a pluralistic space what my own Christian tradition had called "spiritual formation" or "discipleship" for 2,000 years. What had we learned from that history? Second, there was a power dynamic evident in Global North "experts" developing a framework to solve problems most acute in the Global South. A colleague working in Kenya on leadership development for the SDGs said, "Don't colonize my mindset." In some ways, corporate approaches to human development through the IDGs (e.g., the IKEA partnership) can perpetuate the dehumanizing residue in capitalistic systems. Additionally, Mason's approach to centering the personhood of individuals to consider, configure, and catalyze their own learning and development may be difficult to enable in corporate leadership development programs.

I had studied much of the IDG-adjacent work including Peter Senge, Otto Scharmer, Hilary Bradbury-Huang, David Cooperrider, Robert Kegan, and Lisa Lahey, and in practice seen the transformational work of Jonathan Gosling, Kathryn Goldman Schuyler, Katherine Tyler Scott, Janis Balda, and others in that community who had spent decades on these approaches and inner–outer change for sustainability. However, developing leadership towards the SDGs and pointing collective action towards regenerative processes is fraught with difficulties (Balda, Stanberry, & Altman, 2023; Stanberry, Balda, & Balda, 2022). It was clear that managing psychological safety, co-creating as a facilitation mode, and alertness to immunities to change could be effective signposts in the IDG process.

Anna and I met in a doctoral consortium in 2022 and later decided to co-facilitate the workshop because of my use of Q methodology – I became interested in this more critical approach to the IDGs, while also perceiving inner tensions. I had asked similar questions to the "One Question Survey" in the IDGs, which led to some anxieties about presenting Q in a "light touch" way appropriate for a practitioner workshop. At the same time the power of the sorting process and analysis needed to create the conditions for reflexivity at the individual and collective level.

The IDGs, combined with the ability of Q sorting to form a particular kind of reflective moment, introduced new possibilities for group facilitation and empowerment. The kind of collaboration needed for implementation of the SDGs captured in SDG 17 had been missing a focus on vulnerable people and populations, and the IDGs provided a pathway for activating and visualizing this focus (Stanberry & Balda, 2023). Finally I looked forward to working with Anna, as our shared positions and divergent backgrounds offered an opportunity for friendship and for personal growth.

The process of reflecting and writing towards this chapter allowed for these latent tensions to become visible. The confrontation with the IDGs came naturally to me –

raising with Anna my own concerns and echoing hers, for example. The collaboration with Anna also came as an intentional piece of the project, and the workshop and debriefing appropriately concluded this kind of event.

However, focusing these reflections on a piece of writing, and therefore more deeply addressing each other, raised a particular kind of vulnerability. I experienced this as an intentional *slowing down*. Writing, email exchanges, and even reading the relevant literature took on a decelerated disentangling. The narrative continues as "true" or "honest", however the heightened awareness of a performative space – notable in the IDGs – could be seen as an added tool available to the toolbox of the practitioner, and a particular shared manifestation of collective leadership moving from the first person to the second person.

## Second person: Author team

The sense of overlapping and divergent roles and identities emerged as a theme in our discussions. We share important intersections – both are "mature" doctoral students with preceding careers and both parent children of similar ages as mothers. Nevertheless, distinctions emerged to be acknowledged and negotiated – our relationships to norms, faith, and religion, our affinity for certain technologies, and the emphases of our research.

Often, the connections and tensions only emerged through dialogue. At first, our research is similar: we both connect theory and practice researching how to bring about desirable and sustainable futures. We both facilitate collective sensemaking processes applying systems thinking. We both teach about societal impact. But through dialogue, we also uncovered how differently we perceive the world, ask questions, and challenge assumptions due to our diverse cultural background.

To facilitate such a dialogue, the personal statements that we have derived from the IDGs were useful. They offered spaces where we could negotiate how we position ourselves in the world and towards each other. Our discussion changed several times: sometimes we confronted as our views diverged or alternatively contemplated different word meanings or statements creating positive and negative associations simultaneously. We emerged from the process with more comprehensive frames as change agents in a complex world. The IDG statements acted as prompts to facilitate our joint reflection and discussion.

## The workshop

We facilitated the workshop in a hybrid setting during the Relating Systems Thinking and Design (RSD-12) Conference in Amsterdam in October 2023. We used a Miro board to open the workshop, to introduce the IDGs and the Q sorting exercise, and finally, to document a collective reflection process. Additionally, we used software to enable the card-sorting exercise and to collect individual reflections directly after completing the card sort.

The participating group of eight experts was exceptional to the extent that all of them engaged in systemic design. Systemic design connects systems thinking with design approaches, leading to a deeper and more rigorous understanding of problems, advanced approaches in form giving and developing social interactions, as well as more critical reasoning that informs how we shape the world around us (Jones, 2013). By understanding the interconnectedness and emergent properties of systems, specialized designers can become more reflective and impactful in their practice.

Our workshop participants shared a passion to understand complex systems and make an active impact in the world through design research or practice. However, most were unaware of the IDGs. Consequently, in the workshop, we focused on two aspects: (1) scope and limits of the IDGs; and (2) Q methodology as a process for self-reflection. We describe both below.

## Scope and limits of the IDGs

To explore the limits of the IDGs, we shared the largely homogenous culture of their origins. The IDG initial survey (n=861) comprised of roughly half Swedish respondents, of those remaining included only 6% from Africa, Latin America, or developing countries in Asia. Additionally, almost half of the participants worked either as a coach/consultant, as a manager, or as a leadership professional. So, as facilitators we felt that there may be more critical skills that have yet to be identified due to such cultural and/or professional homogeneity. A Colombian farmer, a Kenyan housewife, or an Indonesian waste-picker could have different skill sets than those in the current IDG framework.

To present a more comprehensive picture, we explored other frameworks for inner change towards sustainable development in management, sustainability, spirituality, and indigenous knowledge (cp. Scharmer & Yukelson, 2015; Senge, 1990; Rimanoczy, 2020; Ives et al., 2020; Ives et al., 2023; Pope Francis's encyclicals, 2015; 2023; Development Policy Unit, 2022; Beamer et al., 2021).

The group appreciated the five IDG dimensions but raised questions around the system perspective, the interconnectedness of the IDGs, and also the need for heterogeneous versus homogeneous, specialized skills. We then used Q methodology as a process for self-reflection by taking participants into a confrontation with the IDGs.

## Enabling workshop participants to "confront" the IDGs through Q methodology

We took the workshop participants into a live exercise to demonstrate understanding of self-efficacy by doing a card-sorting exercise based on Q methodology. Q methodology is a research design that allows identifying subjective constructs on a topic via a card-sorting exercise and interviews (Brown, 1980; Stephenson, 1953; 1993). It has been widely used in situations of sustainability governance as a creative and useful tool to assist in cultivating collaborative relationships (Seghezzo et al., 2023).

During the card sort, there are two reflective processes ongoing in parallel. First, the process of considering the salience of each statement. Second, the statements are considered *in relationship to each other*, leading to deeper contemplation and reflexivity. Table 18.1 describes the prompt offered to participants.

**Table 18.1:** Conditions of instruction for participants.

| |
|---|
| Below you find 40 statements on the topic of self-efficacy (*'Selbstwirksamkeit'*, *'Zelfeffectiviteit'*). These are spread across five IDG dimensions: *being, thinking, relating, collaborating*, and *acting*. |
| Consider your ability to create change for more sustainable futures. Sort the statements based on those that best describe your inner world to the right, and those least like you on the left. |
| What most describes the abilities and challenges that *you* are facing when trying to create change towards a more sustainable future? |

The workshop participants first sorted the cards into three stacks – agree, neutral, and disagree – using digital software (one physically sorted the cards). After a final sort they arranged their subjective perceptions of 40 statements into a pattern on a scale from "strongly agree" to "completely disagree" (see Figure 18.2).

The statements (see table in Appendix 1) define constructs around self-efficacy and were based on the IDGs. Each individual Q sort results in a matrix that represents one individual perception of self-efficacy. The matrices can then be used to apply statistical factor analysis. The groupings of factors into distinct and shared viewpoints is conducted with the aid of theoretically informed hand rotation and interpretation of the qualitative responses (Brown, 1980). In the case of the workshop, these were provided in a written survey and through responses on a digital Miro board. The educative potential of Q methodology is realized through the attention and internal reflection applied to each statement and then through narration through placing it on the grid (Stanberry, 2023).

The reflection questions in the follow-up survey included:
–  What was that process like for you?
–  Did you feel that any statements were missing? What would you want to add and where would you sort it?

**Sort 2:** Consider your ability to create change for more sustainable futures.
What most describes the abilities and challenges that **you** are facing
when trying to create change towards a more sustainable future?
Sort the statements that best describe your inner world to the right, and those least like you on the left.

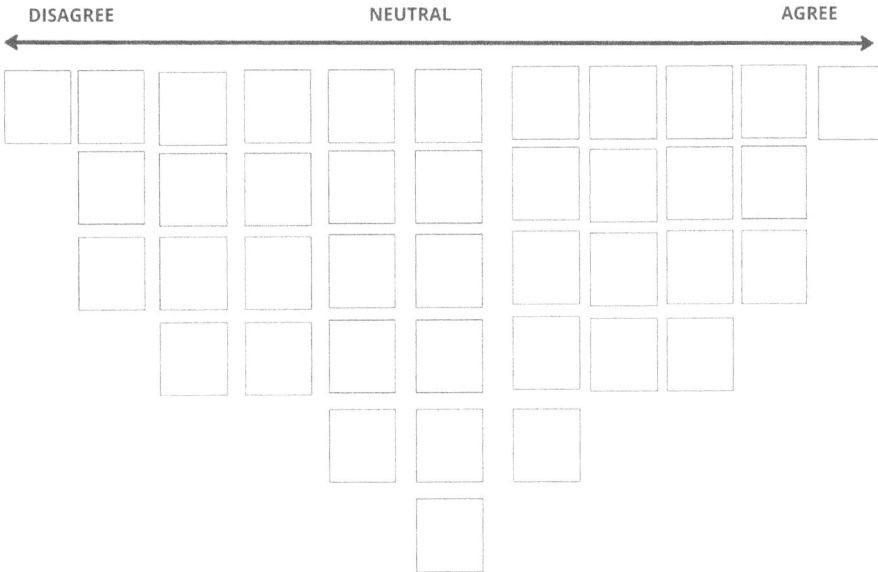

**Figure 18.2:** Q methodology sorting grid for the IDG statements.

–   Write a statement describing your overall viewpoint of the abilities and challenges that you are facing when trying to create change towards a more sustainable future.

The participants considered their overall viewpoint. Using the same questions, this provides qualitative data to understand the Q sorts when composite sorts are created through Q analysis, and these composite sorts are then interpreted to understand viewpoints. The table in Appendix 4 lists the statements included in the Q sorts and the factor scores.

## Findings: Third-person perspectives on the IDGs

To understand the third-person level of the workshop, we draw on the factor analysis in the Q sort, the qualitative survey replies, and the interaction in the workshop and on the Miro board. The final grid placements of eight participants were analyzed using statistical methods associated with Q methodology, and two separate composite viewpoints emerged. We interpreted the meaning of these viewpoints through the statements "most like" and "most unlike" the related viewpoints, including using the survey responses and comments in the workshop to help understand these perspectives.

Below, we describe the overall impressions of the process and the potential for the IDGs to contribute to reflection on self-efficacy, and then give an impression of the two viewpoints present: (1) the perceptive translator; and (2) the relational disruptor.

## General responses

Feedback from participants on how the process was experienced included the following themes:

- **Prioritizing statements relative to other statements**: This was a key interest and challenge of the sorting process. One participant stated, "Weird to see how you change your perception of a certain part of your life, giving it less or more strength." Some even experienced frustration, noticing a tension when thinking in this relative way "It [. . .] surfaces some overestimation of what I want versus how it is." For some this was positive. The two-step process of sorting "makes it clearer where I really stand on my neutral points of view". They liked how "everything changed" after they ranked the statements in the grid causing them to consider these one at a time.

- **Performativity**: Some noted tensions between their actual emotions and other emotions that might be more desirable to choose in this public space. "Sometimes I struggle to answer based on what I 'should' think and how I show up in the world," said one participant.

- **Unfamiliar challenge**: There was a sense that engaging in a workshop in this way felt new, different, and challenging. Many didn't have additional statements they would want to include, noting that this was "pretty extensive and already hard enough to sort". Some liked how their "beliefs and perceptions were challenged".

- **Heightened attention**: The Q sorting processes shifted the way in which they normally experienced their attention and allowed an opening for inner change. One said in this space that they could take the time to learn about themselves. Another enjoyed the time to "really focus and pay attention to each statement" and consider its relative placement.

We believe that these themes, being interwoven through the sharing together of the feedback at the end of the workshop, demonstrates social learning. Additionally, it begins to demonstrate the potential for Q methodology to enable reflexivity at the third-person level towards the IDGs.

As mentioned above, the participants share many similarities: they engage in systemic design either as academics or as practitioners, they live in Europe, and they are interested in sustainability. Still, the factor analysis brought out two distinct viewpoints, which we called the *perceptive translator* and the *relational disruptor*. The two viewpoints share a high empathy orientation but are also distinctive in certain ways. We describe them in more detail below.

## Viewpoint 1: The perceptive translator

This perspective sees personal inner change towards sustainability challenges as a process of figuring out puzzles and bringing different perspectives together as an analytic or critical process (see table in Appendix 2). Both viewpoints see themselves as highly empathetic, but the translating perceiver experiences this through listening and finding adaptable communication styles for various stakeholders, and then finds synergies between these differences.

On the other hand, perceptive translators can easily parse the complexities inherent in systems thinking, locating patterns and iterating their approach. They learn from mistakes. One summarized that "everything in this life is experience, and when you overcome a challenge you learn something that will help you to overcome the next challenge". They see inner skills as the analytic capacity to make sense of their dynamic environment and they feel confident in relaying these diverse perspectives to others.

The challenges here emerge from the perceptive translator's keen sense of system dynamics. They easily perceive system dynamics, notice the gaps between reality and the shifts needed, and experience this as dissonance. One described "feeling helpless and lost in the existing short-term thinking". Another participant expressed this explicitly as the "trade-offs between economic growth and sustainable growth". These inner dimension reflections show the embeddedness of the broad social, environmental, and economic challenges of the SDGs in an inner life. Overall, the perceptive translators experience their own communication and facilitation skills as courageous and adaptable. Aware of systemic complexity, they still desire to untangle the tensions inherent in complex systems.

## Viewpoint 2: The relational disruptor

This perspective approaches systems through the lens of relationships and is particularly focused on how power dynamics and inequities are embedded in those relationships (see table in Appendix 3). One stated, "I can create change by connecting on a deep level, but it's hard to scale this." Another relational disruptor wanted to include the "perspectives of nature, next gen, and more-than-humans" as an added statement as they reflected on their inner world. Through this lens, the relational disruptors express an extensive inner world that is concerned with others, especially those with fewer resources or less of a voice. In their visible actions they challenge the status quo and champion diversity.

Relational disruptors view their disruptive practices as harmonious and improvisational. They acknowledge barriers, such as those "institutions have to the way things 'should' be done and the rules and procedures" and believe that "equity is more important than equality". Their connection to the wider system is rather intuitive, focusing on "reaching synergy" and "being curious, humble, and inclusive". Interested in embodied learning, they give as much attention to bodies as to minds. Overall, the relational disruptor reflects a deep and thoughtful inner world, cued into power dynamics and pointed at intervening on behalf of those "left behind".

# Discussion

This chapter presents how the IDGs can contribute to reflection. In particular, we demonstrated how a different methodological approach enables seeing the IDGs through a new lens. The preparation, facilitation, and post-workshop reflection allowed us to confront the tensions inherent in the IDGs and contemplate what these tensions mean for us (the two authors) as researchers, facilitators, and practitioners. We present these reflections below.

## Comparing the first-, second-, and third-person viewpoints

Both third-person viewpoints consider empathy and continuous learning as critical skills but have different understandings of what this encompasses. The perceptive translator interprets social, technological, and environmental systems leaning on models and knowledge and focuses on bringing this knowledge across to diverse audiences. The relational disruptor is eager to integrate marginalized perspectives from outside the mainstream environment and give a voice not only to marginalized social groups but also to nature, animals, and generations to come. So, while both consider themselves as systems thinkers, their views of how to define a system diverge.

Having these differences spelled out so clearly allowed us to have a follow-up conversation on how we relate to the two viewpoints. For Joanna, the richness of the perspectives supports that Q methodology can locate diversity even where others might perceive sameness.

For Anna, this reflection brought out how important it is to spend enough time in seminars and workshops to reflect the system boundaries – an exercise that is often taken for granted, even in systems thinking. Specifically, for the CBL course, the insights challenged Anna to strengthen the connection between rational and embodied knowledge as both are vital parts of the course. To address this, we invited an additional lecturer to focus on body techniques (e.g., breath, body, acting) that bring out authenticity.

The workshop demonstrated that combining the IDGs with Q methodology (1) triggers individual reflection on self-efficacy and (2) enables deeper lecturer reflection on diverse student needs. The third goal for the CBL course – supporting students in reframing their (individual and collective) potential as change agents towards the SDGs – could be achieved if the Q sorts completed and shared can trigger collective reflection and discussion.

## Limitations and challenges

Q methodology challenges became clear through the process. The participants, genuinely interested in the outcome of their sorting and the analysis of the emergent shared perspectives, could not receive this in the limited time frame. Some resisted mixed methods because of hesitancy with statistics/quantitative data, so we were often searching for other language to convey the process. Anna began using language of data-supported persona analysis to position Q methodology for the systemic design community to present this shared knowledge.

Technology both offered real-time analysis and challenging constraints. The software did not work properly on all laptops, so card sorting faltered. For Anna – being in the room – technology acted as a separator preventing a more collective sorting experience, which hindered approaches to the IDGs and the need to engineer dynamic and smooth collective experiences both online and offline. Hybrid formats in particular provided challenges.

## Conclusion

The workshop was developed for systemic design practitioners to demonstrate how the IDGs could be made useful for reflection and evaluation purposes, bringing into the picture self-efficacy as a unifying theme. Additionally, could Q methodology enable a particular space, focused attention, surfacing of values, and narration or enactment of perspectives? The process catalyzed both individual and group-level sensemaking, so activating viewpoints in this way can approach social learning as third-person reflexivity. Our analysis of the two perspectives, the perceptive translator and the relational disruptor, oriented that third-person reflexivity in a form that we believe can spark further work and wider applications. For example, the IDG One Question Survey asks, "What qualities, abilities, or skills do you think are essential to progress towards a more harmonious, sustainable, and equitable world for people and planet?" (Inner Development Goals, 2024).

Our experience at the first-, second-, and third-person levels deepens appreciation for the diversity of different perspectives. These different views are not limitless, but can be understood as distinct and subjective approaches to inner development for advancing sustainability and the SDGs. Long understood by those working in this space, they support that the ability to slow down, give full attention, and reflect and develop awareness of the inner–outer dimensions of the self, is perhaps the most important precursor and the necessary condition for all other change. A less understood factor – that the substance of the living ideas themselves matter tremendously in the space of reflection – also requires attention to the quality and source of that which we reflect *upon*. In suggesting this, we hope to offer a reminder of the *proportions* of the IDGs needed to bring together change at each level of engagement.

# Appendices

## Appendix 1

**Table 18.2:** Viewpoint 1 – the perceptive translator (three participants).

| Viewpoint 1: "Most like" statements | |
| --- | --- |
| I am good at connecting different perspectives and leveraging synergies. | 5 |
| I am good at recognizing patterns and connections and describing them. | 4 |
| I like to question the statements of others critically and analytically. | 4 |
| I am a good listener. | 3 |
| If things do not work out as planned I adjust my approach and try over and over again. | 3 |
| I adjust my communication style depending on the audience. | 3 |
| **Viewpoint 1: "Most unlike" statements** | |
| I struggle to empathize with others. | −5 |
| I often feel overwhelmed when trying to understand complex content and systemic interdependencies. | −4 |
| It is impossible to align different perspectives. | −4 |
| I often feel provoked and undervalued by others. | −3 |
| I often lack the courage to present and defend my views and values to others. | −3 |
| I often struggle to bring my standpoint across convincingly. | −3 |

# Appendix 2

**Table 18.3:** Viewpoint 2 – the relational disruptor (five participants).

| Viewpoint 2: "Most like" statements | |
|---|---|
| I feel connected and part of a wider community, even of the universe, the world, and human-environment systems. | 5 |
| I reflect a lot about myself and my place in this world. | 4 |
| I am good at recognizing patterns and connections and describing them. | 4 |
| I like to work in interdisciplinary and intercultural teams. | 3 |
| I like to challenge authority, including my bosses and lecturers. | 3 |
| I constantly challenge the status quo and search for novel, better solutions. | 3 |

| Viewpoint 2: "Most unlike" statements | |
|---|---|
| In a difficult situation, I first consider the consequences for myself. Consequences for others are not a priority. | −5 |
| I often feel provoked and undervalued by others. | −4 |
| I struggle to empathize with others. | −4 |
| A career is very important to me – even if sometimes this means compromising on my values. | −3 |
| It is impossible to align different perspectives. | −3 |
| I like strict processes and clear routines. | −3 |

# Appendix 3

**Table 18.4:** Statements with factor scores with corresponding ranks.

| Factor scores with corresponding ranks | | | | | |
|---|---|---|---|---|---|
| | | Factor 1 | | Factor 2 | |
| # | Statement | z-score | rank | z-score | rank |
| 1 | I am here for a purpose. I would like to create value in the world. | −0.40 | −1 | 0.71 | 1 |
| 2 | The world is as it is. I cannot change it. | −0.43 | −1 | −1.08 | −2 |
| 3 | Sometimes I feel uncertain about my values. | −0.88 | −2 | −0.46 | −1 |
| 4 | I remain honest and authentic even in challenging situations. | 0.44 | 1 | 0.69 | 1 |
| 5 | I want to learn. And I am ready to take risks on this learning journey – even if this means feeling embarrassed sometimes. | 0.44 | 1 | 0.89 | 1 |
| 6 | I don't mind failing because I can learn from this experience and grow as a person. | 0.89 | 2 | 0.21 | 0 |

**Table 18.4** (continued)

**Factor scores with corresponding ranks**

|  |  | Factor 1 | | Factor 2 | |
|---|---|---|---|---|---|
| # | Statement | z-score | rank | z-score | rank |
| 7 | I often lack the courage to present and defend my views and values to others. | −1.29 | −3 | −0.35 | −1 |
| 8 | I reflect a lot about myself and my place in this world. | 0.88 | 2 | 1.26 | 4 |
| 9 | A career is very important to me – even if sometimes this means compromising on my values. | 0.40 | 1 | −1.35 | −3 |
| 10 | I like to question the statements of others critically and analytically. | 1.68 | 4 | 0.77 | 1 |
| 11 | I often feel overwhelmed when trying to understand complex content and systemic interdependencies. | −1.70 | −4 | −0.05 | 0 |
| 12 | It is impossible to align different perspectives. | −1.70 | −4 | −1.51 | −3 |
| 13 | I am good at recognizing patterns and connections and describing them. | 1.72 | 4 | 1.58 | 4 |
| 14 | I prefer to focus on short-term goals and tasks. | −0.42 | −1 | −0.70 | −1 |
| 15 | I have a vision for MYSELF. And I am pursuing this vision. | 0.05 | 0 | −0.46 | −1 |
| 16 | I have a vision for the WORLD. And I am pursuing this vision. | 0.42 | 1 | 0.15 | 0 |
| 17 | I often feel provoked and undervalued by others. | −1.29 | −3 | −1.63 | −4 |
| 18 | I am grateful every day to be part of an amazing community of friends, family, and colleagues. | 0.88 | 2 | 0.63 | 1 |
| 19 | I feel connected and part of a wider community, even of the universe, the world and human-environment systems. | −0.01 | 0 | 1.59 | 5 |
| 20 | In a difficult situation, I first consider the consequences for myself. Consequences for others are not a priority. | −0.86 | −2 | −1.73 | −5 |
| 21 | I struggle to empathize with others. | −2.15 | −5 | −1.60 | −4 |
| 22 | I am a good listener. | 1.26 | 3 | 0.94 | 2 |
| 23 | I often struggle to bring my standpoint across convincingly. | −1.28 | −3 | −0.07 | 0 |
| 24 | I prefer to leave the job of facilitating a workshop to others. | −0.42 | −1 | −1.07 | −2 |
| 25 | I adjust my communication style depending on the audience. | 1.28 | 3 | 0.92 | 2 |
| 26 | When engaging in creative work I prefer to be alone. | −0.40 | −1 | −0.57 | −1 |
| 27 | Creative solutions are best found in a team. | 0.01 | 0 | 0.98 | 2 |

**Table 18.4** (continued)

**Factor scores with corresponding ranks**

| | | Factor 1 | | Factor 2 | |
|---|---|---|---|---|---|
| # | Statement | z-score | rank | z-score | rank |
| 28 | I am good at connecting different perspectives and leveraging synergies. | 2.14 | 5 | 1.08 | 2 |
| 29 | I prefer to work with people who are like me. | −0.84 | −2 | −0.52 | −1 |
| 30 | I like to work in interdisciplinary and intercultural teams. | 0.01 | 0 | 1.17 | 3 |
| 31 | I find it difficult to trust others. | −0.02 | 0 | −1.22 | −2 |
| 32 | I'm good at getting others excited about my ideas. | 0.83 | 2 | 0.52 | 1 |
| 33 | I often lack the courage to present and defend my views and values to others. | −0.85 | −2 | −0.74 | −2 |
| 34 | I like to challenge authority, including my bosses and lecturers. | 0.38 | 1 | 1.21 | 3 |
| 35 | I like strict processes and clear routines. | −0.44 | −1 | −1.46 | −3 |
| 36 | I constantly challenge the status quo and search for novel, better solutions. | 0.44 | 1 | 1.20 | 3 |
| 37 | I remain an optimist – even when things get rough. | −0.03 | 0 | 0.35 | 0 |
| 38 | I am a realist – there are certain things that we just cannot change. | 0.42 | 1 | −0.50 | −1 |
| 39 | If things do not work out as planned it is better to stop and do something else. | −0.41 | −1 | −0.29 | 0 |
| 40 | If things do not work out as planned I adjust my approach and try over and over again. | 1.26 | 3 | 0.49 | 1 |

# References

Argyris, C. (2011). *On organizational learning*. Blackwell.

Arkedis, J., Benavides, M., Dessein, L., Kniffin, L., Ospina, S. M., & Priest, K. (2023). *Collective Leadership for Sustainable Development: Evidence from Research and Practice*. People First Community and Lemann Foundation. https://ugc.production.linktr.ee/6bc235de-b0c2-404a-92cf-8d843b291d62_2023.11-Final-People-First-Evidence-Review-.pdf.

Bandura, A. (1982). Self-efficacy mechanism in human agency. *American Psychologist, 37*(2), 122–147. https://doi.org/10.1037/0003-066X.37.2.122.

Balda, J. B., Stanberry, J., & Altman, B. (2023). Leadership and the regenerative economy – concepts, cases, and connections: Leveraging the sustainable development goals to move toward sustainability leadership. *New Directions for Student Leadership, 2023*.(179), 121–141. https://doi.org/10.1002/yd.20574.

Ballen, K., Wieman, C., Salehi, S., Searle, J. B., & Zamudio, K. R. (2018). Enhancing diversity in undergraduate science: Self-efficacy drives performance gains with active learning. *CBE—Life Science Education*, *16*(4), 1–6. https://www.lifescied.org/doi/10.1187/cbe.16-12-0344.

Beamer, K., Tuma, A., Thorenz, A., Boldoczki, S., Kotubetey, K. 'iahonui, Kukea-Shultz, K., & Elkington, K. (2021). Reflections on sustainability concepts: Aloha 'Āina and the circular economy. *Sustainability: Science Practice and Policy*, *13*(5), 2984. https://doi.org/10.3390/su13052984.

Brown, S. R. (1980). *Political subjectivity: Applications of Q methodology in political science*. Yale University Press.

Colombelli, A., Loccisano, S., Panelli, A., Pennisi, O. A. M., & Serraino, F. (2022). Entrepreneurship education: The effects of challenge-based learning on the entrepreneurial mindset of university students. *Administrative Sciences*, *12*(1), 10. https://doi.org/10.3390/admsci12010010.

Cunliffe, A. L. (2018). Wayfaring: A scholarship of possibilities or let's not get drunk on abstraction. *M@n@gement*, *21*(4), 1429–1439. https://www.cairn-int.info/article.php?ID_ARTICLE=E_MANA_214_1429.

Cuppen, E. (2013). Q methodology to support the design and evaluation of stakeholder dialogue. *Operant Subjectivity*, *36*(2). https://doi.org/10.22488/okstate.13.100517.

Development Policy Unit, UNDP Pakistan. (2022). The Sustainable Development Goals (SDGs) and Islam: Contextualising the Sustainable Development Goals in the normative framework of Islamic tradition. *UNDP*. https://www.undp.org/sites/g/files/zskgke326/files/2023-06/undp_balochistan_sdgs_and_islam.pdf.

Edwards, G. & Bolden, R. (2023). Why is collective leadership so elusive? *Leadership*, *19*(2), 167–182. https://doi.org/10.1177/17427150221128357.

Gallagher, S. E. & Savage, T. (2020). Challenge-based learning in higher education: An exploratory literature review. *Teaching in Higher Education*, *28*(6), 1135–1157. https://doi.org/10.1080/13562517.2020.1863354.

Guthey, E., Ferry, N. C., & Remke, R. (2022). Taking leadership fashions seriously as a vehicle for leadership learning. *Management Learning*, *53*(3), 397–416. https://doi.org/10.1177/13505076211009674.

Harris, K., Oatley, C., Mumford, S., Pham, P. K., & Nunns, H. (2021). Introducing Q methodology to program evaluators. *American Journal of Evaluation*, *42*(3), 439–453. https://doi.org/10.1177/1098214020932227.

Hendrickson, P. (2021). Effect of active learning techniques on student excitement, interest, and self-efficacy. *Journal of Political Science Education*, *17*(2), 311–325. https://doi.org/10.1080/15512169.2019.1629946.

Inner Development Goals. (2024). What's missing from the IDG Framework? [Thumbnail with link attached] [Post]. LinkedIn. https://www.linkedin.com/posts/inner-development-goals_welcome-to-the-global-survey-activity-7140943923119661056-079H. [Accessed Nov. 5, 2024].

Ives, C. D., Schäpke, N., Woiwode, C., & Wamsler, C. (2023). IMAGINE sustainability: integrated inner-outer transformation in research, education and practice. *Sustainability Science*, *18*, 2777–2786. https://doi.org/10.1007/s11625-023-01368-3.

Jackson, J. W. (2002). Enhancing Self-Efficacy and Learning Performance. *The Journal of Experimental Education*, *70*(3), 243–254. https://doi.org/10.1080/00220970209599508.

Jones, (2013). Systemic Design Principles for Complex Social Systems. In G. Metcalf (ed.), *Social Systems and Design*. Springer, Vol. 1 of the Translational Systems Science Series.

Jordan, T., Reams, J., Stålne, K., Greca, S., Henriksson, J. A., Björkman, T., & Dawson, T. (2021). *Inner Development Goals: Background, method and the IDG framework. Inner Development Goals Project*. https://drive.google.com/file/d/13fcf9xmYrX9wrsh3PC3aeRDs0rWsWCpA/edit [accessed Nov. 5, 2024].

Mason, C. (1905). *School Education: Vol. III*. Kegan Paul, Trench & Co. London. Available at:

May, T. & Perry, B. (2017). *Reflexivity: The essential guide*. SAGE Publications Ltd.

Middlekauff, A. (2016, Sep. 18). A Revolution in Methods. *Charlotte Mason Poetry*. https://charlottemasonpoetry.org/a-revolution-in-methods/ [Accessed May 1, 2024].

Ramlo, S. (2015). Student views about a flipped physics course: A tool for program evaluation and improvement. *Research in the Schools; Jacksonville, 22*(1), 44–59. https://www.proquest.com/scholarly-journals/student-views-about-flipped-physics-course-tool/docview/1792738527/se-2.

Ramlo, S. (2016). Mixed method lessons learned from 80 years of Q methodology. *Journal of Mixed Methods Research, 10*(1), 28–45. https://doi.org/10.1177/1558689815610998.

Rimanoczy, I. (2020). *The sustainability mindset principles: A guide to developing a mindset for a better world*. Routledge.

Scharmer, O. & Yukelson, A. (2015). Theory U: From ego-system to eco-system economies. *The Journal of Corporate Citizenship, 58*, 35–39. http://www.jstor.org/stable/jcorpciti.58.35.

Seghezzo, L., Sneegas, G., Jepson, W., Brannstrom, C., Beckner, S., & Lee, K. (2023). The use and potential of Q method in environmental planning and management. *Journal of Environmental Planning and Management, 67*(12), 2721–2747. https://doi.org/10.1080/09640568.2023.2207727.

Senge, P. M. (1990). *The fifth discipline: The art and practice of the learning organization*. Doubleday/Currency.

Stanberry, J., Murphy, D. F., & Bragan Balda, J. (2024). Recognising ecological reflexivity: An alternative approach to partnership capabilities for collaborative governance. SSRN. http://dx.doi.org/10.2139/ssrn.4764874.

Stanberry, J. (2023). Q methodology for the Anthropocene: The how and why of educative potential [Paper presentation for the 39th annual conference of the International Society for the Scientific Study of Subjectivity, University of Ulster in Belfast, Northern Ireland, Sep. 13–15, 2023].

Stanberry, J. & Balda, J. B. (2023). A conceptual review of SDG 17: Picturing politics, proximity, and progress. *Journal of Tropical Futures, 1*(1), 110–139. https://doi.org/10.1177/27538931231170509.

Stanberry, J., Balda, J. B., & Balda, W. D. (2022). Xenophon to the Sustainable Development Goals: An interweaving of collective engagement. In S. K. Dhiman, J. Marques, J. Schmieder-Ramirez, & P. G. Malakyan (eds.), *Handbook of Global Leadership and Followership: Integrating the Best Leadership Theory and Practice* (pp. 875–906). Springer International Publishing.

Stephenson, W. (1953). *The study of behavior; Q-technique and its methodology*. University of Chicago Press.

Stephenson, W. (1993). Introduction to Q-Methodology. *Operant Subjectivity, 17*(1/2), 1–13. https://doi.org/10.15133/J.OS.1993.006.

Wolf, A. (2022). Perspectives on Q sorting. In J. C. Rhoads, D. B. Thomas, & S. E. Ramlo (eds.), *Cultivating Q Methodology: Essays Honoring Steven R. Brown* (pp. 242–267). BookBaby.

Freddy Mutanguha
# Chapter 19
# Forgiveness and the missing IDG skill: From surviving genocide to leading the Rwanda Peace Education Programme

**Abstract:** This chapter explores the remarkable journey of Freddy Mutanguha, a survivor of the genocide against Tutsi in Rwanda, who emerges as a tireless advocate for peace and reconciliation. Divided into two sections, it first examines Freddy's personal narrative of loss and resilience, tracing the roots of the genocide back to colonial-era divisions and the subsequent violence endured by the Tutsi community. Through heartbreaking accounts of familial tragedy and personal trauma, Freddy illuminates the enduring scars left by the genocide and the profound challenges of forgiveness and reconciliation.

In the second section, the chapter shifts focus to Freddy's groundbreaking work in leading the Rwanda Peace Education Programme. With unwavering determination, he confronts the perpetrators of violence, seeking understanding and reconciliation through dialogue and empathy. Through his curriculum, Freddy imparts invaluable lessons on peacebuilding and inner development, weaving together testimonies of survivors and perpetrators to forge a path towards healing and understanding.

Drawing on over two decades of experience, Freddy's narrative serves as a powerful testament to the transformative power of forgiveness and the resilience of the human spirit. His efforts not only shape the national discourse on peace and reconciliation in Rwanda but also offer valuable insights for fostering peace in conflict-affected regions worldwide. Ultimately, Freddy's story is one of hope, illustrating the enduring capacity of individuals and communities to overcome tragedy and build a more peaceful future.

**Keywords:** genocide, forgiveness, peace, resilience

## Section 1: Would you like to share a little bit about what we could learn from you?

I am a survivor of genocide. I endured the horrors of the 1994 genocide against the Tutsi, which claimed the lives of a million people. The year 1994 stands as a dark period in Rwanda's history. One morning, we awoke to the stark reality of being orphans, forced to navigate life and shape our destinies without the support of our families. This narrative unravels a lengthy history, with its roots firmly entrenched in the

https://doi.org/10.1515/9783111337913-020

seeds of discrimination, hatred, and division sown during the colonial era around the early nineteenth century as Germany and Belgium successively controlled Rwanda through the early twentieth century.

The most heart-wrenching chapter unfolded in 1959, during the Rwandan Hutu Revolution. Mutara III Rudahigwa, the king of Rwanda, began questioning the viability of divisive policies and the "divide and rule" politics implemented by Belgium. They discerned the inappropriateness of these divisions for Rwanda, recognizing a stark misalignment with Rwandan values. He was killed mysteriously in 1959. Concurrently, the broader African landscape fervently advocated for independence. The Tutsi (primarily cattle herders) individuals advocating for positive advancements in the nation faced discrimination, violence, and the grim reality that more than 20,000 were killed and 330,000 of them were subjected to forced exile.

The persecution persisted after Rwanda gained independence. The colonialists installed extremists in Hutu (farmers) power, perpetuating the ideology of genocide for three decades. The culmination occurred in 1994, a carefully orchestrated final solution resulting in the loss of a million lives in just 100 days. Among them were my parents and four sisters. When I unearthed my parents' remains, I discovered that their skulls had been brutally smashed, revealing the use of machetes and clubs in their execution.

My sister's fate was equally harrowing. I heard their cries as they were killed, their bodies callously discarded into a septic tank, covered with stones. In their innocence, they pleaded for mercy, hoping that their youth would evoke compassion. Sadly, those perpetrating the violence showed no mercy, extinguishing their lives without remorse.

They hurled stones at their heads until they took their own lives. While I was in hiding, I could hear their voices, and those echoes will persist in my mind until my final moments.

On April 14, 1994, I became an orphan at 18 years old, losing everything: my parents, my sisters, and all my relatives – aunts, uncles, cousins, we all lived together. I counted that 80 members of my family were wiped out in just a few weeks. Yes, I lost everything, including my home, my childhood, and my future. Unsure of where to commence rebuilding my life, the silver lining is that I survived with my sister, who is still alive and now has two children. As for me, I have five children.

Before I parted ways with my mother on April 13, she came to my hiding place. She gazed at me and said, "We saw the militias. They are much stronger than us, and we don't know if tomorrow we will see each other." True to her words, she brought beans and passion fruits, even though she knew I didn't like beans. Today, however, I appreciate them. She also knew others liked passion fruits, but my preference was for bananas. Despite this, she looked at me and conveyed that this was all that we had left at home. The underlying message was clear – if I survive and become a man, it saves all in our culture. Unfortunately, the next morning, she was killed. I vividly recall the last meal with my mother and our final conversation. If I thrive today, it's because of her words, which have profoundly influenced many fellow survivors in Rwanda. There's even a song by one of our artists expressing the significance of the last memory. This last memory becomes stronger in our lives, helping us navigate the present. The genocide eventually ceased, and the international community turned its attention to our country. Former refugees, part of the Rwandan Patriotic Front led by the current president of Rwanda, His Excellency Paul Kagame played a crucial role in stopping the genocide. However, they too experienced trauma, witnessing the killing of their relatives. The aftermath left the country and its people devastated, requiring prayers and assistance to rebuild. The good news? With the leadership and courage of survivors, including myself, I chose not to seek revenge. Living with the children of perpetrators, who bear a sense of shame, I, as a teacher by profession, vowed not to pass on such a legacy to my own children. I resisted revenge and embarked on a journey of reconciliation and forgiveness. Although time is limited, I want to emphasize the importance of forgiveness in inner development. Despite being part of the inner development movement for a few months, I feel that I've been part of it for more than ten years. Forgiveness, for me and many other survivors in Rwanda, is intrapersonal, requiring us to navigate through pain, anger, bitterness, resignation, and pride. It is a personal process that takes time, often met with pushback as we question whether those who committed atrocities deserve pardon. The struggle is ongoing, as even joyful moments are tainted by the absence and loss that surround us. Yet, I carry the words of my mother urging me to be a man, pushing me beyond these feelings.

I was tasked with overseeing a memorial and developing a curriculum to prevent future genocides and counter the ideology of genocide. I named it the Peace Education Programme. The irony of imparting lessons on peace while grappling with my own sense of inner peace did not escape me.

You can't teach what you don't have; you must give what you possess. Thus, I realized the importance of testing myself. My transformative journey spanned a decade, requiring several years to truly grasp the necessity of embarking on the journey of forgiveness. It took 17 years to confront my perpetrator and assess if I genuinely had peace, enabling me to teach and develop a curriculum that imparts the values of inner development skills.

Returning to my village and facing the individual responsible for my sisters' deaths was a process that unfolded over 17 years. When I finally went there for the first time in a long while, I met him. He had been released from prison after serving a ten-year sentence, reduced from 20 years as he confessed to his crimes. This reduction occurred through Gacaca courts, a grassroots system of justice aimed at restoring social relationships and administering justice to survivors. When one tells the truth and confesses, the sentence is reduced.

The meeting coincided with the end of his ten-year prison term. Honestly, I couldn't bring myself to greet him. However, one of his relatives, familiar with me from visiting the memorial, asked if I could take them there. This posed another test for me – a survivor leading perpetrators around the memorial I guided. The memorial, the burial place for 250,000 victims of genocide, presented a significant emotional challenge. Despite this, I accepted it, arranging a minibus for 19 of them. I didn't inform my colleagues, unsure of their reactions. I led them around, and among them was someone I knew, someone responsible for many deaths. When he looked at the picture of a child and heard the testimony from the child's mother, he started crying.

In that moment, I questioned why he was crying, assuming he would be indifferent or even satisfied with his actions. To my surprise, I found that perpetrators still retain a sense of humanity – a realization that became the cornerstone of my curriculum. This insight shaped the curriculum, focused on testimonies. What I discovered is that there is a path to genocide, but equally important, there is a pathway to peace. The curriculum I developed is now integrated into the national education curriculum in Rwanda, impacting over two and half million students annually.

We live in a world of conflict, but peace is possible. I believe that Rwanda has much to teach the world about justice, reconciliation, forgiveness, and peacebuilding. Based on 20 years of experience and the impact of the Peace Education Programme, my colleagues and I at Aegis Trust, a non-governmental organization that campaigns to prevent genocide worldwide, are committed to sharing stories of peace to the world through a newly established Isoko Peace Institute with a vision to establish a culture of peace and build resilience against intercommunal violence.

## Section 2: Present and future for the Rwanda peace movement

### An interview with Freddy Mutanguha

Mauricio Campos Suarez: After listening to your story, I sense how much peace, reconciliation, and forgiveness matter to you. Reconciliation is an important element of *relating* with others and reconciliation is supported by forgiveness as part of the individual and collective inner development. I wonder how these principles reflect in your program. How does the work you are doing in your organization, and the program you've put together, leverage those skills and develop them?

Freddy Mutanguha: To promote peace, reconciliation, and forgiveness in my country, we are addressing all IDG dimensions: *being*, *thinking*, *relating*, *collaborating*, and *acting*. We develop these skills in our program because the challenges of peace are not due to a lack of resources or willingness, but rather a lack of skills, knowledge, and ability to implement the IDGs. Some of the key skills we leverage are in the "thinking" category, where we use critical thinking. This is very important because when we talk about peace being possible, it involves developing skills and values that help someone to say, "I'm going to stop my cycle of violence and embrace peace," which comes from the ability to think about the consequences of hate, having values of empathy, and making the right decisions. Empathy and critical thinking help someone make the right choice, which may lead to peace, social cohesion, or forgiveness and reconciliation. And it's very important not to make this an unconscious emotional process; it has to be thought about. Individually we have to become aware of our own emotions of hate, resentment, revenge, and by being aware to be able to think of the best course of action for us, our families, community, and country. You have to have the right skills to sustain this path to peace, reconciliation, and forgiveness. These are the skills that we use to equip the participants in our programs, to have the ability to think critically but also with empathy and compassion so that when they embrace the path of forgiveness or peace and reconciliation, they really understand what this involves. That is how we leverage IDGs.

Eleftheria Egel: You talk about forgiveness. The word seems to be at the center of your work. And forgiveness is a quality that is not in the IDG framework. I wonder, how important is forgiveness for inner development?

Mutanguha: Forgiveness is very important, and it affects all IDG dimensions. Starting with the "being" dimension, that's who you are, you have to understand yourself. Forgiveness starts from here, from your heart.

Let me give you an example. A person who survived Rwanda's genocide against Tutsi. His name was Felicien; unfortunately, he has passed away. He said, "If you really knew me and you really knew yourself, you would not have killed me." This statement made me think that we should know ourselves. We have to cultivate self-understanding first, and then to work on understanding others. Forgiveness starts from understanding yourself, loving yourself, and forgiving yourself. Then you can move to forgiving others.

Forgiveness is also an important part of the "thinking" dimension. It enables you to think critically about your actions and how your actions have an impact in your community and shape your future.

On the "collaborating" side, understanding oneself and others paves the way for joint efforts. In Rwanda, an example is the Reconciliation Village where survivors and perpetrators live side by side. They collaborate on activities such as farming, and they have a single water tank that they have to share, which consolidates forgiveness. Water is a symbol of life and they need to agree on how to share it. The way to this collaboration starts with self-love and self-understanding and continues with empathy and compassion for others, allowing us to act together even when you have done terrible things to me.

Egel: It's clear how important the skill of forgiveness is for Rwanda, to heal the past and collaborate towards a more sustainable future. Do you think that forgiveness is equally important to be developed for individuals and societies that haven't gone through such terrible circumstances? Do you think that forgiveness is equally important all over the world?

Mutanguha: Yes, the skill of forgiveness that I'm talking about is universal and applicable in various contexts, not just specific to Rwanda or other regions with similar tragic histories. It's about how we, as human beings, address our past wounds to collectively heal and progress towards a better future. Hatred and divisions exist worldwide, leading to conflicts in various forms, whether small or large, in our homes, workplaces, and social circles. Forgiveness is crucial in all these scenarios, not just in major conflicts. It's a lifelong practice for individuals because, as humans, we inevitably make mistakes that may affect others, knowingly or unknowingly. Seeking forgiveness helps repair relationships and foster understanding.

For instance, in my own life, as my daughter enters her teenage years, we face new challenges and conflicts. However, practicing forgiveness allows us to navigate these situations, apologize when needed, and rebuild our bond. Forgiveness isn't solely about monumental events like genocide; it's a fundamental aspect of daily life, reflecting our shared humanity and the need for compassion and reconciliation in all interactions.

Campos Suarez: The way you emphasize the importance of self-awareness, understanding others, critical thinking, and collaboration is inspiring. I especially appreciate the metaphor of the water tank, symbolizing the essence of life and the shared responsibility for resources among families that used to be enemies. It's a profound concept that you've integrated into your program, and I'm curious if there's a specific aspect of the program you could share to give readers a tangible understanding of its components. Could you provide some insight into what the program entails and how it works?

Mutanguha: First and foremost, it's essential to understand that we don't explicitly call upon individuals to come and learn forgiveness or critical thinking. That approach would be awkward and ineffective. Instead, as facilitators and educators, we subtly guide participants towards transformative experiences. We employ various techniques such as role-playing, exercises, and real-life stories to stimulate deep reflection and personal growth.

For instance, in our forgiveness-related activities, we often engage participants in role-playing scenarios. Through these exercises, individuals take on different roles, such as perpetrator, survivor, or rescuer, and confront challenging situations that demand forgiveness. By immersing themselves in these scenarios, participants are compelled to contemplate their own capacity for forgiveness and reckon with their personal conflicts.

During these exercises, participants make decisions and take steps forward or backward based on their responses, symbolizing their progress or reluctance towards forgiveness. Through this process, individuals are encouraged to confront their own internal struggles and consider the complexities of forgiveness in their own lives.

We also incorporate real-life examples, such as the story of Maria, a genocide survivor who forgave one of her attackers despite unimaginable loss. By sharing these stories and experiences, we challenge participants to reconsider their preconceptions about forgiveness and explore the possibility of reconciliation even in the most extreme circumstances.

Overall, our approach involves creating thought-provoking scenarios and activities that encourage participants to reflect deeply on their own lives and relationships. While there isn't a specific formula or directive for forgiveness, our aim is to spark meaningful introspection and dialogue that ultimately leads to personal growth and reconciliation.

The normal duration of the program is three days. Despite our preference for a longer duration, we recognize the constraints faced by some individuals who cannot commit to a three-day program. In response, we condensed the content into a single day, albeit feeling it might not be ideal. We liken this condensed format to a marathon sprint, where we strive to pack in as much impactful content as possible within a shorter time frame. Despite the challenges posed by these constraints, we've consistently seen significant results. Moreover, my experience with the Global Leadership for Sustainable Development program has been invaluable. It provided me with insights and tools to enhance our own program, incorporating new inner development methodologies and practices.

Campos Suarez: It's evident how crucial forgiveness is for overcoming, healing, and prospering in the future, especially considering the heavy burden that comes with being a victim of genocide. How does forgiveness compare to forgetting? In your perspective, does forgiveness entail forgetting about what happened, or how do you navigate living with both remembering and forgiving?

Mutanguha: Forgiveness begins with accepting one's own experiences and actions. Asking for forgiveness entails acknowledging the harm caused and the extent of the damage inflicted upon others. This dual acceptance – of the crime committed and the potential for growth – paves the way for reconciliation. However, it's crucial to recognize that the presence of the perpetrator serves as a constant reminder of the past. Forgiveness doesn't erase memories; rather, it reinforces them. When someone forgives, they consciously choose to remember the act of forgiveness itself. The person is constantly reminded, "I forgive you, and I'm not going to forget that I forgave you."

The act of forgiveness strengthens the memory because the forgiven individual becomes a living testament to the reconciliation process. Conversely, refusing to forgive may lead to attempts to forget or deliberately ignore the situation, which ultimately proves unproductive.

In summary, forgiveness doesn't contradict remembrance; instead, it reinforces it in a profoundly positive manner.

Mutanguha: Yeah. I have to say that forgiveness starts with accepting who you are and what you lived through. And to ask for forgiveness is also accepting what you did and how you did it, how much damage you did to someone. And by this acceptance of, on one hand, the crime, and on another hand, of the ability to be beyond your things, it helps to come together. But the fact that the person who did harm to you is a constant reminder of what happened, so forgiveness actually helps to remember because that person is constantly reminding you "I forgive you, and I'm not going to forget that I forgave you". Then you're not going to forget that. Why would you forget that person? We have seen so many instances that when you don't forgive, two things may happen. One, you live with constant remembrance and constant anger and things. There are some people who shy away or try to say "I don't even want to talk about it. I don't want to talk about it. I don't want to hear anyone talking about it". Not forgetting, forgiving, may lead to forgetting or deliberately ignoring of the situation, which is not helpful. So, we have seen this happening, but I have to say that forgiveness strengthens the remembrance because the person you forgive is actually a constant reminder of what happened. And at the same time, when you forgive, you know why you forgave. You provide this forgiveness, so I think it doesn't act against it, but it strengthens it in a very positive way.

Egel: So then, actually, these people who are participating in the program, are they young people? Are they future leaders? Or are they people who lived through the genocide? What type of people participate in the program?

Mutanguha: Our program encompasses a wide range of participants from various backgrounds. We welcome both young individuals, including those in and out of school, as well as community members, local leaders, and policymakers. Additionally, we don't overlook professionals in different fields, such as bankers, lawyers, and teachers. While these individuals excel in their respective professions, they may lack awareness in areas related to forgiveness and reconciliation. For instance, while bankers may understand how to manage finances effectively, they may not necessarily possess the skills needed to foster forgiveness and empathy within their communities. Therefore, we're considering developing a specialized curriculum tailored to the needs of these professionals to ensure that we reach and impact all sectors of society.

Egel: So, focusing on future leaders, how do you believe equipping young people with development skills can empower them to drive change and advocate for peace in their communities and beyond? Specifically, how do you envision the impact of your educational program on young participants? You mentioned incorporating inner development skills into the program – how does this contribute to their capacity to effect change? Essentially, what do young people gain from this training, and how does it influence both their personal growth and their community engagement?

Mutanguha: The impact of developing inner development skills in young people is truly profound and tangible. It's about witnessing positive transformations and navigating complex topics with a deeper level of understanding. Take, for example, the challenge of fostering peaceful dialogue among individuals from diverse cultural backgrounds or conflicting perspectives. This can be incredibly challenging, but inner development skills provide the tools necessary to adapt to these contexts and engage in constructive dialogue. During a recent trip to the United States, I had discussions with both Palestinian and Israeli students who struggled to communicate due to mutual accusations and animosity. However, if our youth are equipped with inner development skills, they can approach such situations with critical thinking, resilience against manipulation, and the ability to foster honest, positive, and peaceful conversations – even across deeply divided communities. So, in response to your question, the answer is a resounding yes.

Campos Suarez: Thank you for sharing your insights. As we conclude, I have a brief question regarding your aspirations for the future of Rwanda. If you could make one wish to drive positive change and progress within your community and across Rwanda, what would that wish be?

Mutanguha: My people have endured immense suffering for far too long. My wish is to witness Rwanda and its people, particularly the younger generation, thrive and serve as a beacon of peacebuilding within our community. I envision Rwanda taking proactive steps to foster peace not only within our nation but also throughout the region. I hope to see Rwanda actively supporting initiatives aimed at promoting collaboration, innovation, and socioeconomic progress, both locally and internationally. Despite the tragedies we've endured, I aspire for Rwanda to emerge as a symbol of resilience and a catalyst for peacebuilding efforts worldwide.

# Integration

As we journey through the profound experiences and insights shared by Freddy Mutanguha, we are invited to explore the complex dynamics of forgiveness, reconciliation, and peace. We propose to reflect by considering the following questions not just as prompts for thought, but as invitations to engage with your own experiences, beliefs, and values. Through introspection, we can uncover new perspectives and insights that may resonate with the profound lessons shared in this chapter and to transform it into action.

- How do Freddy Mutanguha's experiences and insights challenge your understanding of forgiveness and reconciliation?
- Reflect on a time when you faced a conflict or held resentment towards someone. How might applying inner development skills, such as empathy and critical thinking, have influenced the outcome?
- Consider the role of forgiveness in your own life. Are there areas where you struggle to forgive or let go of past grievances? What steps could you take to culti-

vate a greater sense of forgiveness and reconciliation? What commitments do
you need to make to take action on it?

–   Reflect on the concept of forgiveness as a catalyst for peacebuilding on both personal and societal levels. How might fostering forgiveness within yourself contribute to fostering peace within your community and beyond?

# Conclusion

The 1994 Genocide against the Tutsi in Rwanda stands as one of the darkest chapters
in human history, a time when hatred and division led to the systematic slaughter of
nearly one million people. In this chapter, Freddy Mutanguha shares his deeply personal story as a genocide survivor, offering profound insights into the nature of forgiveness, reconciliation, and healing. His reflections emphasize that forgiveness is not
synonymous with forgetting but rather a necessary step in helping both individuals
and societies move forward from the most traumatic of experiences.

His story is a powerful testament to the human capacity to recover from atrocity.
He explains how forgiveness, as an important Inner Development Goal, can be a
transformative force, enabling survivors to begin the process of healing. His message
is clear: forgiveness is not an act of erasure; it does not negate the past or diminish
the suffering that was endured. Instead, it is about recognizing the wrongs that were
committed but choosing to release the anger, hatred, and desire for vengeance that
often accompany such experiences. This distinction between forgiving and forgetting
is crucial, particularly in the context of mass violence and genocide.

One of the central themes of his narrative is the importance of memory in the
process of healing. He argues that it is not only possible but necessary to forgive while
still remembering the past. Forgetting what happened would be dangerous, as it could
open the door for history to repeat itself. By keeping the memory of the genocide
alive, Rwandans and the global community can remain vigilant against the forces of
division and hatred that once led to such catastrophic violence. Memory, in this sense,
becomes a tool for peacebuilding—it allows societies to reflect on past mistakes, learn
from them, and build a future that is not haunted by the specters of the past but
rather informed by them.

Forgiveness, in Freddy's view, is a collective endeavor as much as it is an individual one. When communities embrace forgiveness, they create the conditions for reconciliation, allowing former enemies to live side by side without the constant fear of
retribution. This, in turn, strengthens the fabric of society, fostering resilience against
future conflicts. Rwanda's post-genocide journey, in many ways, exemplifies this process. Despite the horrors of the past, the country has made remarkable strides toward
peace and unity, due in no small part to its commitment to fostering forgiveness and
reconciliation among its people.

Freddy's story is a reminder that forgiveness is not easy, nor is it a one-time event. It is a process—often long and painful—that requires both individual courage and collective commitment. But it is also a process that holds the potential for immense healing. By cultivating forgiveness, individuals and societies can begin to heal the wounds of the past while ensuring that those wounds do not fester and breed further violence. In doing so, they can create a more peaceful, resilient, and compassionate world.

While the scars of the genocide against the Tutsi in Rwanda will never fully fade, the ability to forgive without forgetting provides a pathway toward healing, peace, and the prevention of future atrocities. By embracing forgiveness as a human quality and a societal value, we can learn from the past while working together to build a future where such tragedies are never repeated.

Lara Yasmin Hunziker

# Chapter 20
# Nonviolent Communication is an Inner Development Booster

How letting four simple and proven steps guide your communication can have a profound impact on the Inner Development Goals

**Abstract:** Nonviolent Communication (NVC) is an approach to communication that was designed to help resolve conflicts and to navigate difficult conversations. It was developed by Mashall Rosenberg in the late 1960s and has been most successfully applied in schools that were struck by severe conflicts after starting the dissolution of racial segregation. Today, NVC has been effectively applied in many other realms such as family, business, politics, and especially peace negotiations.

Obviously, learning NVC will enhance the IDG skill of *communication*. But as this text will highlight, it has a much broader impact, touching upon all five dimensions of the IDG framework, making it a powerful and easy-to-implement training resource with the potential to boost inner development at a large scale.

**Keywords:** Communication, collaboration, empathy, nonviolence, personal development

# NVC – a language of understanding

Misunderstandings, disagreements, and conflict are inevitable. They are part of our daily interactions. Most times, they are painful. We are overwhelmed by emotions, separated from those we conflict with, and resolution often involves either sacrificing our interests or our relationship, or overpowering others to get what we want.

Nonviolent Communication (NVC) is an approach to conflict resolution that focusses on authentic self-expression and compassionate listening. Developed by Marshall Rosenberg in the 1960s, NVC has been used in peace negotiations, mediations, and conflict resolution globally. It can be viewed as a communication technique, but it is certainly more than that. Woven into the technique is a mindset fostering empathy and guiding verbal expression. In other words: The technique is a guideline to put into practice the belief that we can all get what we need if we truly listen to each other. And that it can be enough, if one party starts to adopt this mindset.

NVC is structured around four key components: observations, feelings, needs, and requests. These components help clarify communication, increasing the likelihood of mutual understanding and cooperation. The steps are:

https://doi.org/10.1515/9783111337913-021

- **Observations**: Identify the facts of the situation, distinguishing them from judgments and interpretations.
- **Feelings**: Recognize and acknowledge your emotions as indicators of unmet needs.
- **Needs**: Identify the underlying needs driving your feelings and actions.
- **Request**: Make clear, actionable requests to address the situation.

For example, after a near-miss accident with a car while biking, one might be tempted to shout at the driver, making rude gestures and calling them an idiot or other non-flattering things. Which is totally understandable since we might be scared and angry at this moment. NVC can help us to reflect and express: "When you turned in front of me *(observation)*, I felt scared *(feeling)* because I need safety while cycling *(need)*. Could you please check next time before turning *(request)?*" – it is not very hard to imagine that the driver would probably react in a much more understanding way than if we had shouted at them. And even if this exact wording may not be practical, and not feel natural, the four steps the message entails are foundational for true understanding among humans when under stress.

While the four steps are simple, applying them is not as easy as one might think, since our communication patterns and our emotional energy often lead us down another road. It requires time, practice, and patience, and perhaps also some encouragement and guidance, but due to its simplicity, NVC seems to be learnable by anyone. And with it we develop the capacity to navigate conflict, remove blockades in collaboration, and act towards what matters to us, ultimately transforming relationships at personal, organizational, and international levels.

With this overview of NVC[1] let's move on to see how an NVC training boosts inner development.

## NVC boosts all five dimensions of the IDGs

On my journey of becoming more affluent in NVC and of becoming an NVC teacher, I have grown in almost every aspect of the 23 skills of the IDG framework. Of course, some skills were touched more deeply than others, illustrated in Figure 20.1. What I can say for sure is, that all five dimensions are involved.

In the following, I discuss how a training in NVC supports personal growth in the five dimensions. I start with the dimension that is boosted the most, and work down the ladder of suspected impact. Since I am not aware of any scientific evidence, the analysis is based in my own judgment.

---

**1** more can be found on www.cnvc.org.

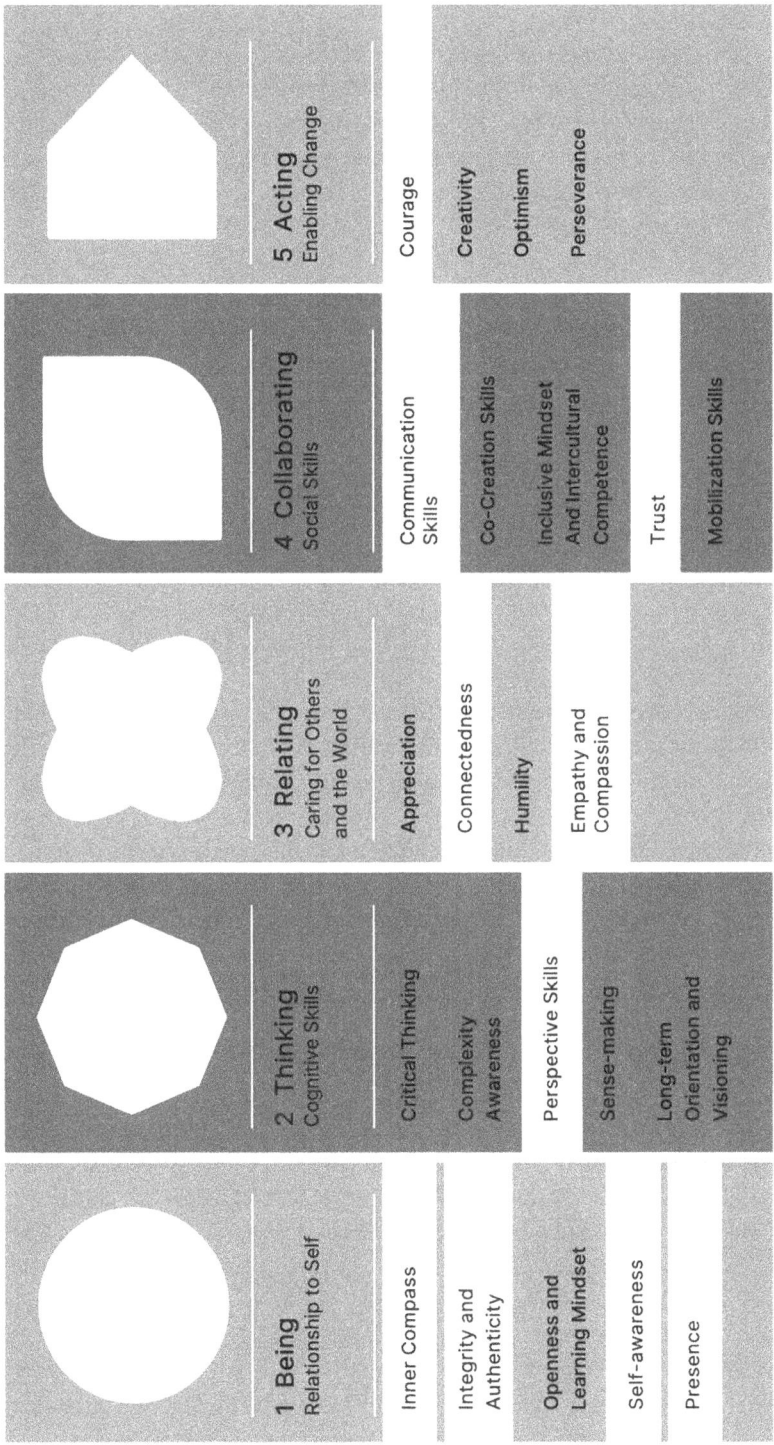

**1 Being**
Relationship to Self

Inner Compass

Integrity and
Authenticity

Openness and
Learning Mindset

Self-awareness

Presence

**2 Thinking**
Cognitive Skills

Critical Thinking

Complexity
Awareness

Perspective Skills

Sense-making

Long-term
Orientation and
Visioning

**3 Relating**
Caring for Others
and the World

Appreciation

Connectedness

Humility

Empathy and
Compassion

**4 Collaborating**
Social Skills

Communication
Skills

Co-Creation Skills

Inclusive Mindset
And Intercultural
Competence

Trust

Mobilization Skills

**5 Acting**
Enabling Change

Courage

Creativity

Optimism

Perseverance

**Figure 20.1:** Ten of the 23 IDG skills where NVC has the strongest effect.
Framework: https://innerdevelopmentgoals.org/framework/, highlighted qualities added by Lara Yasmin Hunziker.

## Collaborating dimension

Looking back in history, humanity has achieved unbelievable things in collaboration, and at the same time, most of us have probably experienced the challenges that come with working alongside other people. An obvious way in which NVC directly tackles those difficulties is by enabling individuals to communicate their needs clearly and honestly, while also listening to others with benevolence. This can on one hand increase trust, on the other also minimize misunderstandings and conflicts, and help resolve them quicker. Therefore, NVC can make teams more effective in navigating challenges and better at working towards a common goal. I will illustrate this with some examples that I have experienced before myself.

## A common goal is not enough

Some years ago I was part of Fridays for Future, a movement fighting for climate justice and net zero emissions while trying to organize itself without hierarchies. While it was inspiring to see so many people united by the same purpose, I quickly realized that having the same purpose is not enough. I was surprised and sad to see how much energy got lost in arguments, disagreements, slamming doors, and frustration. That is when I realized that to collaborate, it is not enough to want to achieve the same thing because we will always have different opinions on how to get there. Especially in situations of shared leadership, we need to find a way to communicate what is important to us and include each other's perspectives and insights into new creative solutions. In the Fridays for Future movement, we finally dedicated an entire team to thinking about how we want to communicate and develop our own decision-making process, which I now know is very similar to the decision-making process inspired by NVC.

## Giving feedback to tap into collective wisdom

NVC can also be very helpful for giving feedback. Usually when we want to give feedback, it means something is important to us. Otherwise, we would not bother giving feedback. But often we are scared that the other person will be offended, take it personally, or think that we dislike their entire work, even when there is just a minor comment that we would like to make. NVC can help to make sure the other person understands what is important to us. Instead of saying, "Your presentation was confusing," one could say, "In your presentation, you started with the topic straight away. I was confused because I would have liked some clarity and orientation. Would you mind including a quick overview of the points that you are going to cover in the presentation, as well as giving a bit of context before jumping into it?" When we can give feedback in a way where other people do not hear it as judgment but as a contribution, we can enter a collective creation process, where we can combine experiences, perspectives, and capacities.

## Getting people to do what we want

When collaborating with other people, we would often like to get people to do what we think is right. However, when being nonviolent, we cannot make another person do something. I have been asked how one can make their child clean up their room but say it in a nonviolent way. Or how to make a subordinate do something but be nonviolent while doing so. The truth is, there is no nonviolent way to force someone to do something. People always have a choice. And when we communicate based on feelings and needs, chances are high that people are willing to do what we ask, because they want to contribute to our life and the fulfillment of our needs. So yes, you can request something from your child or your subordinate at work, but it is still their choice whether they do it or not.

It can feel like a defeat for a moment to realize that people always have a choice. But one thing I realized is that even if it is painful to hear a "no", if people do not want to do what I request from them, I prefer them not doing it. Because if I make someone do something that they do not want, they are going to resent me for it, which is going to damage our relationship, as well as influence the quality of how they do what I asked from them. That is already the case when people give me a "half yes" to things I ask. If a part of them is saying no, it means some of their needs are overlooked if they do what I ask. This circles back to the perspective that feelings are a valuable source of information. Being aware of parts of us that say no enables us to adapt the strategy and search for solutions that cover as many needs as possible. That is why it is my wish to have people only do things where they have a full yes.

## Speaking up

One thing I like about NVC is it gives me the confidence to speak up about what is important to me – even to people who are higher up in the hierarchy. I think it is because once I have inner clarity about what is important to me, and what needs I am trying to fulfill with the request I am making to this other person, I know it is worth it. And I can also empathize with the part of me that is scared to speak up. What is this part telling me? Because these feelings are also signaling that a need is in danger of not being met. The need for safety, for example, or harmony, or we are worried about losing our job if we speak up, so the fear might be protecting our need for stability. In this case, I can hold both parts of me with compassion. I can realize that part of me wants to speak up because something is important to me, and part of me does not want to speak up because other things are important to me as well. And then I have a choice, and when I decide to speak up I know that I weighed my options and I know what I want.

## Listening – an invitation to pause

But here is a more subtle but profound way in which NVC also enhances our communication and co-creation skills: NVC invites us to pause and listen – to ourselves and others. Pausing and listening might not seem adequate given that we want to solve problems. Ironically, it is exactly the deeply ingrained urge in us to do things that is keeping us from listening, form understanding, from connecting, and ultimately from moving forward as one. If we do not listen to each other, we are not only less effective in what we do, we might not understand the problem we are trying to solve in the first place, thus investing a lot of time, energy, and resources into a solution that is not tackling the real problem. In this way NVC can help teams understand problems more deeply and thus become more effective at solving them.

There are numerous stories of projects aimed at supporting developing countries in some way which fail to achieve their goals and lead to unintended side effects. One example was an initiative by Nike to reduce child labor in soccer ball stitching, so they built stitching centers that could be monitored to ensure child labor-free production. Having to go to those stitching centers for work, however, lead to less income and increased verbal and sexual assault for the local women (Boje & Khan, 2009), such initiatives failed to understand the root causes and interdependencies of the problem they were trying to solve. They are fighting symptoms, while the organism stays sick. I do not want to say working on those problems is easy, nor do I want to diminish the efforts and good intentions of those who are trying to soothe the symptoms of an unjust world. What I am saying is until we pause and truly understand the root cause of the problems we are trying to solve, we will only treat symptoms, relocate problems, or shift their burden onto someone else.

Circling back to the initial argument, that it is our urge to do things that is keeping us from solving our problems, I would like to elaborate and add a personal reflection. I have spent most of my life unconsciously wanting to get somewhere. Growing up in a Western capitalist society, I got the impression that I needed to get many things so I could relax and be happy – the right job, enough money, the right partner, the right living situation, etc. I was not chasing money in the sense of working until I collapsed, and I was aware that I did not need a mansion and a big car to be happy, but still, I thought that happiness was somewhere in front of me and that there are things I could and should do to get there. So, I spent my life doing things that I thought would get me there, and if I was not happy, I thought I was probably not doing the right thing, or I was not doing it well enough. As a result, I tried doing something else or doing it better.

Most of us have read quotes about how happiness is within us, that we can't buy it, etc. I find myself rolling my eyes at such quotes: "Yes, yes, I get it, I love myself, of course . . ." – but realizing what that means for our own lives is something else entirely. For a while, I thought I had it figured out. I thought I needed to meditate and become more self-aware, learn NVC and get really good at it, go to therapy and heal the wounds of my past. But even after hundreds of hours of meditation, self-reflection, and therapy, I still catch myself running around doing as many things as possible with the hope that it would make me happy. In fact, I am reproducing the same pattern, simply applied to NVC, meditation, and self-development. And as I do all this, I blame myself for not being good enough at realizing that I do not need to be good enough.

I believe I am not alone in this. I am primarily a product of the society I live in, a society in which achieving and possessing things are at the core of what we believe will make us happy. Many problems humanity is facing are consequences of the lifestyle resulting from this mindset. Why else would we destroy the basis of our own existence if not to drive business, earn money, survive, be successful, and maybe be admired and respected, to feel fulfilled and finally happy? But we fail to see and question what is driving us to live the way we do, why we keep on running, precisely because we do not stop running. So, I believe the first step to making progress is to stop trying to get there for a moment.

# Relating dimension

As mentioned earlier, NVC is centered around the idea that we all have the same fundamental human needs. These are physical needs like the need for rest, food, and shelter, but also psychological needs like the need for love, for being heard and understood, the need for appreciation, or the need for connection. Those needs are all abstract: they do not imply any action or plan on how they might be fulfilled, and that is why they can all be beautiful and coexist without excluding one another.

One of the core distinctions in NVC is the distinction between the needs themselves and the strategies we choose to fulfill them. While needs are abstract and beautiful and can all exist next to each other, strategies are concrete. It is because of their specific nature, that they can collide with each other and lead to conflicts. Here, it is important to understand that conflict does not occur at the level of needs, but at the level of strategies; the disagreement is not with the person, but with the strategy they have chosen to meet their need. This may seem like a small detail, but for conflict resolution and interacting with one another, this distinction makes a crucial difference. Since we all have the same needs, they offer a kind of neutral ground where we can relate to each other and recognize that, fundamentally, we are all the same. Rumi, a Persian philosopher and poet, is said to be the source of the following words:

*"Beyond right and wrong there is a field, I'll meet you there."* This quote beautifully captures the spirit of meeting someone and connecting to this person beyond judgements, beyond what we believe to be right and wrong, but where they truly are, on the level of needs.

## Connectedness through the shared experience of life and needs

Realizing that we all have the same needs can strengthen a sense of connectedness and deepen empathy and compassion. Additionally, by becoming aware of our internal patterns and communicating them openly, we might realize that we are all struggling with similar things in the end. Furthermore, by becoming more aware of our thoughts, judgments, feelings, and internal patterns, we can realize how strongly we are influenced by our subconscious. This may lead to a sense of humility and maybe an increasing willingness to forgive others when they are being trapped in the maze of their own patterns.

A phenomenon that I noticed in all NVC courses I have been part of is a very strong sense of connection between participants. People start sharing what they truly care about, recognizing themselves in each other, and feeling a sense of connection that I believe is only possible when we go beyond right or wrong, beyond opinions and judgements, but see each other as the human beings that we are, all sharing this experience of life. This goes even beyond NVC courses. I find myself looking at people, especially people who are doing things that I do not understand, or I judge as inappropriate, bad, or silly, and I ask myself how might they be feeling? What need might they be trying to fulfill with this strategy that I do not understand? It makes me see more of people then just their behavior. So, the interesting thing about NVC is that the people we are relating with or talking to do not need to know NVC for our relationship to be transformed by NVC. We can listen and think empathically, finding the feelings and needs behind the words of the other person, empathize, and see the beauty of them, without the other party needing to ever have heard about NVC.

## Is investing in relationships a chore?

It can get quite exhausting to do all the "translation work". Towards the end of my first course in NVC, I got quite frustrated. Why is it always me that must be empathetic? Why do I need to learn NVC to then be able to talk to people? Why is it always me who listens first and only then do I express what is important to me? This is unfair, is what I thought. I expressed these thoughts with Yoram, one of our teachers, and he said, "We don't do NVC because it is fair. We do it because we care for the connection to the other person." NVC is not a chore, it is not the dirty work someone in a relationship must do to keep the relationship alive. NVC is a mindset and a practice we do for ourselves because it allows us to have deeper connections to ourselves and others. And yes, it is hard with some people, and sometimes it feels like we are *always* the ones that listen, that we are always doing the emotional labor, while the other person is not putting in any effort to care for the connection. We should never make efforts for a connection in the form of NVC and then add that to our count of things we do for the connection and then hold it against the other person (e.g., "I bring the trash out and I do the dishes and I do NVC and you do nothing"). The only reason we should practice NVC is because it enriches our lives, makes our connections more meaningful and our conflicts more fruitful. It is important to remember that NVC is no magic formula. It does not magically make conversations flow and people more easygoing. It might still very well be that we end up breaking off contact with someone, that we set boundaries. But NVC gives us the tools to ask for things, express what we need, and speak about imbalances, thus allowing us to connect with the other person and possibly resolve the issue instead of diverging. And if the moment comes when we feel that a relationship is not giving us what we want, we will possibly have more inner clarity and know that we made our sincere efforts and that we are taking this decision in connection with ourselves and not out of desperation.

In this way, NVC can impact how we see ourselves, the people, and the world around us and how we relate to them.

## Being dimension

It is easy to think that NVC is something that only happens between people – it is about communication after all. But to be able to communicate clearly about our needs, we need to be aware of them in the first place. NVC is not only about communicating with others, but also just as much about getting into contact with ourselves. Empathy does not only go outwards but also inwards. The framework of NVC with the four steps can provide guidance when reflecting on experiences and bring clarity to internal processes. There is a beautiful exercise called self-empathy which guides the reader in processing situations that can be found at the end of this text.

Most of us spend most of our lives on autopilot. Our brain constantly filters information, directs attention, interprets, and judges. We react to stimuli and situations, and they trigger our internal patterns, which we then reproduce, often without noticing it. This is quite natural and very helpful; it is how we can deal with the flood of information that is coming towards us every second without being overwhelmed. But sometimes these patterns direct us into behaviors that do not serve us. Doing exercises like the self-empathy exercise can help to see behind those patterns. What needs am I trying to fulfill with those patterns? Is the pattern helpful in fulfilling those needs? Can I be compassionate and kind to myself even when I realize that the pattern is not serving me? Becoming aware of our patterns and looking at them with kindness is an act of stepping out of the autopilot. And once we start to step out of it, we start to see how much it dominates our lives, without us even realizing it.

One thing that struck me when I started to become aware of my autopilot was realizing how many judgments I have about myself. Judgements in the form of "I should be more of this" or "I should do more of that". Judgments in the form of comparison, indirectly circling back to "I should be more something", in the form of "I am not enough X" and "I am too much Y". A constant voice in my head judging everything I do. It is quite exhausting at times. In NVC there is a saying that behind every judgment, there is a beautiful, unfulfilled need. The idea is that judgments are tragic expressions of needs that would like to be fulfilled and that they can actually be a very effective signpost, pointing towards our needs. If I, for example, have the judgement that someone is disrespectful, I likely have the need for respect. Empathizing with my judgments and finding out about the needs behind them showed me the core needs that drive a lot of my feelings and behavior and ultimately lead me to understand myself better.

Thus, having the NVC framework in mind while going through life, reflecting on feelings, and trying to find out to which needs they are connected, sharpens our awareness of our internal processes. There is a quote by Viktor E. Frankl: "Between stimulus and response there is space. In that space is our power to choose our response. In our response lies our growth and our freedom." It is a quote I have heard in connection to mindfulness, but in my opinion, it applies just as much to NVC. Even if in the beginning, feelings and needs can only be understood in hindsight, with practice it gets easier to notice them when they emerge, leading to greater awareness and presence. This in turn allows us to act earlier, with choice, and from a more calm and wise position, compared to if we had waited longer and reacted out of impulse. It thus allows us to become more purposeful in choosing strategies to fulfill our needs, almost like an inner compass, while being able to communicate them allows us to live with greater authenticity and integrity.

## Being honest is being kind

A common misconception about NVC is that once I learn NVC, I need to be empathetic, calm, and collected all the time; that NVC is there to create harmony, and that I soften because I empathize with someone, that I become less respected and more vulnerable. My experience is exactly the opposite. Yes, I did become more aware of my emotions, feeling them more strongly, but with that also comes more internal clarity. And internal clarity is what allows us to act with intent and kind determination. NVC is about honesty, and honesty gives agency and is a sign of respect to other people. Counterintuitively, that often means becoming aware of and setting boundaries more clearly and enforcing them with more intent. Of course, NVC opens the possibility to have a conversation and to explore possible ways forward, to pick up the metaphor from earlier on, to meet on the field of needs, beyond right or wrong. But that does not mean that we cannot decide, that we do not want something, which connects strongly to the next paragraph on saying no.

## Staying true to ourselves – saying "no"

One example where NVC has helped me a lot is with saying no. Personally, I find saying no quite hard. First of all, I do not want to hurt or disappoint anyone. I know from myself how fast it happens that we interpret a "no" to what someone suggested as a "no" to us as a person. And secondly, I often have several needs, some of them making me want to say no to protect my energy, for example, while some of them make me want to say yes, like my need for adventure and fun. Holding both those parts of me at the same time can be challenging and confusing. But what I realized is that saying no to something always means saying yes to something else. Saying no to someone else means saying yes to my boundaries. Saying no to company means saying yes to time for myself. Saying no to helping someone means saying yes to honoring my capacities. Additionally, NVC provides a way to say no while stating the need I am trying to fulfill with this no, and it also allows us to empathize with the feelings triggered in the other person by this "no". As an example, if a friend asks me whether I would like to go for a hike on the weekend, my normal response would have been, "I'm quite busy, maybe some other time." With NVC I could also say, "The idea of going on a hike with you sounds very intriguing and there is a part of me that would love being outside and with you and go on this adventure and at the same time I need some rest and time for myself right now, so I prefer to stay at home this weekend. How is that for you to hear?"

# Acting dimension

Conflicts often block or slow action. NVC can help to remove those blocks, but NVC also requires time. Taking time is sometimes the last thing we want when we are already delayed in our plans because of a conflict. I think it is necessary, however, to take this time to reach our long-term goals and lay the basis for long-term collaboration. Here are some ways in which NVC can help to get back into action.

## Removing the blocks to action

A core thought of NVC is that if we are allowed to relax and connect with our needs, we will automatically start developing our own strategies to fulfill those needs. Therefore, a simple exercise such as the self-empathy exercise (which can be found at the end of this chapter) can help to reconnect with our needs, reorient ourselves, and get back into action. But NVC can also help support others to get back into action. This introduces the concept of empathetic listening.[2] The idea of empathetic listening is to remove the blocks to action by allowing the other person to fully relax, while feeling seen, heard, and fully accepted. We are present with the other person, listening without judgments, fully accepting them where they are, such that they can let go of their judgments and accept themselves as well.

The base for empathetic listening is simply being present, not saying anything at all. Anyone who has ever tried this might have realized how unfamiliar it feels. We are so used to giving opinions, comforting the other person, and giving advice. We want to help, or maybe share a similar story. Empathetic listening, however, tries to keep the entire attention on the other person. While listening empathetically to someone we can make guesses about what they are feeling or what their needs are with the goal of lending our sense of them to them. We do not, however, share our own thoughts, experiences, and emotions. The goal is to make those guesses with the framework of NVC in mind, to allow the other person to relax and ultimately settle on their unmet need. From there on, new strategies for action can be developed, leading to new, purposeful action. This process can support people who feel stuck with a dilemma, a decision they need to take, or a situation that is bothering them, where they do not know what to do. Empathy can remove blocks to action and get things moving again.

## Decision-making

I had a striking experience when I had to decide about whether to sign up for a certain master's program. I was taking an NVC course at the time and volunteered to do the demo when we practiced the dilemma process. We followed the process of listening to both voices, the one that says yes, and the other that says no, and finding out what needs lie behind both of those voices. We found out that the part of me wanting to do the master's wanted safety, orientation, and learning, while the other part wanted freedom, spontaneity, and flow. And when the facilitator of the course repeated the needs of both sides combined in one sentence, I started to cry. It was so beautiful to realize that there was no right or wrong decision to take. I was not being silly or annoying for struggling with this decision, but there are parts of me that care for different beautiful needs. And the needs do not have to exclude each other. It was incredibly relieving to get out of the mindset of "either-or" and embrace one of "and".

---

2 This explanation of empathetic listening is strongly based on a video by Dominic Barter. The video can be found using the following link: www.youtube.com/watch?v=-olmJVxNvYo.

It is one thing I keep reminding myself of whenever I am struggling with a decision. There is no right or wrong, there are just different needs I am trying to fulfill. And maybe I can include all of them in a creative strategy. The exercise helped me to switch from a defensive mindset and a feeling of being overwhelmed to a creative mindset of curiosity and exploration. And that, I believe, is a superpower.

With this area of *acting* we conclude our exploration of how the mindset and practices that lay at the base of NVC can support and transform various areas of our lives. We have seen how NVC acts within different areas of the IDGs and thus contributes to the individual and collective growth necessary to tackle today's challenges.

# Thinking dimension

When it comes to training cognitive skills, one would probably not first think of training in NVC. And yes, critical thinking is not what one specifically learns since NVC is more about empathy, but perspective skills are also part of the thinking dimension. In the IDG Framework, perspective skills are skills in "seeking, understanding and actively making use of insights from contrasting perspectives".[3] And these skills are substantially augmented by NVC in several ways.

Regarding the seeking of contrasting perspectives, I have observed in myself that in conflicts I have developed a tendency of curiosity toward the other person, whereas my initial tendency was to avoid, push away, devalue, and certainly not to listen. This seems most powerful since it is key to everything that follows and since it is not an intellectual step: everybody knows they should listen to other people's perspectives, but only actually doing so when under stress oneself is transformational.

When it comes to understanding contrasting perspectives, NVC delivers a simple structure to understand. So, if you do not understand, it is easy to ask questions that will help you to do so fast.

And lastly, NCV helps in making use of insights from contrasting perspectives. There is certainly an intellectual part in making use of insights from contrasting perspectives that is not covered by an NVC training like the analysis of power structures, but there is a psychological, an emotional part, to drawing conclusions from different perspectives and it a powerful one. This part is certainly enhanced by NVC training.

Thus, I conclude, even the thinking dimension is substantially touched by NVC, and therefore all five dimensions of the IDGs.

---

**3** https://innerdevelopmentgoals.org/framework/.

# Better communication supports leadership for sustainability

While there is good reason to believe that supporting the IDGs is what is needed for reaching sustainability, we might want to have a closer look at how exactly this is happening. Since NVC is about communication, let me point out how better communication contributes substantially to achieving the SDGs, the Sustainable Development Goals set by the UN: It is by supporting better leadership on a personal and on a cultural level.

The personal level is obvious. Leaders who are better conflict resolvers are better at finding sustainable solutions. But the cultural level is less obvious, yet it might be even more powerful.

In a complex and rapidly changing world, no single leader can have all the answers, however good she or he might be at conflict resolution. Thus, we see collective leadership structures on the rise. Collective leadership is a powerful approach, but it comes with a big challenge: dealing with conflicts. Collective leadership does not work if there is no culture of dealing well with conflicts. NVC not only boosts the qualities of collective leadership team members, but it also helps develop the culture of need to successfully engage in collective leadership.

How important this is may become clearer if you think about where collective leadership is called for. I think of families or leisure clubs, of schools or health care organizations, of nonprofits or business firms, or even of international negotiations regarding carbon dioxide reduction.

# Conclusion

A training in Nonviolent Communication (NVC) boosts all five dimensions and many of the individual 23 skills of the IDG framework. Since NVC is a well-proven and established concept, training for NVC seems like a good strategy for individuals, schools, and institutions who want to contribute to the sustainability of the world.[4]

---

4 If you are interested to learn more, I recommend the book *Nonviolent Communication* by Marshall Rosenberg which dives deeper into the concept of NVC. But just like you cannot learn how to swim without getting into the water, NVC cannot be learned without real-life practice. That is why I highly recommend taking a course in NVC where you will get the chance to practice and reflect together with like-minded people.

# Acknowledgements

Thanks to Andy Balmer for the inspiring conversations about NVC and their connection to the IDGs and sustainability.

Thanks to Yoram Mosenzon, Tanja Walliser, Sonja and Barbara Wolfensberger, Livio Lunin, as well as all the amazing assistants and friends, whom I have had the pleasure to learn NVC from and explore NVC with.

Thanks to my family for their unwavering support on my path of (self-)exploration.

Thanks to my father, Alexander, for supporting me in writing this text.

Thanks to Mauricio Campos Suarez, Eleftheria Egel, Michael Bieder, and Lutz Hempel for all the wonderful work on IDG Switzerland!

# References

Boje, D. M. & Khan, F. R. (2009). Story-branding by empire entrepreneurs: Nike, child labour, and Pakistan's soccer ball industry. *Journal of Small Business & Entrepreneurship*, *22*(1), 9–24. https://doi.org/10.1080/08276331.2009.10593439.

Rosenberg, M. B. (2015). Nonviolent communication: A language of life (3rd ed.). Puddledancer Press.

# Self-empathy exercise

Good to do when:
- You realize that something is not going well (but also when everything is wonderful).
- When you feel a bit off, but don't know why.
- As preparation for a difficult conversation.
- As a form of self-care, it can help to bring clarity about what is going on internally and help you understand what you need right now.

## Exercise

1.  Name the feelings: Write down all the feelings that resonate with you right now, use the list if you want (see table 20.1). Take your time, and ask yourself for every feeling on the list whether you are feeling it right now. Often, we feel a physical reaction and know instinctively whether a certain feeling fits or not. Write down all the feelings, there might be many, and they can be quite different as well. When you're done, write them into thematical blocks.

2. Pick one of the feelings/blocks and try to find out what the trigger for this feeling was. Was there a specific situation/observation? If not, you can skip this step.

3. Write down all the thoughts and judgments you are having in connection with this situation and write it as closely to what it sounds like in your head, with no filter.

4. Ask yourself the question: "When I feel . . . (feeling) and think . . . (thought), am I needing . . . (need)?" Insert the feelings and thoughts from before and guess the needs that you might have. You can use the needs list (see table 20.2). Write down all the needs that are connected to your feelings.

5. Observe if any ideas pop up in terms of what could be the next steps. If there is nothing, that is totally okay as well. Is there something that you could do yourself? Is there something you could request from another person? It does not have to be something big.

6. How are you now? Do you notice any difference from before you did the exercise?

**Table 20.1:** List of feelings for self-reflection in NVC.

| FEELINGS In NVC | | | |
|---|---|---|---|
| **CALM** | **ALIVE** | **CONCERNED** | **PAIN** |
| relaxed | awake | nervous | guilty |
| grounded | lively | restless | shameful |
| comfortable | excited | stressed | lonely |
| relieved | enthusiastic | | grieving |
| centered | ecstatic | **CONFUSED** | suffering |
| calm | sensual | torn | regretful |
| | | lost | jealous |
| **HAPPY** | **COMPASSIONATE** | hesitant | envious |
| joyful | warm | baffled | |
| amused | open | | **BODY SENSATIONS** |
| cheerful | touched/moved | **ANXIOUS** | lump in the stomach |
| fulfilled | tender | fearful | narrow throat |
| playful | | paralyzed | fast heartbeat |
| grateful | **CONFIDENT** | panicky | breathless |
| | empowered | mistrustful | |
| **CURIOUS** | proud | | **SAD** |
| fascinated | hopeful | **TIRED** | melancholic |
| inspired | optimistic | overwhelmed | depressed |
| focused | | exhausted | hopeless |
| engaged | **ANNOYED** | burnt out | longing |
| | irritated | tired/ sleepy | desperate |
| **REFRESHED** | frustrated | | |
| rested | impatient | **VULNERABLE** | **ANGRY** |
| regenerated | uncomfortable | fragile | angry |
| clear | | insecure | furious |
| | | sensitive | raging |

Source: The lists are loosely based on the book: Nonviolent Communication a language of life by M. B. Rosenberg.

**Table 20.2:** List of needs for self-reflection in NVC.

| NEEDS in NVC | | | |
|---|---|---|---|
| **CONNECTION** | **HONESTY** | **PHYSICAL WELL-BEING** | **PURPOSE** |
| Love | Self-expression | Air | Goals / Dreams/ Meaning |
| Closeness | Authenticity / Genuineness | Nourishment | Contribution / Generosity |
| Intimacy | Integrity | Relaxation | Presence |
| Empathy | Transparency | Physical recreation | Centeredness |
| Appreciation | Truth | Exercise | Hope |
| Acceptance | | Health | Clarity |
| Recognition | **PLAY** | Touch | Knowing / being in reality |
| Openness | Liveliness | Sexual expression / Sexuality | Learning |
| Trust | Flow | Home | Awareness |
| Communication | Passion | Safety / Protection | Inspiration / Creativity |
| Attention | Spontaneity | Emotional safety | Challenge / Stimulation |
| Tenderness / softness | Fun | Comfort | Growth / Progress |
| Respect | Lightness / Humour / Laughter | | Being in power |
| Being seen | Variety / Diversity | **HARMONY** | Competence / Capacity |
| Being heard | | Peace | Self-worth / Self-confidence |
| Being understood | **FREEDOM** | Beauty | Efficiency |
| Consideration / Care | Independence | Order | Being important / Playing a role |
| Belonging / Participating | Having the choice / Voluntariness | Closeness to nature | Having my place in the world |
| Supporting | Having space and time | Tranquility/ Calmness | Spirituality |
| Cooperation/ Community / Partnership / Friendship | Follow your own pace / rhythm | Stability | Being part of a greater whole |
| Reciprocity | Living your own truth / conviction | Lightness | Simplicity |
| Consistency / Continuity | | Processing / Integration | Regret (mourning) and |
| | | Predictability | celebration |
| | | Justice / Fairness | Ecstasy |

This list is inspired by Empathiestadt Zürich (empathiestadt.ch)
Source: The lists are loosely based on the book: Nonviolent Communication a language of life by M. B. Rosenberg.

# List of figures

https://doi.org/10.1515/9783111337913-022

# List of tables

https://doi.org/10.1515/9783111337913-023

# Index

Abram, D.  57
acting, IDG framework
– Chinese model  144–145
– connectedness in  25, 244–245
– reverent action  53–54, 60–61
– social-emotional learning (SEL)  145
– summer, Seasonal Circles of Change  187–188
– Zhao's circle  145
adult development, Experience Cube
– Clear Leadership framework  285–286
– constructivist developmental theory  283
– conventional stages  284
– post-conventional stages  284–285
– self-differentiation  285
– stages  283–284
African Forest Landscape Restoration Initiative
    (AFR100)  93
*ahimsa* (nonviolence)  21
Ames, R. T.  146
ancient wisdom  4, 105, 110, 129, 137, 147, 180
Andrade Azevedo, A.  193–206
animacy  50, 51, 62
anthropocentrism  65–67, 79, 80
appreciation  59, 75, 90, 116, 186, 242, 279, 340
art-based approaches  244
Art Basel Week (2024) Show  88, 93
*The Artistic Attitude* (Coumans)  45
artists of life  44–46
art-making process
– creation phase  95–96
– ideation phase  94–95
– learning phase  97
– reflection phase  96–97
– wrap-up  97–98
Artmann, M.  79
assurance stage  121–122
attunement  134, 222, 244
average sentiment score, blockage/action
    stickers  228–229
"awesome blossoms" pod  186

Bach, J. S.  38
Barroso, M.  193–206
Bateson, G.  22
Beer, T.  244
being, IDG framework  4, 9, 13, 14, 22, 25, 68, 69,
    105, 134, 230

– connectedness with ecological self  15, 57–58,
    239–240
– constraints  22–23
– core  179–181
– descriptions  15–19
– examples  26–28
– and group cohesion  99
– heart-mind  135–136
– inter-becoming  17
– interconnectedness  53
– omnipresence of  15
– profound shift  21
– and rhythms of life  181
– self-cultivating tool  134–135
– superpositions  21
– Western psychology and science  18–19
Bennett, N. J.  244
biophilia  61, 62, 68
Block, P.  185
Boyatzis, C.  238
bread trail narratives
– "bread is religion"  42
– community engagement  37
– digital artefact  36
– educational tool  36
– embeddings  36
– IDG framework  35–37
– personal growth and reflection  36
– policy and advocacy  37
– professional development  36
British Columbia Health Leadership Development
    Collaborative (BCHLDC)  178
broaden-and-build theory  219
Bucher, A.  238
Buddhism  16, 17, 25, 94, 112, 149, 159–170,
    214–216, 231
Burckhardt, X. D.  87–102
burned-out changemaker  179–181
Bushe, G. R.  269–288

Campos Suarez, M.  1–6, 9–12, 87–102, 209–212
Caniglia, G.  244
care  1, 2, 46, 58, 65–70, 122, 180, 183, 186, 238,
    244, 330, 334
challenge-based learning (CBL)  291–294. *See also*
    Q methodology, confrontation and
    contemplation

https://doi.org/10.1515/9783111337913-024

# Contributor Biographies

BOOK 1: From "I" to "We"

**Andrade Azevedo, A.**
Triconsult
Brasil
Founding Partner and Director of TriConsult, and Co-founder of HUB IDG Alinhar. He serves on the boards of Conscious Capitalism Brazil and the Family Business Network. A professor at Fundação Dom Cabral (PDA Program) and in Conscious Capitalism's leadership programs, he teaches leadership, purpose, and organizational culture. With 30+ years in strategic alignment consulting across sectors, he holds degrees in Business and Accounting, with specializations in finance, strategy, Gestalt training, coaching, and mediation. Creator of "ALINHAR: Love to Results:and author of multiple e-books, he is dedicated to lifelong learning and meaningful impact.

**Barroso, M.**
University of St. Gallen,
Switzerland
Senior Researcher, Lecturer and Project Lead at the Sustainability Innovation Lab (Institute of Technology Management) and Head of Executive Education of the Competence Center for Social Innovation, both at the University of St. Gallen, Switzerland. She has extensive experience as a lecturer and facilitator, and in consulting organizations with respect to sustainable business models and sustainable leadership in the context of corporate social responsibility, multistakeholder management, impact-oriented organizations and systems thinking. Mônica holds a PhD in Social Policy from the London School of Economics and Political Science, and was a postdoc Kleinhans Fellow of the Rainforest Alliance leading a project on "Linking Market Intelligence and Remote Villagers" in the Brazilian Amazon, where she also facilitated a number of learning journeys for executive audiences. She was also Head of Learning and senior lecturer at The School of Life Brazil, having facilitated emotional intelligence workshops for individuals and corporations. She has additionally co-founded local hubs of the Inner Development Goals in Brazil and Switzerland, supporting business students and leaders in developing inner skills that will equip them to better lead the sustainability transition from inside out.

**Björkman T.**
Founder of the Ekskäret Foundation & Chair of the Inner Development Goals Foundation
Sweden
Tomas Björkman is founder of the Ekskäret Foundation, Stockholm, with the aim of supporting sustainable development for individuals, organizations and society. He is also the chair of the Inner Development Goals Foundation, the co-founder of the research institute Perspectiva in London, of the Co-creation Foundation and the media platform Emerge in Berlin and 29k.com personal development platform. He is the author of three books: The Market Myth (2016), The Nordic Secret (together with Lene Rachel Andersen, 2017) and The World We Create (2019). He divides his time between London, Stockholm and Berlin.

**Burckhardt, X.D.**
Burckhardt HR Consulting GmbH
Switzerland
Xuan Dung Burckhardt is the founder of FLOW and Managing Director of Burckhardt HR Consulting GmbH. With more than 20 years of experience in various industries, particularly in the pharmaceutical

https://doi.org/10.1515/9783111337913-025

sector in both established companies and start-ups, she is passionate about a people-centric approach to HR. As a well-rounded HR leader, Dung has managed the entire employee lifecycle – from talent acquisition and development to organisational development and post-merger integration. Her ability to translate business objectives into actionable HR strategies has consistently led to improved business performance, making her a trusted advisor to senior executives and leadership teams. Beyond her HR achievements, Dung is also a dedicated artist whose work has been exhibited in galleries since 2018. This creative passion not only fuels her artistic endeavours, but also inspires her to create FLOW, a methodology that uses art as a medium in team or individual interventions to foster collaboration and innovation. Her art can be viewed at www.xdart.ch.

### Bushe, G.R.
Beedie School of Business, Simon Fraser University
Canada
Gervase R. Bushe is the Professor of Leadership and Organization Development at the Beedie School of Business, Simon Fraser University in Vancouver, Canada. His career spans four decades of transforming organizational structures, cultures and processes away from command and control toward more collaborative work systems. An award-winning author of over 100 papers and four books on organizational change, leadership, teams, and teamwork, Gervase has consulted with a wide variety of organizations. In 2019, he co-founded the Bushe-Marshak Institute for Dialogic OD, which offers in-house courses and certification in Dialogic OD, and is the editor of the BMI Series in Dialogic Organization Development. A chapter on his life and work appears in the Palgrave Handbook of Organizational Change Thinkers.

### Campos Suarez M.
Co-Founder Inner Development Goals
Switzerland
Mauricio is a transformative leader with over 20 years of experience across healthcare, technology, and digital innovation in 40+ countries, having held key roles at Pfizer, Merck & Co., and Novartis. As a certified bilingual Integral™ & Systemic Team Coach (ICF PCC, EMCC Senior Coach), Mauricio helps leaders and teams align their inner development with business strategies through long-term cultural transformation. His expertise spans executive coaching, innovation management, and Agile methodologies. Mauricio's passion lies in empowering organizations to embrace change, fostering collective leadership, and driving both personal and systemic growth to meet the challenges of a rapidly evolving world.

### Clarke, D.
Ever Being Movement
Canada
Danielle holds a master's degree in Environmental Education and Communication from Royal Roads University in British Columbia, Canada. Residing amidst the vibrant ecosystems of the Pacific Northwest on the unceded lands of the Musqueam, Squamish, and Tsleil-Waututh nations, she is deeply committed to fostering connections between humans and the natural world. As the Founder of Ever Being, Danielle creates offerings that help individuals navigate the climate crisis by reconnecting them with themselves, each other, and the more-than-human world. She is passionate about merging ecological awareness with embodied practices to deepen our relationship with the Earth and reveal a more profound sense of inner knowing.

**Cody, M.**
Clear Leadership
Canada
I have a Ph.D. in Law. My thesis was about Dialogic Law and Regulation – or how would you get a large system of people (say 10,000 or so) to learn a new desired behaviour – and I mean really learn so that it becomes a part of them. I was the Gold Medallist of my law school and have won numerous scholarships and academic awards and I have published multiple articles and book chapters on business ethics, corporations, and corporate governance.

**Contreras, I.**
ICON coaching / AO Foundation
Switzerland
Irene Contreras is a Spanish-Swiss coach, facilitator, and Health Professions educationalist based in Winterthur, Switzerland. She holds a License in Translation, a MAs in International Relations and is an ICF certified professional coach. Irene's work as a coach mainly focuses on helping the millennial generation overcome their unique challenges, build confidence and create meaningful change. She also helps organizations bridge the gap between cultures and generations. Her coaching philosophy revolves around deep listening, compassion, creativity and curiosity. Outside of work, she is mom of two wonderful girls, a life-long learner, a creative handcrafter, and a passionate traveler and explorer.

**Feldman, B.**
Harvard University
USA
Boaz B. Feldman (MSc, SEP, FSP, PgD) is a pragmatic visionary, clinical psychologist, trainer, researcher and contemplative acting for worldwide positive change. A depression in his early 20's led him to ordain as a Buddhist monk in Thailand, where he practiced meditation and studied the teachings for 3 years. He returned to Geneva, Switzerland to train as a clinical psychologist and led a number of psychological first aid programs with International NGO's (UNOCHA, Doctors Without Borders, International Medical Corps), specializing in staff welfare. After missions in conflict affected regions (Afghanistan, Burkina Faso, Myanmar) and low-income regions, he designed a 3-year CARE training program (Clinical Abilities for Resiliency & Empowerment) and founded NeuroSystemics, a Geneva-based NGO. Boaz studied the effects of compassion meditation for conflict resolution at the Interdisciplinary Centre for Affective Science at the University of Geneva, and currently holds positions of Research Associate at Life Itself (France) and Research Scholar at Harvard University's Graduate School of Education focusing on implementation and community-based sciences with youth.

**Förster, R.**
Dr. Ruth Förster, training & counselling,
Switzerland
Dr. sc. ETHZ Ruth D. Förster is a passionate advocate for change towards more regenerative ways of living and working. Her practice is rooted in more than 25 years of experience and expertise in innovative, creative, transdisciplinary ways of adult education and collaborative leadership inside and outside academia. Nowadays, she is working as lecturer, counsellor, trainer or coach for individuals or organizations in transformation processes. Particularly, she tailors and holds outdoor learning spaces for deep experiential, embodied learning fostering connectedness and creativity. Selected degrees: Doctoral Degree in Environmental Engineering ETH Zurich, Tamalpa Live Art Practitioner, Vision Quest Guide (tradition School of Lost Borders).

**Hunziker, L.**
Switzerland
Lara Yasmin Hunziker, born in 1998 in Bern, Switzerland, is a passionate advocate for empathy, emotional intelligence, and conscious communication in every day life and expecially when addressing global challenges. During her bachelor's in physics at ETH Zurich, she discovered that solving complex mathematical problems honed her curiosity, persistence, and logical thinking. Recognizing the limits of logic alone, Lara pursued studies in Sustainable Management and Technology at EPFL/HEC/IMD, while actively seeking to explore resilience, self-awareness, and strong communication skills through meditation, Nonviolent Communication and a commitment to personal development and sustainability. She is dedicated to finding integral approaches to today's pressing issues.

**Jansen, P.**
University of Regensburg
Germany
Petra Jansen, full Professor at the University of Regensburg, is an experimental psychologist who also works in sports science. Her main research interests include investigating the relationship between motor, emotional, and cognitive aspects. She is also interested in the role of inner sustainability in well-being and sustainable behavior.

**Jeffcutt P.**
Seramus Heaney Centre, Belfast
Ireland
Paul Jeffcutt is a writer, with three full collections of poetry: 'True', Black Spring Press (2024), 'The Skylark's Call', Dempsey & Windle (2020), and 'Latch', Lagan Press (2010). He has recently completed his first novel. Paul has won thirty three awards for poetry in competitions in Ireland, the UK and the USA. His poems have been published in literary journals and anthologies in three different continents. He has been featured five times on BBC Radio and has appeared at major arts festivals in Ireland and the UK. Paul was an academic; he published a series of books and journal articles on behaviour in organisations. www.pauljeffcutt.net

**Kempkes. C.**
FingerSpitzen Kollektiv
Belgium
With an extensive background in finance, Christophe brings a wealth of experience to his role as a transdisciplinary facilitator of systemic change. Inspired by Pippi Longstocking's adventurous spirit, he values experimentation and growth through discomfort and curiosity, advocating for human modesty over tailored solutions. Christophe emphasizes the importance of rising above systems to unlock human potential. His "relationist manifesto" champions the idea that relationships, not individuals, shape culture and drive social change. With clear analysis and an open heart, Christophe nurtures a network of self-aware individuals and organizations, aiming for deep impact.

**Kouji, M.**
IDGs Kamakura Zen Lab
Japan
After he receiving a Master's degree from Keio University, he joined Fujitsu Ltd. and pursued a PhD while working as an IT venture director. Restructured due to business decline, he began daily zazen to recover. His zazen practice inspired 'zenschool,' an innovation management method using mindfulness. He led Japan's first international mindfulness conference, 'Zen2.0,' at Kenchoji Temple, which grew into the world's largest Zen and mindfulness conference. From 2020, he launched 'zenschool Metaverse' and now lectures on the 'AI and IKIGAI' in the AI era.

**Läubli, M.**
xcg executive consulting group ag
Switzerland
Matthias Laeubli, Professional Certified Coach (PCC), builds on extensive hands-on business experience as Senior Consultant, HR Leader and Business Partner. He has a proven track record in organizational transformations, global mobility, mergers and acquisitions, restructuring, international recruitment, and providing trusted advisory to the C-Suite in international organizations. Following his career in HR, Matthias has become an expert in identifying and developing senior executives and high potentials. He has worked with clients from multiple industries, countries, and cultures. Matthias holds a master's degree in psychology and is a certified coach. Furthermore, he has served as president of the ICF Switzerland Chapter.

**LeCorre, C.**
IDG Vancouver Island Co-Inspire Hub
Canada
Cathryn provides leadership solutions and coaching for changemakers who want to thrive. With over 20 years of experience co-creating leadership and coaching cultures in healthcare organizations, she is passionate about expanding wellbeing, collaboration and innovation through partnership. A collective leadership coach, organizational development consultant and yoga teacher, she is also the founder of the IDG Vancouver Island Co-Inspire Hub. Cathryn partners with leaders, teams and organizations who want to embody their leadership, innovate toward global goals, and co-create thriving communities so we can thrive, together.

**Margolis, A.**
University of Hamburg | IST University of Applied Science
Germany
Anna Margolis is a doctoral candidate at the Chair of Circular Economy and Systems Innovation at Hamburg University and a lecturer at the IST University of Applied Science. Her research focuses on how organisations and society can innovate towards more desirable, sustainable, and circular futures. She builds on theories from systems thinking, innovation, collaboration, transitions research, and sociology to design science-based tools for practitioners. Before, she worked as a change program facilitator at Henkel and founded a social start-up. She is a fellow of the Foundation of German Business (sdw).

**Mata Carrera, A.G.**
Mexico
I'm a photographer with a passion for capturing the stories behind the moments and storytelling through imagery (@agabriela_m). In addition to photography, I'm also an entrepreneur, founded SurYNor Art to promote the development of true aborigine communities and create awareness in fair trade and responsible consuming especially from my country, Mexico.

**McNichol, T.**
Ren Associates
USA
Theresa (Terri) McNichol, an award-winning artist, arts administrator, former curator and museum director, is President, Ren Associates. She studied traditional and classical Chinese language along with Chinese, Japanese and South Asian art history. To share her passion for the arts of Asia with American undergraduates, she has taught a non-Western art history survey and studio for over thirty years. Her consulting, research, international conference presentations and publications highlight arts-based pedagogy, wise management and aesthetic imagination.

**Mutanguha, F.**
Aegis Trust
Rwanda
Freddy Mutanguha is the CEO of the Aegis Trust and Director of the Kigali Genocide Memorial. He developed Aegis' peace education program in Rwanda and is expanding it to regions at risk, such as the Central African Republic, South Sudan, and Kenya. Freddy joined Aegis in 2004 and became Country Director in 2006. He holds a master's degree in project management and a bachelor's degree in education. A survivor of the 1994 Genocide Against the Tutsi, Freddy has received numerous accolades for his peace efforts and lectures internationally on genocide impact and the importance of forgiveness in post-conflict reconstruction.

**Raysz, J.**
Super
USA
Jochen Raysz is a mentor, coach and meditation teacher. He supports founders, leaders and coaches to develop inner sustainability and live fully aligned with their deepest essence, values and purpose in life and business so they don't burn out while changing the world. After his Masters in Psychology, Neuroscience and Management, Jochen worked as change manager and leadership coach. He took a break to travel, lived in the Himalayas, and went on to cofound and grow several impact-driven organizations in Europe and the US. Jochen lives in California with his wife. He loves surfing and making Italian food and espresso.

**Ruth, D.-M.**
Ruth is a systemic coach and mixed-media artist of British-Trinidadian heritage, based in Switzerland. Her art draws inspiration from her early years on a Caribbean island, where she was raised by her grandmother and aunts, and primarily centres on the theme of women. The art pieces she creates feature vibrant colours and graceful curves, celebrating women who are unapologetically bold and comfortable with themselves.

**Sägesser, A.**
scaling4good
Switzerland
Dr. Anaïs Sägesser is a process steward dedicated to societal transformation. Rooted in Switzerland, she integrates transdisciplinary research, systems thinking, and embodied practices to deepen connections to self, others, and the more-than-human. As reflective practitioner she draws from multiple disciplines and weaves together different perspectives and ways of knowing. As custodian of land, she is dedicated to regenerating ecosystems and fostering meaningful relationships with place. Committed to systemic change for a thriving planet, Dr. Sägesser co-founded scaling4good and serves also in advisory and governance roles across various initiatives.

**Santolini, M.**
Learning Transitions Research Unit, Learning Planet Institute, Paris
France
Marc Santolini is a practitioner-researcher specializing in open innovation and collective intelligence for Sustainable and Inner Development Goals. His work explores how groups innovate and collaborate, particularly in citizen science and open-source communities. Holding a PhD in Statistical Physics from École Normale Supérieure Paris, he specialized in network science at the Barabási Lab and now leads the Interaction Data Lab at the Learning Planet Institute. He co-founded the Just One Giant Lab Foundation to support large-scale open

research communities. His research integrates network approaches and participatory methods to enhance collaborative dynamics and relational well-being, supported by national and international organizations.

**Stanberry, J.**
Initiative for Leadership and Sustainability, University of Cumbria
UK
Joanna Stanberry lives in Lancaster, UK where she is a Sustainability Research Fellow and postgraduate researcher at the Initiative for Leadership and Sustainability at the University of Cumbria. She has published on historical, governance, ethical, and cross-sector approaches to sustainability leadership. Previously, Joanna has taught at the MacArthur School of Leadership at Palm Beach Atlantic University, also working for 15 years in New York City in non-profit marketing, tech, finance, and philanthropy. She has an MA in Organizational Leadership from Eastern University, PA, and a BA from Claremont McKenna College in Claremont, CA.

**Vogel, L.**
Institute for Systemic Management (IMP-HSG)
Switzerland
Lukas is a systems scientist and group facilitator. By utilizing the framework of Inner Development Goals (IDGs), he supports individuals, teams and communities in the process of building sustainable businesses. He places a strong emphasis on cultural sensitivity, ecosystems-centric design and enhancing social skills. His methodology incorporates process-oriented psychology, developmental theory, and evidence-based mindfulness practices.

**Von Wirth, T.**
Frankfurt University of Applied Sciences & Erasmus University Rotterdam
Germany
Timo von Wirth is Full Professor of Sustainability Science with Frankfurt University of Applied Sciences, Visiting Professor at Erasmus University Rotterdam, and Invited Research Fellow with the Center for Sustainability Transitions at Stellenbosch University, SA. His work addresses Transformative governance, Human Well-being and epistemic justice in Sustainability transitions.

# Endorsements

"For humanity to address the great interconnected challenges of the world there needs to be a fundamental shift in human consciousness. This international collection of chapters on how we do the inner development necessary is a valuable contribution for all leaders, coaches, consultants and educators who all have a prime responsibility in this transformation of human consciousness."

**Professor Peter Hawkins**

Chairman of Renewal Associates and author of *Beauty in Leadership, Coaching and the Transformation of Human Consciousness* and many other best-selling books.

"I enthusiastically endorse Inner Development Goals: Stories of Collective Leadership in Action, a transformative two-volume anthology. This collection offers invaluable insights and practices from global Inner Development Goals (IDGs) gatherings, highlighting the power of collective leadership in advancing the Sustainable Development Goals (SDGs).

The Caux IDG Forum, held in July 2024, exemplifies the integration of inner development and systemic change, showcasing practical approaches that strengthen networks and capacities essential for achieving the SDGs. The book and the forum connect by the depth of study with the richness of dialogue.

This collection is more than a book; it's a call to action. Accompanied by a digital workbook, it fosters dialogue between authors and readers, empowering collective action. Each chapter explores the multifaceted dimensions of systemic change through academic insights, case studies, and artistic expressions.

For anyone dedicated to the SDG movement, this collection is both a guide and an inspiration, underscoring the critical role of inner development in creating a sustainable and just world."

**Ignacio Packer**
Executive Director
CAUX INITIATIVES OF CHANGE

"Inner transformation and outer transformation complement one another. Mostly we focus on outer transformation. Therefore the publication of Inner Development Goals: Stories of Collective Leadership in Action is a powerful and inspiring step in the right direction. This is a timely book. The authors have brought together stories full of great insights and wisdom. It is an outstanding contribution to a holistic worldview that is urgently needed at this critical time."

**Satish Kumar**
Founder, Schumacher College
Editor Emeritus, Resurgence & Ecologist

https://doi.org/10.1515/9783111337913-026

**INNER** DEVELOPMENT **GOALS**
**Switzerland**

The Digital Workbook enhances the book's vision, offering a dynamic platform for on-going learning, collaboration, and personal transformation. Through exclusive resources, reflections, and community engagement, the Hub extends the journey beyond the book's pages, fostering a global exchange of insights and practices to support inner development and the SDG agenda.

The Digital Workbook serves as an evolving, interactive space where authors and readers collaborate to co-create inner development narratives. It goes beyond documenting insights from these journeys, aiming to cultivate deeper connections and collaborative learning within a supportive community. In this space, participants engage in meaningful conversations, share reflections, and contribute their unique perspectives to enrich our collective understanding of inner development.

The Digital Workbook is free for readers of the book.

Simply scan the QR code below

**Use the coupon code 'IDGSTORIES' for free access**

idgworkbook.sutra.co

# Digital Workbook

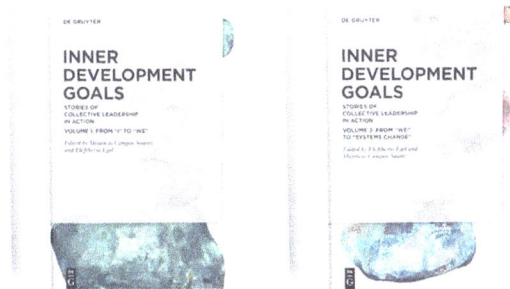

www.ingramcontent.com/pod-product-compliance
Lightning Source LLC
Chambersburg PA
CBHW080548270326
41929CB00019B/3228